STATE OF REPRESSION

STATE OF REPRESSION

Iraq under Saddam Hussein

LISA BLAYDES

PRINCETON UNIVERSITY PRESS

Princeton and Oxford

Published by Princeton University Press,
41 William Street, Princeton, New Jersey 08540
In the United Kingdom: Princeton University Press,
6 Oxford Street, Woodstock, Oxfordshire OX20 1TR

press.princeton.edu

Jacket image: Baghdad, Iraq, 2002
Photography by Eric Bouvet. Courtesy of Getty Images.

Library of Congress Control Number: 2018936379
ISBN 978-0-691-18027-4

British Library Cataloging-in-Publication Data is available

This book has been composed in Garamond Premier Pro and Scala Sans

Printed on acid-free paper. ∞

Typeset by Nova Techset Pvt Ltd, Bangalore, India
Printed in the United States of America

1 3 5 7 9 10 8 6 4 2

FOR JOSH

CONTENTS

FIGURES AND TABLES

PREFACE

Some readers of this text will see it as two books in one. While I have sought to make my core contribution the promulgation of a new theory for how political identities are reinforced through authoritarian regime repression, a second narrative lurks just beneath the language of theories, hypotheses, and empirical tests. The "shadow" book is one about the everyday lived experience of individuals managing the high-stakes political world of autocratic Iraq during the dictatorship of Saddam Hussein.

The qualitative stories embedded in this book appear as evidence for assumptions, empirical implications of hypotheses, and as tests for my theoretical expectations. These narratives reflect the complex interactions between a regime and a citizenry, both struggling for survival. Some of the qualitative accounts are mundane, focused on the ways that Iraqis sought opportunities for social, educational, or political advancement. Other narrative accounts are more profound in their implications. In all cases, the Baʿthist regime's aspirations for political hegemony were thwarted by a lumpiness in the regime's ability to monitor its own society and, eventually, declining state capacity.

When fiscal conditions were favorable—like during the 1970s after nationalization of the oil industry—the Baʿthist regime managed emerging political threats with relative ease. The 1980s and 1990s, however, brought an entirely new set of challenges, first with the tremendously costly Iran-Iraq War and, later, with the humanitarian catastrophe of the international economic embargo. Understanding how the Baʿthist regime managed Iraqi politics during good economic times is not as puzzling as comprehending how the regime managed domestic threats during tough times. The burdens associated with war and sanctions increased individual acts of political non-compliance. A primary argument of this book is that the way citizens were punished in response to these behaviors forged and reinforced meaningful, actionable forms of political identity.

Communities that were culturally distant from the Baʿthist regime were difficult to penetrate from a monitoring and intelligence-gathering perspective. When the Baʿthists could not accurately distinguish between those individuals who had complied with and those who had resisted regime dictates, punishment was meted out imprecisely. In other words, the regime meted out punishment based on the precision of its intelligence. Communities that were culturally distant from the Baʿthists presented a monitoring challenge and group-level punishment reinforced the salience of group identities. Highly penetrated communities that were culturally close to the Baʿthists were punished with a high degree of accuracy; the result was political atomization for members of those communities.

The struggle to make the Iraqi population legible to the Baʿthists was a core regime pursuit. While countries across the Middle East were seeking to stem growing urbanization and the associated expansion of urban slums, the Baʿthists were clearing the Kurdish countryside, moving tens of thousands of Iraqi Kurds into cities to increase the regime's ability to monitor and penetrate northern society. One of the richest sources of data used in this project emerges as a response to the regime's failure to accurately "read" Iraqi society. Prior to the regime-shaking 1991 Uprisings, the regime collected only basic data about Iraqi high school students, like name, address, and political orientation. After 1991, however, the regime significantly expanded information collection with the goal of identifying which young people and, by association, which families were politically trustworthy. In both the example of the creation of Kurdish urban settlements and the enhanced information collection on high school students, separating out "good" from "bad" citizens was a preoccupation of the regime. The documents that comprise the empirical content of this project are themselves a manifestation of the bureaucratization of autocracy that the Baʿthist regime epitomizes.

How does the Baʿthist regime in Iraq compare to other authoritarian regimes? And how broadly might the lessons of this book be applied? The idea that group-level punishment reinforces communal identity has wide applicability. In the democratic context, there are countless examples of cases where governments or local authorities criminalize entire communities because investigators did not possess or invest in the capacity to differentiate between law-abiding residents from law breakers. During World War II, Japanese Americans were less legible to the US government than German and Italian Americans; as a result Japanese Americans were collectively imprisoned based on their ethnic identity, while German and Italian Americans were investigated individually, with subsequent implications for the development of a Japanese American cultural identity.[1] In the runup to the 1984 Olympic games in Los Angeles, the Los Angeles Police Department engaged in widespread sweeps of areas of South-Central Los Angeles in a bid to crack down on gang violence. Thousands of young people were arrested as part of "Operation Hammer," the overwhelming majority of whom were never charged with a crime.[2] My arguments suggest that a shared sense of salient identity would emerge among residents of South-Central Los Angeles as a result of the way the area was repressed by a state that could not effectively discriminate among individual actors within that population. This period of collective repression spawned new forms of anti-system artistic expression, and in 1992 South-Central Los Angeles was the epicenter for major ethnic riots.

While my arguments might be applied to democratic contexts, the theoretical implications of the book are particularly apt for the study of political behavior in autocracies. In countries where a dictator rules a homogeneous population that is culturally similar to the ruling clique, effective monitoring of the population means citizens are constantly worried about members of their own social network who may inform on them. The result is a relatively low degree of interpersonal trust between individuals and no reinforcement of a salient identity around which political mobilization might organize. For example, North Korea is a relatively homogenous society where the ruling elite comes from the majority cultural group. There are few barriers to intelligence gathering within the population and the regime has the capability to mete out punishment with precision. North Korean prison camps are full of would-be defectors and others who ran afoul of the regime for any variety of offenses.

Collective punishment heightens group identity, even when such identities were not particularly salient for group members in advance of the repression. Stalin's collective repression of Ukrainian peoples during the 1930s is thought to have given birth to Ukrainian national consciousness.[3] Bedouin populations in the Egyptian Sinai have been the victims of collective punishment masquerading as counterterrorism policy. Mass, indiscriminate arrests and the wanton destruction of hundreds of homes have led to an increased salience

1. See Ngai (2004) for a discussion of this case.
2. See John Mitchell, "The Raid That Still Haunts LA," *Los Angeles Times*, March 14, 2001 for a discussion of the enduring aftermath of one such raid.
3. See Stephen Kotkin, "Stalin, Father of Ukraine?" *New York Times*, November 27, 2014.

of Bedouin identity. Examples abound in the Middle East and beyond. And while this project cannot account for how certain types of identity came to exist as social constructs in the first place, I do seek to explain how and why identities become emboldened and reinforced.

Finally, while scholars have long described state repression—including harassment, surveillance, arrests, and mass killings—as a key lever of political power, the study of repression has developed unevenly with core concepts left undertheorized.[4] Repression studies have especially neglected systematic analysis of the targets of state violence, creating an intellectual blind spot with regard to our understanding of how repression influences individuals and their communities.[5] This is particularly troubling since the number of people who have died at the hands of their own governments likely exceeds the number who have died in either interstate conflicts or civil wars.[6] Within the study of authoritarian regimes, we also know much more about the politics of cooptation when compared to our understanding of state repression. What explains the use of repression and the deployment of state violence? And how does repression impact citizenries? There is a dearth of scholarship on these subjects relative to studies focused on either interstate conflict or political patronage. This book is the product of my efforts to dig a little deeper into the causes and consequences of repression as well as to understand how repression fits into a broader conceptualization of power in autocratic regimes.

Lisa Blaydes
Stanford, CA
September 24, 2017

4. Davenport 2007.
5. Davenport 2015, 9.
6. Rummel 1997.

ACKNOWLEDGMENTS

There is virtually no end to the debts that I have incurred while writing this book. My first thanks go to the Hoover Institution, which brought the Iraq Memory Foundation collection to Stanford University and supported my research on the materials as a National Fellow during the 2012–2013 academic year. It was during that year that I was able to put together many of the datasets that form the empirical core of this project. Richard Sousa, former director of the Library and Archives at the Hoover Institution, and Eric Wakin, current director, have been important sources of support for my scholarship. At Hoover, Carol Leadenham was always helpful in the reading room, and Haidar Hadi has been a lifeline for me as I have sought to navigate the collection and understand more about Iraqi society. The Iraq Memory Foundation has its roots in the tireless work of Kanan Makiya, without whom the materials would never have been preserved and digitized for research.

The archivists at University of Colorado's Norlin Library were both kind and welcoming. Many thanks to David Hays and Bruce Montgomery for facilitating my work on the Iraqi Secret Police files. David Palkki and the staff of the now-closed Conflict Records Research Center assisted with my access to the Saddam Hussein Collection at National Defense University. Michael Brill and Abby Fanlo helped me to fill in gaps in my research following my visit there.

A number of institutions and programs provided me with various forms of research support. The Institute for Research in the Social Sciences at Stanford offered me initial seed funding for the project. The Smith Richardson Foundation generously extended a Junior Faculty Research Grant. The staff at the Monterey Institute of International Studies arranged a course of study in Iraqi Arabic that was extremely valuable.

The Stanford Summer Research College was critical for the completion of this project. Between 2010 and 2016, more than a dozen outstanding undergraduate student researchers assisted me with various aspects of this project, from data collection to coding variables and reviewing various literatures. I am grateful to each of them for their cheerful attitudes and willingness to dedicate a part of their summer to working with me on this project. I am also appreciative of students associated with the Stanford International Policy Studies Program for their kind assistance.

Much of this book was written while I was a fellow at the Center for Advanced Study in the Behaviorial Sciences. Many thanks to Margaret Levi for her mentorship and encouragement. I am also thankful to Mary Murphy, who generously shared her knowledge of social psychology with me at a critical juncture in my writing.

The Stanford Department of Political Science has been an ever-reliable source of intellectual inspiration and feedback. David Laitin continues to be the most helpful of colleagues. Gary Cox and Lachlan McNamee generously read and provided important feedback on chapters. Jim Fearon, Steve Krasner, Yuki Takagi, and Barry Weingast talked me through difficult puzzles. I am grateful to each of them.

The Center for International Security and Cooperation at Stanford's Freeman Spogli Institute hosted a book conference for me with funding from the Carnegie Endowment for International Peace. Martha Crenshaw convened an outstanding group of colleagues who gave me a clear sense of direction for how to move forward with my manuscript. Many thanks to Barbara Geddes, Anna Gryzmala-Busse, Beatriz Magaloni, Neil Narang, Christiana Parreira, David Patel, Scott Sagan, Ken Schultz, and Jeremy Weinstein for their participation and helpful advice.

Kind audiences at a number of universities provided me with feedback and guidance. Many thanks to my hosts, discussants, and audience participants at the University of Virginia, Stanford University, Rice University, University of Wisconsin, University of Rochester, Columbia University, UCSD, Yale University, MIT, Harvard University, UCLA, Berkeley, NYU Law School, University of Chicago, Princeton University, and University of Konstanz. Among the many useful comments I received, some interventions stand out in my memory. John Ferejohn encouraged me to think more carefully about the assumptions underlying my project. Paul Staniland challenged me to state my claims more boldly. Jim Robinson pushed me to think more carefully about the implications of my work for the study of state failure. Laia Balcells, Carles Boix, Fotini Christia, Dan Corstange, Clark Gibson, Kevan Harris,

Sam Helfont, Amaney Jamal, Lewis Kornhauser, Steve Kotkin, Timur Kuran, Gerry Munck, Sebastian Schutte and Victor Shih all offered intellectual support and encouragement.

Tareq al-Samman and Sarah Ghattas were research assistants without parallel. During the time he worked with me on this book, Tareq and I watched his native Syria descend into civil war. I learned much from our conversations, about life in authoritarian Syria but also about the pursuit of economic justice, Tareq's passion. I also have Tareq to thank for designing the maps that appear in this book. Sarah was a model research assistant, responding kindly and patiently to my requests for information. While working together, we shared many conversations about her native Egypt during the tumultuous months after the 2011 Uprisings. Sarah also generously shared her knowledge about social practices within Egypt's Coptic Christian community, insights that were important for other aspects of my research.

I was fortunate to have had Alissa Walter proofread the manuscript and assist with the transliteration and indexing. Omar Shakir graciously provided me with introductions to members of the Iraqi community in the San Diego area who shared critical insights. Eliana Vasquez provided outstanding faculty support throughout research and writing.

Many thanks to Eric Crahan at Princeton University Press for his enthusiasm for the project. He has been a thoughtful and supportive editor. I am also appreciative of Karen Verde for her careful copyediting and Leslie Grundfest for assistance with the book's production.

My family provided the loving support and patience I needed to finish this project. My exceptionally kind brother, Bernard, read and edited portions of the manuscript. My children, Jonah and Ethan, are endless sources of joy for me. My greatest debt goes to my husband, Josh, whose reliable support helped me at every step along the way. It is to Josh that this book is dedicated. Infer nothing about him from the fact that I have dedicated to him a book about repression, as he exemplifies the opposite.

STATE OF REPRESSION

CHAPTER 1

INTRODUCTION

Citizens of few countries have experienced a recent political history as calamitous as that suffered by Iraqis. In the 1970s, Iraq was a middle-income country with a significant and growing class of educated and cosmopolitan elites. Endowed with both oil and water resources, Iraq was on a path to economic modernization, particularly in the years following the 1973 surge in the price of petroleum. Increasing Iraqi oil rents paralleled the rise of an ambitious, yet ruthless, political leader, and the relative prosperity of the 1970s was disrupted by war and repression. The pain of political oppression was compounded by crippling economic sanctions followed by foreign occupation and the violent unfolding of a sectarian civil war. During this time, Iraq became a destination and breeding ground for Islamic extremists.

The Iraqi state that emerged from this trauma has struggled to reestablish territorial integrity. Its governance structures are fragile and prone to sectarian favoritism. In 2006, then-Senator Joseph Biden suggested that an Iraq of autonomous regions split along ethnic lines might bring an end to the civil war.[1] More than ten years later, US policymakers continue to debate whether a unified Iraq will ever again be governable.[2] This project explores the conditions that led to the breakdown of the Iraqi state through an examination of Iraqi political life during Saddam Hussein's time in power.

There is little doubt that the recent history of political trauma Iraq has experienced has its roots in the Baʿth Party's governance. Yet understanding how and why nation-building failed in Iraq has been challenging, at least in part, because of difficulties observing the inner workings of autocratic

---

1. Joseph Biden and Leslie Gelb, "Unity Through Autonomy in Iraq," *New York Times*, May 1, 2006.

2. Tim Arango, "With Iraq Mired in Turmoil, Some Call for Partitioning the Country," *New York Times*, April 28, 2016.

governance structures. The internal workings of a dictatorship are often described as taking place within a "black box"—while some of the input and output characteristics are known, the inner dynamics of how power coalesces and is maintained remains opaque. And because collecting information in a nondemocratic setting is so challenging, relatively little scholarship has sought to explain the mechanics of autocratic control in the world's most repressive regimes. It is virtually impossible to study the internal politics of such regimes while the dictator is in power.[3] Even after regimes have been overthrown, new holders of political power may have an incentive to hide information about the repressive and control apparatuses due to the political implications of exposing the often widespread nature of societal complicity with the ancien régime.[4] And although the existing literature on nondemocracies has grown tremendously in the last twenty years, it tends to be sparse when compared to scholarly work that seeks to explain political life in democracies.

Despite these barriers, determining the specificities of everyday political life in Iraq during the Saddam Hussein era has become possible as a result of the recent availability of millions of documents recovered following two pivotal events—the establishment of Kurdish self-rule in northern Iraq in the wake of the 1991 Uprisings and the overthrow of Saddam Hussein's Ba'thist regime in 2003. The first cache of government documents was salvaged following large-scale popular demonstrations that took place following the Iraqi military withdrawal from Kuwait. This collection—known as the Iraqi Secret Police Files—is housed at the University of Colorado Boulder. These files provide detailed information about Ba'th Party and government operations in northern Iraq leading up to 1991. At the time of my visit to this archive in December 2013 to January 2014, I was the only researcher to have visited the collection.[5]

The second cache of government documents is composed of two collections that were captured during the 2003 US invasion of Iraq. The first collection

3. See Ahram (2016) for more on how the opacity and brutality of the Ba'thist regime, in particular, negatively impacted the way research was conducted in Iraq before 2003.

4. See Nalepa (2010) for a discussion of this dynamic in Eastern Europe following the fall of Communism.

5. Although the collection had not been utilized by an academic researcher prior to that point, documents from the collection were used by Human Rights Watch to generate an influential report published in 1993 entitled "Genocide in Iraq: The Anfal Campaign Against the Kurds: A Middle East Watch Report."

consists of the tapes and associated transcripts of conversations between Saddam Hussein and various advisors and underlings. Until recently this collection, which is no longer available to the public, was housed at the Conflict Records Research Center at the National Defense University.[6] The second collection consists of documents assembled by the Iraq Memory Foundation. The Hoover Institution acquired the Iraq Memory Foundation collection in 2008, and these files became available for scholarly research in 2010.[7] The documents in this second collection include both print and video materials which provide a rich picture of the everyday practices of Iraq's highly repressive autocracy.[8]

6. First open in 2010, the Conflict Records Research Center (CRRC) at the National Defense University housed both documents and audio files captured in Iraq and Afghanistan as part of the Iraq War (2003–2011) and the War in Afghanistan (2003–2014). The collection contained more than 1,000 individual documents comprising more than 30,000 pages and is described by the CRRC management team in Woods et al. (2011). The center was closed for budget reasons in June 2015. For more on the closing of the CRRC see Michael Gordon, "Archive of Captured Enemy Documents Closes," *New York Times*, June 21, 2015.

7. The records of the *Hizb al-Baʿth al-ʿArabi al-Ishtiraki* in Iraq, or the Baʿth Party Records (1968–2003) compose an approximately 11 million document collection at Stanford University's Hoover Institution. The collection includes correspondence, reports, membership and personnel files, judicial and investigatory dossiers, and administrative files relating to political conditions in, and governance of, Iraq. Most documents are part of the Baʿth Regional Command Collection (BRCC). While there are files that are drawn from both the earlier and later periods of Baʿthist rule, the collection skews strongly toward the 1990s and early 2000s in terms of the sheer number of documents. There are a number of reasons why this may be the case, including the possible purging of older documents, the tendency for older documents to be lost or not to survive and the increasingly common use of computer technologies which made it easier to produce documents (versus the use of handwriting and typewriters from the earlier periods).

8. Working with the Baʿth Party Records proved to be challenging, in part because of the sheer size of the collection. I began my research on the collection initially by browsing through the documents to get a sense of their internal organization. The collection is formally divided into a series of discrete file groupings including the North Iraq dataset, the Kuwait dataset, the School Registers, the Baʿth Party Boxfiles, and the Membership dataset. The School Registers and the Baʿth Party Boxfiles make up the largest two groupings within the collection. The School Registers are organized by governorate-year. Within each governorate-year file, data are organized by school where each "sheet" within the Registers includes information on dozens of students. The Baʿth Party Boxfiles, while not organized in a straightforward geographic or temporal manner like the Registers, frequently exhibited forms of internal coherence within each electronic boxfile. For example, a boxfile typically included the contents of a binder or folder of materials. The first page of the electronic boxfile often includes a scan of the descriptive label that might appear on the outside of the binder. As a result, I was often able to scan the descriptive binder labels to identify boxfiles on topics of political significance.

Reliance on collections of Iraqi government documents no doubt allows for only a partial, incomplete picture of political life in Iraq under Saddam Hussein. Another important source of information comes from the first-hand testimony of Iraqis. Between 2003 and 2008, documentary film-makers associated with the Iraq Memory Foundation recorded the experiences of 190 individuals who lived through Baʿthist rule as part of an oral history project. These testimonials aired on *al-ʿIraqiyya*—an Arabic-language satellite and terrestrial public television network in Iraq that serves 85 percent of the country's population.[9] I include the first-hand testimony of individuals interviewed for this project at various points in the book.[10]

Using data from these three collections, as well as material from a vast secondary source literature on Iraqi politics and history, I have sought answers to a series of foundational questions related to autocratic governance in Iraq. What did the Baʿthist regime actually know about its citizens? Why did it use blunt, seemingly suboptimal, forms of punishment against its population? And what explains variation in the types of compliance and resistance behaviors undertaken by Iraqis during Hussein's dictatorship?

While some of my findings affirm a conventional narrative about citizen behavior in autocratic Iraq, in other cases the archival evidence demands we update the accepted wisdom about Iraqi political life. I find that, despite pretensions to political hegemony, the Iraqi regime frequently lacked important information about its population, and this problem of intelligence gathering varied in magnitude across ethnic, religious, and communal groups within Iraq. When rebellious behaviors occurred, inadequate information about the specific identity of the perpetrators led the regime to engage in forms of collective punishment that reinforced and cemented identity cleavages

9. The testimonials, including material not included in the original television broadcasts, are available for viewing in the Library and Archives of the Hoover Institution.

10. On the one hand, the individuals selected for participation in the oral history project were chosen because of their experiences with regime repression. Clearly not all Iraqis were subject to the type of abuses described in the footage. On the other hand, Saddam Hussein is believed to have killed as many as one million of his own citizens (see Dexter Filkins, "Regrets Only?," *New York Times*, October 7, 2007). Countless international human rights reports and journalistic accounts describe the widespread nature of Iraqi human rights abuses under the regime of Saddam Hussein (See "Endless Torment: The 1991 Uprising in Iraq and Its Aftermath," *Human Rights Watch*, June 1992, and "Iraq's Brutal Decrees: Amputation, Branding, and the Death Penalty." *Human Rights Watch*, June 1995, for two examples). I am also not aware of any circumstance under which the testimony of these individuals has been refuted.

precisely among those groups about which the regime was least informed. Ethno-sectarian and communal identities alone, therefore, cannot explain the wide range of behaviors observed on the part of Iraqi citizens.

My argument is state-centric in the sense that it suggests states create the political behaviors that they face as a result of their policies toward their citizenries. While my theoretical focus is squarely upon the actions of the state, the state itself is constrained in a number of ways that limit its ability to pursue its preferred policies and achieve its desired outcomes. Most important, states are constrained by their financial and infrastructural, or bureaucratic, resources as well as by the inability of state political leaders to accurately predict or anticipate the response of international actors to their foreign policy initiatives.

In particular, the Iraqi state under Saddam Hussein faced three key constraints on its power. First, Hussein was unable to render all parts of the country politically "legible" to the central government in Baghdad. What is meant by the term legible? Scott suggests that a central problem of statecraft involves effective "mapping" of a country's terrain and its people to aid the basic functions of the state, including taxation, conscription, and the prevention of rebellion.[11] From a political economy perspective, relatively illegible citizens and regions are those for which monitoring costs are high.[12] This was a problem particularly for Iraqi government efforts to politically penetrate the three most northern provinces in Iraqi Kurdistan. Second, despite a well-educated population and abundant oil reserves, the Iraqi state proved to be highly vulnerable to economic shocks, many of which were induced by foreign policy crises. The devastating human and financial costs associated with the Iran-Iraq War and the catastrophic suffering caused by the international sanctions regime of the 1990s were two key contributors. Third, the Iraqi state under Hussein—not unlike other dictatorships which struggle to accurately assess the incentives and motivations of foreign governments—miscalculated the international response to key foreign policy decisions with important knock-on effects for domestic politics. For example, when Iraq invaded Iran in 1980, Hussein expected a war lasting weeks, not years. These three constraints—which are both structural and contingent in nature—form the political context for Iraqi politics in the late twentieth century.

11. Scott 1998, 2.
12. Attempts to increase legibility are state-driven efforts to reduce the cost of monitoring the population.

The arguments that I put forward relate to the literature on state-building and, ultimately, state breakdown. While most of the literature on state-building has focused on the European experience associated with the development of strong territorial states,[13] and on the African experience associated with states struggling to project political power across territory,[14] I seek to understand how state power is projected in a context that might be more favorable for state development—the contemporary Middle East. Middle Eastern states—endowed with the financial resources to invest in governance structures and a conflict-prone external environment conducive to nation-building—would seem to present a relatively favorable set of conditions for creating robust states. Yet within the Middle East, there has been considerable variation in the strength of states despite a broad similarity of structural economic and international conditions. My findings suggest that certain parameters—like the difficulties associated with policing a diverse ethno-sectarian population—were built into the creation of the Iraqi state and proved difficult to manage over time. This was particularly the case as the state faced a tightening budget constraint as a result of poor foreign policy decision making. Although the dissolution of the Iraqi state was, indeed still may be, avoidable, the forces working against a unified Iraqi state are strong and self-reinforcing.

The weakness of the Iraqi state has its roots in the construction of political identity and social cleavage structures both during and directly after Hussein's dictatorship. While most scholarly accounts of the determinants of societal cleavage structures have focused on the experience of democratic countries and emerging democracies,[15] my arguments suggest when and why certain identities become salient across communities within an autocratic regime. My findings also challenge a conventional narrative about sectarianism in Iraqi society. The myth of monolithic Sunni, Shi'i, and Kurdish populations in an eternally and hopelessly fractured society belies both the multi-sectarian nature of collaboration with the regime, as well as the tremendous threat posed to regime stability by rivals within Hussein's own Sunni community.[16]

13. Tilly 1992.
14. Herbst 2000.
15. E.g., Lipset and Rokkan 1967; Rogowski 1989; Posner 2004.
16. See Kirdar (2009) for more on why it is misleading to characterize the Hussein regime as a Sunni regime. Similarly, Zeidel (2010) argues that it is problematic to think about activities of the regime as being carried out on behalf of the Sunni community. For example, he asks,

And perhaps most pernicious, this conventional narrative has, and likely will continue to have, a harmful influence on the formation of US policy in Iraq.

COMPLIANCE AND RESISTANCE UNDER AUTOCRACY

While the dynamics associated with compliance and resistance to autocratic rule are closely tied to issues of authoritarian legitimacy, regime duration, and the existence and success of secessionist movements, recent scholarly work on authoritarianism has been focused primarily on authoritarian institutional type with little attention paid to the everyday practices of governance. The most influential work in this tradition has focused on generating typologies of authoritarian regimes. Geddes argues that single-party, military, and personalist regimes are distinctive institutional types and that the strategic factors guiding politics in each context are different.[17] One tension in this literature relates to how one should characterize those regimes that combine aspects of party organization, military rule, personalism and, sometimes, even hereditary succession.[18]

The focus on institutional type (e.g., military, party, personalist regime, or monarchy) represents a step away from a previous literature on nondemocratic rule that offered reflections on how power was projected under autocracy and the lived experience of autocratic rule for citizenries. Arendt's work on the origins and outcomes associated with totalitarianism is seminal; she defines totalitarianism as a "form of government whose essence is terror and whose principle of action is the logicality of ideological thinking."[19] For Arendt, the use of terror and ideology are an outgrowth of a regime's desire to dominate all aspects of citizen life. Although Arendt's use of the term

---

"would the activities of a handful of officers, all of them Sunnis, to topple a Sunni regime be branded 'Sunni'?" (Zeidel 2010, 160).

17. See Geddes (2003). Hadenius and Teorell (2007) contend that all dictatorships exhibit greater or lesser degrees of personalism, often in combination with more institutionalized governance structures. Magaloni (2008) concurs and develops a schematic that reintroduces monarchies as a distinctive regime type and focuses on a key difference within the set of party autocracies, particularly the distinction between single-party regimes and hegemonic-party regimes.

18. Geddes describes many of the regimes in the Middle East—like those in Egypt or Syria—as "hybrid" regimes exhibiting multiple institutional forms simultaneously.

19. Arendt 1966, 474.

totalitarian has been criticized by scholars who argue that truly totalizing forms of social control are not possible even in the most repressive regimes,[20] the ambition to create totalizing forms of social control would seem to be one dimension by which to distinguish such regimes from other types of autocracy.

Linz focuses on the distinction between totalitarian and authoritarian regimes without regard for the precise institutional form. While he defines authoritarian political systems as ones with limited forms of political plural-ism, he sees totalitarianism, on the other hand, as having an ideology, a single party, and "concentrated power in an individual and his collaborators or a small group that is not accountable to any large constituency."[21]

While scholars of dictatorship have recently eschewed discussion of the totalitarian-authoritarian distinction, a core debate in the literature on Iraq under Saddam Hussein relates to whether the regime should be categorized as authoritarian or totalitarian. Complexities associated with understanding the role of repression, fear, and terror in the Iraqi case contribute to differences of interpretation.[22] In *Republic of Fear*, Makiya argues that fear was "not incidental or episodic," but rather constitutive of the regime itself.[23] Dawisha writes that "unlike earlier authoritarian periods in Iraq ... Saddam's Iraq was a country that was held hostage to the will and whim of one omnipresent tyrant."[24] For Dawisha, the authoritarianism of Hussein's predecessors be-comes dwarfed by "Saddam's procrustean totalitarianism."[25] Sassoon, on the other hand, does not consider the regime totalitarian, despite the Baʿth Party's involvement with almost all aspects of life from birth to death.[26] Sassoon

20. Wedeen 1999, 44.
21. Linz 2000, 67. In Linz's conceptualization, the party is a critical component of totalitarianism; he writes that "only when the party organization is superior or equal to the government can we speak of a totalitarian system" (2000, 94). In addition, "propaganda, education, training of cadres, intellectual elaboration of the ideology, scholarship inspired by the ideology, rewards for intellectuals identified with the system" (Linz 2000, 71) are frequently associated with totalitarian rule. Totalitarian regimes also tend to be ones where a single leader is the "object of a cult of personality" (Linz 2000, 75). Although totalitarian systems are often characterized by violent coercion, for Linz (2000, 74) terror is neither a necessary nor sufficient condition for defining a regime as totalitarian.
22. See Faust (2015) for more on this debate.
23. Makiya 1998, xi.
24. Dawisha 2009, 241.
25. See ibid., 240. Baram (2014, 5) offers a slightly different perspective, arguing that Hussein aimed for "totalitarian omnipotence," but failed in this effort.
26. Sassoon 2012, 5–9.

points out that "many Iraqis did not accept the Baʿth regime."[27] Further, some who did support the regime did so not as a result of duress, but rather out of a desire for power and privilege. For Sassoon, Iraq under Saddam Hussein—while brutal and controlling—should be classified as authoritarian, not totalitarian.[28]

Part of the reason for this disagreement among various scholars relates to the differential treatment of citizens and groups of citizens across time and geographic region within the context of a single Iraqi "regime." For example, tolerance of dissent declined for certain populations over time. This variation in treatment across groups within a single country, as well as for particular groups over time, is not unique; yet, empirical studies that use "regime" as the unit of analysis may place less emphasis on the issue of variation in governance forms within the borders of a single state.

These concerns are especially salient for the undifferentiated conceptualization of repression or "punishment" in works of political economy. Punishment, as it typically operates in autocratic regimes, is differentiated across groups and individuals and is also context-specific. This suggests the existence of *individualized autocracy*, or the idea that autocracy, as it is experienced by an individual citizen, is conditional on a variety of factors including the identity of that individual and his or her location within the broader political schema.

IDENTITY IN IRAQI POLITICS

A starting point for most studies of Iraqi politics emphasizes the importance of the country's multi-ethnic, multi-sectarian population. This is a sensible line of reasoning. Iraq's geographic position on the historical boundary between the Sunni Ottoman Empire and Shiʿi Safavid Empire, as well as contemporary Iraq's adjacency to the historical homeland of the Kurdish people—an ethnic and linguistic group indigenous to southwest Asia—would suggest the relevance of ethno-sectarian concerns. Indeed, as the Ottoman Empire came to consolidate its political control over the region that would become contemporary Iraq, the area was divided into three provinces centered

27. ibid., 221.
28. Similarly, Alahmed (2009) criticizes portrayals of the Iraqi government as totalitarian since those depictions attribute undeserved omnipotence to the Baʿthist regime.

around the area's major population centers—Mosul, Baghdad, and Basra— which came to roughly correspond to the centroids of a Kurdish north, Sunni center, and Shiʿa south, respectively.[29]

Prominent academic accounts focus on how historical antagonisms between the Ottoman Empire and its Persian geopolitical rival generated a legacy of uneven distribution of positions in the military and bureaucracy across ethno-sectarian groups. Disparate access to state employment across groups is an undeniable feature of the postcolonial Iraqi state and a fact that has taken on a decisive role in many scholarly accounts. Wimmer, for example, describes Iraq as an example of an "ethnocracy" where Sunni nationalists ruled over Iraqi Kurds and Iraqi Shiʿa, who were largely excluded from bureaucratic and other opportunities.[30] Osman argues that "the failure... to resolve inherent tensions between primordial sectarian identities" has been a defining feature of the modern Iraqi state.[31]

Journalistic accounts of Iraq also describe sectarianism as an enduring, seemingly inescapable feature of the country's identity politics. Similarly, references to ethno-sectarian identities are ubiquitous in Western diplomatic and intelligence reports about internal Iraqi politics. Yet this narrative assumes both too much and too little about the salience of ethno-sectarian identities. Such a narrative suggests that ethnic and sectarian identities have been the defining, overriding identity concern for the majority of Iraqi citizens. And such a narrative says almost nothing about when and how ethno-sectarian schisms emerge as salient when they do.

Increasingly, scholars specializing in Iraqi history have resisted the idea that ethno-sectarian conflict served as the country's primary driver of political tension. Jabar argues against the characterization that Iraq is made up of self-contained ethno-sectarian communities, focusing instead on the tremendous economic, religious, and political heterogeneity within the Sunni, Shiʿi, and

29. Conversions from Sunni to Shiʿi Islam took place in Iraq throughout Shiʿi history but it was not until the late eighteenth century that the proportion of Shiʿa grew to a significant portion of the Iraqi population. Many of these conversions were of nomadic tribesmen whom Sunni clerics viewed as "barely Muslims prior to their conversion" (Nakash 1994a, 456). Conversions were thought to take place for a variety of reasons including as a way to evade military conscription or as a form of opposition to Ottoman rule (Nakash 1994a). These conversions were most common in southern areas of Iraq which would have been influenced by Shiʿi pilgrims traveling from the East to the holy cities of Najaf and Karbala.

30. Wimmer 2013, 28–29.

31. Osman 2014, 266.

Kurdish populations.[32] Davis rejects essentialist claims about Iraq's ethnic diversity, emphasizing how historical narratives about the nation have been constructed by political actors.[33] And Visser warns against trying to "shoe-horn" analysis of Iraqi politics into a sectarian "master narrative," as such an approach tends to systematically overlook forms of intrasectarian tension which exist at multiple levels for the case.[34] Scholars who take such a perspective extend a variety of evidence: relatively high levels of intermarriage across ethno-sectarian groups, promotion and advancement opportunities for Baʿth Party loyalists regardless of ethno-sectarian identity, and the perpetration of political oppression within, and not only across, ethnic groups and sects.

In addition, a stream in the literature on political identity in Iraq has increasingly focused on the constructed and contingent nature of identity formation. Haddad argues that a variety of factors have created sectarian tension including the influence of external actors and economic competition between sectarian groups.[35] Khoury links post-2003 sectarianism in Iraq to forms of physical and bureaucratic violence perpetuated by the Baʿthist regime.[36] For Khoury, regime-perpetrated violence was not sectarian in nature but, instead, driven by security concerns. Helfont concurs, arguing that even if sectarianism was a product of Baʿthist governance, the regime strove to treat Sunnis and Shiʿa equally.[37] Yousif suggests that sectarianism arose in Iraq as a result of an interaction between unfavorable underlying conditions and damaging government policies where economic sanctions elevated the salience of sectarian identities.[38]

While existing accounts are compelling and empirically informed, there is little consensus regarding the specific mechanisms underlying identity salience or a more generalizable frame for understanding these issues. My argument creates a unified, theoretical framework for thinking about the form and timing of identity salience that might be applied to a variety of cases.

32. Jabar 2003a.
33. Davis 2005, 24.
34. Visser 2012c.
35. Haddad 2011.
36. Khoury 2010.
37. Helfont 2015, 70.
38. Yousif 2010.

ARGUMENT AND EMPIRICAL STRATEGY

The case of Iraq provides unique opportunities for the study of political behavior under autocracy, and for reasons that go beyond the availability of the new Ba'th Party archival materials. Through an examination of the Iraqi case it is possible to explore the broad scope of repression intensity and government distributive strategies, as well as a wide variety of behaviors undertaken by a diverse citizenry operating in a high-stakes political environment. In Iraq, one's political life came to be synonymous with life itself.

While beliefs, ideological or otherwise, are critical for determining the described outcomes, the empirical focus of this study is on behaviors, those actions that might be observed or leave a bureaucratic record. Part of the reason for this focus is the untenability of accurately measuring beliefs for a period of time that has passed and for which there were no reliable ways to collect information, even if we could go back in time. Another part is equally practical—the data that I use to test the main theories laid out in this book are not attitudinal, but based on the observable, or quasi-observable, actions of individuals as collected or documented by the regime's single party. There is also a tangible quality to behaviors, as behaviors reflect a commitment to action that is not always reflected in attitudes, which can be fast-changing and without clear consequences. While behaviors, too, are highly contextual and made under conditions of extreme political pressure, I believe that they reflect complex political calculations.[39]

Theoretical Contribution

This project focuses on how state actions explain citizen political behavior. In particular, I seek to endogenize the political beliefs and behaviors of citizens through a focus on the actions of states and their leaders. I argue that the policy choices of the state are constrained in a number of meaningful ways and that these constraints limit the action set available to state leaders, forcing them to deviate from their optimal political strategy. The actions that I am most

---

39. Kalyvas (2006, 101) argues that it is important not to infer support based on behaviors, a point with which I concur; he argues that inferring preferences from behaviors is difficult for a variety of reasons including the tendency for beliefs to be manipulated and falsified as well as the ever-changing nature of political support. Petersen (2001, 9) also chooses to focus on observable behaviors and not attitudes in his study.

concerned with are related to distributive practices, particularly the intensity and precision of monetary rewards offered to citizens, and practices related to punishment for political transgressions that threaten regime interests.

From the perspective of an autocratic regime, the state's ideal financial resources would be functionally unlimited, allowing for private payouts to regime insiders and public goods for the general population.[40] In such a setting, citizens would grow to be invested in the state's political leadership where citizen investment in the regime resembles a capital asset—providing more and more rewards to citizens grows public investment in the political status quo. But what happens if the state's financial resources decline? Or even worse, the state begins to demand costly service of the citizenry as a result of a foreign war or other external shock? As investment in the regime declines, or even becomes negative, citizens harmed by the negative shock may engage in anti-regime behaviors that the state seeks to punish. In such a setting, states attempt to sanction political transgressors, but often face an information problem—it is difficult to identify precisely who committed the transgression, yet the behavior demands a punitive response. This situation leads states to use forms of collective punishment, particularly directed against those segments of the population that are less legible to the state.

A primary argument of this book is that the use of collective punishment has important implications for both the beliefs and behaviors of citizens living in autocracies. When citizens are punished collectively (i.e., in a relatively imprecise manner), a number of processes unfurl. First, citizens know that the state's ability to monitor them is weak, and this knowledge allows them to organize in relative safety, encouraging the creation of dense networks with high degrees of social cohesion. Second, when information-poor states punish citizens as a result of their membership in an identity group, this encourages the likelihood of in-group policing within that identity group as the actions of one group member are tied to the outcomes for all members. Finally, when punishment is both severe and collective, individuals increasingly come

---

40. Recent research on distributive politics in the Middle East has tended to focus more on the distributive consequences of electoral authoritarianism (e.g., Koehler 2008; Lust 2009; Blaydes 2011; Masoud 2014; Corstange 2016); the impact of sectarianism on public goods provision (e.g., Cammet and Issar 2010; Salti and Chaaban 2010; Clark and Salloukh 2013; Cammett 2015); and the distributive policies of oil-exporting states of the Persian Gulf (e.g., Herb 2009; Harris 2013; Harris 2016; Hertog 2016). Less attention has been paid to the distributive economic policies of countries with the most repressive authoritarian regimes.

to believe that they share a "linked fate" with their fellow group members, further enhancing group solidarity and encouraging all-in strategies of political resistance.[41]

The level at which these processes take place depends on how punishment is meted out by the state. When the state punishes at the level of the "nation"—impacting a collective with common characteristics like language, customs, and ethnicity—the result is *nationalism*. When punishment takes place at the level of a smaller social group—impacting a collective that falls short of constituting a national group—the result is *communalism*. By communal, I mean related to a group or community including a cultural group, a religious community, or an extended kinship group, regardless of whether the kinship ties are actual or fictive.[42] What determines the state's choice to punish at the level of the nation or the subnational group? I argue that there exists variation within countries regarding the legibility of certain populations and this factor determines the precision with which punishment is delivered.

This argument suggests that states create the citizen behaviors that they confront as a result of policy action, but the constraints that states face are real and binding. The first constraint relates to the evenness with which populations within society are legible to the state. A number of factors contribute to the legibility of sub-populations to the bureaucracy; language group and terrain or geographic accessibility are two highly salient factors. When groups speak a different language than the dominant language of the state and its bureaucracy, this increases the monitoring costs for the government. Similarly, when groups are located in or near geographic regions that are relatively inaccessible to the government, this also decreases the

41. Scholars have argued that African Americans, and members of other minority groups, often believe that their individual fates are linked to those of other African Americans, even substituting group utility for individual utility when making political evaluations (Dawson 1994). While research has suggested that the salience of linked fate is contextual (Gay 2004), it is a salient political narrative when considering the attitudes and behaviors of minority groups living under conditions of political repression. Relatedly, Levi and Olson (2000) describe workers associated with organized labor movements as being part of a shared "community of fate" as their interests are bound up with one another.

42. My use of the term communalism differs, then, from those who focus on the principles and practices of communal ownership, often related to the study of communes and other forms of collective ownership. For the purposes of this study, communalism refers to the salience of group identity where such groups might include collectives associated with a variety of characteristics including ideological attachment, religious beliefs, or organizational and tribal identity.

ability of the state to monitor. Schutte (2017) uses a distance-decay model to show that violence becomes more indiscriminate with distance from the state's power center. While physical distance is a powerful proxy for the use of indiscriminate punishment, *cultural distance* hinders a state's ability to monitor to a degree greater than geographic distance alone.[43]

That said, both of these problems can be overcome with a sufficiently large financial investment in monitoring. In some cases that means developing the bureaucratic capacity to effectively police less legible areas. While geographic factors would seem difficult or even impossible to impact for a state, the experience of Iraq under Saddam Hussein suggests otherwise. Although unable to raze the mountains in the Kurdish regions of the country, the Iraqi state sought to depopulate villages near the northern mountains and went so far as to drain the marshlands in southern Iraq.[44] These extreme and costly measures were done with the goal of increasing the legibility of the Iraqi citizenry to the state.

The other binding constraint faced by states beyond the heterogeneous legibility of its population relates to the limited and variable financial resources that are available for governance. Proponents of rentier state theory have long argued that state-controlled natural resources provide countries with the means to distribute wealth to their populations in exchange for political support.[45] Yet even countries that are endowed with such a favorable rent stream are subject to internationally driven commodity price fluctuations

43. Fearon (2003) uses the structural distance between languages as a proxy for the cultural distance between groups; Blaydes and Grimmer (2017) determine cultural groups based on shared values (measured using public opinion survey responses) and then estimate the distance between groups. Cultural distance has been shown to be an important predictor of military effectiveness. For example, during the Second Chechen War large numbers of Chechens crossed ranks to work with the Russians. Lyall (2010) finds that Chechen soldiers were more successful at conducting counterinsurgency raids than their Russian counterparts. The implication is that cultural distance—as exhibited between Russian soldiers and Chechen civilians—resulted in less targeted and effective forms of punishment. Within sociology, scholars discuss social distance as multidimensional, with a cultural basis (Karakayali 2009). Bhavnani et al. (2014) define social distance as encompassing a variety of intergroup differences including class, ethnicity, religion, race, and variants associated with normative, cultural, and habitual perceptions of difference. Social distance might also be assessed in an empirical setting. Bakke et al. (2009) employ a social distance perspective, mapping the unobserved dimensions of social distance among survey respondents in Bosnia-Herzegovina and the North Caucasus region of Russia.

44. Prior to their draining, the Iraqi marshlands were the largest in western Asia.

45. See Ross (2012) for a discussion of recent literature on this subject.

and other sources of financial instability. For states that aspire to regional leadership or other foreign policy objectives, shocks to financial resources are potentially even greater should a state become embroiled in a costly war.

The idea that citizen preferences are endogenous to state action is not new and, indeed, recent scholarly work has emphasized the way behaviors respond to government policy. Kalyvas, for example, suggests that while existing accounts of civil conflict tend to focus on preexisting ethnic, sectarian, or nationalist cleavages as the key determinant of conflict outcome, there exist a variety of endogenous, micro-historical mechanisms that influence the behavior of individuals.[46] Lyall argues that, despite the fact that there is no consistent empirical relationship between state repression and collective mobilization, state repression can reinforce certain forms of group identity.[47] Lawrence argues that French colonial subjects who were offered the full rights of French citizens were less likely to engage in anti-colonial protest; in other words, movements for political equality that emerged in the French empire were endogenous to the policies of the metropole.[48]

Mylonas considers the determinants and impact of three nation-building policies—accommodation, assimilation, and exclusion—on nationalism, particularly among noncore groups (i.e., those groups that do not share the ethnic, religious, or sectarian identity of the host state).[49] For Mylonas, noncore groups can be effectively assimilated if this is compatible with the host state's external relations. Like Mylonas I argue that because individual behaviors are influenced by state actions, it is important to develop an account that can explain variation in policies toward various societal groups. Where I diverge from Mylonas is with regard to the locus of activation. While Mylonas argues that state policies are externally activated, I argue that attitudes toward noncore groups may also be activated *internally* as a result of government policies promulgated in the context of various constraints, limitations, and unforeseen (indeed, unforeseeable) external shocks.[50]

---

46. For example, Kalyvas (2006, 132) argues that the most important factor favoring collaboration with the state is the level of territorial control where territorial control requires a "constant and credible armed presence."

47. Lyall 2006.

48. Lawrence 2013.

49. Mylonas 2012.

50. This is not to say that external factors are not important; I would argue that their relevance needs to be considered in the context of domestic political constraints, however, and

Outcome Variables of Interest

A first task for this project relates to defining the outcome to be explained—the range of observable behaviors undertaken by citizens in relation to the state. Previous scholarship has pointed to the complexities associated with understanding forms of political assent, dissent, and passivity. Levi argues, for example, that "compliance and non-compliance are not the simple dichotomous variables they at first appear to be," suggesting a range of possible activities that reflect varieties of consent, volunteerism, and resistance.[51] Scott makes the case for the existence of subtle forms of resistance to economic domination that go beyond characterizations of "blind submission and homicidal rage."[52] Indeed, Scott points out that rebellions—particularly among rural populations—are rare and that everyday forms of resistance among peasants tend to stop short of collective defiance. In his work on resistance to autocracy in Eastern Europe, Petersen describes the continuum of activities that might reflect an individual's collaboration with or resistance to the regime.[53]

What are the concrete behaviors that I seek to explain in this book? First, I attempt to explain variation in pro-regime behaviors or those behaviors that enhance the power or reach of the state. In many autocratic settings, a primary way by which citizens might do this is by supporting or joining the regime party. Whether in single or hegemonic party systems, providing support for the regime party is an important marker of the regime's political access and control.[54] I provide detailed information about party identification based on tens of thousands of individual records of Iraqi high school students at four different points in time.[55] I also provide evidence on the regional distribution of party rank based on the Baʿth Party's internal membership records.

---

concur with Mylonas regarding the importance of endogenizing nationalist sentiment by taking state strategies into account.

51. Levi 1997, 17.

52. Scott 1985, 304.

53. See Petersen 2001. Sassoon (2012) also takes a broad view of resistance in Iraq under Hussein to include: desertion, sheltering deserters or opposition members, absenteeism from work or party activities, fleeing the country, subversive intellectual or artistic work, petition writing, and joke telling.

54. This is even more true because these parties are often devoid of meaningful ideological content.

55. The Baʿthist regime considered the political loyalty of Iraqi youth an important indicator of consent and control.

Citizens may also seek out or accept honors and distinguished status vis-à-vis the regime. This can take a number of forms and might include special bureaucratic designations, medals, or distinguished service awards. Acceptance of such an award signals a willingness to associate oneself closely with the authoritarian regime. Using lists collated by the Baʿth Party, I am able to identify the tribal affiliation for thousands of Baʿth Party "badge" recipients. Because tribal affiliation provides indication of an individual's sectarian and regional identity, I am able to make inferences about the distribution of the regime's core constituencies. I can also identify the geographic distribution of the "friend of the president" bureaucratic status, a designation that provided special privileges to holders.

Another way that citizens can support regime objectives is to inform on fellow citizens or engage in other forms of regime collaboration. While this is often a private act, there are important political implications as widespread collaboration creates a climate of mistrust and fear. Citizens also seek out ways to become part of the inner-circle autocratic apparatus itself. In such cases, individuals may volunteer for regime-sponsored militias. Baʿth Party documents provide information about the many thousands of individuals who volunteered for militias—like the Jerusalem Army—both at the aggregate level, across regions of Iraq, as well as at the individual level for the Iraqi high school student population.

An alternative to active complicity is the possibility for acquiescence or more passive forms of collaboration. Kalyvas surveys existing literature on conflicts between incumbent regimes and opposition groups and finds that only a small percentage of citizens actively support the armed opposition; this leads him to conclude that "most 'ordinary' people appear to display a combination of weak preferences and opportunism, both of which are subject to survival considerations."[56] Levi raises the possibility that "perhaps what we have come

---

56. See Kalyvas 2006, 103. Schedler (2013, 42) argues that most authoritarian contexts include the "bad, the good and the guilty—regime supporters, their opponents and the silent masses in between." Yet such a characterization glosses over the difference between individuals who may appear to be supporters or fence sitters but who are actually quiet resisters. Scott (1985, 315–316) describes how economic and political oppression elicits certain, often quiet, types of political and economic resistance. In particular, Scott (1985) suggests how class rule might be enforced through the passive compliance of a subordinate economic class rather than more straightforward forms of coercion.

to describe as compliance is actually a means of expressing consent."[57] In other cases, political elites create institutions that encourage compliance, including "rituals, symbols and propaganda."[58] Schedler argues individuals often "adapt to the realities of authoritarian governance by taking part in public rituals and official discourse, by applauding and falling silent at the right moments, by going into inner or outer exile, by ciphering or self-censoring their political disagreements."[59] For Scott, compliance can be the result of either resignation or more active forms of support. In either case, class rule is not enforced through sanctions or coercion so much as through passive compliance of society's economic subordinates.

On the other end of the behavioral spectrum are anti-regime and anti-government protest activity as well as other, more private, forms of political resistance. The existence of revolutionary social movements represents the most forceful and politically risky form of citizen non-compliance since collective action of this type deeply threatens either the existence or the territorial integrity of the state itself. In some cases, it might be defined as a civil war or sometimes even as domestic terrorism. For the Iraqi case, I am able to identify numerous memoranda documenting the nature of protest and resistance activities as well as regime documents outlining strategies for handling political transgressions of this type.

Much smaller in scale, but often more impactful, are attempts to seize political power via overthrow of an existing ruler or assassination of that ruler. An attempted or successful coup d'etat is often instigated by a small group; as a result, it lacks the scale of an insurgency. Political protest represents a third act of anti-regime activity that can take place either on a large or small scale.[60] This

57. See Levi 1997, 18. The public transcript gives the impression that subordinate groups endorse their continued subordination within the prevailing power structure, while the private transcript might provide a totally different interpretation of political preferences (Scott 1990, 4–5). In such a setting, conventional behavioral measures may be "nearly indistinguishable from behavior that arises from willing consent" (ibid., 67). More quiet forms of political and economic resistance rely on coordination within the community of subordinate people where even the "social spaces where the hidden transcript grows are themselves an achievement of resistance" (ibid., 118–119).

58. Levi 1988, 52.

59. Schedler 2013, 42.

60. Existing accounts of public protest that focus on the organizational factors associated with protest occurrence tend to emphasize the importance of coordinated action and informational gaps in predicting behaviors. Coordination is critical for overcoming the collective

activity also takes both public and private forms.[61] Using both public reports and internal regime documents, I report on suspected coup attempts, assassinations targeting regime leaders, and political protest in a variety of forms.

Anti-regime political activity that undermines the objectives of an authoritarian leadership in less overt ways includes behaviors like draft dodging, which has the effect of undermining the capability and morale of an authoritarian army.[62] Using internal security reports, I discuss the geographic distribution of draft dodgers as well as regime efforts to handle that problem. In the strictly controlled information environment of many authoritarian regimes, the circulation of rumors represents another way that regime objectives are subverted. While some of these rumors may have explicitly anti-regime content, the mere circulation of unsanctioned information on almost any topic of social concern breaks the information monopoly dictators seek to maintain. I collect and report on the content of more than 2,000 rumors collected by the Baʿth Party, the most common locations where rumors circulated, as well as the typical vectors of rumor dispersion.

Approach to Inference

My approach to making inferences relies on two factors—first, the short-term exogeneity in citizen legibility across different regional groups within Iraq and, second, the unanticipated impact of a series of externally driven shocks that forced coalitional realignment for the regime. Neither of these strategies approaches the gold standard for causal identification in the social sciences—the randomized control trial. Within the world of observational data analysis,

action problem for a number of reasons. First, citizens are loathe to be alone in their anti-regime behavior, preferring the protection of crowds. In addition, protest behavior on the part of activists can trigger protest participation of more moderate individuals who differ from extremists in terms of how costly it is for them to falsify their preferences (Kuran 1991). Lohmann (1994) and Kricheli et al. (2011) both consider how incomplete information impacts the possibility for public protest participation.

61. The behaviors that I am highlighting are not an exclusive list; rather they are emblematic of behaviors along a spectrum of possible behaviors. The specific types of behaviors that represent active collaboration, acquiescence, or resistance differ as a function of political and cultural context. Behaviors that are seen as resistance in one regime may be viewed as supportive in another, requiring a context-specific approach to defining the range of relevant behaviors for examination.

62. While it is impossible to discern the political motivations of a single individual evading military service, there is little doubt of the net effect of the act when taken collectively.

true natural experiments are rare, as are instrumental variables that meet the exclusion restriction. As a result, the strategy that I have proposed represents, in every way, a compromise of the ideal inferential setting. That said, given the realities of empirical analysis of observational, archival data, I believe that my approach provides meaningful analytic leverage.

A key dimension of cross-sectional variation explored in this project is geographic, where geography tends to be correlated with ethno-sectarian identity. While some parts of the country tend to be highly diverse with regard to the ethno-sectarian background of the citizenship, there are many areas of Iraq that were dominantly homogenous, allowing me to make some inferences about the behavior of citizens belonging to particular ethno-sectarian groups without much concern for problems of ecological inference. My goal is not to claim that ethno-sectarian groups behave in monolithic ways. Indeed, the evidence that I provide offers details about the within-group variation in political behavior. Rather, I take a regional approach to the study of Iraqi politics. One reason for this is practical; much of the data that I have collected suggest important forms of regional variation in political behaviors. More important, however, is the fact that prominent scholars of Iraqi politics have endorsed such an approach.[63]

Figure 1.1 provides maps displaying information about the ethnic breakdown of the Iraqi population.[64] This map suggests that the southern portions of Iraq are predominantly Shiʿi, while the northern portions of the country are primarily Kurdish. The central portion of the country is populated by Sunni Arabs, while the area surrounding Baghdad and Baghdad itself is a mix of Shiʿi and Sunni Arabs. The key distinction between Kurds and Arabs is linguistic, as Kurds typically speak one of two (some say three) main Kurdish dialects. Religious belief is a second dimension of potential cleavage. The

63. For example, Zeidel (2008, 80) argues that "regional identity" holds particular importance in the western areas of Iraq, including towns like Tikrit, Samarra, Haditha, and Ana, whose townspeople are not drawn from a single dominant tribe. In Tikrit, regional identity is highly salient and a function of the relative weakness of local tribes as well as the geographic isolation of the area (ibid., 80). Visser argues that "in Iraq south of Baghdad, two non-sectarian ideological currents have historically been far more important than the idea of Shiite consolidation in a territorial bloc" (ibid., 29).

64. The map for ethnicity in Iraq in 2003 was produced using a shapefile available on the ESOC website (https://esoc.princeton.edu/), which relied on data from the Gulf/2000 Project at Columbia University's School of International and Public Affairs.

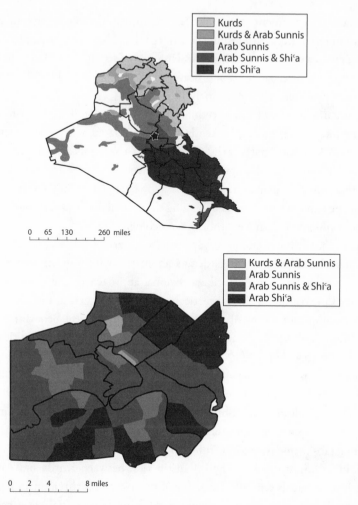

Figure 1.1. Ethno-religious population distribution across Iraq (top) and Baghdad (bottom).

majority of Iraqi Kurds are Sunni.[65] As a result, Kurds and Sunni Arabs have a shared religious framework that distinguishes those groups from Shiʿi Arabs, who have historically been the plurality of Iraqi citizens. Sunni Arabs, then, might be viewed as the ethno-sectarian "pivot" group[66] as well as the group inhabiting the geographic center of the country.

65. While numerically small, the Fayly Kurds—Kurdish Shiʿa—have been historically important in commerce.
66. Posner 2005.

The linguistic difference that stood between Arabs and Kurds proved to be very difficult for the Baʿthist regime to overcome. The regime attempted a variety of measures to bureaucratically control northern Iraq. And while sometimes successful, the difficulty in determining the identity of anti-regime activists, and those who abetted them, plagued the regime.[67] Sunni Arabs, on the other hand, shared the religious and linguistic characteristics of the regime's core, thus making that community legible to the Baʿth Party. The ease with which information could be gathered about opposition to the regime among Arab Sunnis left disgruntled individuals with less incentive to hide their beliefs. And while the Sunnis of Iraq typically were less aggrieved than either the Shiʿa or the Kurds, there did exist variation within the Sunni community on this dimension. For the Shiʿa, however, a shared language made their community more legible than the Kurds, but still less accessible than the Sunni, given the regime's own origins within the Sunni community. Barriers to legibility were intensified within insular, Shiʿi religious communities.

The challenges physical geography posed for state penetration of society mapped onto the Iraqi population in a similar fashion; Kurdish areas of the Iraqi north tended to be mountainous and difficult to penetrate and, similarly, the wetlands of southeastern Iraq also proved to be a safe haven for anti-regime activists, including Shiʿi Daʿwa Party members and draft evaders.

A central shortcoming of my analysis is that even as I analyze variation in the salience of group identity, the project begins with ethnic groups.[68] In

67. Cultivating and maintaining local informants from within groups that are culturally distant would seem to be part of an effective strategy for increasing the legibility of hard-to-read segments of society. This strategy has been widely used by autocrats in a variety of contexts, including multi-ethnic societies like the USSR. In Iraq, the regime engaged in surveillance of the population both through its own agents as well as through the use of informants (Faust 2015, 155). Yet informants are unable to completely replace the infrastructural capacity of the state. For example, given the clandestine nature of much of the political activity in northern Iraq, the regime would have been required to have informants within relatively small units of Kurdish militants or be able to observe civilian support for Kurdish fighters that often took place under cover of darkness. An escalation of policing capacity, on the other hand, allows for forms of monitoring that are more effective against organizational compartmentalization, a common feature of militant groups. See della Porta (2013) on the issue of how clandestine groups are often both fragmented and hierarchical in their organization, which may help to avoid penetration by the state or to increase the difficulty of recruiting informants.

68. Fearon (2006) defines an ethnic group as socially relevant when people notice and condition their everyday behaviors on ethnic distinctions; ethnicity becomes politicized when political coalitions are organized based on ethnicity.

particular, I posit the existence of groups and then analyze the conditions under which group identity becomes salient. Like other scholars who study the salience of ethnic identification, I struggle to explain why certain ascriptive identities would be viewed as a dimension of difference to begin with.[69] The challenge of analyzing "ethnicity without groups"[70] is a real one that exists beyond my scope.

My characterization of the relative legibility of the three ethno-sectarian groups is time-invariant in the short-term, but surmountable with a long-term investment in state-building. Indeed, the positive economic conditions enjoyed by Iraq during the mid- to late 1970s proved to be favorable for handling such concerns. In the 1970s, Iraq was a rapidly modernizing state, flush with foreign currency reserves as a result of rising oil prices. The Iraqi state spent freely in a bid to extend its reach through the building of roads and schools and new job creation in the public sector. While the political elite was dominated by the regional and tribal kinsmen of Hussein, the benefits associated with the economic boom were felt by large swaths of the Iraqi population.

But the economic expansion of the 1970s was interrupted by a costly war in the 1980s, followed by more than a decade of debilitating economic sanctions. Rapidly declining economic conditions had important political implications. And while there is little doubt that Ba'thist-initiated foreign policy actions were undertaken with domestic political considerations in mind, evidence from a variety of sources suggests that the regime leadership often anticipated vastly different reactions by foreign powers than those actually observed. In fact, the Iraqi leadership was poorly positioned to predict many of the domestically relevant externalities associated with these foreign policy choices. In some cases, Hussein may have been insulated from high-quality estimates of success as a result of incompetent or sycophantic advisors. In other cases, he and his advisors may have misread signals from international actors or failed to make accurate predictions about how international actors would respond to his actions.

For example, Hussein invaded Iran in 1980, just months after the 1979 Islamic Revolution in Iran. Although there had been long-simmering grievances between the two countries, Hussein believed that the Iranians were

69. E.g., Marx 1998.
70. Brubaker 2004.

weak, geopolitically isolated, and likely to capitulate quickly. Rather than lasting for six weeks—as had been anticipated by the Iraqi side—the war lasted for eight years. Chapter 4 discusses both Iraqi regime expectations going into the conflict as well as the uneven distribution of human casualties on the Iraqi side. I argue that the political implications of war costs undermined investment in the regime among Iraqi Shiʻa who disproportionately bore the burden of war.

A second, critical strategic error relates to the Iraqi regime's decision to invade Kuwait in August 1990. Some accounts have suggested that Hussein believed the United States would not intervene in inter-Arab disputes based on his July 25th meeting with then-US Ambassador April Glaspie, just eight days before the Iraqi invasion of Kuwait.[71] Although accounts of that particular meeting vary, the result was that Hussein "seriously miscalculated Arab and Western opposition to Iraq's annexation of Kuwait."[72] The 1990–1991 Gulf War between Iraq and the United States (with its coalition partners) was a military conflict that Iraqi leaders did not anticipate would take place but, nonetheless, had far-reaching consequences for domestic Iraqi coalitional concerns. Most important, in March and April 1991, an anti-regime insurgency erupted in Shiʻi and Kurdish regions of Iraq that left fourteen of eighteen Iraqi governorates outside of government control at its peak. These protests led Iraq's three northern governorates to political autonomy and to a markedly different relationship between the regime and Shiʻi populations of the country after 1991.

Finally, the United Nations Security Council sanctions imposed upon Iraq beginning in 1990 and continuing until 2003 were among the most stringent financial and trade restrictions ever inflicted on a developing country. The economic contraction associated with sanctions impacted all Iraqis, creating tension at many levels of society. Public sector employees saw huge income losses, increasing political dissension for Iraq's large class of party and civil servants. And as state sector expenditures fell, Hussein and his immediate family increasingly monopolized income-generating economic opportunities, like smuggling. The net result was a decline in the financial benefits to all

71. The historical record on this issue is not entirely clear, in part because of the difficulty associated with knowing Hussein's beliefs and expectations during the meeting. See Stephen Walt, "WikiLeaks, April Glaspie and Saddam Hussein," *Foreign Policy*, January 9, 2011 for more on this issue.

72. Davis 2005, 227.

Iraqis, including Sunni Iraqis who were not part of Hussein's inner circle. In chapter 5, I argue that the sanctions regime drove a political wedge within the Sunni community with important implications. Hussein had not anticipated such a vociferous, negative response to his invasion of Kuwait and had no prior belief that sanctions of such magnitude would be imposed. Decisions about the sanctions were made by international actors, only indirectly influenced by Iraqi diplomacy.[73]

PLAN FOR THE BOOK

Part I of the book describes my theoretical framework and provides an empirically focused discussion of Iraq's recent history. Chapter 2 details the theoretical arguments of the project and enumerates a series of empirical implications of the theory. Chapter 3 describes the nature of political life in Iraq before the start of the Iran-Iraq War. Understanding how the Ba'thist regime fared during times of economic plenty provides a basis for evaluating an implicit counterfactual in this book—that were it not for the massive financial shocks associated with the Iran-Iraq War and 1986 crude oil price collapse, Iraq might have remained an "ordinary developing country" rather than a "republic of fear."[74]

Chapter 4 establishes a key empirical point using new data; I demonstrate that ethno-sectarian communities within Iraq paid a differential cost associated with the Iran-Iraq and Gulf Wars and that this differential war burden created the conditions for the 1991 Uprisings. While scholars have sought to estimate aggregate death tolls using census and other data, previous scholarship has failed to empirically demonstrate the within-Iraq variation with regard to war casualties. Chapter 5 discusses the political impact of the international sanctions regime instituted after the Iraqi invasion of Kuwait. Data from a variety of sources suggest differential costs borne within Iraq's Sunni community, with implications for the vulnerability of the regime from "insider" threats.

Part II of the book examines the political behaviors that are the core focus of this volume. Chapter 6 provides details about the behaviors of

73. For example, during the 1990s, there existed a great deal of uncertainty about when the sanctions would end or eventually be eased with the Oil-for-Food provisions.
74. Makiya 1998, vii.

Iraqis in the three northern governorates of Iraq leading up to the creation of an autonomous political zone in Iraqi Kurdistan in 1991. Chapter 7 discusses a wide range of behaviors related to participation in the Baʿth Party, including the political orientation of Iraqi students, the distribution of party members across party ranks, and the regional distribution of the "friend of the president" bureaucratic status and other party honorifics. Chapter 8 shifts to an examination of the "hidden" political transcript through analysis of rumors circulating in Iraq covering a variety of subjects. Chapter 9 describes the rise of religious communalism and also details how the Baʿth Party sought to monitor and control the country's clerical establishment. Chapter 10 explores the relationship between the state and the military through an examination of three subjects, (i) evasion of compulsory military service, (ii) volunteerism for state and party militias, and (iii) coup attempts, the majority of which were initiated by members of the Iraqi military.

And, finally, chapter 11 recapitulates the main arguments of the project, discusses how my conclusions relate to existing scholarly work on Baʿthist Iraq, and describes the process of sectarian identity formation in Iraq after 2003. I also explore the theoretical and empirical generalizability of my arguments and findings.

PART I

THEORETICAL AND
EMPIRICAL
FOUNDATIONS

CHAPTER 2

COMPLIANCE AND RESISTANCE UNDER AUTOCRACY

When Iraqi government officials initiated the Anfal Campaign against targets in Iraqi Kurdistan, Iraq had been locked for five years in a costly, seemingly endless war of attrition against Iran.[1] In private meetings with commanders of the armed forces, Saddam Hussein expressed frustration with how to handle the problem of saboteurs (*mukharribun*), or anti-regime militants, in northern areas.[2] He was particulary upset that rebel groups were taking advantage of the regime's relative weakness while the Iraqi army was focused on the Iranian enemy. Organizing military strikes against insurgents posed a challenge since collecting accurate information on the positions of the saboteurs was difficult and high-quality intelligence was deemed a necessity.[3] Despite years of state investment in extending its scope to Iraq's Kurdish regions, the regime's intelligence-gathering capacity in the area continued to be weak.

By the spring of 1988, communications between high-ranking members of the regime suggested an air of panic. Kurdish resistance groups were making political control of northern areas problematic. Monitoring their activities was challenging as they operated through private networks and closed organizations. Helicopters were deployed to surveil movement on the roads, but monitoring activities on the ground proved difficult. Anti-regime militants were continually encouraged to return to the "national fold" with intensive messaging of promises for pardons in exchange for handing over

---

1. Literally, *anfal* means "booty" or spoils and was the code name used by the regime for its military campaign against Kurdish civilian populations in northern regions of Iraq during the final years of the Iran-Iraq War.
2. CRRC Doc. No. SH-SHTP-A-001-045, c. 1985.
3. Ibid.

weapons.[4] In March of 1988, the Kurdish resistance had improved its position in the town of Halabja.[5] Halabja appeared at risk of falling into Iranian hands, forcing a redirection of Iraqi army brigades to the North despite a desperate need for the troops on the southern front. Halabja, and other towns and villages in northern Iraq, were attacked with "special" ammunition (i.e., chemical agents), killing both members of the Kurdish resistance and non-combatants.[6] While these attacks did not lead to complete regime control in northern areas, resistance groups were forced to scatter, diminishing their effectiveness.[7]

The unfolding of the security crisis leading to the use of chemical weapons in Halabja illustrates a fundamental challenge facing the Iraqi regime, and authoritarian regimes more generally. Monitoring the behaviors of noncompliant citizens is costly; when times are tough, monitoring capacity might be diminished exactly at the moment stakes of failure are rising. This can lead regimes to undertake forms of punishment that work against their broader state-building interests.

This chapter provides a theoretical framework for understanding forms of both cooperation and non-compliance in an oppressive political context.[8] State action, which is subject to a variety of constraints and shocks, shapes both the incentives faced by citizens calibrating their behaviors as well as the less tangible beliefs held by individuals that inform their actions. These beliefs include ideational commitments like nationalism—the view that the interests of the nation are of primary importance—and communalism—the view that the concerns of tribes, religious communities, or other groups are core interests. I present my conceptualization of distribution and punishment regimes and discuss how rewards and punishment vary in intensity and precision over time and place. Resources, including informational gaps, underlie the use of collective repression which subsequently plays a determining role in the behaviors of citizens.

---

4. CRRC Doc. No. SH-GMID-D-000-859, Spring 1988.
5. CRRC Doc. No. SH-GMID-D-000-468, March 15, 1988
6. CRRC Doc. No. SH-GMID-D-000-859, Spring 1988.
7. CRRC Doc. No. SH-PDWN-D-000-678, 1988.
8. Legal scholars define compliance in the context of conformity to law or other official requirements. A broader definition, however, considers compliance as satisfying a demand or a desire. In this text, I adopt a definition that goes beyond compliance with the law to also include compliance with expectations and norms of behavior either demanded or desired by an autocratic regime.

A THEORY OF COMPLIANCE AND RESISTANCE

A rich and influential literature offers theoretical insights into when and why citizens comply with government directives and expectations. Scholarly consensus suggests that multiple motivations play into individual behavioral choices with regard to the state. For example, in the context of democratic regimes, Levi asks: "when are individuals actively consenting and when are they more passively engaged in conforming and acquiescing?"[9] While both sanctions and incentives play a role in determining citizen behavior, Levi makes the case that at least some portion of observed compliance reflects belief in the "rightness of the policies and of the trustworthiness of the government actors implementing them."[10]

Levi's arguments about citizen behavior in democratic contexts reflect a vastly different set of conditions when compared with the behavior of citizens living under dictatorship, particularly highly restrictive autocratic regimes.[11] In dictatorships, trust in government is often less salient than concerns about government sanctions or rewards. Some of the most influential work in the existing literature suggests that uncertainty about the preferences of others in society breeds compliance—until it doesn't, when citizens engage in massive, and often violent, periods of popular revolt.[12] Where existing scholarly work does point to quiet forms of resistance to political power, scholars suggest the importance of reading a society's "hidden transcript."[13] But a great deal of political resistance exists between the realms of open insurgency and the subtle modes of resistance exercised by the weak.

9. Levi 1997, 16.
10. Levi 1997, 18.
11. Ermakoff (2008) presents a series of explanations for the process of "collective abdication," or why a group would surrender its fate and ensure its political submission to another actor. A first explanation is related to fear and coercion where political abdication takes place in the shadow of intimidation. Ermakoff points out, however, that resistance often takes place under highly intimidating political conditions, suggesting a more complex narrative. For Ermakoff, the key to understanding collective abdication is considering how the actions undertaken by individuals are conditioned on the behaviors of other actors, where individuals highly value coordination with others. Through a process of "collective alignment," members of a group facing the same decision align their behavior with one another. Alignment takes place sequentially where risks are assessed in light of the behaviors of others and political isolation is viewed as a bad outcome (182).
12. Kuran 1995.
13. Scott 1985.

Beyond resistance activity, there also exist important puzzles regarding when and why citizens actively cooperate with autocratic governments or engage in public behaviors that signal their support for the regime. Co-ethnic status would seem to be an important factor influencing support for incumbent authoritarians; existing work suggests that shared ethnic status with a ruler often leads to meaningful gains in public goods that an individual or community may not enjoy under an alternative leadership. Levi finds that under some circumstances, politically compliant behavior relates to habits of conformity.[14] Common sense suggests that beyond material considerations, personal security would also be a powerful driver of collaboration with a sitting autocrat, particularly when a person or group shares some responsibility for past violence or atrocities. Yet, the literature in political science remains underdeveloped regarding the conditions under which citizen cooperation is most likely to occur.[15]

Other studies consider the role played by technocrats and party apparatchik who carry out the directives of the dictator. Without the collaboration of these individuals, the business of oppressive rule would not be done.[16] Studies

14. Levi 1997. While some of these habits may be learned, others could be the result of personality traits. Altemeyer (1998, 48) argues that individuals who exhibit an authoritarian submission trait tend to "believe strongly in submission to established authorities and the social norms these authorities endorse."

15. Schedler (2013) argues that political collaboration with an autocratic regime can take many forms—formal and informal collaboration as well as collaboration that exists within or outside of state institutions. Existing work that seeks to explain the provision of political support for dictatorship typically focuses on various classes of political actors. One class of studies emphasizes a dictator's reliance on a small, trusted circle of political elites. This inner-circle might be built around a military academy class or as a result of shared co-ethnic, tribal, or regional status. By appointing individuals with close ties to serve as high-level advisors, dictators may miss out on the opportunity to appoint more competent bureaucrats, trading competence for loyalty. These individuals are often significant beneficiaries of the regime's financial resources.

16. Scholars in the field of social psychology have made the largest advances in understanding the conditions under which non-sociopathic individuals might participate in activities that would seem to be morally objectionable. For example, in his study of the Nazi doctors who sought to rationalize their participation in Hitler's genocidal campaign, Lifton (2000 [1986]) argues that evil behavior needs to be understood in its context, arising out of "atrocity-producing situations" even in the absence of mental illness or a psychopathic disorder on the part of the perpetrators. Goldhagen (1996, 11–12) argues that there exist a number of different explanations for why individuals commit atrocities—that these behaviors were coerced, that perpetrators blindly followed orders, that they were subject to social psychological pressure to conform, that perpetrators were soulless bureaucrats pursuing their own career objectives,

focused on political elites and their support for autocratic regimes tend to say little about how and why regular citizens collaborate with or reinforce forms of hegemonic control in autocracies.[17] While material payoffs are a part of the conventional explanation, scholars have also pointed to the importance of the rituals of autocracy for encouraging forms of complicity and political domination.[18]

The primary argument of this book is that citizen behaviors in autocratic contexts are determined by the intensity and precision of expected rewards and punishments administered by the state. In this setting, the intensity and precision of rewards and punishments are subject to conditions and shocks that may be beyond the immediate control of the autocrat. In the next section, I discuss the basic assumptions of my project regarding the importance of incentives in motivating human behavior as well as how incentives shape beliefs. I also define two dimensions of punishment and reward—intensity and precision. I describe how the intensity and precision of a given punishment or reward influence both investment in the authoritarian regime and beliefs about community cohesion. The section that follows discusses the theoretical framework as applied to the case of Iraq with a focus on the specific empirical implications of the project.

Incentives, Beliefs, and Behaviors

I take for granted that Iraqis, like other individuals, are motivated by incentives that can take a number of forms, particularly financial and coercive incentives. Financial incentives exist when an individual expects a material reward in exchange for a particular mode of behavior. Coercive incentives exist when failure to adopt a particular mode of behavior leads to an expectation that an individual, or his or her family or community, will be punished in some

---

or that tasks associated with abuse were so fragmented, individuals did not understand their role in the atrocity. In the case of ordinary Germans carrying out the tasks associated with the Holocaust, Goldhagen (1996, 14) argues that anti-Semitism motivated the actions of Nazi and state apparatchik.

17. Kalyvas (2006, 180) distinguishes between collaboration and denunciation where denunciation refers to the provision of information about specific individuals while collaboration involves a much wider set of activities. Importantly, individuals may simultaneously publicly collaborate with the regime while engaging in private resistance activity.

18. See Wedeen 1999. Also, see Faust (2015, 67) for a discussion of this point in the Iraqi context.

way. These punishments might include bodily harm, imprisonment, expropriation of property, or forced relocation.[19] The idea that financial and coercive incentives motivate citizen behavior with regard to government directives and expectations aligns with what Levi calls "opportunistic obedience." In this setting, individuals calculate the costs and benefits of actions and engage in "compliance due to fear of sanction or promise of inducements."[20]

A second key assumption of this project is that citizen behaviors in authoritarian regimes are governed by the interaction between incentives and beliefs. In particular, reward and punishment structures influence citizen beliefs and, when taken together with incentives, beliefs and incentives generate behaviors. What does it mean to say that incentive structures generate beliefs? By this, I mean that the manner in which citizens are rewarded or punished by the government influences the personal convictions that make up their worldview, including beliefs about government and also about the preferences and beliefs of others in their community.[21] While state incentive structures influence multiple domains, in this project I focus on two main areas. The first is related to an individual's beliefs about the performance, efficacy, and legitimacy of the political regime. The second relates to the politically relevant level and degree of social cohesion within one's community.[22]

19. Grant (2006) considers the ethical implications of various incentive systems. She argues that while some incentives reflect a form of voluntary, economic trade from which both parties benefit, coercive incentives reflect a display of power that makes them ethically objectionable.

20. See Levi 1997, 28–30. The assumption that individuals respond behaviorally to selective incentives, whether they be positive or negative inducements, is associated with Olson (1965) and has been applied most vigorously to the study of the free rider problem associated with collective action dilemmas. For Olson, selective incentives might take the form of less tangible benefits like social status or social acceptance. My argument differs, however, as I am suggesting that the incentive structure impacts beliefs about social factors.

21. For example, in the field of sociology the "Pygmalion," or Rosenthal, effect refers to a series of studies which show that the ways that teachers treat students influence the way that students behave, perform, and think about school. Work in the field of law and society suggests that perceived legitimacy regarding procedural justice by the government toward an individual and his or her group can strongly affect that individual's beliefs about the legitimacy of the system (Tyler 2006). System justification theory suggests that individuals hold positive beliefs toward status quo social structures of which they are beneficiaries. Effort justification theory suggests that people place a greater value on an outcome when they put a great deal of effort into acquiring it (like being admitted to a club that subjects its prospective members to unpleasant treatment). In all of these cases, the way one is treated impacts beliefs about oneself or the world.

22. My approach is related to that taken by Elster (2015), who argues that attempts to understand utility maximization need to be put in the context of psychological and other

Why is it important that incentives are not the sole drivers of human action? Beliefs are particularly important factors when discussing behaviors that are jointly produced, or rely on the collaborative effort of multiple actors. Beliefs about the preferences and expected behaviors of others in society may allow citizens to solve collective action problems, like the provision of a costly public good. Common knowledge encourages successful coordination of behavior by individuals who rely on shared understandings. A focus on incentives alone fails to take into account the types of social forces that allow individuals to aggregate their efforts into complex, and potentially costly, behaviors like rebellion or political subversion.

This text also assumes that government policy can be understood through an examination of systems of rewards and punishments administered by states. While this focus is narrow as it under-emphasizes the importance of factors like individual leader attributes and political ideology and culture, I believe the categories of reward and punishment to be sufficiently broad as to capture the dynamics I see as core determinants of citizen behavior under conditions of autocracy. Relatedly, I make some critical assumptions about the differential ways in which rewards and punishment operate.[23] For example, while inaccurately administered rewards giving would likely be welcomed by individual recipients as a windfall, the costs associated with imprecision in administration of punishment suggest a core asymmetry between the two concepts.

Finally, I presume that indiscriminate punishment by political regimes tends to backfire and, knowing this, regimes prefer targeted punishment, all else being equal. Scholarly consensus suggests that this is a widely held belief.[24] This assumption also seems appropriate for the Iraqi case. Dimitrov

---

constraints, like the challenges associated with estimating risk, aversion to loss, and emotional reactions to unfair treatment. But while Elster (486) is focused on the way that "preferences and beliefs of an individual jointly induce actions," I place greater emphasis on the role of incentives in shaping beliefs about government and the preferences of others in society. These beliefs are less related to psychological constraints on human cognition and more a function of reasonable inferences that one might make given a particular state of the world.

23. For example, like Dari-Mattiacci and de Geest (2010), I assume it is harder to economize on rewards compared to punishment, as the threat to punish enjoys a multiplication effect while reward gets used up every time compliance occurs. This appears to be the case mostly when the threat to punish is meted out against individuals sequentially, limiting their ability to coordinate their actions.

24. Greitens (2016), for example, sees indiscriminate violence as self-undermining. In the study of insurgent violence and civil wars, scholars generally agree that indiscriminate violence

and Sassoon argue that information scarcity in Iraq led to more totalizing forms of political repression, while increased security service penetration was associated with decreased violence and repression.[25] Johnson has argued that "Saddam's group knew that political repression alone would generate more resistance."[26] Faust finds that "Hussein and the Ba'th never pursued a policy of indiscriminate terror toward the Iraqi population at large," but that "structural and extralegal characteristics" of the system often led innocent civilians to suffer as a result of regime action.[27] In other words, the optimal punishment regime for states would be one where non-compliance is accurately observed and punishments are meted out with perfect precision at a penalty value that would completely deter violations.[28]

In some cases, the Ba'thist regime went to great effort and expense to determine whether an individual was guilty or innocent.[29] For example, following the 1991 Uprisings, the regime expended considerable energy to identify those responsible. A university professor who was a suspected organizer of the protests described his experience in a prison memoir.[30] The regime planted informants in his prison cell and incentivized others to provide evidence

---

is counterproductive as it generates new grievances and decreases the opportunity cost of collaborating with the rival actor (Kalyvas 2006; Lyall 2009). Kocher et al. (2011) find that bombing civilians systematically shifted control in favor of the insurgents during the Vietnam War. Condra and Shapiro (2012) find that collateral damage hurts both insurgent and regime sides during conflict. Downes (2007) argues that indiscriminate violence can be effective under specific circumstances, including situations with a small population supporting the insurgents or a smaller geographic domain.

25. Dimitrov and Sassoon 2014.
26. Johnson 2011, 32.
27. Faust 2015, 153.
28. Indiscriminate punishment of civilian populations can arise for a variety of reasons. A number of studies focus on why insurgent groups engage in indiscriminate punishment. Weinstein (2006) argues that rebel strategies regarding the use of indiscriminate violence differ for ideologically and materially motivated groups. Humphreys and Weinstein (2006) argue that the determinants of civilian abuse during civil wars are often internal to the structure of the warring factions themselves. In this project, I focus on indiscriminate violence undertaken by the state rather than insurgent groups, though some of the same mechanisms connecting collective punishment to identity formation may be relevant in the context of insurgent behavior as well.
29. This is not to say that mistakes were not commonplace, a function of regime intelligence failures. For example, a case of mistaken identity—specifically the arrest of someone with almost an identical name—forms the plot of Mahmoud Saeed's fictional account in the 2004 novel, *Saddam City*.
30. Albrisem 2013.

against him. But if someone "fingered" a person who was not actually guilty, or found not to be guilty, the accuser himself would be executed.[31] His account suggests that the regime desired to obtain accurate information when they believed they had the capacity to do so.[32] A similar sentiment was expressed by a party official speaking to Hussein in 1994 about treatment of suspected draft dodgers. The party official says it would have been easy to simply charge anyone captured and suspected of draft evasion, but instead, a thorough and time-consuming investigation was undertaken for each case.[33]

To summarize, I assume that individuals are motivated by both coercive and financial incentives. Incentives and beliefs, together, generate behaviors, many of which require coordination across societal actors. I focus on two beliefs in particular, a citizen's investment in the regime, and his or her beliefs about societal cohesion. I argue that these beliefs are influenced by the systems of reward and punishment administered by governments where there exist important asymmetries in the way that rewards and punishment operate.

Distribution and Punishment Regimes

There are two key dimensions to the systems of distribution and punishment used by dictatorships.[34] The first dimension involves the intensity of punishment or reward. The second relates to the precision with which it is applied. I argue that while distribution and punishment regimes are both subject to budget and legibility constraints, budget constraints are more salient for systems of reward while legibility constraints are of higher salience for systems

31. There was also a reluctance to believe confessions that were made under torture; for example, when poorly trained military personnel elicited a confession from a subject, these confessions were not accepted as evidence or believed by more professional interrogators (Albrisem 2013).

32. In addition to the sentencing and execution of individuals believed to be guilty of disloyalty to the Baʿthist regime, the dehumanizing and unsanitary conditions of Iraqi prisons led to the deaths of tens of thousands. Individuals who did not comply with prison rules were also often executed, though the random (i.e., completely indiscriminate) killing of prisoners appears to have been most commonly a practice used to elicit truthful confessions from prisoners (or, in some cases, the actions of sadistic higher-level regime insiders like Saddam Hussein's son, ʿUday).

33. CRRC Doc No. SH-SHTP-A-001-238, September 3, 1994.

34. My conceptualization bears similarities to Greitens (2016, 65), who focuses on the scope of state violence, its intensity, and its indiscriminacy. In my account, I consider intensity and precision, two dimensions of interest as applied to both punishment and reward.

of punishment. In this section, I attempt to explain how states influence behaviors as well as why regimes choose (or are saddled with) particular types of punishment and reward systems.

Distribution and Its Impact on Investment in the Regime

There is a broad consensus that material benefits incentivize individuals to support authoritarian regimes. Wintrobe observes that dictators do not rule through repression alone and, as a result, must "pay" for loyalty.[35] In this setting, repression and co-optation are substitutes.[36] For Gandhi and Przeworski, dictators share rents and make policy concessions to avoid rebellion.[37] Magaloni argues that individuals are constantly updating their expectations about economic growth, and holding authoritarian regimes responsible for recession.[38] Blaydes sees informal rights to rent streams as important for maintaining elite coalitions; likewise, elites are forced to engage in downward provision of rewards to mobilize voters they have promised to the regime.[39] Distribution of state wealth streams, services, and rents constitutes a key strategy for politicians to protect themselves from dissent and, maybe, even removal from office.[40]

Rewards influence behaviors in two ways. First, the rewards, or rents, themselves induce compliance as individuals enjoy the material benefits associated with that transfer. Second, receiving private or public goods from the regime also increases an individual's investment in the regime, both from a psychological perspective and from a forward-looking anticipation of future rent streams. If an individual is receiving private or public goods from the regime, that individual begins to assess the regime in a positive way. At the same time, individuals become more invested in the regime as they seek to maintain anticipated future benefits that they hope to enjoy. In other words, actors are not just thinking about their contemporaneous payoff but also the

35. See Wintrobe 1998. In the context of authoritarian Iraq, scholars have discussed the idea of "*tarhib wa targhib*," or "terror and enticement," as the twin pillars used to cement loyalty to the Baʿthist regime (Faust 2015, 15–16).

36. Some formal theoretic models of authoritarianism focus on issues of power and power sharing with less focus on the way that rent distribution matters for regimes (Svolik 2012).

37. Gandhi and Przeworski 2006.

38. Magaloni 2006.

39. Blaydes 2011.

40. Golden and Min 2013.

value of all future payoffs. In many ways, this framework relates to existing literature in the study of democratic politics on retrospective voting. In democracies, citizens evaluate performance of incumbents with implications for vote choice. In authoritarian settings, meaningful vote choice is not an option, but citizens nonetheless engage in processes of evaluating government and acting on the beliefs these evaluations generated. Objective performance indicators like GDP growth and unemployment matter for voters in democracies, but individuals are also concerned with their own personal well-being.[41]

My conceptualization differs from backward-looking evaluations, however, as investment in the regime also depends on expectations about future benefits. In this conceptualization, investment acts like loyalty as described in Wintrobe.[42] For Wintrobe, loyalty—defined as attachment to an organization or institution—is a capital asset that a dictator might invest in through the provision of public goods and patronage. Like Wintrobe, I see investment in the regime as acquired through the provision of material benefits including property rights to various rent opportunities. Unlike Wintrobe, however, I do not view loyalty, or attachment, as the key conceptual factor influencing behaviors; rather, I see investment in the regime as contributing to an individual's belief about the value of current and future income streams. Part of this calculation is conditional on the extent to which others in the society also hold a high level of investment in the regime. This suggests that an individual's investment in the regime depends, in part, on the evaluation of the regime by others in society.

There are two dimensions along which reward can vary—in its intensity and in the precision with which it is distributed. Individuals who receive more goods increase their level of investment in the regime, though perhaps not in a linear fashion. Eventually, citizens who receive private and public goods often begin to approve of the government to some degree, or at least do not feel as strongly that the government needs to be opposed or replaced.[43] They also know that more people in their community feel that way, creating common

41. As Ferejohn (1986) points out, incumbents are judged on growth, avoiding major wars and providing public and private goods to constituents.

42. Wintrobe 1990.

43. Within democratic contexts, Birnir (2007) argues that restrictions on ethnic access to the executive—and its associated rents—create incentives for an ethnic group to deviate from peaceful electoral participation.

knowledge about the investment of others in the government. In other words, investment in the regime is endogenous to the intensity of the reward one receives.[44] And, unlike in the case of punishment, legibility is not an issue when it comes to rewards as everyone shows up to collect their reward.[45]

In the Iraqi case, investment in the regime was often unrelated to ideological support for Baʿthism and its principles, particularly during Saddam Hussein's period in power. Rather, individuals were offered privileged financial opportunities as a result of their "closeness" to Hussein where proximity was often determined by regional and tribal ties (Baram 2003, 99).[46] For example, coveted party positions were often filled by individuals drawn overwhelmingly from the provincial towns neighboring Tikrit.[47] This was particularly the case for staffing the Iraqi Republican Guard, as Hussein felt confident in his ability to rely on tribal relations for stalwart support. The opportunity for well-paying jobs and quick promotions afforded these individuals social status which invested them in the perpetuation of the regime.[48] Indeed, some have suggested that many Baʿth Party apparatchik during Hussein's time in power were poorly educated individuals from impoverished families who owed their economic affluence entirely to the regime.[49]

It is possible to imagine situations where there exist high-intensity, collective rewards and, likewise, low-intensity, individualized rewards. Budget constraints often make collective, high-intensity rewards too costly for most

44. The most common and effective way to access private information is via "consensual provision" (Kalyvas 2006, 176). Kalyvas focuses on allegiances in civil wars as endogenous to war outcomes. My focus is a little different. I argue allegiances are endogenous to reward systems. Kalyvas (178) views denunciations as motivated by either political or personal vendettas but tends to downplay the importance of material exchange or payment for denunciations. Kalyvas's focus is on control, not information, even though he acknowledges that information is important and a key determinant.

45. Even if they do not want to be publicly recognized for their actions, the person who is undertaking the desired behavior for the government wants to make that action legible.

46. Costly demonstrations of loyalty might also lead individuals to be "close" to Hussein.

47. See Marr 2004, 264. Hussein was born in the village of Awja, which is located to the south of Tikrit. Within the environs of Tikrit, some locals have argued that residents of Awja were privileged over Tikritis. For example, Bengio (1988, 363–364) argues that "although Tikrit formed an important base of support for Hussein, not all the Tikritis supported him." Yet despite the existence of variation in support for the regime within the area around Tikrit, most individuals from the Tikrit region came to see their future prospects tied to Hussein's even while questioning aspects of his authoritarian rule (ibid.).

48. Baram 2005.

49. Al-Khafaji 1992.

TABLE 2.1. Conceptual scheme for relationship between distribution regime and form of compliance. Above the dotted line represents the "rewards" or benefits offered to citizens; below the dotted line represents the costs imposed on citizens by the government.

Distribution Regime	Investment in Regime		Form of Compliance
Individualized Reward High Intensity	Strongly Positive	⇒	Active Cooperation
Collective Good Low Intensity	Mildly Positive	⇒	Acquiesence & Depoliticization
- - - - - - - - - - -	- - - - - - -	- -	- - - - - - - - - -
Collective "Tax" Low Intensity	Mildly Negative	⇒	Dissatisfaction & Disaffection
Individualized Loss High Intensity	Strongly Negative	⇒	Grievance & Disloyalty

regimes. As a result, this is largely an unoccupied "cell" in the analysis. In addition, when rewards are low intensity, regimes may not deem it worthwhile to make the effort to identify the worthy recipients with a high degree of precision given the costs associated with bureaucratic investment. In other words, most of the empirical observations tend to exist along the axis involving rewards that are individualized/high intensity and collective/low intensity.[50] It is also possible to imagine conditions under which states need to apportion burden as part of distributive politics.[51]

The framework I have described suggests a number of empirical implications, summarized in table 2.1. The first is that for conditions of high-intensity, individualized reward, citizens are likely to be invested in the regime and engage in active cooperation with regime expectations of behavior. When the recipient receives broadly provided, low-intensity rewards—in other words, public goods—this will induce, on average, acquiesence and

50. It would be untenable to offer everyone high-intensity, individualized rewards unless the regime was unlimited in its wealth.

51. Material loss or disincentives differ from a punishment in that punishment is a response to transgression while state-distributed burden is a "tax" that falls on citizens as a result of state circumstances.

depoliticization as the citizens enjoy some material rewards from the autocratic regime. If the state begins to distribute negative goods, in other words burdens upon a population, those burdens can also vary in their intensity and precision. In some cases, a "tax" might be levied on the population where everyone pays. The "tax" need not come in the form of a monetary assessment, but could instead include things like removal of subsidies, or a degrading of other public services, resulting in dissatisfaction and disaffection. Finally, when losses are individualized and high intensity, the result is disloyalty that may or may not be expressed depending on the cost of doing so.[52]

There are a number of implications of these arguments. Because autocratic regimes are vulnerable to economic and external shocks, such events have serious implications for their ability to maintain previous rent streams and associated investment in the regime. In good times, there might be sufficient rents to provide high-intensity, individualized rewards to core supporters of the population and less intense, more diffuse forms of benefit and public goods to others. Indeed, in Iraq during the 1970s, this was the case and, as a result, the country witnessed relatively high levels of active cooperation on the part of core groups and either passive collaboration or acquiesence on the part of others. One of the key arguments of this book is that a series of severe, prolonged, and largely unanticipated external shocks made it difficult for the Iraqi regime to maintain previous high levels of reward distribution with implications for political coalitions over time.

Punishment and Its Impact on Social Cohesion

For individuals who enjoy high-intensity, individualized rewards from an autocratic regime, the incentives for active collaboration are strong. While there are some individuals who engage in political transgressions at any level of reward, it seems reasonable to assume that the number of such individuals increases—on average—as rewards, and associated investment in the regime, decrease. While many individuals who receive low, or even "negative," rewards from the regime maintain a stance of passive neutrality, others will engage

---

52. What distinguishes a high-intensity, individualized loss from a punishment? Punishment is a penalty imposed for an outcome or behavior. A high-intensity, individualized loss may come about independently of a retributive logic. For example, a government policy that imposes a severe distributive cost on individual citizens—like a draft, for instance—should be thought of as a loss rather than a punishment.

in behaviors that the state seeks to punish. Underlying this perspective is the assumption that individuals derive utility from voicing their negative opinions about an authoritarian regime honestly, as doing so allows one to enjoy a feeling of self-respect and personal integrity.[53] Indeed, a large literature in social psychology would suggest that individuals suffer forms of mental distress if they are not able to maintain a coherent sense of self where one's actions are in line with one's beliefs.

But what happens when an individual acts upon the impulse to disobey an autocratic regime? Consider a situation where an individual citizen transgresses a regime directive. When a transgression occurs, a major challenge for an autocratic regime can involve identifying the individual or set of individuals deserving punishment for their actions. In other words, high monitoring costs are a key constraint on regimes in their efforts to disincentivize anti-regime behaviors.[54] While monitoring costs might be decreased with technological improvements—for example, the introduction of better surveillance methods—the challenge associated with identifying those responsible for unwanted behaviors is an enduring one.[55] In the context of insurgency, Fearon and Laitin argue that "if government forces knew who the rebels were and how to find them, they would be fairly easily destroyed or captured."[56] Kalyvas concurs, arguing that selective violence is costly as it requires an intelligence-gathering infrastructure to locate enemies through the use of civilian collaborators.[57] According to Greitens, "intelligence enables precise, selective, lower-intensity violence, against the right people and only when necessary."[58]

53. Kuran 1995.
54. For the Iraqi case, there seems to have been a desire on the part of the regime to make the punishment fit the nature of the transgression. For example, individuals who were believed to have chanted slogans against Hussein during the uprisings had their tongues cut out, individuals who shot weapons at party apparatchik had their fingers cut off, and those who urinated on pictures of Hussein had their genitals removed (Albrisem 2013).
55. Lyall and Wilson (2009) suggest one avenue by which indiscriminate targeting may be increased as a result of technological improvements. They argue that mechanization of military forces inadvertently fuel insurgencies because mechanized armies cannot easily deploy coercive power in a selective way.
56. Fearon and Laitin 2003, 80.
57. See Kalyvas 2006, 165. Kalyvas (145) writes that "the choice of whether to use selective or indiscriminate violence is heavily dependent on the quality of information available—one cannot discriminate without the information to discriminate—which itself is heavily dependent on the nature of the sovereignty exercised."
58. Greitens 2016, 43.

While the regime generally learns that the noncompliant behavior has occurred, it only observes a noisy signal of any particular individual's behavior. For the regime, then, the dimension of relevance is the smallest group for which behaviors can be observed with precision. I call this the *minimum legible group* and punishment is meted out at this level.[59] My argument provides the inverse insight when compared to that offered by Bates.[60] If Bates sees an ethnic group as a minimum winning coalition, large enough to win benefits for group members while simultaneously small enough to maximize value to members, my definition of an "ethnic" group reorients focus from distributive benefits to repressive punishments. Identity emerges or is reinforced at the level of the minimum legible group. Since the regime cannot distinguish between members within it, group-level punishment increases identity for the group through a mechanism that is distinct from the distribution of goods to a winning coalition.

A starting point for this analysis assumes differential costs for collecting information about opposition across societal groups.[61] In the extreme, forms of collective punishment that target entire villages or regions might be observed. Knowing that repression has the potential to radicalize individuals, autocratic regimes—all else being equal—prefer targeted to indiscriminate forms of repression. The cost to the state of information collection has important implications for the forms of social cohesion that emerge across communities.

There are at least three mechanisms by which this occurs. First, when acts of non-compliance are unobservable by the regime, individuals—knowing this—can organize relatively safely, encouraging the creation of dense networks with higher degrees of social cohesion. In other words, lack of state penetration of society creates the opportunities and incentives for coordination between individuals.[62]

59. The minimum legible group size takes a value of one when an individual is perfectly observed; group size is large if the regime only knows that the perpetrator lives in a certain area or has a certain ethno-religious identity.

60. Bates 1983.

61. Greitens (2016, 45) argues, for example, that shared ethnicity carries a demonstrated informational advantage in authoritarian settings.

62. Petersen (2001, 15) argues that strong communities encourage individuals to engage in more high-cost political activities through a number of mechanisms. Information costs are reduced in more cohesive social units and recruitment for political action is more successful (ibid.). In addition, communities with high levels of face-to-face contact and dense networks of social interaction tend to weigh positive and negative status rewards for behavior more highly, leading individuals to be more likely to engage in potentially costly political activity (ibid.).

Second, punishment of the collective creates incentives for individuals to develop closer bonds with those in their community.[63] When information-poor states punish citizens as a result of their membership in an identity group, this encourages the likelihood of "in-group" policing as the actions of one group member are tied to the outcomes for all members.[64] In the Iraqi context, poor monitoring capacity sometimes led the regime to use a dragnet approach to finding insurgents and other political dissidents. This served to "warn prospective offenders and their relatives to think twice before committing a crime or hiding their family member's transgressions"; the net result was to induce the population to "police itself."[65]

Relatedly, when punishment is both severe and collective, individuals increasingly come to believe that they share a "linked fate" with their fellow group members, further enhancing solidarity and collective political resistance.[66] Under such circumstances, social networks increase in density, encouraging a strategy of "all-in" resistance that can cascade into full-fledged rebellion. Individuals know that their own outcomes are contingent on the behaviors of their fellow co-"ethnics," enhancing incentives to coordinate. In the Iraqi context, this mechanism applies most clearly to the emergence of Kurdish nationalism. Iraqi Kurds had historically been organized around

63. The idea of dense social networks between co-ethnics is supported by experimental evidence that individuals, when interacting with co-ethnics, expect that they will be sanctioned for non cooperative behavior (Habyarimana et al., 2009).

64. See Fearon and Laitin (1996) for a discussion of in-group policing. For Fearon and Laitin, asymmetry of information makes it much easier for people to monitor and punish within their own ethnic groups as social networks are often more dense within ethnic groups compared to across groups. I make a similar assumption in this project. But while Fearon and Laitin are concerned with everyday inter-ethnic interactions that have the potential to spiral into broad forms of inter-ethnic conflict, I am focused on interactions between citizens and the state.

65. See Faust 2015, 154. According to Faust (149), "if families did not disown their deviant individual members, more family members might die or be tortured, and the entire extended family would therefore fall under heightened suspicion." In the extreme, if there were noncompliant members within an extended family whose actions posed a danger to the rest of the group, those individuals might be killed (Baram 2014, 110). Faust (2015, 3–4), for example, relates stories about individuals turning in or sometimes even killing their own sons and relatives for deserting from the army or failing to turn oneself in after deserting from the army. See Khoury (2013, 172–178) for a discussion of punishment at the level of the kin group.

66. My argument also suggests that social bonds are critical determinants of citizen behavior in dictatorships, a perspective shared by a number of scholars. Gurr (1970) argues that when grievances are large and societal groups have elaborate networks with strong, cohesive identities, then anti-regime rebellion is a possible outcome.

tribal or ideological interests. According to Bengio, the chemical attacks on Halabja and other Kurdish towns were "a major turning point in the crystallization of Kurdish identity."[67] Why was the regime driven to take such destructive measures? Ahram summarizes this perspective, arguing that the chemical attacks were undertaken because local informants were not providing sufficiently good information regarding collaboration between Kurdish insurgents and Iranian forces at the height of the Iran-Iraq War.[68]

The level at which these processes take place depends on how punishment is meted out by the state. When the state punishes at the level of the "nation"—impacting a collective with common characteristics like language, customs, and ethnicity—the result is *nationalism* for that collective.[69] When punishment takes place at the level of a smaller social group, the result is *communalism*. Punishment of this sort impacts a collective which shares actual or fictive kinship or ancestral ties, in which case the communalism takes the form of tribalism or "clannishness."[70] In other cases, the community of interest is not kin-based, but instead based on common religious training or beliefs. For example, the followers and seminary students of prominent religious leaders can develop a salient communal identity based on their shared adherence to the teachings of a particular cleric. None of this is to say that communalism emerged in some segments of the Iraqi population exclusively as a result of the punishment strategies employed by Hussein. Rather, communal identity was one of a repertoire of plausible latent identities that increased in salience as a result of the nature of state punishment.[71]

67. Bengio 2010, 62.

68. See Ahram 2011, 80. This perspective is consistent with Faust (2015, 7), who argues that "the production of fear was not the primary purpose for the Baʿth's violence." Indeed, Faust (148) finds no evidence that the Baʿthist regime under Hussein "purposefully meted terror randomly in order to instill fear," in contrast to Makiya's description of the regime (1998, xi–xii).

69. More precisely, when the relevant collective is an ethnic group, the result is ethnonationalism.

70. Throughout the project, I refer to nationalism in reference to Kurdish ethnonationalism and tribalism in reference to identity considerations associated with group ties that rely on beliefs of shared kinship or ancestral ties.

71. Existing work highlights this statement. Balcells (2011) finds that severe victimization during the Spanish Civil War and the Franco dictatorship impacted political identities, particularly identities that were related to the relevant cleavages when the violence was perpetrated. Rozenas et al. (2017) find that indiscriminate violence directed against civilian populations can have a long-lasting impact; in Ukraine, large-scale exposure to violence during

This argument suggests that the politically relevant cleavage structure may differ across communities within an autocratic regime. In addition, the most impactful determinants of societal cleavage structures may differ for autocracies and democracies. While societal cleavage in democracies, and emerging democracies, is highly influenced by relative factor endowment[72] and electoral institutions,[73] or may have been "frozen" into place at critical historical junctures,[74] existing theories hold less resonance for contemporary autocratic regimes where elections may not be focused on representing political constituencies.

What determines the state's choice to punish at the level of the nation or the communal group? And what types of factors increase or decrease a group's "legibility" from the perspective of the regime?[75] Shared language is one critical factor. Geographic accessibility—particularly the existence of mountainous terrain or other difficult to penetrate territories—also influences a government's ability to map an area, take a census, or engage in other forms of information collection. In some cases, such factors might be overcome with a large investment in bureaucratic expertise; even then, however, costly investment may not readily translate into local knowledge. In Iraq, for example, the regime faced challenges monitoring Shiʿi religious learning circles which tended to have dense social networks and sometimes even Persian-language instruction.

According to Faust, northern provinces were also hard for the Baʿth Party to penetrate "due to cultural and linguistic differences."[76] It was also difficult to staff certain parts of the country that were less desirable for Baʿth Party apparatchik.[77] In part, this was because few Baʿthists spoke Kurdish well, but it was also the case that Baʿthists who worked in northern areas were more

---

Stalin's rule affected the political preferences of communities generations later. Lupu and Peisakhin (2017) find that the indiscriminate deportation and victimization of Crimean Tartars in 1944 impacted the attitudes and behaviors of descendants.

72. Rogowski 1989.
73. Posner 2004.
74. Lipset and Rokkan 1967.
75. See Scott (1998) on the efforts of high modernist states to render society as "legible."
76. Faust 2015, 161.
77. Rotation systems were often employed to staff undesirable locations. Greitens (2016, 46) argues, however, that rotation policies create "social distance between police and society" since these policies "prevent bureaucrats from building bonds with local residents or locally recruited grunts."

likely to be killed in the line of duty than in other parts of Iraq.[78] Challenges of this type were compounded by the existence of mountainous hideouts in northern Iraq which provided a location for anti-regime insurgents to mount attacks on Ba'th Party headquarters. In response, the party offered incentives to encourage Ba'thists to work in northern provinces, including shortened assignment times, free housing and vehicles, and accelerated promotions and bonuses.[79] In one case, a security service official asked to be moved back to his home city following his posting in the northern city of Sulaymaniyya. It was revealed that he had lied about how long he had been in Sulaymaniyya (one year and eight months rather than his full two-year assignment) and was punished by having to remain in Sulaymaniyya longer.[80]

At the opposite extreme, a high level of regime penetration into a community means that punishment for transgressing regime expectations tends to be more individualized. Segments of society with more individualized punishment and lower levels of punishment intensity are able to publicly express forms of dissent with less risk, but have a more difficult time fostering social cohesion. Further, the ease with which information is gathered about opposition to the regime leaves disgruntled individuals with less of an incentive to hide their beliefs; agents of the regime are likely to ferret out their preferences anyway. Citizens recognize that regime penetration of their network means that even close associates might report their opposition beliefs to the government. For highly penetrated parts of Iraqi society, trust between individuals was very low. An individual would expect to be punished for failing to turn in an associate who committed even a minor transgression.[81] Ba'thification in this context had the tendency to "atomize" individuals from one another.[82] Low levels of interpersonal trust were common even within the set of people who had close relations with Hussein, as they were often subjected to intense and effective scrutiny.[83] In such a context, even subtle forms of political resistance were likely to be detected.[84]

78. Faust 2015, 161–162.
79. See Faust 2015, 161. For example, during the Iran-Iraq War, party cadre who worked in Kurdish areas would receive the benefits of participation in the Popular Army, even receiving the benefits of state martyrdom if the individual died during the course of service (ibid.).
80. North Iraq Dataset Doc. No. 21454-101-39.
81. Faust 2015, 155.
82. Ibid., 149
83. CRRC Doc. No. SH-INMD-D-000-657-5, August 1995.
84. Machain et al. (2011) develop a formal model where individuals make a decision about whether or not to engage in anti-state rebellion. In this model, individual decision-makers

For middling levels of legibility, dissent tends to move underground into the realm of furtive behavior. In these cases, the regime may have some idea about who perpetrated the transgression, but not enough information to identify an individual transgressor. Under such circumstances, trust and social cohesion develop at the group level, often to include members of a tribe or a communal religious society. It is also at the level of the group that transgressors might be reined in by those in their community in a bid to avoid group-level punishment.

Punishment precision and punishment intensity do not necessarily increase together. Indeed, communities are regularly sanctioned or deprived of resources in autocracies for non-compliance with government directives or expectations. For example, in Egypt under Mubarak, districts that voted for the Muslim Brotherhood in parliamentary elections received smaller improvements to their physical infrastructure.[85] Similarly, a close associate of the dictator might receive an individualized reprimand for a transgression which would represent a low-intensity, high-precision punishment.

Yet cultural distance may be driving both the legibility of communities as well as a willingness to use intensive forms of punishment. This is, in part, because groups that are highly legible are often closely connected to the dictator. Citizen populations that are legible to a regime tend to be those that have the closest ties to the ruling elite; citizen populations that are less legible to a regime—as a result of language difference, geographic distance, or difference in ethnic identity—are typically less central coalition partners. Therefore, while all "cells" associated with levels of precision and intensity are feasible, precision and intensity are often inversely correlated, particularly for the most repressive regimes.

Table 2.2 provides a conceptual scheme for the relationship between the prevailing punishment regime and the form of non-compliance observed. Low-intensity, individualized punishment is associated with minimal social

---

do not know whether the government will punish indiscriminately, regardless of whether the individual participates in the rebellion, or only as a function of participation in rebellion. In this setting individuals decide whether to engage in rebellion knowing there is some probability that the government will punish them even if they do not rebel. For Machain et al. (2011) states come in two types, the "nasty" type which punishes indiscriminately, and the type that only punishes if acts of violence are committed and will only punish those who commit the rebellious acts. In my conceptualization, indiscriminate punishment emerges as a result of limitations to state capacity rather than as a function of state "type."

85. Blaydes 2011.

TABLE 2.2. Conceptual scheme for relationship between punishment regime and form of non-compliance.

Punishment Regime	Social Cohesion		Form of Non-compliance
Individualized Low Intensity	Low (Individualism)	⇒	Public Non-cooperation
Group ("Communal") Middling Intensity	Middling (Communalism)	⇒	"Underground" Transgression
Collective ("National") High Intensity	High (Nationalism)	⇒	Nationalist Rebellion

cohesion and small-scale, public forms of political non-cooperation. As the punishment regime intensifies in both its precision and intensity, citizens shift from public to underground acts of political non-compliance. Many of these less public acts of non-compliance require at least some degree of complicity from those in one's community.[86] Social cohesion emerges strongly in the least legible communities, generating conditions suitable for rebellion. In contrast to the reward regime, the effect of punishment on behavioral outcomes is discontinuous in that citizens move from small-scale public defiance to quiet transgression to the potential for open rebellion.[87]

Feedback Loops

I have argued that collective punishment impacts populations in a number of ways—by signaling the opportunity structure around coordination, by creating incentives to police the collective internally, and by linking the outcomes of group members in ways that encourage their coordinated behavior. There is nothing about the theoretical argument I have presented that suggests a

86. In other words, what seem to be dyadic relationships between citizen and state are often mediated by an individual's social interactions with other citizens.

87. The question of how conflict impacts group cohesion has long been a topic of scholarly discussion. Stein (1976) finds that there is no clear empirical relationship between conflict and group cohesion, in part, because the core concepts of conflict, group, and cohesion are not subject to a uniform definition. In this project, I offer a more specific definition of conflict—focused on state repression—and its impact on social cohesion, at various levels of "group-ness."

particular starting point, however, complicating the issue of determining an empirical beginning for the analysis.

Greitens argues that the punishment repertoire of autocratic regimes reflects the design of the regime's coercive institutions.[88] For regimes that were founded under conditions of a high potential for coup risk, coercive institutions tend to be fragmented and exclusive, both factors that hinder the collection of intelligence that allows for more discriminating forms of repression; this contrasts with unitary and inclusive security institutions, which are able to gather intelligence in a way that minimizes the use of indiscriminate violence. For Greitens, coercive institutions get locked into place based on the "dominant perceived threat" facing an autocrat at the time they come to power.[89] For the Baʿthist regime in Iraq, coup risk would have exceeded threat from popular revolt at the time of the regime's founding, suggesting a preference for multiple, overlapping coercive institutions built around a narrow cadre of regime loyalists.

A more flexible approach allows for the possibility of feedback loops, which are a common feature of complex political and social interactions. The interaction between punishment regime and the behaviors that punishment induces in a population undoubtedly exist in a dynamic system. In this setting, a regime's system of punishment and reward serves as a key determinant of citizen beliefs and behaviors; those systems, in turn, are influenced by a state's resources, bureaucratic capacity, and vulnerability to external shocks, which can lead to discontinuities in how rewards and punishments are meted out. Societal actors surely enter into interactions with the state with differing levels of investment in the regime and social cohesion. This suggests that for any given time period, levels of investment in regime and social cohesion reflect previous interactions with the state. In other words, a historical legacy of investment in state-building impacts citizen interactions with the state even after a new political regime has come to power.

In an optimal setting, dictators would know exactly how much reward to distribute in order to maintain the relevant coalition, as well as exactly who was deserving of punishment and how much punishment would be required to deter individuals from transgressing. But because the autocrat's technologies for monitoring are imprecise, particularly in the case of increasingly

88. Greitens 2016.
89. Ibid., 18.

binding budget constraints, dynamic processes would seem relevant. Indeed, an initial condition of weak state penetration of a community might lead to a spiraling of punishment and, potentially, rebellion. Similarly, reliance on a narrow, and narrowing, set of coalition partners might lead those individuals to become increasingly invested in an autocratic regime, particularly if they believe that their high level of investment in the regime may be costly for them should the regime collapse. As a result, autocratic regimes may begin, over the medium to long term, to exhibit the types of centrifugal and centripetal forces that lead groups of citizens further "inward," toward the regime core, or "outward," toward behaviors of private resistance, and potentially violent collective action.

I will make the case in the next section for an empirical strategy that suggests the two key determinants of the reward and punishment regimes—the legibility of various ethno-sectarian groups and the position of those groups within a dictatorship's coalition configuration—enjoy either a degree of short-term exogeneity (in the case of the group's legibility) or are subject to unanticipated external shocks (in the case of the coalition configuration) that allow for forms of both cross-sectional and temporal comparison. These features of the Iraqi case permit me to engage in empirical analysis, despite the presence of complicated feedback channels in the state-society relationship.

APPLICATION TO THE CASE OF IRAQ

The goal of the preceding section was to provide a structured framework for understanding the political behaviors of individuals living in autocratic contexts, broadly, and in Iraq under Saddam Hussein, more narrowly.[90] Much

90. This project does not emphasize the important and interesting ideational and political cultural concerns that are discussed in prominent studies. For example, Baram (1991) describes how the regime used references to Mesopotamian history as a legitimizing political and cultural frame. Davis (2005) argues that historical memory plays an important role in ideology which, itself, is core to hegemonic projects like Ba'thism. Podeh (2014, 145) discusses symbolic celebrations related to Hussein's birthday or other milestones; the goal was for these events to reach all parts of the country. The Ba'thist documents also provide details about the regime's cultural concerns. In some cases, public works of art depicting Hussein were discussed in committee meetings where badly painted murals were scheduled for removal (BRCC Doc. No. 01-2665-0002-0166 to 0170, 1993). Hussein announced a decision in 1998 suggesting that schools and villages that did not include a national symbol should be renamed for well-known martyrs from the area; these names would be chosen by local councils and political leaders (BRCC Doc. No. 01-2804 0000-0242, September 29, 1998).

of the existing work that seeks to explain citizen resistance to government directives focuses on factors like co-ethnicity, where co-ethnic status encourages compliance for a variety of reasons, some of which are material. On the other hand, having a different ethnic status than that of the autocrat might induce individuals to work actively or passively against the interests of the autocrat, again, for material and other reasons. While it may seem that Iraq would be a prime case for such an argument, citizen behavior in Iraq under Saddam Hussein exhibited tremendous variation within ethno-sectarian groups as well as for particular groups over time.

Part of the reason for the failure of naive cultural explanations is that they tend to overstate the homogeneity of co-ethnic behavior. And while the empirical analysis that I conduct is not sufficiently fine-grained to demonstrate the entire range of behaviors across individuals, groups, and regions, over time, I am able to describe empirically meaningful forms of both cross-sectional and temporal variation. In some cases, I am also able to provide outcomes of interest associated with variation across Iraqi tribes, both Arab and Kurdish.

The empirical predictions for the project emerge directly from the theoretical framework as applied to the two core dimensions of empirical variation—cross-sectional variation associated with ethno-sectarian differences across regions, and temporal variation associated with unanticipated shocks that impacted the nature of the Iraqi political coalition. A first prediction to emerge, then, relates to the behaviors of Iraqi citizens during the 1970s. A variety of evidentiary sources suggest high levels of private and public rewards during this period following the nationalization of Iraqi oil resources in 1972 and increasing global oil prices, especially in 1973. Relatively high levels of public cooperation, or at least political acquiesence, were common during this period. Where acts of political resistance did emerge, they were subdued with relative ease by the autocratic regime.

During the Iran-Iraq War (1980–1988), the regime witnessed relatively high levels of both political collaboration and acquiesence by ordinary Iraqis. This was particularly the case for the first half of the conflict when the regime was able to provide politically meaningful forms of economic compensation for those individuals who lost family members in the war. During this period, ethno-sectarian identity did not make any Iraqi, including Kurds and Arab Shiʿa, automatic enemies of the regime.[91] Public forms of non-compliance,

---

91. A notable exception to this statement relates to the experience of Iraqis of Persian, or Iranian, descent. On the basis of Persian ethnic background alone, the Baʿthist regime deported

like refusal to self-identify as a Ba'thist, were discouraged but did not result in an immediate threat to life and livelihood. As a result, areas subject to negative reward shocks were more likely to witness acts of non-cooperation. Sunnis from Tikrit and its environs received the largest benefits from having a Ba'thist political orientation while simultaneously enjoying the lowest levels of grievance against the regime; as a result, we should expect those individuals to exhibit the lowest levels of small-scale public defiance.

Over time, however, the duration and cost associated with the Iran-Iraq War unleashed a number of dynamics that proved costly for the Ba'thist regime. First, as the budget constraint tightened with the duration of the conflict—a process exacerbated by a global drop in the price of oil in 1986—the Ba'thists were no longer able to provide the same levels of public and private goods to Iraqi citizens. As a result, citizens decreased their investment in the regime. Second, the cost of conflict was born disproportionately across the population where Iraqi Shi'a shouldered a greater burden than other groups on a per person basis. This created an underlying level of grievance that eventually generated conditions conducive to rebellion. For Kurdish Iraqis, declining public goods provision as a result of a tightening budget constraint also decreased investment in the regime. In addition, when anti-regime activists engaged in cross-border collaboration with Iranian forces, the regime's low levels of bureaucratic penetration in the Kurdish communities meant that the regime had difficulty identifying the responsible parties. When those associated with resistance activity could not be identified accurately, the Iraqi regime punished Kurdish citizens collectively in a manner that increased feelings of "linked fate" among Iraqi Kurds.

The 1990–91 Gulf War and associated Shi'i and Kurdish protests in March of 1991 were a turning point for the coalitional politics of the regime. Indeed, the uprisings represented among the most serious challenges to Hussein's survival as a political leader. Spontaneous protests by Shi'i Iraqis in the areas most devastated by the Iran-Iraq War and Gulf War were eventually put down by the Ba'thists. Kurdish populations took advantage of regime weakness during the Shi'i uprisings to organize protests in the North, which led to the eventual establishment of an autonomous Kurdish zone. The key military

---

first tens and then hundreds of thousands of such individuals, many of whom had families that had lived in Iraq for generations. Shi'i Iraqis of Arab, rather than Iranian, descent were not targeted in these forced deportation campaigns.

units of the Iraqi regime—overstretched as a result of the Kuwaiti occupation and twin uprisings—relied on military and security service militias made up of individuals from both within and outside of Hussein's home area of Tikrit to put down the southern rebellion. When the southern rebellion was suppressed, virtually all Iraqi Shiʿa came to be viewed by the regime with increasing suspicion.[92]

Because Iraqi Shiʿa remained governed by the Baʿthists after the 1991 Uprisings, we can compare behavior of the Shiʿi community over time. Before 1991, political non-compliance was a costly—but not necessarily devastating—act on the part of Iraqi Shiʿa. Once the regime was able to reconsolidate forms of political power in the mid-1990s, however, severe punishment became the norm for even relatively small acts of non-cooperation. For the Shiʿa, a shared language with the regime—Arabic—made their community more legible than the Kurds, but still less accessible than the greater Sunni community, given the detailed knowledge of Sunni communities possessed by the regime. As a result, punishment was often meted out on the level of the tribe or religious group, typically associated with the followers of a particular Shiʿi cleric. One observable implication of this narrative is that levels of public non-compliance should decrease in Shiʿi areas of southern Iraq replaced by acts of underground resistance.[93] The use of collective punishment at the level of the extended family or religious affinity group encouraged forms of social cohesion that supported the spread of rumors, draft evasion, and circulation of banned materials, all of which rely on dense networks. Draft dodgers are dependent on the financial support and protection of those who hide them or provide them with resources while they are in hiding. Rumors only spread as a result of conversations between people who believe that they enjoy—at least to some degree—trust with one another, as rumormongering was criminalized by the Baʿthists, a strategy typical in autocratic regimes.

Changes in Iraq's Sunni community behaviors might also be observed over time as well as in comparison to other groups. In the years immediately after

92. See Khoury (2013, 135) for a discussion of the Baʿthist regime's public response to the 1991 Uprisings, including a series of newspaper reports that depicted southern Iraqi populations in sectarian terms.

93. For example, by the late 1990s, the expected punishment from having an independent political orientation among Shiʿa was so high that I expect to observe a type of "pooling" equilibrium where everyone signals that they have a Baʿthist political orientation despite strong anti-regime sentiment among Shiʿa.

the 1991 Uprisings, Sunnis from across Iraqi believed that the regime was weak and highly susceptible to either domestic or foreign overthrow. As a result, cooperation with the Baʿth Party waned. In addition, Sunnis peripheral to Tikrit saw significant declines in quality of life under the sanctions regime despite the instrumental role non-Tikriti elites and soldiers had played in putting down the 1991 Uprisings. Western Sunnis, for example, did not enjoy the same levels of access, employment, and privilege as Sunnis from in and around Tikrit.[94] Sunnis living at some distance from Tikrit—particularly in the Upper Euphrates region of Anbar governorate—were less likely to suffer punishment for transgressions against the regime as a result of their status as Sunnis and were unlikely to be punished collectively. As such, outlying Sunni populations had less to gain from joining the Baʿthists, but also less to fear in terms of potential punishment for failing to comply with regime expectations. As quality of life for non-Tikriti Sunnis declined during the sanctions period, individuals from this community were more likely to engage in acts of political non-cooperation and resistance. The result was an increasing number of Sunni-initiated overthrow attempts emanating from the military, all of which were thwarted as a result of regime penetration of those communities.

SUMMARY OF EMPIRICAL EXPECTATIONS

This chapter has provided a theoretical framework for understanding citizen behavior under conditions of autocracy. My arguments suggest that the determinants of the politically relevant cleavage structure may differ for typical autocracies and democracies. While factor endowment, electoral institutions, or historical legacy would seem to be the most important determinants of the political cleavage structure in democracies, in the autocratic context differential monitoring capability across heterogeneous communities leads to the emergence of individualism, communalism, and nationalism.

Applied to the case of Iraq, I am able to generate a series of empirical expectations which are summarized in table 2.3. The first column identifies the time

94. Since the early days of Hussein's rule, the regime showed a preference for placing family members and geographically based tribesmen from Tikrit and its environs in sensitive positions of government, including the military, bureaucracy, intelligence, and security services. This preference intensified over time as a result of the sanctions-related budget constraints, to the detriment of Sunnis from outside of the Tikriti heartland.

TABLE 2.3. Summary of Empirical Expectations across Time Periods.

Time Period	State Fiscal Resources	State-Society Relations	Expected Citizen Behaviors
early 1970s to mid-1980s	High following state nationalization of oil and 1973 OPEC-induced oil price shock	Individualized rewards for Baʿth Party loyalists and broad-based provision of public goods increase citizen investment in the Baʿthist regime	Reduced incentives for public and private dissent; instances of anti-regime revolt and political organization are effectively suppressed by the regime
mid-1980s to 1990	Declining with mounting war costs and expenses associated with provision of compensation for war martyr families; collapse in world oil prices in 1986	Declining citizen investment in the Baʿthist regime, particularly for Shiʿi communities with high war casualties; cross-border collaboration between Kurdish peshmerga and Iran leads to increased collective punishment of Kurdish populations	Increasing public dissent for Shiʿa, especially communities with high war casualties; collective repression of Iraqi Kurds leads to increasing Kurdish nationalist sentiment
1991 to mid-1990s	Extremely limited as a result of the United Nations-imposed international sanctions regime	Far reaching and intense public dissatisfaction with economic conditions; increasingly repressive environment for Shiʿa in the wake of the 1991 Uprisings	Widespread public disaffection, both at the elite and mass levels; surge in number of Sunni-led coup attempts; increasing number of communal, "underground" political transgressions by Shiʿa
mid-1990s to 2003	Limited but improving as a result of United Nations-sponsored Oil-for-Food program, introduced in 1996	Improvement to state fiscal resources allows regime to invest in new distributive channels—like paramilitary organizations—encouraging forms of regime reconsolidation	Continued public non-cooperation by some Sunnis, especially non-Tikritis; continued "underground" dissent by Shiʿa

period, with information about state fiscal resources in the second column. The third column summarizes key developments in state-society relations. Chapters 3, 4, and 5 provide more information about how these important changes came about as well as their political implications. In these chapters, I will validate some of the key assertions of my historical narrative—using new archival data where possible. The final column of the table summarizes the empirical expectations which will be explored in part II, which focuses on variation in Iraqi citizen behavior. These observables should not be thought of as predictions derived directly from my theoretical framework. Rather, they represent the cumulative set of empirical suppositions which I generated while developing my theoretical framework and during my exploration of the archives.

CHAPTER 3

STATE- AND NATION-BUILDING IN IRAQ, 1973–1979

When Saddam Hussein was interviewed in February 2004 at a US military detention facility at Baghdad International Airport, lead interrogator George Piro felt that he was developing a good personal rapport with Hussein. Hussein spoke to Piro at length on a number of topics. He shared his belief that he had served the Iraqi people well. He was proud of the many social programs that he had created, particularly in the fields of education and health care.[1]

From Hussein's perspective, when the Baʿth Party returned to power in 1968, the Iraqi people were impoverished and uneducated. Food was scarce, agricultural methods were primitive, and infant mortality was common, as was illiteracy. Over the course of the 1970s, however, the Baʿth Party oversaw huge improvements in the employment opportunities and public goods provided to the Iraq populace. Beyond that, Hussein stated that the Baʿth Party at that time was not even particularly cognizant of the sectarian identity of its party members. According to Hussein, he had not initially realized that one of his top officials, Tariq Aziz, was a member of Iraq's Christian minority. When contemplating his legacy, Hussein said he believed that history would view him favorably for his fair treatment of all Iraqis.[2]

While it is easy to dismiss Hussein's statements as the delusional account of a cruel dictator hoping to curry favor with his captors, there is little Hussein stood to gain by misrepresenting his beliefs. And despite the indisputable abuses of power displayed during his tenure, Hussein's statements do

---

1. FBI Interview Session 1 with Saddam Hussein, Baghdad Operations Session, US Department of Justice, February 7, 2004.

2. FBI Interview Session 6 with Saddam Hussein, Baghdad Operations Session, US Department of Justice, February 16, 2004.

carry a kernel of truth which hints at an alternative view of state- and nation-building in Iraq.

The decade leading up the Iran-Iraq War represented a period of unprecedented government spending in Iraq. While the Iraqi state had long aspired to gain greater control over its the domestic economy, the nationalization of the Iraqi oil sector in 1972 followed by the sharp increase in world oil prices after the 1973 OPEC embargo provided the means by which state intervention in the economy might be achieved. The net result was that the Iraqi state was able to distribute wealth across society in a way that increased both citizen investment in the regime as well as citizen dependence on the state as standards of living improved. Sanford writes that "flush with mounting oil revenues, Iraq was able for some years to pursue its socialist model without having to make hard choices between solvency and other priorities such as welfare benefits, infrastructure development, and even armed forces modernization."[3] In other words, the state spent on everything in a way that increased its relevance in the eyes of the Iraqi population across the board. And because this spending was possible as a result of a natural resource windfall, no sectors were taxed in order to generate the revenue to spend.

How does the experience of Iraq during the 1970s speak to the theoretical arguments that I have advanced? The implicit counterfactual that this chapter considers is as follows: how would Iraqi political development have progressed in the absence of the negative external shocks of the 1980s and, later, the 1990s? And if the state-building opportunities of the 1970s had continued, how might this have influenced Iraqi political identity in the decades to follow? The answer advanced in this chapter is that Iraq would have continued to develop along the lines of a typical authoritarian regime in the Middle East—repressive and corrupt, but intact and functional.

My answer to this counterfactual also has implications for our understanding of Iraqi identity politics. A conventional narrative about the salience of ethno-sectarian politics in Iraq suggests the Ba'thist regime pursued a sectarian agenda that systematically excluded Iraqi Shi'a and Kurds, creating forms of deeply held resentment that would eventually become politically insurmountable. While Iraqi Shi'a and Kurds may have been shut out of the very highest levels of political power, non-Sunnis did reach high levels of influence within the regime and were major beneficiaries of state distributive

3. Sanford 2003, 5.

networks. In addition, when transgressions against the regime did occur, these actions were managed relatively effectively from the perspective of the regime. Thus, state- and nation-building in Iraq during the 1970s continued along a historical trajectory that long worked against sectarian identities. Why and how that trajectory was disrupted is the subject of the rest of this book.

EXPANDING THE IRAQI STATE

Efforts at state- and nation-building in Iraq have faced serious challenges, many of which have been well-documented in a number of excellent country studies.[4] A series of economic and political shocks over the course of the twentieth century, for example, encouraged forms of social instability associated with a breakdown of traditional social classes.[5] Scholarly works also point to how the 1958 overthrow of the Hashemite monarchy introduced a period of increasing political instability which hindered state-building. Forms of political control in Iraq followed a pattern quite similar to those found in neighboring Arab states. Military overthrow of foreign-backed monarchs established Arab republics that repressed political opponents, only to be overthrown themselves by other military or political party factions.[6]

This relative instability ended with the formal consolidation of political power in the hands of Saddam Hussein, who successfully sidelined his fellow Baʿthist, Ahmed Hassan al-Bakr, in 1979. Although it was at this point that Hussein took over formal control of the state as President, he had been highly influential in Iraqi governance since the 1968 Baʿthist coup. In 1972, Hussein—Iraq's Vice President at the time—nationalized Iraq's oil industry. While not yet officially head of state, Hussein was widely believed to be the country's dominant political actor, serving as a de facto president because of the influence he wielded. During the 1970s, and contemporaneous with Hussein's rise to power, oil fueled Iraq's economic expansion and was critically important in the nation-building process.

---

4. E.g., Batatu 1978; Farouk-Sluglett and Sluglett 1990; Tripp 2000; Marr 2004; Dawisha 2009.

5. Batatu 1978, 12.

6. During this time, the state grew in response to demands for job opportunities and reformist social programs aimed at assisting the poor (Al-Khafaji 2000, 262).

Oil-Fueled Public Goods Provision and Development

Exports of oil increased significantly for Iraq over the course of the 1970s, dramatically expanding the capacity of the state to influence politics through economic distribution. Oil output increased from 1.5 million barrels per day in 1972 to 3.5 million barrels per day in 1979. This occurred during a period of rising oil prices leading Iraqi government revenues to increase ninefold during the oil boom.[7]

State spending during this period sought to modernize Iraq's infrastructure and industrial capacity. Yousif finds that public investment was the main driver of physical capital formation in the 1970s, which doubled between 1970 and 1975 and doubled again between 1975 and 1980.[8] Investments were made into a variety of sectors, including mining, industry, construction, and communications. Ozly writes that "the Iraqi government spent $14.2 billion on economic development in the 1974–80 period," including on "heavy industrial complexes... iron and steel mill(s)... the development of sulphur and phosphate extraction and processing and the fertilizer industries."[9]

In addition to large industrial and infrastructure projects, the Iraqi state also invested in basic public goods which had the potential to dramatically improve citizen quality of life. Schools, universities, hospitals, and military bases were built and expanded.[10] While Iraq had made major strides in the provision of public education leading up to the 1970s, momentum toward widespread literacy and higher educational opportunities increased after 1972. In 1978, the Ba'th Party initiated a new program to eradicate illiteracy for all Iraqis between the ages of fifteen and forty-five. The program was ambitious in scope and accompanied by a mass media campaign; even opponents of the regime acknowledged the positive impact the program had on thousands of Iraqi citizens.[11]

Growth of the domestic economy led to accelerated demand for education by Iraqis; and the nationalization of schools in 1975 equalized access to education by making schooling free of charge. The number of primary schools increased from 5,617 in academic year 1970–1971 to 11,316 in academic

7. Ehteshami 2013, 55.
8. Yousif 2012, 55–59.
9. Ozly 2006, 15.
10. During the 1970s, the regime also spent considerably to upgrade facilities for pilgrims at the holy shrines in Najaf and Karbala (Baram 2014, 96).
11. Heine 1993, 42–43.

year 1979–1980, while secondary schools increased from 921 to 1,774 over that same time period.[12] In addition to building schools, funds were also spent on providing meals to schoolchildren to make school attendance more appealing.[13] This investment in development projects transformed large parts of the country, particularly areas that had been previously underserved.

During the 1970s, the Iraqi state built a modern sanitation and sewage disposal system that covered major cities and most rural areas.[14] The government also played a significant role in improving the quality of housing, subsidizing affordable residences both directly and through low interest loans.[15] Between 1970 and 1980, the number of health facilities in Iraq increased from 1,125 to 1,845 and per capita hospital beds increased at a similar rate; the number of hospitals grew from 145 in 1970 to 167 in 1975 to 200 by 1978 and could be found across the country.[16]

Public sector employment also became an increasingly available workforce option for Iraqis during this period. According to Ayubi, the non-defense bureaucracy grew from 319,000 in 1967 to 558,000 in 1976 and 663,000 by 1978.[17] In this setting, the state was a favored employer for many, including university graduates, and by the end of the 1970s the Iraq state was, by far, the country's largest employer.[18] Another large portion of the adult workforce was employed in the defense sector. State expenditure as a proportion of GDP grew from 44 percent in 1970 to 51 percent in 1975 to 81 percent in 1978.[19]

The state also represented an important economic resource for contractors and brokers—a core of Iraq's bourgeois class—who received subsidized capital, machinery, and raw material from the state, investing them politically in the regime.[20] State spending associated with the increased value of oil rents elevated GDP per capita during the 1970s. Yousif finds that GDP per capita grew from $670 in 1970 to $1,384 in 1979.[21] Private industrial firms grew as well and the standard of living increased for the entire population with

12. Yousif 2012, 75.
13. Ibid.
14. Al-Jawaheri 2008, 119.
15. Yousif 2012, 88.
16. Ibid., 101.
17. Ayubi 1995.
18. Workman 1994, 104.
19. Ayubi 1995.
20. Workman 1994, 109.
21. Yousif 2012, 49.

meaningful gains in real income that considerably benefited Iraq's poorest citizens.[22] Between 1977 and 1980, economic growth was so robust that Iraq reached full employment, requiring the import of Egyptian guest laborers.[23]

State investment in public goods provision had a particularly positive impact on Iraqi women. For example, elementary education was made compulsory in 1976 for all Iraqi children up to the age of ten, a policy that brought many more girls into the classroom.[24] The state's aggressive expansion of educational opportunities benefited women significantly, as measured by a number of indicators including a narrowing of the literacy gap between men and women.[25] Female employment in the public sector expanded as well, with state-sponsored child care and maternity leave facilitating women's labor force participation.

These new state policies had the effect of replacing traditional influences— like tribal allegiances—with the welfare state, and women's rights became an important area of contestation.[26] Aggressive efforts to increase female labor force participation took place across all economic sectors.[27] This is not to say that Hussein was intrinsically progressive in his attitudes toward women, but rather that he undertook "paternalistic attempts to widen his basis of support" through his policies toward women.[28] Nonetheless, women benefited from these employment opportunities. One female informant recalls how she and her friends all expected to work, even after having children and that, within her social group, men increasingly expected to have wives who were able to earn a salary.[29]

Spending and Citizen Investment in the Regime

State spending strongly increased citizen investment in the Ba'thist regime. Expansion of the public sector in so many different domains—education,

---

22. Alkazaz 1993, 216–218.

23. Ibid., 220.

24. Ismael and Ismael 2007.

25. Ibid. By the end of the sanctions period, illiteracy rates among adults were higher than they had been in the 1970s, with particularly dire effects on female illiteracy (Al-Jawaheri 2008, 60).

26. Ismael and Ismael 2007.

27. Ibid.

28. Al-Ali 2007, 131.

29. Ibid., 132.

employment, health services, and industrial development—led Iraqi citizens from various segments of society, and across the country, to evaluate the regime positively, even at a time when the security sector was increasingly deploying violence against its political opponents. During this period, Iraq developed a welfare state that took on a central place in the lives of its citizens, encouraging the growth of a new middle class.[30]

The benefits of state expansion extended broadly and facilitated incorporation of a wide swath of citizens into the Baʿth Party orbit. One Shiʿi informant said that she and her family became sympathetic to the party and regime because of the dramatic upward social mobility and income improvement they experienced during this period.[31] She also supported the regime because the Baʿth Party was thought to be fair in its treatment of different sectarian groups. While Sunnis from Tikrit were noticeable beneficiaries of party largesse at the highest levels, Shiʿa also rose in the party and government. During this period, corruption and graft were thought to be relatively low and state money was "being put to good use."[32]

Incorporating rural classes into the state posed a challenge that required a different approach. Collective farms on state-owned land were developed in a bid to engage the rural population and to "transfer the people's allegiance to the Iraqi nation state."[33] Both the Baʿth Party and the state apparatus were deployed to implement these changes, which reached virtually every corner of the country.[34] Rhetoric from Hussein complemented the policies. In a November 1978 speech to the Baʿth Party leadership, Hussein emphasized the regime's recent achievements in reaching the citizenry and his desire to increase societal capacity across the country.[35]

Even citizens who were highly critical of the regime during this period, or who had suffered at the hands of the regime, were appreciative of the state-sponsored programs.[36] Part of the reason for this was that the vast majority of the goods provided were public and non-excludable in nature. For example, Baghdadi women from a variety of ethnic and religious backgrounds

30. Al-Jawaheri 2008, 8.
31. Al-Ali 2007, 129.
32. Al-Ali 2014, 9.
33. Rohde 2010, 25.
34. Dawisha 2008, 221; Rohde 2010, 25.
35. CRRC Doc. No. SH-PDWN-D-000-938, November 8, 1978.
36. Al-Ali 2007, 136–137.

welcomed and acknowledged the state-sponsored modernization projects, which were viewed as constructive and important.[37] According to one informant, "by the end of the 1970s, all of Baghdad was modernized... although the mayor was cruel, and Baghdadis hated him, he managed to make Baghdad very clean."[38]

During this period, repression of political opponents was taking place, but without a vocal, broad-based public outcry. According to Sassoon, Hussein believed that "if there was economic growth and prosperity, then the Iraqi people would accept Ba'th rule even if it used bloody methods."[39] Al-Ali finds that the regime "managed to silence dissent and even obtain people's approval by providing a prospering socio-economic context in which many Iraqi families flourished."[40]

Despite the emergence of armed rebellion between Kurdish Democratic Party troops and the Ba'thist regime in 1974, the 1970s witnessed widespread incorporation of Iraqi Kurds into the state apparatus. Kurdish populations, for example, were major beneficiaries of regime-provided public goods and employment. Ba'th Party documents from this period suggest many Kurds sought to join the police force, for instance.[41] One administrative report from the northern districts describes the needs of the local population as well as regime plans for handling them.[42] Top priorities included employment, housing, public safety, and improving the quality of roads to rural villages.[43]

The same report documents existing programs for improving employment opportunities in northern areas and governmental participation in local public celebrations and occasions of mourning.[44] Gifts from Hussein himself, new televisions for instance, were distributed throughout the area. Attempts were underway to make more Iraqi Kurds aware of the literacy centers the regime had created. And the Ba'th Party was seen as a primary institution by which the population could provide feedback to the regime through channels of

37. Ibid., 128.
38. Ibid.
39. Sassoon 2016, 160.
40. Al-Ali 2007, 128.
41. Iraqi Secret Police Files Doc. No. 40261 to 40262, April 20, 1977.
42. Iraqi Secret Police Files Doc. No. 10380 to 10397, July 17, 1980.
43. Ibid.
44. Ibid.

reporting and accountability. One Iraqi informant summarized the situation in the following way:

> In the beginning of the 1970s, there was reconstruction in the north and there was peace with the Kurds. Kurdish was taught even in schools in Baghdad. You can't have a perfect situation. You have to use force to bring some good.[45]

While it is impossible to know whether the regime extended these public goods for ideological or tactical reasons, historians have suggested that the net result was a depoliticization of the population, even in the face of continued repression against some groups.[46] According to Rohde, the regime preempted internal dissent through its creation of a salaried middle class dependent on employment by the state bureaucracy or public sector enterprises.[47] Economic conditions were good and "by and large the Iraqi population was optimistic."[48]

CULTIVATING AN IRAQI NATIONAL IDENTITY

Alongside efforts at state-building through oil-fueled public goods expansion, the Baʿthist regime also undertook a renewed effort at cultivation of a national identity. Throughout this period, the Baʿthists made considerable efforts to encourage feelings of national unity.[49] This is not to say that nation-building in Iraq was new or exclusively part of a Baʿthist repertoire. The Iraqi state had long since created the symbols of nationhood, including a national army and school curriculum designed to cultivate national allegiance.[50] The Baʿthists deployed two main strategies for the cultivation of national identity. The first was to seek national integration through the success of the country's

45. Al-Ali 2007, 128.
46. Rohde 2010, 23.
47. Ibid.
48. Alkazaz 1993, 221.
49. Chartouni-Dubarry 1993, 35.
50. Osman 2014, 69.

development programs.[51] The second was a deliberate de-emphasis on sectarian identity in regime rhetoric and policy.[52]

Despite the use of non-sectarian state rhetoric and promotion of economic development initiatives, regime concerns about coup-proofing led the security apparatus to recruit heavily from the tribal and regional allies of Hussein. Sunni Iraqis from the areas in and around Hussein's home region of Tikrit came to enjoy particular benefits from the Ba'thist regime. These political appointments were made on the basis of loyalty and trust rather than out of sectarian affinity, but the patterns of political appointment gave the appearance of sectarian nepotism.[53] In other words, the Sunni appearance of the regime did not necessarily reflect an anti-Shi'i or anti-Kurdish policy, but rather a desire to make appointments to those with the closest ties to Hussein—many of whom happened to be Sunni Arabs.[54]

Indeed, during this period of time, it would have been difficult to locate a distinctly Iraqi Shi'i identity or shared set of interests. Iraqi Shi'a were a highly diverse group, which included a class of religious elites, urban merchants, and artisans, as well as tribal communities.[55] During the 1970s, largesse extended to all needy Shi'i areas.[56] Shi'i-owned small businesses were also able to accumulate wealth.[57] The Ba'thists did not view Shi'ism as a problem in and of itself, and Shi'a were not targeted because of their sectarian identification. Because such large numbers of party cadre were themselves Shi'a, in many places anti-Shi'i discrimination would have amounted to Shi'i prejudice of other Shi'a.[58] Batatu summarizes the relationship between the regime and Iraqi Shi'a more generally:

> Saddam Hussein does not discriminate against Shi'is. He thinks in Arab rather than in sectarian terms. This is not without appeal to many in Baghdad or the southern part of the country who are Arabs first and

51. Chartouni-Dubarry 1993, 34.
52. Ismael and Fuller 2008.
53. Helfont 2015, 69.
54. Davis (2005) has argued that Hussein was keen to solidify his basis of support within the Sunni community. While Hussein enjoyed deep support within his core constituency, his greatest threat of overthrow came from non-Tikriti Sunnis.
55. Zubaida 2002, 208.
56. Dawisha 2008, 221.
57. Al-Ali 2007, 128.
58. Helfont 2015, 68.

Shiʻis after. Few Shiʻis hold crucial threads in his regime, but this is not attributable to sectarian influences. Rather, the relative thinness of his domestic base and the repressive character of his government have driven him to lean more and more heavily on his kinsmen or members of his own clan or old companions from his underground days. Over the last five years or so, he has spared no effort to recruit Shiʻis into the Baʻth Party or to associate them with his regime.[59]

Efforts at cultivating an Iraqi national identity were also evident in Kurdish areas of Iraq. The regime sought to reach accommodation with Kurdish communities during the 1970s, recognizing past political conflict and implementing measures to reverse prior wrongs.[60] Al-Ali writes that government offices and the military worked to ensure equal access to employment and education.[61]

One regime file from June 1975 describes a meeting among government insiders to discuss the Kurdish situation, noting that many countries have citizens belonging to two different "national" identities.[62] While in the Iraqi case, it was Arabs and Kurds, such a situation was also apparent in Morocco and Somalia where Berber and Somali nationalities eventually came to think of themselves as Arabs.[63] The stated goal for the regime was to bring more and more Kurdish Iraqis into the national fold. While the document suggests that it was important to acknowledge Kurdish identity as being culturally unique, over time it would be possible to encourage a greater Arabization of Kurdish populations through intermarriage and education.[64] It was also suggested that the regime should provide greater public goods to Kurdish areas and encourage party cadre to learn the Kurdish language in order to deliver the Baʻthist message effectively.

The 1975 Algiers Accord between Iran and Iraq ended Iranian support for Kurdish rebels in northern Iraq in exchange for Iraqi concessions along the southern border. Attempts at Baʻthification of Iraqi Kurdistan were pervasive

59. Hanna Batatu, "Iraq's Underground Shiʻi Movements." *Middle East Report*, 102 (January/February 1982).
60. Al-Ali 2014.
61. Ibid., 29.
62. CRRC Number Doc. No. SH-MISC-D-000-508, June 1975.
63. Ibid.
64. Ibid.

after 1975.[65] Ba'th Party documents from between 1975 and 1980 also suggest important forms of collaboration on the part of Kurdish Iraqis. A series of documents from 1977, for example, describe some of the forms of citizen-regime collaboration in northern Iraq. One file discusses how the village headman (*mukhtar*) serves as an important source of information about local affairs.[66] The village headman was known to provide intelligence on the types of weaponry held by insurgents as well as details about the financial situation of the rebels and the nature of their communications equipment.[67] At this time, the Ba'th Party was also highly invested in cultivating ideological commitment toward the party, particularly by working through schools. The Ba'th Party paid close attention to the political orientation of teachers and university professors in northern Iraq.[68]

Rhetoric out of Baghdad also increasingly suggested the possibility of the successful integration of Kurdish interests with the Iraqi state. Hussein publicly stated that he did not believe that the Kurdish rebel groups—like the Kurdish Democratic Party (KDP)—represented all of the Kurdish people,[69] signaling a desire to differentiate between ordinary Iraqi Kurds and political activists who were willing to use violence in pursuit of their aims. In a 1977 public address, Hussein encouraged Iraqis not to think of themselves as Kurdish or Arab, but rather, as Iraqi with a Kurdish or Arab national identity.[70]

Quarterly administrative reports from the Ba'th Party branch leadership in Erbil detail the concerns and goals of the regime for northern Iraqi areas. Reporting from 1979 describes strategies for improving the loyalty of Kurdish constituencies. One report suggests that better practices, like leadership visits and the pardoning of prisoners, had recently improved attitudes toward the party.[71] The regime also sought to rehabilitate former political prisoners by providing them with employment opportunities; the goal was to turn these individuals into productive and loyal citizens under Ba'th Party leadership.[72]

65. Aziz 2011, 74.

66. North Iraq Dataset Doc. No. 02477-101-55, February 3, 1977.

67. North Iraq Dataset Doc. No. 02477-101-12, November 29, 1977.

68. North Iraq Dataset Doc. No. 05007-103-22; North Iraq Dataset Doc. No. 05007-103-55.

69. McDowall 1996, 335.

70. Natali 2005, 57.

71. Iraqi Secret Police Files Doc. No. 10518 to 10539, July–September 1979.

72. Ibid.

Increasing public trust in political institutions was deemed important in northern areas. Seminars for citizens were viewed as a strategy for educational outreach where Baʿth Party achievements might be shared with the population. The reports further suggest that it would be possible to increase public loyalty to the regime by providing gifts; participating in local celebrations; offering housing for citizens; finding jobs for the unemployed; listening to local problems and seeking solutions for those issues; strengthening relations with both religious clerics and local headmen; building schools in the countryside; fixing streets; and organizing sporting activities.[73]

An administrative report from the first quarter of 1980 suggests how the Baʿth Party used political, organizational, and cultural seminars to encourage support for party principles in northern areas.[74] At that point in time, the public was described in the report as having high morale, attributed to the relatively strong financial situation in the area and reliable availability of everyday consumer goods. With the goal of improving Baʿth Party performance in the Kurdish region, strategies for improvement were also discussed.[75] The party was called upon to provide more efficient responses to citizen demands. It was also suggested that a lack of meeting space for Baʿth Party student and youth meetings was an area for improvement and that the regime should speed up school building efforts, as the new schools could serve as places where meetings might take place.[76] Another proposal suggested that party cadre make more frequent visits to mosques and other local institutions. Cooperation between the Baʿth Party and the Kurdish Democratic Party at this time was described as very positive.

RESISTANCE ACTIVITIES AND STRATEGIES OF PUNISHMENT

Thus far, I have argued that oil-fueled development reduced political opposition as ordinary Iraqis were the beneficiaries of state-provided public goods. Contemporaneously, the Baʿthist regime promulgated non-sectarian rhetoric and engaged in policies with the goal of increasing Iraqi nationalist sentiment. During this period, political opposition to the regime existed and, at times,

73. Ibid.
74. Iraqi Secret Police Files Doc. Nos. 20110 to 20121, April 14, 1980.
75. Ibid.
76. Ibid.

was highly vocal. At the same time, however, these oppositional movements were relatively limited in scope and politically manageable for the regime, given the resources of the state.

During the 1970s the Da'wa Party—an Islamist, Shi'i party—grew in strength and popularity. It is difficult to know precisely why the Da'wa Party enjoyed increased support and mobilizational capacity. On the one hand, Islamist political organizations benefited from increases in popularity during the 1970s across a variety of Muslim countries.[77] It is also likely that increased Da'wa mobilization was driven by dissatisfaction with the avowedly secular nature of the Ba'thist regime.

Rioting by Shi'i activists in 1974 and 1977 led to a repressive crackdown by the regime. Indeed, the mass protests in Najaf and Karbala in 1977 have been considered unprecedented, urban-based spontaneous demonstrations.[78] Although these upheavals were a massive challenge to the Ba'thist regime, the government crackdown was relatively focused, limited in scale and scope. The Da'wa Party could not compel a majority of Iraqi Shi'a to become politically engaged and mobilized. This was likely due to a combination of skepticism toward religious appeals as well as a recognition that the growth of the state sector provided meaningful benefits to large swaths of the Shi'i community. The behaviors of most Iraqi Shi'a during this time period, then, might be characterized as somewhere between active collaboration and political acquiesence.

The next section examines regime efforts to monitor populations suspected of politically transgressive behaviors. I then focus on punishment and resistance for a particular ideological group—Iraqi Communists. The regime's total suppression of political activity by Iraqi Communists suggests the ease with which the Ba'thists were able to eliminate an ideologically rival group during this period.

---

77. The salience of nationalist, sectarian, Islamist, and other political identities is, to a large extent, a regional phenomenon that transcends any particular Middle Eastern state or a single state's policies. This suggests that transnational trends influence the development of political identity in important ways. Understanding how and why certain regional trends emerge when they do is complex and beyond the scope of this project. Instead, I look at subnational variation in the influence of regime and state actions on identity formation, conditional on the existence of broad regional trends.

78. Jabar 2003a, 208–209.

Monitoring and Punishing Suspected Dissidents

Monitoring the opposition was an important part of Ba'thist strategy, particularly for segments of the population deemed to be of questionable loyalty.[79] Artists, scholars, and writers came under considerable suspicion and scrutiny, according to statements given by informants who provided testimony to the Iraq Memorial Foundation documentary efforts.[80] A university professor who refused to join the Ba'th Party was subject to harassment and arrested in 1977, accused of being a Da'wa Party sympathizer.[81] In another case, an artist and journalist—whose father had run a literary salon—was expelled from the Institute of Fine Arts in 1979 and forced into the military for refusing to join the Ba'th Party.[82] In yet another case, a writer said that members of his Basra-based cultural forum were arrested and sent to prison.[83] A Kurdish informant said that his brother, who was a poet, was arrested and executed in 1979.[84]

While artists, writers, and poets were often viewed with suspicion as a result of their occupational status, in other cases, the regime had more concrete information about individuals accused of specific political infractions, like insulting the regime. Punishment varied depending on the nature of the transgression and the identity of the perpetrator. In 1977, a secretary for a provincial security directorate was sentenced to two years in jail for anti-regime statements. Officers arrested him, while drunk, for speaking out against the ruling party, the revolution, and security officials. A man from Najaf reported he was arrested in 1978 for insulting then-Vice President Saddam Hussein. He was eventually transferred to the Revolutionary Court, where he received a three-year sentence that he spent in Abu Ghraib Prison.[85]

79. For example, the regime maintained lists of individuals who were reported to be Fatimi Party members (see Iraqi Secret Police Files Doc. No. 100015 to 100016, October 18, 1969). The Ba'th Party was also highly concerned with keeping the names of individuals presumed to be Muslim Brotherhood members (see Iraqi Secret Police Files Doc. No. 10007 to 10014, November 27, 1972).

80. When referring to the testimony of individuals who participated in the Iraq Memory Foundation documentary project, I use the term informant to mean a person who provides cultural data or other information to a researcher or documentarian.

81. Testimony of K. Al-Awad, recorded January 2007.

82. Testimony of M. Al-Musawi, recorded May 2007; Another individual claimed that he was rejected from the Institute of Fine Arts because he was not a member of the Ba'th Party. See testimony of I. Husayn, recorded December 2006.

83. Testimony of A. Al-Basri, recorded January 2007.

84. Testimony of A. Khodr, recorded December 2007.

85. Testimony of M. Al-Mimar, recorded January 2008.

In another case, a female suspect was sentenced to one year in prison for anti-regime activities, but was only made to pay a fine of 50 Iraqi dinars and three years of probation due to her very young age and and status as a student.[86] A Kirkuk-born man was arrested in 1979, accused of being a member of a Turkmen organization and charged with writing anti-Baʿthist slogans.[87] A year after his arrest, the only evidence brought against him was the fact that he owned unauthorized books.

Repressing Communism

Iraqis—particularly those associated with urban, low-income neighborhoods—were drawn to leftist parties that promoted forms of economic redistribution (Jabar 2003a, 129). The relationship between the Baʿth Party and the Iraqi Communist Party was not always hostile. There existed significant threads of ideological commonality that fostered cooperation between the groups.[88] Those commonalities, however, may have eventually led the Baʿthists to view the Communists as potential rivals.

With the encouragement of the Soviet Union, the Communist and Baʿth parties worked together in the early 1970s. For example, the Iraqi Communist Party agreed to participate in the National Patriotic Front in 1973. Iraqi Communists engaged enthusiastically in political activities during this period, writing articles and mobilizing party cadre.[89]

The alliance with the Baʿth Party did not favor the Communists, however. Communists became marginalized as Communist student federations and women's groups became co-opted by the Baʿthists. Communist Party supporters were heavily pressured to became Baʿthists. One Communist Party affiliate reports being arrested on his way to his school exams, causing him to

86. CRRC Number SH-IDGS-D-000-576, 1979.
87. Testimony of A. Omar, recorded December 2006.
88. Scholarly accounts have documented the historical origins of Communist Party support within Iraq over the course of the twentieth century. Ismael (2008, 311–312) argues that economic domination by a land-owning aristocracy created a large class of landless peasants, many of whom emigrated to Iraqi urban centers because of lack of opportunities. For example, in 1958, 1 percent of the population held 55 percent of agricultural land, while 64 percent of the rural population owned less than 4 percent of all cultivated land (313). Marxist groups began to organize in cities, making political connections to the urban poor and increasing the salience of Marxist ideas (318).
89. Al-Ali 2007, 118.

fail for that year; he was eventually forbidden from finishing his studies for refusing to join the Baʿth Party.[90] Career paths were also increasingly available to Baʿthists, often to the exclusion of Communist Party sympathizers. According to one informant who was affiliated with the Communist Party, as a schoolteacher she came under pressure to join the Baʿth Party and was eventually forced to flee Iraq as the the crackdown on Communist Party activists intensified.[91]

The Baʿth Party monitored Communist Party meetings, keeping lists of the names of those in attendance.[92] By the late 1970s, outright repression of Communists was widespread and Communist Party activism was increasingly forced to operate underground.[93] Relations between the Communists and Baʿthists deteriorated to the point where Communists were systematically arrested, tortured, and killed. Sassoon writes that the Communist Party serves as an exemplar for "how the Baʿth regime made an alliance with an opposition party, only to trap it, execute many of its members, and reduce its influence dramatically."[94] One informant, who was an active Communist Party member during the period of Communist-Baʿthist cooperation, was forced into hiding with her family for almost ten years.[95] She eventually gave herself up when a political amnesty was offered.

Dozens of narrative accounts document the repression of Iraqi Communists. Informants born into Communist-leaning families were often swept up in the repression. One journalist from a Communist family reports that he was under constant surveillance and that his children were hassled because of their refusal to join the Baʿth Party. The informant's son was eventually arrested and executed.[96] Another informant reports that her father was arrested in 1978 for being a member of the Communist Party. Eventually the rest of the family was also detained after security officers occupied their home.[97] An informant from Najaf reports that he was a student when the Communists came under attack in 1978; he was arrested, along with other schoolboys, leading him to eschew politics and focus on his studies instead. Despite his

90. Testimony of H. Jawad, recorded April 2007.
91. Al-Ali 2007, 119.
92. See, for example, Iraqi Secret Police Files Doc Nos. 100004 and 100005, March 2, 1979.
93. Ismael 2008, 201.
94. Sassoon 2016, 50.
95. Testimony of S. Al-Fatalawi, recorded May 1, 2007.
96. Testimony of H. Atabi, recorded February 2007.
97. Testimony of S. Nasir, recorded May 2007.

conscious decision to avoid political activism, the informant was eventually arrested again and tortured.[98]

CONCLUSIONS

In this chapter, I have argued that oil revenue enabled the Baʿthist regime to engage in spending on public goods, industrial development, and state sector employment that invested Iraqi citizens in the state and the Baʿth Party. This interpretation is consistent with scholars who suggest that the 1970s witnessed profound transformations in the Iraqi economy as the Baʿth Party took the lead in national development.[99] Faust concurs, arguing that oil allowed the Baʿthists to "diversify and deepen their bases of support," encouraging forms of allegiance that extended to large segments of the Iraqi population.[100] It was during the 1970s that "the welfare state in Iraq" became a central aspect of life, investing more and more Iraqis in the regime from which they accrued material benefit through the regime's resource allocation programs.[101] In the words of Al-Khafaji, "in an oil-rich economy, state expansion proved to be a relatively easy task ... the growth of state institutions dramatically altered the balance of power between state and society, to the detriment of the latter."[102]

For some beneficiaries of regime largesse, particularly those associated with the inner circle of politics, this translated into active cooperation with Hussein's regime. For the vast majority of Iraqis who benefited from the state's social spending in a less intensive and more diffuse manner, however, the result was an increasing tendency toward political acquiescence and depoliticization. Ethno-national and tribal identities were less salient during this time period as the regime promoted a strongly nationalist rhetoric. One possible exception to this statement relates to the increased salience of Tikriti identity as the regime sought out tribal and regional kinsmen to install in positions that demanded high levels of loyalty to the regime.

At the same time, the need to punish large groups of citizens during the 1970s was minimized due to the relatively high level of citizen investment in

98. Testimony of M. Abu Ghunaym, recorded January 2008.
99. Owen 2007.
100. Faust 2015, 23.
101. Al-Jawaheri 2008, 8.
102. Al-Khafaji 2000, 262.

the regime. Where repressive abuses did occur, public outcry was relatively muted. As one Iraqi explained it, "during the early and mid 1970s the majority of the population in Iraq was content and enjoyed some economic benefits from the Ba'th government... if they knew of atrocities, they chose to look the other way as did many Western and regional governments."[103] By the end of the 1970s, Hussein had successfully consolidated political power, culminating in his accession to the presidency in 1979.

103. Quoted in Faust 2015, 23.

CHAPTER 4

WAR BURDEN AND COALITIONAL POLITICS, 1980–1991

During the course of the Iran-Iraq War, Baʿth Party officials began to notice that exceptionally large numbers of young men drafted and sent to the front lines were from Basra, Iraq's largest southern city, located at the entrance of the Persian Gulf.[1] The conflict had evolved into a war of attrition. Attrition warfare typically favors the side with greater resources and Iran had a population size three times as large as Iraq. On the battlefield, Iraqi troops were subjected to human wave attacks by Iranian paramilitary volunteer militias, like the *basij*. Huge numbers of Iranian fighters were killed in these offensives and when the attackers could surround an Iraqi unit, they stood to capture large numbers of Iraqi fighters.

In 1984, the Baʿthist regime commissioned a special report on the number of war martyrs, missing in action, and prisoner of war soldiers from Basra governorate.[2] The purpose of the investigation was to provide special benefits to areas that had suffered the largest war burden. The report suggested that top leaders, like Saddam Hussein, should visit the neighborhoods that had lost the largest numbers of residents to the war.

The report also related neighborhood or village population estimates to give party officials a sense of the relative war burden given the size of the community.[3] For example, the Hadi neighborhood located in northern Basra was divided into two areas: al-Hadi al-Ula, with 16,000 residents and al-Hadi al-Thaniyya, with 9,000. Both suffered approximately the same number of residents killed (62 and 59, respectively). The smaller neighborhood had almost three times as many prisoners of war and more than twice as

1. BRCC Doc. Nos. 01-2202-0001-0044 to 0053, 1984.
2. Ibid.
3. Ibid.

many soldiers missing in action. In other words, even for geographically proximate and otherwise similar areas, the war burden could vary and the Iraqi regime was keen to identify those differences with the goal of recognizing and rewarding sacrifices in the interest of the nation.

From an empirical perspective, I seek to address a series of questions: Which ethnic and geographic groups within Iraq bore the greatest burden associated with the wars? In what ways did the regime respond to declining citizen and soldier morale as a result of the losses associated with the conflicts? And how did conflict ultimately impact Iraqi citizen investment in the Baʿthist regime?

To preview the main empirical findings, I show that Iraqi Shiʿa were more likely than their Sunni counterparts (and much more likely than Iraqi Kurds) to have died during the Iran-Iraq War, even after taking into account the size of different sectarian groups within Iraq's population. Government efforts to counteract declining citizen morale during the course of the war took a number of forms, including compensation for families of fallen soldiers, educational programs, and symbolic displays. I argue that despite expending considerable political and material capital in response to concerns about morale, the differential war costs significantly undermined investment in the regime, setting the conditions for the 1991 Uprisings which represented a critical political rupture.

While Iraq's Kurds were not subjected to high casualty rates in the Iran-Iraq War when compared to Iraqi Shiʿa, the conflict between Iraq and Iran had a comparably profound impact on political sentiment in the Iraqi North. Because of cross-border military and intelligence cooperation between Iran and Iraqi Kurdish groups, the Baʿthist regime felt compelled to engage in a series of massive and devastating acts of collective punishment that alienated Kurdish populations to an extreme extent. The nature of the Iraqi punishment regime also encouraged forms of social cohesion within the Kurdish community as Kurds came to increasingly see themselves as sharing a common fate at the hands of the Baʿthist regime. While Iraqi Kurds did not achieve effective autonomy until the 1991 Uprisings, the Anfal Campaign represented a seemingly insurmountable challenge to the possibility of Kurdish support for conventional forms of Iraqi nationalism.

The evidence presented in this chapter also speaks to the heterogenous effects of war on state- and nation-building. A conventional narrative suggests that war has a positive impact on the growth and consolidation of states.[4] But when the costs of war are not shared across a country's regional and communal groups, the differential impact of conflict on the citizenry can actually work against efforts at nation-building.

IRAQ AT WAR

During Saddam Hussein's almost thirty years of de facto rule, the Iraqi regime initiated a series of externally oriented military interventions. Indeed, Iraqis lived under conditions of nearly continuous war for much of the time the country was governed by Hussein.[5] At the start of the Iran-Iraq War, multiple potentially relevant cleavages existed within Iraqi society. One officially recognized designation was based on "national" identity where Arabs and Kurds were the two main identity groups. Sectarian identity—Sunni or Shi'i—was also salient for some Iraqis, though this distinction did not officially exist in party or state discourse. In addition, important differences persisted between urban Iraqis, who were less likely to rely on tribal identity, and rural Iraqis, for whom tribal affiliation was more politically salient. A primary argument of this chapter is that political and social developments that took place during the Iran-Iraq War and later, the Gulf War, placed a burden on particular communities within Iraq with implications for the salience of certain identities.

The Iran-Iraq War

The Iran-Iraq War lasted eight years, a comparatively long time for a conventional modern war. One reason for the long duration was that each side had a significant, countervailing advantage. While Iraq enjoyed a military technology edge over Iran, Iran was able to deploy its much larger population in battle.

Why did the Iraqi regime enter into such an unpredictable and potentially destabilizing political conflict in the first place? There is little doubt that the 1979 Islamic Revolution in Iran had a profound effect on the political calculus of Hussein and his advisors. The Islamic Revolution represented

4. Tilly 1992.
5. Al-Khafaji 2000, 258; Khoury 2013.

an ideological threat to Sunni-ruled Iraq as Hussein was consolidating political power. This was even more so in the context of growing Iraqi Shiʿi activism on the part of a religiously minded minority. The Iraqi regime feared that Iran would act on its self-stated goal of exporting its revolution to Iraq.[6]

When an Iraqi of Iranian origin attempted to assassinate Deputy Prime Minister Tareq Aziz in April of 1980, the regime responded with the execution of Shiʿi cleric Muhammad Baqir al-Sadr and his sister, Amina bint al-Huda. Thousands of Iraqi Shiʿa were deported and, in September 1980, Iraq preemptively attacked Iran, citing a series of border disputes as a primary motivation for the instigation of hostilities.[7] The Iranian province of Khuzestan was a target of interest for Hussein because of both its large Arab population and its extensive coastline, which would enhance Iraq's ability to export oil.[8]

While the theocratic nature of the new regime in Iran surely influenced Hussein's decision to invade, arguably even more important were tactical, rather than ideational, considerations. Iraq had long held a series of specific grievances against the Iranian regime. Among these was the need to reclaim Iraqi rights associated with the Shatt al-Arab waterway and a desire to obstruct Iranian military support for Kurdish rebels in the Iraqi north. Iraqis also felt that the Iranians had failed to meet their obligations under the 1975 Algiers Agreement.[9] And the Islamic Revolution was viewed as a period of political vulnerability for Iran during which the new leadership would be unable to mount an effective defense. When later directly asked by US interrogators about why he went to war with Iran, Hussein responded that he felt like a farmer who had an annoying next-door neighbor—one day that neighbor beats up your son, the next day he bothers your cows and, even after receiving warnings to desist, the neighbor continues to provoke until you take action against him.[10]

6. Baram and Rubin 1993, xii.

7. Al-Khafaji (2000, 279) argues that it was only "possible for the regime to deport... a quarter of a million Iraqi Shiʿa to Iran, confiscate their properties, and resell them to favorites of the regime for a fraction of their value" as a result of a strong and growing Iraqi nationalist sentiment.

8. Johnson 2011, 6.

9. CRRC Doc. No. SH-SHTP-A-000-835, September 16, 1980.

10. FBI Interview Session 2 with Saddam Hussein, Baghdad Operations Session, US Department of Justice, February 8, 2004.

Iraqi officials believed that they would enjoy a quick and relatively easy victory over the new Iranian regime.[11] At the time, the Iranian army was deployed to battle separatists at a variety of geographic locations; in addition, the Iranian air force had been grounded at the Nojeh air base since a July 1980 coup attempt.[12] Hussein imagined the possibility of a "blitzkrieg," but these expectations were confounded as the conflict degenerated into a prolonged war of attrition resulting in hundreds of thousands of casualties.[13] Hussein later conceded that he had not understood Khomeini's thought process very well.[14] Chubin and Tripp argue that "divisions in Iranian politics seemed to prevent the formulation of a consistent, and as the Iraqis would see it, 'reasonable' response to the Iraqi use of force."[15] This suggests that even if the Iraqi regime had detailed information and analytic capabilities, it still may have been difficult to anticipate the Iranian response. The Iraqi regime was unprepared for the challenge of handling the political implications of war casualties and declining citizen and military morale.

Chubin and Tripp describe the war as fought "for political gain through territorial concession, initiated at a moment of apparent political and military opportunity."[16] The Iraqi leadership seemed interested in compelling the Iranians to offer "official recognition to Iraqi might."[17] When this recognition was not forthcoming and Iranian forces invaded Iraq, the conflict became an effort to defend the territorial integrity of the Iraqi state. According to Chubin, "Iraq's miscalculation was nearly total in that it overestimated its own

11. Al-Marashi and Salama (2008, 134) write that the Iraqi regime expected a "walkover" of Iran but that this assessment was based on both faulty military intelligence and an inflated sense of Iraqi military prowess. The Iraqi regime also failed to anticipate the impact of the invasion on encouraging Iranian nationalist sentiment. Iraq may have also overestimated the military value of new technology it had acquired from France and the USSR (ibid.).

12. Razoux 2015, 6. Also see Murray and Woods (2012, 47) for more on Iraqi reports prior to the invasion of Iran. They argue that Iraqi intelligence thought that Iran did not have the ability to launch a wide-scale offensive operation against Iraq or defend itself effectively from foreign assault.

13. Razoux 2015, 10. In Middle Eastern autocracies, leadership stability has often come at the expense of conventional military capabilities as the methods used to ensure military loyalty often conflict with the principles of efficient organization (Brooks 1998, 10). These issues are discussed to a greater extent in chapter 10.

14. Chubin and Tripp 1988, 56–60.

15. Ibid.

16. Chubin and Tripp 1988, 28–29.

17. Ibid., 54.

capabilities while misconstruing the nature of its adversary and the sources of power at the latter's disposal."[18]

During the course of the Iran-Iraq War, the Iraqi ruling elite attempted to define and redirect identity as a function of the regime's political needs at that moment.[19] While it would have been within Hussein's repertoire to promote an Iraqi or Mesopotamian identity, instead the focus was on promoting Iraq's Arab identity with the goal of emphasizing the difference between Arabic-speaking Muslims and Iran's Persian population.[20] Dawisha has argued that Iran's Persian identity was the "main point of weakness" and the optimal focus of identity differentiation given the regime's strong need to convince Iraqi Shiʿa to battle the Persian enemy.[21]

The regime increasingly embraced Shiʿi symbols and iconography with the goal of cultivating the nationalist feelings of Iraqi Shiʿa. Although nationalistic sentiment was already high among Iraqi Shiʿa,[22] the regime sought to enhance this sentiment by celebrating the largely Shiʿi-led 1920 anti-British tribal uprisings,[23] paying for gold leaf to decorate Shiʿi shrines, paying respect to Shiʿi holidays,[24] and maintaining a strictly non-sectarian discourse about religion.[25]

Many Iraqi Shiʿa—co-religionists with Iranian Shiʿa—feared cultural and political subjugation at the hands of Iran.[26] When the conflict was initiated, Iraqi Shiʿa occupied both high and low positions within the Iraqi regime and, in general, were themselves worried about the rise of Khomeini.[27] Large segments of the Iraqi Shiʿi population "feared that an Iranian invasion would result in a violent disruption of their lives that had also improved materially since the war began."[28] Even Iraqi Shiʿa who disapproved of the Baʿthist regime generally felt unsupportive of creating a Shiʿi theocracy.[29]

18. Chubin 1988, 14.
19. Dawisha 1999, 554.
20. Chubin and Tripp 1988, 103.
21. Dawisha 1999, 558.
22. Cockburn 2008, 61.
23. Reid 1993.
24. Cockburn 2008, 61.
25. Helfont 2015, 70.
26. Baram 2014, 163.
27. Johnson 2011, 122.
28. Al-Marashi and Salama 2008, 151.
29. Khoury 2010.

Iraqi Shiʻa who were initially reluctant to fight in the war found that after friends and family were killed or wounded at the hands of the Iranian forces, their hesitancy disappeared.[30] One Shiʻi army captain from Karbala reported that while he initially opposed the war, upon hearing about the ill treatment of Iraqi captives in Iranian prisoner of war camps, he fought hard against Iran and found himself recommitted to Iraqi national unity.[31] The Iranian occupation of the strategically important Faw peninsula—located at the head of the disputed Shatt al-Arab waterway—further galvanized Iraqi national sentiment.[32]

The Gulf War and Iraqi Uprisings

The Iran-Iraq War triggered what has been called an "economic free-fall" for Iraq, which went from $35 billion in foreign currency reserves prior to the start of the war to a debt of at least $80 billion by the end of the conflict.[33] Despite this, historians have argued that Hussein felt confident of citizen loyalty to the regime, as evidenced by the huge sacrifices Iraqis of different ethnic and religious groups had made during the course of the Iran-Iraq War.[34] The Iraqi leadership also took for granted that Gulf monarchies would offer strategic rents to offset the costs of the conflict.[35]

The 1990–1991 Gulf War between Iraq and the United States (with its coalition partners) was precipitated by the August 1990 Iraqi invasion of Kuwait. The most common explanation given for the invasion of Kuwait points to fear of debt burdens Iraq had accumulated during the Iran-Iraq War. In 1989, Kuwait had refused to forgive billions of dollars of Iraqi debt and failed to comply with an OPEC decision to slow production as part of a plan to drive up oil prices.[36]

---

30. Cockburn 2008, 57.
31. Ibid., 58.
32. Ibid., 59.
33. Abdullah 2006, 42.
34. Chubin 1988, 63; Baram 2014, 171.
35. Al-Khafaji 2000, 273–274. Transcripts of meetings between Hussein and his advisors also suggest that he truly believed that Iraq had enjoyed a victory over Iran in the conflict (Jabar 1992). There is no evidence to suggest that following the war Hussein was anticipating or preparing in any way for what would soon became the most significant threat to his regime.
36. Alnasrawi 1994, 117

The war proved to be particularly costly for citizens of the Shiʿi South. Much of the aerial bombing by coalition forces hit targets in the South where many of the country's oil refineries and petrochemical complexes were located. Eventually, more than 90 percent of power stations in Iraq were destroyed, as well as bridges, roads, and railroads.[37] Southern areas were also impacted by the land invasion of coalition troops moving in from Kuwait and Saudi Arabia. According to one analyst, the Shiʿa bore the brunt of the war in terms of both casualties and damage to infrastructure.[38] And although there was considerable discontent in southern areas before 1991, there was no "hint at the scale of events" that were to follow.[39]

Following Iraq's humiliating defeat and hasty retreat from Kuwait, General Wafiq al-Samarrai reported that Hussein was on the verge of a psychological collapse.[40] Uprisings broke out across southern Iraq in March of 1991. Most were violent protests, without a clear leader, and spontaneous. The most common story regarding the origins of the uprisings point to when an Iraqi tank driver aimed at and shot a mural of Hussein in Basra.[41] Other scholars have also pointed to "angry and disillusioned elements of [the] retreating army" as the key trigger of the southern uprisings.[42] Khadduri and Ghareeb write that the uprisings were "a disorganized popular movement in areas which had a Shiʿi majority and which armed itself in the early stages with weapons taken mostly from the army or from the weapons distributed by the regime to defend against Coalition attacks."[43]

Participants in the rebellion included not just officers and soldiers, but also civilians and, reportedly, Iranian resistance groups that had crossed the border.[44] Baʿth Party headquarters and party officials were attacked and killed by mobs across the Iraqi South. In some cases, lower ranking Baʿth Party officials joined the uprisings rather than be killed by rioters.[45] Eventually, the

37. Rouleau 1995.
38. Rohde 2010, 34.
39. Graham-Brown 1999, 154; Woods 2008, 247; Baram 2014, 162.
40. Graham-Brown 1999, 154.
41. Mackey 2002, 287.
42. Graham-Brown 1999, 153.
43. Khadduri and Ghareeb 1997, 191.
44. Graham-Brown 1999, 154.
45. Rohde 2010, 63; Khoury 2013, 139. During the course of the uprisings, the Baʿth Party struggled with how to handle party members who failed to support the regime during the protests. For example, there are reports of individuals who sought to escape from the

insurgency spread to all of the major Shiʻi cities. Shortly thereafter, Kurdish Iraqis in the North also rebelled. Many of the anti-regime insurgents believed that US assistance would be forthcoming as a result of statements made by US President George Bush.

Notably, many Iraqis chose not to participate in the uprisings. There were soldiers, civilians, and tribal leaders in rural areas who supported the regime as well as "instances when the rebellion collapsed after defections to the government side."[46] The vast majority of ordinary Iraqis living in southern provinces stayed at home, trying to avoid becoming embroiled in the rebellion.[47] Others fled their homes in the wake of the uprisings out of fear of reprisals. A decision was made to focus the efforts of regime loyalists from the "geographic spine" of the Baʻth Party—the Sunni heartland—on repressing the southern uprising.[48] In particular, troops from Anbar province were instrumental in putting down the revolts.[49] Audio recordings of a high-level meeting convened at the time suggest Hussein's belief in the crucial loyalty of citizens in Anbar governorate which had remained "clean" in the eyes of the regime.[50]

A number of scholars of Iraqi history point out that despite the widespread nature of the protest uprisings, there was no centralized leadership for the movement, nor was there any meaningful coordination of activism. Al-Khafaji writes:

> The fact that the rebellion took place in predominantly Shiʻa regions does not mean that the Shiʻa acted in unison. They constitute the single largest confessional community in Iraq, but were dispersed over the whole political spectrum, from individuals occupying leading posts in the Baʻthist governing machinery, to liberals, monarchists and communists. Those Shiʻa who maintained a religious posture, or opposed the regime because of its anti-Shiʻa stance, also showed a wide array of loyalties.[51]

---

government. When caught, these individuals were often executed for their "weakness" or "collapse" in the face of adversity. See BRCC Doc. Nos. 024-5-2-0096 and 0097, March 17, 1991 for examples.

46. Graham-Brown 1999, 154.
47. Ibid.
48. Mackey 2002, 289.
49. Dawisha 2009, 236.
50. Woods et al. 2011, 200.
51. Al-Khafaji 2003, 82-83.

In other words, even though Iraqi Shiʿa were the majority of participants in the southern uprisings, Shiʿi identity did not predict who would participate given that large numbers of Iraqi Shiʿa did not rebel. In addition, the grievances were not explicitly Shiʿi even though the primary protagonists of the rebellion were Shiʿa.[52] Yousif also points out that a principal oppressor of Shiʿa in the wake of the uprisings was, in fact, a Shiʿi himself.[53]

Khoury describes the spread of the uprisings from the perspective of the Dhi Qar branch of the General Federation of Iraqi Women.[54] She finds that in places like Suq al-Shuyukh, participants in the rebellion were clan members, former Communists, and Da'wa sympathizers; in Nasiriyya, members of the political opposition and army deserters were leaders in the rebellion. A number of reports detail violence against Baʿth Party members during the course of the uprisings, though these reports are likely not exhaustive.[55] The tally of Baʿthist dead varied considerably across regions of the South. This included 66 dead in Babil, 53 in Basra, 17 in Karbala, and smaller numbers killed in the areas of Wasit, Dhi Qar, and Maysan. The military office of the Baʿth Party reported 59 additional casualties. The number of Baʿthist dead also varied across northern provinces, including 86 dead in Erbil, 28 in Duhouk, 23 in Ta'mim (i.e., Kirkuk), and 12 from the northern organizing office. The most common tribal names of the individuals killed were Juburi, Dulaimi, Obeidi, Khafaji, and Hamadi.[56]

One report describing the uprisings in the northern city of Sulaymaniyya suggests that the security directorate was overrun by opponents of the regime after running out of ammunition.[57] Once the security directorate fell, rebels began conducting trials of regime officials, at which point party cadre were executed, in some cases after being mutilated.[58] One Baʿthist party cadre who survived the 1991 Uprisings in the North reported that many police and army officers as well as Baʿth Party members were kidnapped, tortured,

52. Haddad 2011, 81.
53. Yousif 2010.
54. Khoury 2013, 138.
55. BRCC Doc. No. 01-3134-0004-0001, May to August 1991.
56. Chapter 7 will identify some of these tribes as major beneficiaries of regime distributive benefits.
57. CRRC Doc. No. SH-MISC-D-000-947, March 1991.
58. The protesters even killed the daughter of Sulaymaniyya's mayor.

and executed and, in some cases, their bodies dismembered.[59] The Iraqi government never fully regained control over the northern, Kurdish part of the country.[60]

In the wake of the uprisings and violence perpetrated against Baʿthist cadre, the regime moved swiftly to assess guilt and punish the rioters. Yet the regime initially lacked high-quality information about the perpetrators. Special forces units of the Republican Guard undertook a variety of counterinsurgency strategies that reflected a lack of precise information about the identity of the perpetrators.[61] All civilian vehicles were ordered to be searched out of fear that insurgents were hiding ammunition in cars. One individual who reported both Communist and religious sympathies said that he was rounded up in the wake of the uprisings even though he did not take part in the events.[62] Another informant reports that during the uprisings, members of his military unit ran away, leaving their weapons unguarded. When he moved the weapons to a safe location, he was mistakenly charged with having taken part in the protests and arrested.[63]

A shortage of high-quality intelligence about the enemy was a clear blind spot of the regime, increasing the propensity for the use of indiscriminate punishment.[64] Artillery units reportedly played a key role in combating the riots. Dawisha finds that "purposeful bombardment was aimed at houses with little regard for its occupants, and people were indiscriminately shot in the streets... within less than three weeks, over 30,000, including women and children, had been killed, and some 70,000 had fled the country, mainly to neighboring Iran."[65] Eyewitnesses in cities like Basra and Karbala reported

59. North Iraq Dataset Doc. No. 39514-101-18 and 19, June 30, 1991.

60. The question of why the revolts failed to unseat Saddam Hussein has been explored by numerous scholars. Mackey (2002, 296) argues that one important factor was that some of the important Shiʿi tribes did not participate in the uprising or remained neutral during the rebellion. Dawisha (2009, 236) suggests that the tribally oriented Sunni Iraqis from Anbar and Salah al-Din had too much to lose should the uprising succeed and, as a result, "savagely put an end to the rebellion." He also points out the importance of the neutrality or even regime support offered by some Shiʿi tribes of the south.

61. CRRC Doc. No. SH-RPGD-D-000-581, March–April 1991.

62. Testimony of Q. Hadi, recorded March 2007; at the time informant testimonies were taken, Iraqi Shiʿa would have little incentive to lie about their involvement in the 1991 Uprisings if, in fact, they had participated.

63. Testimony of T. Al-Shahrani, recorded October 2007.

64. CRRC Doc. No. SH-RPGD-D-000-581, March–April 1991.

65. Dawisha 2009, 226.

soldiers conducting house-to-house searches and public executions by the Republican Guard.[66] Haddad argues that distinguishing between Shi'i rebels and non-rebels was difficult for the regime as it sought to regain control of southern cities, leading to the use of the destructive, collective targeting unprecedented for the Euphrates region of Iraq.[67]

By late March, the security situation in southern governorates was beginning to stabilize. Telegrams describe how ordinary life was returning to Karbala.[68] Army units and special committee members, however, continued to search for rioters in the province. The mayor of Karbala was replaced and the regime assigned a Republican Guard special forces unit to the area to continue purging rebels.[69] There were many local-level party members—including a number of women—who served as informants and witnesses, providing long and detailed reports about uprising participants, their place of residence, and their family affiliation.[70] During this period, Hussein suggested that the most loyal individuals should be praised while acknowledging that it was difficult to find reliable supporters.[71]

Following the regime's repression of the southern uprisings, families of Shi'a suspected of anti-regime activities were increasingly targeted in a bid to elicit confessions and information. Disappearances became common and even individuals who were not involved with the uprisings became victims of state abuse. Makiya writes that beginning in 1991 Iraqi Shi'a became a "target" of the regime for the first time in modern Iraqi history.[72] For example, one man from Najaf reported that his son fled to Saudi Arabia following the uprisings.[73] The son eventually returned to Iraq and reported for military service, at which point he was arrested and executed. When given his son's corpse, the man was barred from holding a funeral.[74]

66. Graham-Brown 1999, 156.
67. Haddad 2011, 73.
68. CRRC Doc. No. SH-GMID-D-000-621, March 1991.
69. Ibid.
70. Khoury 2012, 251.
71. CRRC Doc. No. SH-SHTP-A-000-614, March 1991.
72. Makiya 1993, 100. It was also at this time that regime media outlets promulgated, for the first time, a series of newspaper articles that spoke of the Shi'a in sectarian terms; the writings pointed to Iraqi Shi'a as "ungrateful recipients" of the benefits of state-led development and modernization policies (Khoury 2013, 135–136).
73. Testimony of G. Al-Da'mi, recorded December 2007.
74. Denying the family of an executed political prisoner the ability to hold a funeral was a common practice in Iraq at this time.

In the years after the uprisings, "the Shiʻa would fall subject to a level of ruthlessness previously applied only to the Kurds."[75] Individual accounts suggest that for Iraqi Shiʻa, punishment became more intense after the 1991 Uprisings and was also meted out imprecisely, two factors that had important implications for the political behaviors of citizens in the Shiʻi community. These cases are consistent with Khoury's observation about the increasing use of "family networks to exact punishment for individuals' infractions."[76]

The tendency to engage in punishment at the level of the extended family helps to explain the "mobilization of clan networks against or in support of the regime."[77] According to one Iraqi from Najaf who was serving in the military in 1991, when he returned to his family home following the war, he found his family's property seized and his brother arrested (and remained missing) even though his family did not take part in the uprisings.[78] An Iraqi from the town of Rumaytha reports that his elderly father was arrested following the 1991 Uprisings and it was not until 2003 that he found his father's remains in a mass grave, identifiable by an ID card, prayer beads, eyeglasses, and other personal items.[79]

Regime officials continued to discuss the events around the uprisings in the weeks, months, and even years to follow.[80] During one post-mortem discussion of events, Hussein praised military leaders for their success in controlling the situation.[81] He said that one of the challenges in putting down the uprisings was that the regime did not know how best to find the guilty parties and, as a result, was forced to use air strikes or artillery fire targeted at a general region, both very blunt tools of repression.[82] In another meeting, Hussein met with military commanders and conceded that he had failed to anticipate the uprisings, a fact that required a new focus on internal security issues and emergency preparedness in case another revolt took place.[83] He felt

75. Mackey 2002, 289.
76. Khoury 2013, 139.
77. Khoury 2013, 139.
78. Testimony of H. Najim, recorded December 2008.
79. Testimony of M. al-Zalimi, recorded May 2008.
80. For example, military and intelligence officials deliberated over what to do about families that had fled to bedouin encampments in the desert during the uprisings, but were waiting for a suitable opportunity to return to their homes (CRRC Doc. No. SH-GMID-D-000-502, April 27, 1991).
81. CRRC Doc. No. SH-SHTP-A-000-739, April 1991.
82. Ibid.
83. CRRC Doc. No. SH-RVCC-D-000-610, February 1992.

that his biggest personal weakness was placing too much trust in the Iraqi people, and he was worried about future rioting in the Euphrates region, the South, and the area around Kirkuk.[84]

Uncertainty about how to view the loyalty of Iraq's southern citizens plagued the regime. Seven months after the uprisings, the University of Basra, together with Iraqi intelligence, prepared a classified report about the participants in the revolts based on questionnaires that had been administered to prisoners. The results of the report suggested that urbanites, including marsh Arabs who had relocated to urban areas, were much more likely to have participated in the revolts than Iraqis living in rural areas. According to the report, income was not a significant predictor of participation. National and party organizations had failed to offer adequate support to soldiers withdrawing from Kuwait, particularly psychological services, a fact that spurred discontent.[85] From the perspective of Hussein, the uprisings represented a failure of the Ba'th Party, which was supposed to serve as a societal bulwark against anti-regime sentiment.[86]

MEASURING THE HUMAN COST OF CONFLICT

While it is difficult to estimate the absolute number of military and civilian casualties as a result of the Iran-Iraq War and Gulf War, Iraqi archival sources provide important evidence regarding the relative distribution of war costs across the Iraqi population.[87] This section describes the evidence regarding this distribution of war casualties in Iraq. I focus on war costs conceptualized in three different ways. The first is the individuals killed, missing in action, and taken as prisoners of war between September 1980 and October 1984. The second section examines the distribution of "distinguished" families, or those families with three or more first-degree family members killed in conflict. A

---

84. Ibid.

85. Baram 2014, 245-46.

86. For years after the uprisings, Ba'th Party officials continued to discuss how to handle the issue of party members who failed to join the resistance in the first hours after the protests began versus later, when the regime had gained the upper hand over protesters. See BRCC Doc. No. 01-3564-0002-0131, September 7, 1995, for example.

87. See Kurzman's October 31, 2013 blog post, "Death Tolls of the Iran-Iraq War," for a summary of his cohort analysis using Iraqi and Iranian Census data (http://kurzman.unc.edu/death-tolls-of-the-iran-iraq-war/).

final section reports on casualty counts for the Iran-Iraq War and the Gulf War using data from a census of secondary school students.

Iran-Iraq War Casualties through October 1984

Iraqi Shiʿa were believed to make up 80–85 percent of the military rank and file in the early 1980s.[88] The vast majority of Shiʿi soldiers fought honorably for the Iraqi nation, even if they opposed the Baʿthist regime. On the other hand, Kurdish conscripts made reluctant soldiers and, as a result, Kurds were frequently channeled into government-run paramilitary organizations responsible for internal security in the North.[89] These units were often unreliable agents of Iraqi governmental prerogatives.

There is little doubt that the Iraqi regime was concerned with the heavy cost of war for the population. The regime collected a great deal of information about the war burden with an eye toward compensating the families of war martyrs. Using this information, I have sought to provide more precise data regarding the relatively uneven distribution of war burden across Iraq's multiethnic community. Information about war casualties in the first four years of the Iran-Iraq War were found in a series of Baʿth Party memoranda from October of 1984 that provide provincial, and in some cases, district- or village-level information on three dimensions: number of individuals killed, number missing in action, and number taken as prisoners of war.[90] Khoury has argued that after 1984–85, desertions among rank-and-file members of the Iraqi military increased exponentially,[91] suggesting that the casualty estimates generated in October 1984 would not be impacted as significantly by desertions. In order to estimate the number of casualties per capita, I calculate a weighted average of the 1977 and 1987 province-level population estimates from the Iraq census.

Table 4.1 presents the distribution of war burden. Column 2 shows the number of individuals killed in the Iran-Iraq War by October 1984; column 3 shows the number of prisoners of war and missing in action for the same period. Columns 4 and 5 show these same indicators per 1,000 population for

88. Heller 1993, 45; Cockburn 2008, 57.
89. "Genocide in Iraq: The Anfal Campaign Against the Kurds," Human Rights Watch, July 1993.
90. See BRCC Boxfile Doc. No. 01-2202-0003.
91. Khoury 2013, 73.

TABLE 4.1. Iraqis killed, missing in action, and prisoners of war in the Iran-Iraq War by October 1984.

Location	Killed	POW and MIA	Killed per 1,000	POW and MIA per 1,000
Baghdad	10,314	18,182	2.8	5.0
South				
Basra	5,252	6,294	5.7	6.9
Dhi Qar	4,003	5,832	5.9	5.1
Maysan	1,742	2,177	3.9	4.8
Wasit	3,064	2,616	5.9	5.1
Euphrates				
Muthanna	1,275	1,563	4.5	5.5
Qadisiyya	2,471	3,230	4.8	6.3
Najaf	1,663	3,435	3.2	6.5
Karbala	2,255	2,958	5.6	7.3
Babil	4,929	5,110	5.3	5.4
Central				
Anbar	1,934	2,433	2.7	3.5
Salah al-Din	1,454	1666	3.0	3.4
Diyala	937	963	1.5	1.5
North				
Ninawa	5,012	4,344	3.7	3.2
Ta'mim	1,576	1,372	2.8	2.4
Erbil	315	306	0.5	0.4

the provinces of Iraq.[92] Southern provinces, which are predominantly Shi'i, saw between 3.9 and 5.9 individuals killed per 1,000. In the Iraqi North, which has a large Kurdish population, per capita war deaths were much lower. In predominantly Sunni provinces like Salah al-Din and Anbar, the average number killed was 3.0 and 2.7 per 1,000, respectively. Similar trends are apparent when examining the number of prisoners of war (POWs) and missing in action (MIA) from across Iraqi provinces. Areas like Basra, Karbala, and Najaf—all of which are overwhelming Shi'i—saw the largest number of per capita POWs and MIA soldiers. Kurdish and Sunni majority areas had much lower per capita POWs and MIA soldiers at the end of 1984. These data suggest that the predominantly Shi'i southern areas of Iraq not only saw

92. The number of civilians killed in the Iran-Iraq War was relatively small, representing less than 3 percent of overall casualties. See Razoux (2015) for more on this point.

higher rates of war deaths, but also more overall casualties, including soldiers who were missing in action or taken as prisoners of war.[93] The Kurdish areas saw the smallest number killed, missing, or taken prisoner.

The war had a very different impact on Iraq's Kurdish population. Cross-border alliances between Iran and, at first, the Kurdish Democratic Party (KDP) and, later, the Patriotic Union of Kurdistan (PUK), represented a major threat to the Iraqi regime. At the start of the Iran-Iraq War, animosity between the KDP and PUK gave the Iraqi regime confidence that Kurdish factions were so busy fighting each other that they would not pose a challenge to regime interests.[94] The Iranian offensive into Kurdistan in 1983, however, changed the value of Kurdish loyalty and resistance. When the KDP assisted Iranian forces, the regime "vanished" more than 8,000 civilians affiliated with the Barzani tribe.[95] The PUK was engaged in negotiations with the regime in 1983 and 1984; these negotiations ultimately broke down, however, when the group failed to obtain its primary objectives of political autonomy and fixed oil revenue.[96] Eventually both groups came to be engaged in harassment of Iraqi forces, at times with assistance from the Iranians.[97] By 1985, the regime had lost control over parts of the northern Iraqi countryside to Kurdish insurgents, but was able to retain influence in northern towns and cities.[98] Chapter 6 focuses on the experience of Iraqi Kurds and explores how conflict impacted conceptions of both Iraqi and Kurdish nationalism.

Wartime's "Distinguished" Families

A set of files in the archival collection describes a special bureaucratic designation known as the "distinguished" families ('awa'il mutamayyiza). Distinguished families had between three and seven first-degree family members killed in conflict, where a first-degree relative is defined as a father, son, or brother. Table 4.2 provides information about the number of distinguished

93. It was reported that Iraqi Shi'i soldiers who were captured by Iranians typically were not treated very well (Baram 2014, 163).
94. Chubin and Tripp 1988, 105.
95. Kirmanj 2013, 144.
96. Chubin and Tripp 1988, 106.
97. Ibid.
98. Kirmanj 2013, 145.

TABLE 4.2. Geographic distribution of "distinguished" families, those that lost three or more first-degree relatives in the Iran-Iraq War.

Governorate	3	4	5	6	7+	Total	Per 100,000 Population
Baghdad	54	3	4	0	1	62	1.6
South							
Basra	39	9	3	1	0	52	6.0
Dhi Qar	35	1	0	0	0	36	3.9
Maysan	13	1	0	0	0	14	2.9
Wasit	16	2	0	0	0	18	3.2
Euphrates							
Muthanna	13	1	0	0	0	14	4.5
Qadisiyya	19	1	0	0	0	20	3.6
Najaf	9	1	0	0	0	10	1.7
Karbala	15	0	0	0	0	15	3.2
Babil	27	1	0	0	0	28	2.5
Central							
Anbar	20	1	0	0	0	21	2.6
Salah al-Din	6	0	0	0	0	6	0.8
Diyala	22	2	0	1	1	26	2.7
North							
Ninawa	24	1	0	0	0	25	1.7
Ta'mim	16	0	0	0	0	16	2.7
Sulaymaniyya	8	5	0	0	0	13	1.4
Erbil	1	0	0	0	0	1	0.1
Dohuk	0	0	0	0	0	0	0
Total	337	29	7	2	2	377	

families by Iraqi province.[99] Because large families were common across all of Iraq at this time, it was unlikely that differential family size is driving these differences. Notice the relatively large number of distinguished families in the predominantly Shiʿi southern and Euphrates regions compared to other parts of Iraq.

In table 4.2, the eighth column shows the population-adjusted figures for the relative distribution of distinguished families. Basra governorate saw six distinguished families per 100,000 population compared to only 1.6

99. BRCC Doc. No. 004-2-2-0008, March 9, 1989. Province-level population estimates for 1984 were estimated using data from 1977 and 1987 figures.

TABLE 4.3. Geographic distribution of "distinguished" families, for the Gulf War and 1991 Uprisings.

Governorate	Total	Per 100,000 Population	Designation Rescinded
Baghdad	32	0.8	1
South			
Basra	37	4.2	7
Dhi Qar	20	2.2	2
Maysan	7	1.4	0
Wasit	12	2.1	1
Euphrates			
Muthanna	9	2.9	0
Qadisiyya	15	2.7	4
Najaf	7	1.2	1
Karbala	8	1.7	0
Babil	22	2.0	0
Center			
Anbar	13	1.6	0
Salah al-Din	1	0.1	0
Diyala	15	1.6	0
North			
Ninawa	17	1.1	0
Ta'mim	10	1.7	0
Sulaymaniyya	7	0.7	7
Erbil	NA	NA	NA
Dohuk	NA	NA	NA
Total	233		23

distinguished families per 100,000 population in Baghdad, for example. Northern governorates typically saw fewer distinguished families when compared to other parts of the country, consistent with arguments about the unreliability of Kurdish fighters. Notably, governorates in the central part of Iraq saw relatively fewer distinguished families than in the southern regions. Indeed, Salah al-Din—the home province of Saddam Hussein—saw one of the lowest number of distinguished families in the country.

Table 4.3 includes information collected by the regime on the number of families who lost three or more first-degree relatives in the Gulf War and subsequent 1991 Uprisings. An initial list was compiled that included 233 families. This information was gathered with an eye toward giving families a cash award of between 1,000 and 1,500 Iraqi dinars and a special badge or medal, though some families appeared not to have received any compensation. Later, military intelligence investigations were conducted which revealed that some of the distinguished families had been given the designation as a result of the deaths of individuals who were participants in the 1991 Uprisings rather than those killed trying to put down the anti-regime protests. As a result, about 10 percent of the families had their designation rescinded following the investigation.[100]

Handwritten notes on the regime documents provide more details regarding why the designation was rescinded.[101] For example, Sulaymaniyya families that fled to Iran were removed from the list even if members did not actively participate in the anti-regime protests. In other cases, the family may have come under suspicion because an uncle or other second-degree relative participated in the riots. In Basra, Dhi Qar, and Qadisiyya, however, families that were removed typically had a father or a son who participated in the protests, carried weapons, or joined a mob that had attacked Ba'th Party cadre.

There are a number of key inferences to draw from these data. The southern and Euphrates regions saw the largest numbers of casualties from the Gulf War and 1991 Uprisings. This is the case even after taking into account the possibility that some of the fatalities were due to anti-regime participation in the 1991 Uprisings. Again, Basra governorate saw the largest number of killed during the Gulf War and 1991 Uprisings, with 4.2 distinguished families per 100,000 population. This might be compared to Salah al-Din province, where there was only one distinguished family. This suggests that southern governorates bore a larger war burden than other parts of the country, and even within the predominantly Sunni parts of Iraq, Salah al-Din region suffered the fewest conflict-related fatalities.

Iran-Iraq War and Gulf War Casualties

A final source of evidence regarding the distribution of Iran-Iraq War casualties comes in the form of information gathered as part of a student census

---

100. See BRCC Doc. Nos. 01-2199-0001-0001 to 0018, August 1991.
101. Ibid.

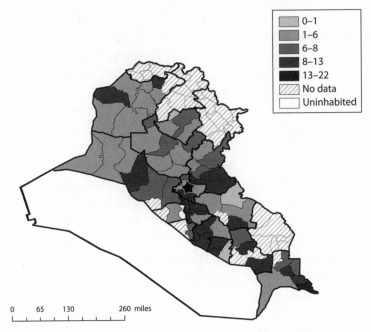

Figure 4.1. Percentage of families with a father or brother killed in either the Iran-Iraq War or the Gulf War based on 2001–2002 academic year school registers.

undertaken by the Ba'th Party in 2001–2002.[102] Data were collected for each student regarding whether or not the student's father or brother had been killed in either the Iran-Iraq War or the Gulf War. Because the Iran-Iraq War was much longer than the Gulf War and had many more casualties, most of the deaths can probably be attributed to the Iran-Iraq War, although casualties in both conflicts contributed to levels of grievance that fueled later political behaviors.

Figure 4.1 depicts the district-level average number of students who had a father or brother killed in either conflict. These figures range from less than 1 percent to 22 percent. The largest concentrations of war casualties appear to have been in Basra governorate and in the Shi'i areas just south of Baghdad. Again, Sunni and Kurdish areas both had fewer war martyrs than Shi'i areas. The information about war burden gathered from the student census data, then, aligns with the patterns observed in the government casualty statistics and the "distinguished" families files.

102. Details about this survey are discussed in chapter 7.

REGIME RESPONSE TO WAR LOSSES

Surviving the Iran-Iraq War became a defining political challenge for the Iraqi regime during the 1980s.[103] As a result, major efforts were made to promulgate policies that would help to mitigate the political damage associated with war costs. This included disseminating political propaganda that promoted the image of Hussein as a dedicated public servant, holding general elections in October 1984 where 40 percent of seats were reserved for Shiʿi deputies, and providing state support for the manufacture of consumer goods, despite wartime austerity.[104] The conflict also provided opportunities to encourage nationalist sentiment. Taking advantage of war populism, Hussein was able to raise his profile in society while at the same time sidelining alternative political organizations.[105] Special effort was made to keep military officers happy. High performers in the military could receive a Mercedes Benz for their service.[106] The next sections focus on three main government activities: providing financial and other forms of compensation for martyr families, inflicting punishments on the families of deserters, and state-sponsored efforts at boosting citizen and military morale through various forms of educational and nationalist programming.

Compensating Martyr Families

Maintaining the morale of both the population and the army itself became an important priority of the regime. In the early years of the war, when Iraq was still flush with cash reserves, Hussein recognized the hardship associated with war casualties and provided generous financial compensation. Indeed, families of fallen soldiers received thousands of Iraqi dinars and a car—originally a

103. A number of scholars focused on the military history of Iraq have asked why Iraq waged war so poorly during the Iran-Iraq conflict. Scholars have pointed to a number of factors, including the ineptitude of commanders who were primarily party cadre rather than trained military tacticians; the tendency of Hussein to micro-manage combat operations from Baghdad with poor knowledge of military strategy or on-the-ground conditions; and the lack of horizontal communication within the army, which would have facilitated cooperation across units (Pelletiere 1992, 42–43). Murray and Woods (2012, 7) have suggested that the Iraqi military was kept weak intentionally, arguing that "Iraq's military, in the 1980s, was as effective as Saddam wanted it to be, but not as effective as he needed it to be."

104. Razoux 2015, 312–313.

105. Workman 1994, 2.

106. Razoux 2015, 313.

Toyota Corona and, later, the less expensive Volkswagen Passat.[107] Families of dead or disabled soldiers also received the right to a pension, a plot of land, and interest-free loans to build a house.[108]

Economic conditions became increasingly difficult for many Iraqis during this period. Households where adult males had been drafted into the army found that military salaries were insufficient to meet a family's basic needs. To make do, poor families sold assets—like furniture or bedding—to purchase food while middle-class families impoverished themselves more slowly.[109] Citizens planted small gardens to help with the food shortages.[110] But despite their best efforts, citizens could not maintain their standards of living and the regime eventually came to the realization that the welfare state it had created was not sustainable.[111]

In 1982, Hussein met with his Cabinet to discuss the budget.[112] Even at this relatively early point, financial austerity was required given rising defense expenditures. In general, budget allocations were to be reduced by 10–15 percent, particularly if they reflected an increase over the 1981 allocations.[113] Al-Khafaji argues that 1982 reflected a turning point in terms of escalating costs.[114] Inflation and food prices also emerged as areas of concern. Hussein expressed an interest in maintaining the patriotic sensibility of the Iraqi people and specifically asked about the distribution of 70 million Iraqi dinars' worth of televisions.[115] Fearing abuse of his generosity, however, he reportedly inspected households and if he found any with more than one of the gifted televisions, he would order the seizure of all of the televisions from those families.[116]

Iraq came under increasing financial strain as a result of the costs of war as well as the drop in world oil prices in 1986. According to Davis, it was at this point that the Ba'thist regime became hard pressed to provide

107. Bashir 2005, 59.
108. Razoux 2015, 313-314.
109. Ismael and Ismael 2008.
110. Al-Ali 2007.
111. Alnasrawi 1994.
112. CRRC Doc. No. SH-SHTP-A-000-635, 1982.
113. Ibid.
114. Al-Khafaji 2000, 272-273.
115. CRRC Doc. No. SH-SHTP-A-000-635, 1982.
116. Ibid.

both "guns and butter."[117] Investment in education slowed and workers were increasingly moved from productive sectors to the front, worsening the investment climate.[118] Iraq fell behind neighboring countries in terms of health, education, and per capita food production.[119] The number of primary schools in Iraq declined from 11,316 in academic year 1979–1980 to 8,141 in 1985–1986.[120] Public funds for school breakfast programs were diverted in favor of military needs.[121] University students no longer received free room and board during their studies, burdening middle-class families.[122]

Despite increasing strain on the government and declines in important economic indicators, the regime continued its efforts to support the families of martyred soldiers. In 1985, for example, the amount of money given to bury a fallen soldier increased from 250 to 500 Iraqi dinars.[123] Regime officials also discussed protocols for Medal of Courage winners, including whether they should receive a live audience before Hussein and whether the award service should be televised or not.[124]

If martyr families were not compensated appropriately, this became a subject of legitimate grievance for discussion with party representatives. During Ba'th Party visits to families of fallen soldiers, it was reported that some families had not received badges or honors commemorating a soldier's death and, in some cases, the families had not received a 10,000-Iraqi dinar honorary gift from Hussein even though they believed that they were eligible.[125] Among the factors that might lower morale within the population was the perception that the distribution of honorifics and rewards for service was unjust. In one instance, a Ba'thist attempted to provide feedback to the regime in a letter to Hussein.[126] Writing very politely, he pointed out that some individuals deserving of a courageous service medal were not honored while others who were not even involved in combat received the medal. According to this individual,

117. Davis 2005, 182.
118. Alkazaz 1993, 222–223.
119. Abdullah 2006, 44.
120. Yousif 2012, 76.
121. Ismael and Ismael 2008.
122. Ibid.
123. BRCC Doc. No. 3048-0002-0286, May, 2 1985.
124. The Iranians were praised for being much more effective than Iraqis at providing commendations of this type. See CRRC Doc. No. SH-SHTP-A-001-023, March 6, 1987.
125. BRCC Doc. No. 3687-0001-0062, June 18, 1986.
126. BRCC Doc. Nos. 01-3388-0001-0240 to 0249, August 12, 1988.

these discrepancies were creating confusion and having a negative impact on morale in the provinces, as people perceived the situation to be unfair.[127]

Concern over enumerating the missing and the dead led the Ministry of Defense to create computerized records to identify the martyrs according to ethnic identity, religion, and mother's name.[128] The Revolutionary Command Council ordered that families of martyrs would be eligible for special benefits including a 20 percent discount to martyrs' families seeking to purchase houses, apartments, or land from the state; families of martyrs were also made eligible for a first payment of just 5 percent of the total property price, with the rest of the discounted purchase price to be paid in monthly installments over a period of 20 years.[129]

Efforts at Boosting Morale

A variety of party memoranda describe the challenges associated with improving morale on the part of citizens and soldiers in the face of mounting war casualties.[130] A state dictate from February 1981 allowed all members of the armed forces to purchase a car without having to pay customs duties.[131] Soldiers who killed more than twenty-five Iranians were given gift cards.[132] During a meeting between Hussein and military officers in 1982, it was suggested that personalized letters be provided to the families of Iraqi soldiers.[133]

Declassified CIA assessments from 1981 and 1983 provide details about US government beliefs regarding the public mood in Iraq. According to one assessment, there were multiple groups that sought to overthrow Hussein, but these groups were unable to cooperate with each other on even the most basic level.[134] According to this assessment, there existed a kind of quiet resignation

127. Ibid.
128. BRCC Doc. No. 2162-0001-0117, February 13, 1989.
129. BRCC Doc. No. 2162-0001-0162, March 12, 1989.
130. Iraqi citizens also responded to changes in the military balance of power between Iran and Iraq. For example, a major public mobilization took place after Iranian shelling of Basra led to the deaths of dozens of civilians and damage to homes, businesses, vehicles, and government offices. After the shelling, thousands of individuals volunteered to join the military or donated blood for the war cause. See BRCC Doc. Nos. 01-3388-0001-0109 to 0111, 1984.
131. Al-Khafaji 2000 286-287.
132. Ibid.
133. CRRC Doc. No. SH-SHTP-A-001-359, 1982.
134. Declassified CIA National Foreign Assessment Center, Research Paper, "Iraq's Dissidents," July 1981.

on the part of the Iraqi public regarding the war as well as a belief among the citizens that the regime was working hard to shield people from severe economic hardship.[135] In 1983, CIA assessments suggested that the Daʿwa Party, for example, was little more than an irritant to Hussein and the Iraqi Communist party was "decimated."[136] The CIA analysis suggested that Iraqi Shiʿa consistently "turn a deaf ear to Iran's persistent calls to revolt."[137]

A regime memorandum from January 1983 describes meetings held with Kurdish special forces fighters. The goal of the meetings was to make fighters feel more confident and less hesitant about their participation in policing the North and fighting the Iranians.[138] During the meeting, regime officials emphasized that Iraq had equalled Iranian fighting capacity despite Iran's much larger population and that Kurdish detachments fought with honor and courage.[139] A special point was made by officials that Kurdish units that had fought on behalf of the Iraqi state would never be abandoned or forgotten, nor would their children and families.[140] Regime officials implored Kurdish populations to only listen to official government mouthpieces and to avoid rebel propaganda. Special forces fighters were encouraged to have confidence in the party and the revolution while emphasizing that any defector who returned to the "national side" would live as a normal citizen.

Southern areas received regime messaging as well. A report put together by party officials in Wasit highlighted events and programs used to increase nationalist sentiment during the period from 1983 to 1985.[141] The report emphasized the strong commitment of the people of Wasit to the war effort as evidenced by donations of money and gold as well as popular participation in national celebrations. The party also awarded a commendation to a citizen who shot and killed his own son for deserting from the army. The man, who was described as a model Iraqi citizen, considered desertion to be a betrayal of honor and nationalist spirit. The party highlighted various programs for increasing morale in the province, including finding employment for 300 women from families with missing sons or disabled family members and

135. Ibid.
136. Declassified Directorate of Intelligence, Intelligence Assessment, "Iraqi Opposition: Status and Prospects," December 23, 1983.
137. Ibid.
138. Iraqi Secret Police Files Doc. Nos. 30703 to 05, January 11, 1983.
139. Ibid.
140. Ibid.
141. BRCC Doc. Nos. 01-2961-0001-0326 to 0343, April 11, 1985.

giving away fabric to martyr families.[142] The party apparatus also succeeded in increasing the number of public portraits of Saddam Hussein in the area from forty-four in 1983 to ninety in 1985.

Recordings of a 1986 meeting of the political and military leadership, including Hussein, suggest that the regime was worried about the emotional state of the population. Hussein expressed concern that the effect of Iranian missile attacks on Iraqi cities could cut one of two ways—either nationalist sentiment would be encouraged with patriotic energy directed to the battle-fronts or, alternatively, citizen anger might lead Iraqis to distance themselves from the regime.[143] In another meeting, Hussein sought a more intense level of political mobilization and expressed concern about the weak commitment of some Baʿthists since party cadre were supposed to serve as exemplars for the Iraqi people.[144]

Maintaining soldier morale during the war was also an issue of major concern. A series of memoranda sent from an educational committee to the secretary of the military office expressed concern with safeguarding the mental state of soldiers.[145] Morale was considered of critical importance to avoid the problem of soldiers surrendering without fighting. While the memoranda describe these types of incidents as unusual, they do acknowledge that such failures had occurred and needed to be remedied.[146] In general, problems of morale among the rank and file were considered to be more common than within the officer corps.

According to the regime's internal analysis, problem soldiers fell into five major categories: (1) those politically affiliated with the opposition, (2) those who pursued their own agendas even if not affiliated with the opposition, (3) those who were hesitant, confused, and lacking in determination, (4) those who were driven only by survival instincts, and (5) those who prioritized their traditional tribal or other personal commitments over the interests of the country.[147] Wide-ranging educational programs were believed to be the solution to these problems. Soldiers were to be instructed about the achievements of the regime, including the cleansing of the internal front of

142. Ibid.
143. CRRC Doc. No. SH-SHTP-D-000-411, September 1986.
144. CRRC Doc. No. SH-SHTP-A-001-023, March 1987.
145. BRCC Doc. Nos. 2479-0004-0259 to 0273, October 22, 1986.
146. Ibid.
147. Ibid.

spies, agents, and vandals and the achievement of equality for all citizens (regardless of race or sect) as well as regime-sponsored advancements in the areas of petroleum, agriculture, education, and health development.[148]

Another regime memorandum considers the use of special seminars with fighters for discussion of key party principles.[149] Indeed, raising the commitment levels and nationalist feelings of Iraqi soldiers was given priority over all other concerns to be discussed in meetings and seminars. The memorandum acknowledged that solving the tactical and administrative failures of the military would increase confidence on the part of the rank and file.[150]

Wartime Repression

Negative inducements were also common. During the Iran-Iraq War, party members who exhibited cowardice might be forced out of the party and have their party-related privileges taken away. One Baʿth Party memorandum describes those benefits as including special loans and contracts, life insurance benefits, housing, health care, the right to travel, acceptance into colleges or institutions of higher learning, the right to facilitate tourism investment, and licenses to work with foreign companies.[151] This memorandum makes clear the benefits of party membership during the early 1980s, particularly access to opportunities that were not widely shared.

Despite the weakness of opposition groups, the regime continued to repress suspected Daʿwa and Communist Party members. One informant reports that during his agronomy studies at Baghdad University he refused to join the Baʿth Party and began to be harassed immediately afterward.[152] He was eventually accused of being a Daʿwa Party member and was sentenced to life in prison. Even individuals that worked in the service of the state came under suspicion. One informant, arrested in 1980 out of his military unit, was charged with belonging to the Daʿwa Party.[153] A naval college officer who refused to join the Baʿth Party was accused of being a Daʿwa Party member.[154]

148. Ibid.
149. BRCC Doc. Nos. 2479-0004-0277 to 0289, October 9, 1986.
150. Ibid.
151. BRCC Doc. No. 01-3388-0001-0171, January 18, 1982.
152. Testimony of J. Kassar, recorded March 2007.
153. Testimony of Z. Jassem, recorded February 2008.
154. Testimony of A. Nasser, recorded July 2007.

He was forced to spend eleven years in prison. Another informant, arrested in 1985, was accused of belonging to the Communist Party.[155] His father and other family members were also arrested, including his brothers.

Repression also crossed class lines. One medical doctor from Basra reports that her brothers, each of whom was a student or professional, were arrested and either executed or imprisoned as a result of suspected Da'wa Party sympathies.[156] Another informant reports that she was born into a wealthy family and was interested in religious education but did not belong to a political party.[157] While a student, she was harassed for wearing a veil and for refusing to join the Ba'th Party. Eventually she was arrested, charged with working for Iran and Israel, and given a life sentence until she was pardoned in 1991.

In November 1986, Hussein signed a presidential decree that punished with life imprisonment and confiscation of property anyone who insulted the president, the Revolutionary Command Council, the Ba'th Party, or other government organs.[158] One individual, a well-known artist of Turkman origin, was persecuted for his poems and songs and eventually arrested and sentenced to life in prison for refusing to sing for Hussein.[159]

IMPACT OF WAR ON INVESTMENT IN THE REGIME

Ba'thism sought, at least in rhetoric, to rid society of all social structures other than the party. Ba'thist ideology, with its emphasis on Arab nationalism, sought to Arabize Kurdish populations of the North while reducing emphasis on the religious distinction between Sunnis and Shi'a. Instead, state discourse focused on the distinction between authentic and inauthentic Iraqis rather than drawing distinctions between Iraqis of different sects.[160] Despite the regime's attempts to reduce the salience of ethno-sectarian identity in Iraqi political life, the probability of dying in war or becoming a casualty of collective punishment was correlated with the very identity groups that the regime tried to nationalize in its rhetoric. As a result, state efforts to erase

155. Testimony of A. Al-Sahlani, recorded January 2008.
156. Testimony of S. Al-Salman, recorded January 2007.
157. Testimony of S. Al-'Ubaydi, recorded March 2007.
158. CRRC Doc. No. SH-PDWN-D-000-590, November 4, 1986.
159. Testimony of A. Tozlo, recorded March 2008.
160. Saleh 2013.

sectarian distinctions were ultimately unable to counteract the effects of the war burden and punishment policies inflicted on these groups.

Within the scholarship on Iraqi politics, there exist multiple perspectives regarding the impact of war on efforts at state-building and cultivation of nationalist sentiment. Some scholars have argued that the only way Iraq could have sustained such a long period of conflict with so many casualties was through a surge in nationalist sentiment.[161] This perspective was shared by the Iraqi regime itself, which attempted to forge "a new Iraqi national community out of the ethnically diverse population."[162] Others have argued that the war had a tendency to undermine nationalist sentiment and, instead, "atomize Iraqi society, throwing its members back on the security of primordial loyalties and collective identities."[163] Jabar argues that in the years immediately following the Iran-Iraq War, for instance, "cracks in the union of popular and official nationalisms began to surface among the restless war generation."[164] According to Al-Khafaji, the Iran-Iraq War triggered an economic crisis that introduced both a more brutal style of government and an associated negative impact on the Ba'thist strategy of rule.[165]

The data and information that I have presented cannot speak to the net impact of the war on nationalism in Iraq, but provide some evidence for the communities within Iraq that were most likely to see declining investment in the regime given the war costs. It is perhaps not surprising, then, that in the wake of the Gulf War, uprisings first emerged in the Shi'i areas of southern Iraq that had witnessed the largest casualty counts during the Iran-Iraq War.

A preliminary piece of evidence is presented in figure 4.2. In this figure, the y-axis is the number of days after the first uprising that protests broke out in areas of southern Iraq; in other words, the number of days between February 28, 1991 to when protests occurred in a given district. The x-axis measures the percentage of high school students who said, in 2001–2002, that they had a father or brother die in either the Gulf War or the Iran-Iraq War.[166] Though

161. Jabar 2003b.
162. Chubin and Tripp 1988, 84.
163. Ibid.
164. Jabar 2003a, 118. This occurred at the same time that the regime had to pull back on its funding for the public goods provision that had helped maintain political stability during the 1970s.
165. Al-Khafaji 2000, 272.
166. Not all districts that witnessed protest activity appear in this figure because I did not have corresponding war mortality data for those areas.

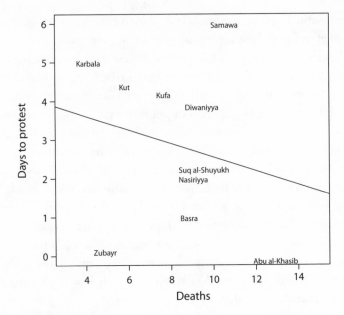

Figure 4.2. Scatterplot of relationship between district-level war deaths and days to protest during 1991 Uprisings.

there are only a very small number of observations reflected in this plot, a fitted line suggests a downward relationship between war deaths and days to protest. In other words, southern areas with more war deaths seem to have been more likely to have been early protest areas. This empirical observation is consistent with Khoury, who finds that the key participants in the protests "were those sectors of Iraqi society that had suffered most during the Iran-Iraq War and the First Gulf War."[167]

CONCLUSIONS

Who bears the costs associated with the foreign policy decisions of dictators? And to what extent are the burdens of war borne by particular ethnic groups in a multi-ethnic society? It is difficult to overstate the impact of conflict on social, economic, and political life in Iraq during the late twentieth century.

167. Khoury 2013, 133.

Hussein, a secularist and strongman, was seen as a bulwark against a growing regional trend of Islamic activism, particularly the Iranian Islamist threat. While the Baʿthist regime was initially able to insulate itself from the political damage of the Iran-Iraq War through a robust program of compensatory spending, war costs eventually overwhelmed the regime. The collapse of world oil prices in 1986 meant that the regime struggled to provide payoffs to citizens at precisely the time they were bearing the largest burdens associated with the conflict. By the end of the Iran-Iraq War in 1988, the Iraqi state was shackled with a debt in excess of $80 billion, much of which was owed to Arab Gulf states. According to Alnasrawi, Iraq spent 254 percent of all the oil revenue it had earned over almost sixty years in just the eight years of the Iran-Iraq War.[168]

In this chapter, I provide empirical evidence for the unequal distribution across population groups of war costs associated with the Iran-Iraq War and the Gulf War and discuss the political implications of these costs for the Iraqi state. While it is generally accepted that Iraqi Shiʿa were the majority sectarian group represented in the army, particularly among the lower ranks, the extent of Shiʿi casualties in the two conflicts had not been measured previously. I show that Shiʿi families were much more likely to have had a son, brother, or father killed in either the Iran-Iraq War or the Gulf War than their Sunni or Kurdish counterparts. In some cases, the losses suffered by Shiʿi families and communities were staggering, particularly in southern districts like Basra. And despite regime fears of Iraqi Shiʿa acting as a "fifth column," there are strikingly few reports of Iraqi Shiʿa seeking to undermine the country's war effort in any way.[169] These trends provide evidence for the existence of a hierarchy of burden associated with the foreign policy decisions of the Baʿthist regime.

According to Kubba, political awareness among Iraqi Shiʿa was relatively low before the Iran-Iraq War but increased significantly as a result of the conflict when it became clear that state policies would have such a profound effect on the well-being of so many citizens.[170] And despite regime attempts to mitigate the costs associated with the war, the mounting financial and social costs of conflict imposed a tax on the Iraqi citizenry that encouraged political dissent, which took a number of forms.

168. Alnasrawi 1994, 100.
169. Kerry 2008, 17. See also Chubin and Tripp (1988, 98).
170. Kubba 1993, 50.

CHAPTER 5

POLITICAL IMPLICATIONS OF ECONOMIC EMBARGO, 1991–2003

In 1996, then-US Ambassador to the United Nations, Madeleine Albright, appeared on TV news show *60 Minutes* for an interview with correspondent Lesley Stahl. At one point, Stahl cited a study which reported that half a million Iraqi children had died as a result of the United Nations-imposed sanctions.[1] Stahl went on to ask, "that's more children than died in Hiroshima… is the price worth it?" In response, Albright replied, "I think this is a very hard choice, but the price … we think the price is worth it." The public outcry to the callous sentiment she expressed in her statement tarnished her reputation around the world. In her 2003 memoir, *Madam Secretary*, Albright explicitly addressed her statement in the *60 Minutes* interview, writing "I must have been crazy… as soon as I had spoken, I wished for the power to freeze time and take back those words… nothing matters more than the lives of innocent people."

Analysts of Iraq have argued that the international sanctions regime levied in the wake of the Iraqi invasion of Kuwait constituted an "invisible war" against the civilian population that resulted in the loss of hundreds of thousands of innocent lives.[2] This chapter does not seek to directly address the efficacy of sanctions for achieving foreign policy outcomes, but instead explores the political implications of the UN-imposed economic embargo on internal Iraqi political coalitions. Like the differential negative impact of war mobilization associated with interstate conflict, it is possible to consider

---

1. This figure remains highly disputed, though few estimates suggest fewer than hundreds of thousands of child deaths as a result of the sanctions. For one perspective on the controversy see Michael Spagat, "The Iraq Sanctions Myth," *Pacific Stanford*, April 26, 2013.

2. Gordon 2010.

the geographic distribution of economic suffering in Iraq as a result of the sanctions regime.

In this chapter, I seek to measure the dispersion of economic grievance in Iraq during the period of the 1990s with the goal of identifying cross-sectional and temporal variation in the quality of life for ordinary Iraqis.[3] Citizens in areas that suffered bad health and nutritional outcomes during the sanctions period were less invested in the Ba'thist regime and this was associated with non-cooperative political behaviors. I find that Sunni Arabs from western provinces like Anbar, who had previously been beneficiaries of state largesse, were increasingly shut out of economic opportunities at both the elite level and in terms of assistance afforded to the general population. A narrowing of the regime's base created incentives for attempts to unseat Saddam Hussein. In chapter 7, I show that political non-cooperation was higher in Anbar than other parts of Iraq; in chapter 10, I discuss the increasing frequency of coup attempts during the toughest years of the sanctions period, with a particularly large number of such attempts emanating from military leaders with ties to Anbar governorate.

INTERNATIONAL SANCTIONS AS AN ECONOMIC SHOCK

The scale and scope of sanctions on Iraq were unusually severe vis-à-vis norms within the international community. Unlike sanctions imposed by one country (or set of countries) on another, the sanctions on Iraq were imposed by the United Nations Security Council and binding on all UN members.[4] Historically, it has been difficult for the Security Council members to agree on imposing sanctions of this scope, making sanctions of this type rare.

The sanctions were also unique in terms of the speed with which they were adopted. According to one analyst, "the unanimity of response with the UN Security Council was unprecedented" and the result was a comprehensive and

---

3. Although United Nations sanctions were technically imposed in 1990 within days of the Iraqi invasion of Kuwait, this chapter focuses primarily on the period after the end of the Gulf War.

4. Gordon 2010, 10. Iraq did not have the option of shifting to an alternate trade bloc, as was common during the Cold War when sanctions were imposed on countries like Cuba, which still had developed trade relations with the Soviet Union.

complex economic embargo that was implemented within just weeks.[5] At the time sanctions were implemented, none of the key actors, either on the Iraqi side or in the international community, anticipated the embargo would remain in place for as long as it did.[6] As a result, the case of Iraq provides a unique opportunity to explore how a dictatorship struggles with a severe, unanticipated, and prolonged economic shock.[7]

Iraq was unusually vulnerable to sanctions as a result of its heavy dependence on oil as a major source of foreign revenue, in particular, and trade reliance, more generally.[8] In fact, Iraq has historically been dependent on imports for two-thirds of foodstuffs.[9] Iraq also suffered a double blow as a result of the political fallout associated with Hussein's invasion of Kuwait in August 1990.

In addition to the comprehensive nature of the international sanctions, the embargo was imposed at a time when Iraq had just suffered the effects of a major bombing campaign. According to one observer, the aerial campaign during the Gulf War "destroyed nearly all of Iraq's infrastructure, industrial capacity, agriculture, telecommunications, and critical public services, particularly electricity and water treatment."[10] All of this took place in the context of a country that had already suffered an estimated US$126 billion in infrastructure damage as a result of the Iran-Iraq War.[11] Sanctions, then, made it difficult for the country to import any of the spare parts or equipment needed to restore infrastructure capacity with serious implications for the health and well-being of the Iraqi population.

5. Graham-Brown 1999, 7.
6. Ibid., 57.
7. Not only were sanctions an economic shock outside of the control of the regime (Rohde 2010, 102), it was also very difficult for the regime to estimate the economic consequences of the embargo. According to the Duelfer Report of the Iraq Survey Group, Hussein severely underestimated the likely economic consequences of the embargo, in part because of a poor reading of precedent cases from the 1980s, like the case of South Africa.
8. Gordon 2010, 21; Graham-Brown 1999, 157.
9. Khoury 2013, 44.
10. Gordon 2010, 1.
11. Graham-Brown 1999, 157. In addition, the sanctions on Iraq were "the first time such a draconian UN embargo had been imposed on a state which had just suffered severe infrastructural damage in the course of a war."

The Socioeconomic Effects of Sanctions

Sanctions impacted the health and well-being of ordinary Iraqi citizens in a variety of ways. Among the most devastating effects related to the country's physical infrastructure. For example, a report issued after the Gulf War suggested that in Basra only one-quarter of sewage pumping stations were operating.[12] Loss of electrical power in many areas made it impossible to run pumps and generators, including for water treatment.[13] Iraqis reported that directly after the conflict there was no water, electricity, telephone, or gas service.[14]

The combined impact of damage to the electrical plants, water purification facilities, and sewage systems directly affected the rise of both typhoid and cholera, which were at very low levels of prevalence prior to the Gulf War.[15] Because hospitals did not have proper illumination, hygiene equipment, and water supply and disposal, the medical system was poorly positioned to assist the ill.[16] Although the government undertook a series of campaigns to repair damaged infrastructure, these efforts were only partially effective.

While the damage to infrastructure affected Iraqis across the income spectrum, other aspects of the economic fallout impacted specific segments of the population more than others. Sanctions severely limited state income streams and left the Iraqi state reliant on about $800 million per year earned through smuggling oil to Turkey and Jordan, as well as liquidation of hidden assets, and government gold reserves.[17] Middle-class Iraqis, particularly state employees, experienced economic strain as the government struggled to pay civil service salaries. Relatively soon after sanctions were imposed, the Iraqi state laid off large numbers of workers.[18] Demobilization of the armed forces alone meant a decline in forces from 900,000 to 300,000.[19]

Monthly security reports provide a time line of the progression of events. Reports from 1990 suggest that economic conditions and food availability at

---

12. Gordon 2010, 35.
13. Graham-Brown 1999, 158.
14. Ismael and Ismael 2008.
15. Gordon 2010, 34.
16. Ibid., 36.
17. Ibid., 91.
18. Al-Jawaheri 2008, 9.
19. Graham-Brown 1999, 161.

the markets were good.[20] In the spring of 1991, it was reported that food was being distributed effectively via the ration card system, but high prices were reported for meat and chicken being sold by private vendors.[21] The regime continued to control prices, but by the end of 1991, it was determined that meat and chicken had become too expensive.[22]

For those who continued to be employed by the state, regime-induced hyperinflation led civil servant salaries to fall to an average of US$2–3 per month from 1993 to 1999.[23] Inflation eroded family savings, leaving middle-class Iraqis with no safety net beyond that which was offered by the state.[24] By the late 1990s, unemployment was estimated at around 40 percent.[25] Iraqis observed that otherwise "respectable-looking" people were found begging in the streets as a result of the embargo.[26]

Middle-class Iraqis probably saw the largest absolute declines in living standards, but sanctions were felt most painfully by its lowest classes. Prior to the Gulf War, Iraq had one of the highest per capita food availability ratings in the Middle East; indeed, a 1988 survey of Baghdad residents suggested that undernourishment was not a major public health problem.[27] But after the imposition of sanctions, the price of food increased so precipitously that large segments of the population struggled to maintain basic food security.[28] In 1991, it was found that a five-pound bag of flour cost US$80 and a dozen eggs was US$50, for instance.[29] Malnutrition of pregnant women emerged as a major cause of pregnancy-related morbidity and low birthweight infants.[30]

20. For example, see BRCC Doc. No. 01-3773-0002-0826, November 1990.

21. For example, see BRCC Doc. No. 01-3773-0002-0703 and BRCC Doc. No. 01-3773-0002-0728, March 1991.

22. BRCC Doc. No. 01-3773-0002-0582, November 1991; BRCC Doc. No. 01-3773-0002-0439, April 1992.

23. Gordon 2010, 92.

24. Mazaheri 2010, 264.

25. Rohde 2010, 68.

26. Al-Radi 2003, 85.

27. Gordon 2010, 33.

28. Food was thousands of times more expensive in December 1995 compared to August 1990 (Gordon 2010, 13), for example.

29. Gordon 2010, 151.

30. Al-Jawaheri 2008, 123.

Regime Response to Economic Embargo

In order to prevent mass starvation, the Iraqi government implemented a food rationing system. Monthly allocations included staples like flour, rice, sugar, cooking oil, tea, and soap.[31] The rations system was operated through a network of government warehouses, silos, and distribution points.[32] Scholars agree that, despite its flaws, the rationing system "was completely essential to the survival of the Iraqi population."[33] It is credited with successfully avoiding an even more severe humanitarian crisis. But the rationing system was also a highly effective "instrument of control" for the Baʿthist regime.[34]

One result of citizen reliance on rations as a primary source of basic sustenance was that the regime became an even more important part of people's lives. Rohde argues that "the increasing dependence of most Iraqis on a government-run food rationing system actually strengthened state power vis-à-vis the weakened Iraqi society and created considerable breathing space for the regime."[35]

Part of the reason why the regime enjoyed increased political control related to the method by which ration cards were distributed. According to Graham-Brown, "when applying for a ration card each person or family is required to produce a civil status identity card, and confirmation of domicile, endorsed by the neighborhood headman, plus a card containing security information."[36] These checks of security service status and residence created difficulties for families who had members at odds with the Baʿth Party or who had failed to complete their compulsory military service. According to one Iraqi refugee, "the need to have a ration card is a form of pressure on families to do what the government wants."[37]

31. Graham-Brown 1999, 168.
32. Mazaheri 2010, 257.
33. Ibid. Both scholars and contemporary observers have found that food rations were distributed to all Iraqis in the provinces controlled by the regime regardless of sect or geographic location (Dreze and Gazdar 1992; Walter 2016). While rations could be temporarily withheld as punishment to deserters, absentee public employees and opposition members (and—from 1994 to 1996—to their entire families), the Baʿthist regime was concerned that a failure to distribute food rations in an equitable way could lead to food riots (Walter 2016).
34. Rohde 2010, 68.
35. Ibid.
36. Graham-Brown 1999, 169.
37. Quoted ibid., 170.

A conversation among high-level Iraqi officials in 1994 suggests the critical importance of the rations system in controlling the population through strategies of "policing" within families.[38] Government control of the ration card system was thought to be decisive in implementing policies against military desertions. According to one official, the regime was able to take advantage of obligations between family members as a potential deserter would not want to be held responsible for his family losing their ration card, resulting in their starvation.[39]

To what extent did political or other factors influence the ability of individuals to receive allocations of staple goods? Speaking to his cabinet, Hussein said that even though the international community believed that the regime was trying to starve certain elements of society, he emphasized that all people were treated equally with regard to foodstuffs and ration cards.[40] Relatedly, Walter finds that the rations distribution system had the effect of flattening societal differences, including sectarian differences, particularly since the rations were distributed without regard for identity markers.[41] Sassoon argues that the regime invested considerable resources into "administering and maintaining food rationing"; while each citizen was supposed to receive the same amount of food, party members, senior army officers, and civil servants were often eligible for a larger allocation, suggesting a political but not sectarian logic.[42]

In addition to dependence on the rations system, the devaluation of salaries, rising unemployment, and collapse of state service provision meant that Iraqis were also increasingly dependent on the gifts, donations, and even presidential philanthropy distributed by the regime.[43] Handouts from local and provincial leaders became ever more important and another lever of political control.[44]

38. CRRC Doc. No. SH-SHTP-A-001-238, September 3, 1994.

39. Ibid.

40. CRRC Doc. No. SH-SHTP-000-774.

41. Walter 2016, 59. The categories of people who were denied rations included military deserters, absentee public employees, and members of opposition groups. For a two-year period, families were punished collectively for the behavior of individual deviants on their ration card, but eventually this practice was abandoned when the regime realized that "the policy of collective punishment was counteracting the regime's efforts to win over the support of the population and alienating families who otherwise supported the regime" (ibid.).

42. Sassoon 2012, 243.

43. Rohde 2010, 68–69.

44. Sarah Graham-Brown, "Intervention, Sovereignty and Responsibility," *Middle East Report*, 193 (March/April 1995).

Charity distribution programs took a variety of forms. For example, according to one Baʿth Party memorandum from 1996, some female heads of households (*al-nisaʾ al-muʿilat*) were recipients of a special food program which gave them additional flour and lentils, although the memo also suggests that some of the women only received the lentil allocation.[45]

Monthly security reports provided detailed information about the economic situation across Iraq. In addition to reporting on political activism in each area, these reports also discussed economic conditions in depth. One report from Anbar governorate described the quantity of food provided by the rations system as insufficient for the population and reported that grocers were trying to sell at prices above those set by the government.[46] A report from Diyala governorate suggested that prices were largely stable except during Ramadan, when the price of eggs, meat, beans, vegetables, and fruits increased.[47] Increases in food rations were described as having a strongly positive effect on public attitudes.[48]

Despite the government food allocation system, one United Nations report from 1993 suggested that Iraqis had food intake lower than that which was found in many sub-Saharan African countries.[49] In 1995, as the state began to run out of funds, the basic food rations were reduced by a third.[50] Gordon argues that at this point the ration system was only providing 1,100 calories per person per day.[51] The state's ability to provide for education, health, water, and sewerage had also declined. In one area in southern Iraq, health departments were tasked with coordinating implementation of a health program for malnourished children.[52]

At multiple points in the mid-1990s, Hussein believed that international sanctions would be lifted,[53] only to be disappointed and left politically vulnerable. In a discussion about sanctions with his cabinet, Hussein acknowledged that his country was in a dark tunnel in which there was not a glimmer

45. BRCC Doc. Nos. 024-5-3-0163 to 0171, October 24, 1996.
46. BRCC Doc. Nos. 01-3773-0002-0435 to 0436, 1992.
47. BRCC Doc. Nos. 01-3773-0002-0026 to 0027, 1993.
48. BRCC Doc. No. 01-3773-0002-0012, 1993.
49. Gordon 2010, 36.
50. Ibid., 135.
51. Ibid., 25.
52. BRCC Doc. Nos. 024-5-3-0163 to 0171, October 24, 1996.
53. Woods et al. 2011, 265.

of light.[54] In terms of its ability to buy loyalty with rewards, the early to mid-1990s represented a low point for the regime and dissatisfaction with it was widespread. Intelligence reports and directives from Hussein indicate the importance to the regime of canvassing the public to determine reaction to the embargo.[55]

Eventually, the deteriorating humanitarian conditions in Iraq led the international community to support an "Oil-for-Food" program that would allow Iraq to sell oil in exchange for food and medicine. The program allowed imports of $130 per person per year; prior to the implementation of Oil-for-Food, Iraqis had been importing only $20 per person per year during the early sanctions period.[56] As a result of the program, average calories per person per day rose from 1,295 in 1993–1995 to 2,030 in 1997–1998.[57] By the late 1990s, food prices had stabilized, in contrast to the uncertainty and hyperinflation of the early 1990s.[58] The regime also began to successfully reconsolidate forms of political power.

Jabar argues the Oil-for-Food program made the population even more dependent on the state than before as it put more resources in the hands of the regime.[59] Hussein used the ability to import goods as a profit opportunity, subsidizing gifts and handouts to loyal subjects.[60] These resources allowed the regime to reconsolidate its political standing as economic conditions improved.

Controlling Dissent

International sanctions against Iraq were implemented with the goal of containing Hussein while simultaneously destabilizing his political rule. And while scholars have argued that sanctions eroded popular support for the

54. CRRC Doc. No. SH-SHTP-A-000-774.
55. CRRC Doc. No. SH-PDWN-D-000-720, January 1996.
56. Gordon 2010, 25.
57. Graham-Brown 1999, 169. According to one source, daily available calories in Iraq averaged 3,375 kilocalories per capita in 1987–1988 (Pellett 2002, 188).
58. Mahdi 2007.
59. Jabar 2003b, 271.
60. Sada 2006. The Oil-for-Food program in the semi-autonomous Kurdish region was not regulated by Hussein's federal government, but instead by UN agencies and Kurdish officials (Dreze and Gazdar 1992). The net result was that Kurdish areas witnessed less malnutrition and more economic growth during this period (Stansfield 2003b).

Iraqi regime,[61] the embargo had the simultaneous effect of enervating the population to the point where anti-regime collective action was highly challenging. One Iraqi intellectual speaking in October 1994 was quoted as saying, "you are looking at a people whose energy is drained simply looking for the next meal."[62] Because Hussein was able to implement a system of food rationing and associated political patronage that became a lifeline for ordinary Iraqis, his citizenry came to simultaneously depend upon and fear him. Indeed, Arnove argues that while the sanctions were intended to weaken the ruling elite, the net result was a strengthening of the status quo "political hegemony."[63]

Where political protest did persist, the regime strove to increase its ability to effectively monitor the activities and predilections of the population. According to Khoury, the regime engaged in two main activities to counter the threat of another rebellion—systematic collection of politically relevant information about individuals and families and the alteration of the physical features of the southern marshes.[64] For example, after the 1991 Uprisings, the regime considerably expanded the nature of data collection on Iraqi high school students. Before 1991, information was collected about a student's political orientation, but after 1991 the battery of questions expanded considerably to include details about any role a student or his family may have played in the uprisings and whether or not the student had participated in training exercises to prepare for handling possible future uprisings. The regime saw it as essential to distinguish between individuals who were amenable to political rehabilitation and those who constituted a future security threat.[65]

The question of how to increase the legibility of the marsh areas plagued the regime.[66] A major study on the marshes was produced by the military and intelligence community in 1992.[67] According to the report, the marsh

61. Pasha 2003, 100.

62. Youssef Ibrahim, "Iraq Is Near Economic Ruin But Hussein Appears Secure," *New York Times*, October 25, 1994.

63. Arnove 2002, 90. Also see Drezner (1999, 13) who argues that "for economic coercion to work, target elites must suffer as much as target populations" which does not appear to have been true in the Iraqi case.

64. Khoury 2013, 141–142.

65. Ibid.

66. See Ahram (2015) for a comprehensive discussion about counterinsurgency in the Iraqi marshes.

67. CRRC Doc. No. SH-GMID-D-000-591, May 1992.

area had long provided refuge to outlaws and deserters. Marsh dwellers were also allegedly in contact with Iranian forces, carrying out sabotage operations against military units, government headquarters, and other establishments in proximity to the marshes. The report provided detailed information about various tribes in the marshes as well as the villages they lived in, their main economic activities, and their living conditions. The report also described the difficulties associated with monitoring the waterways, a challenge that made it easy for deviant individuals to hide and make a quick retreat into the marshes.

During this time, governorates in this area were increasingly governed by military, rather than civilian, leaders.[68] In 1995, Hussein directed his national security staff to prepare an emergency plan to flood the marshes for security reasons.[69] While this strategy was successful at destroying the ecosystem of the marshlands, many areas of southern Iraq were only tenuously controlled by the Ba'thist regime.[70]

Another strategy deployed for controlling dissent related to increasing reliance on tribal networks for population management.[71] The security apparatus sought to delegate some aspects of social control to clan leaders and the regime implored these individuals to send their sons to work in the service of the state.[72] Clan leaders were expected to monitor members of their clan with the idea that they would be held responsible for transgressions by individuals in their groups.[73] Clan leaders were expected to provide intelligence, keeping the regime abreast of relevant issues, including the tracking of rebels. The clans were also expected to support the state and refuse to support or shelter deserters and other fugitives.[74] Faust argues that the regime relied on tribes for policing areas where the state had less capacity; at the same time, tribal leaders could obscure acts of political transgression within their areas, suggesting a citizenry that was not highly legible to the regime.[75]

68. Khoury 2013, 142.
69. See CRRC Doc. No. SH-RVCC-D-000-358, January to April 1995.
70. Khoury 2013, 144–145.
71. Baram 1997.
72. CRRC Doc. No. SH-IDGS-D-000-370, 1991–92.
73. Ibid.
74. CRRC Doc. No. SH-MISC-D-000-327, 1994–95.
75. Faust 2015, 141–146. Management of violence also took place between the regime and tribes. Beginning in 1993, the regime introduced a policy of paying "blood money" to tribes whose members it accidentally or wrongfully killed during security operations in order to avoid trouble with the rest of the tribe (see BRCC Doc. No. 029-1-3-0096). In 1997, tribes became

TABLE 5.1. Childhood malnutrition across Iraqi governorates measured by underweight (low weight-for-age) and wasting (low weight-for-height) in 1996 and 2003.

	Underweight 1996	Underweight 2003	Diff.	Wasting 1996	Wasting 2003	Diff.
Baghdad	28.0	7.9	−20.1	11.0	3.8	−7.2
South						
Basra	34.0	15.6	−18.4	13.0	5.4	−7.6
Dhi Qar	23.0	15.6	−7.4	14.0	4.4	−9.6
Wasit	25.0	13.2	−11.8	14.0	3.8	−10.2
Euphrates						
Muthanna	32.0	12.4	−19.6	14.0	5.0	−9.0
Qadisiyya	23.0	12.6	−10.4	11.0	4.8	−6.2
Najaf	25.0	10.8	−14.2	11.0	4.2	−6.8
Karbala	28.0	8.8	−19.2	14.0	3.3	−10.7
Babil	20.0	15.1	−4.9	8.0	3.4	−4.6
Center						
Anbar	22.0	15.0	−7.0	11.0	7.3	−3.7
Salah al-Din	15.0	13.1	−1.9	7.0	4.9	−2.1
Diyala	19.0	11.2	−7.8	9.0	3.3	−5.7
North						
Ninawa	26.0	12.2	−13.8	12.0	6.3	−5.7
Kirkuk	19.0	11.4	−7.6	7.0	2.2	−4.8
Sulaymaniyya	18.4	7.2	−11.2	4.3	3.0	−1.3
Erbil	21.3			3.0		
Dohuk	17.7			4.1		

Cross-section Variation in Sanctions Impact

How might we measure the impact of sanctions on the Iraqi population both before and after the introduction of the Oil-for-Food program? Table 5.1 provides information on two indicators related to childhood nutrition across Iraqi governorates at two points in time: 1996, before the first Oil-for-Food program deliveries arrived, and in 2003, immediately after the US invasion of Iraq. The indicator "underweight" provides information on the percentage of children who are low weight given their age. The indicator "wasting" provides information about children's weight given their height.[76]

---

prohibited from taking revenge against regime officials who had acted in their official capacity (Faust 2015, 145).

76. Other important indicators relate to human capital development during the sanctions period. For example, while female enrollment in primary education was virtually universal

In terms of the cross-sectional variation for these indicators as well as their relative change over time, a number of patterns emerge. Shiʿi-majority governorates (like Basra, Muthanna, and Karbala) have larger percentages of underweight and wasting in 1996 than Sunni-majority governorates (like Anbar and Salah al-Din). However, within the Sunni areas, there is a large discrepancy between outcomes in Salah al-Din (Hussein's home province) and Anbar. While percentage underweight in Anbar was 22 percent in 1996, this figure was only 15 percent for Salah al-Din. And while 11 percent of Anbari children were described as wasting in 1996, that figure was only 7 percent for children from Salah al-Din. This suggests health disparities across ethno-sectarian communities, but also within them.

When examining the data for 2003, percentages of underweight and wasting decline as a result of the introduction of the Oil-for-Food program. Baghdad and autonomously governed Kurdish areas witnessed major improvements. In the case of the former, this was almost certainly a result of robust distribution networks in the capital city; for the latter, it was widely believed that the Kurdish areas were more capable and less corrupt in getting resources to their citizenries when compared to areas governed by the Baʿth Party. Another notable pattern, however, relates to how poorly Anbar fared relative to other parts of the country. By 2003, Anbar had the highest percentage of children described as wasting and among the highest described as underweight. In many cases, the children of Anbar compare poorly to children in Shiʿi-dominated areas of Iraq. Poor health and wellness outcomes for Iraqi Sunni children defy popular characterizations of Hussein's regime as one that benefited Sunni Arabs to the exclusion of others.

POLITICAL IMPLICATIONS OF SANCTIONS

The international sanctions regime had far-reaching political implications for the Baʿthists. For example, Jabar argues that between 1991 and 2001, the Iraqi regime was forced to restructure its formal governmental institutions as a result of economic conditions.[77] Sanctions also ensured that the state

---

before 1990, by 2003, 31 percent of female children did not attend school at all (Ismael and Ismael 2007).

77. Jabar 2003d, 121.

would be able to serve a key role in the Iraqi economy through control of the distribution of rations and the ability to fix prices, particularly for basic goods.[78] In terms of the informal economy, illicit activity became increasingly controlled by individuals with close connections to the ruling regime. This has led some analysts to argue that sanctions had the effect of widening "the gap between a small number of privileged, who have managed to maintain their living standards or even profit from the crisis, and the majority of the population."[79] From an ideological perspective, the sanctions provided Hussein with powerful rhetoric to accuse external actors of threatening the national interests of Iraq.[80] This section discusses the political implications of the sanctions regime in two domains.

Narrowing of the Regime's Support Base

Although the Baʿthist regime has often been described as having a Sunni basis, the relative standing of various Sunni tribes and geographic groupings has varied over time. In particular, Baʿthist rule under Hussein increasingly came to rely on clans from in and around his home region of Tikrit, particularly over the course of the 1990s.[81] The reliance on Iraqis from Tikrit and neighboring areas represented a decrease in political importance for those from western towns, like Ana and Ramadi, in Anbar governorate.[82] The net result was that tribes that had been previously loyal to the regime—many of which were Sunni—"reacted against the economy's continued deterioration."[83]

78. Al-Jawaheri 2008.

79. Sarah Graham-Brown, "Intervention, Sovereignty and Responsibility," *Middle East Report*, 193 (March/April 1995).

80. Rohde 2010, 68. See also Drezner (1999, 12–13), who argues that the existence of a "rally-around-the-flag" movement can make economic sanctions less effective. The Iraqi regime took every opportunity to remind the citizenry of the US role in the embargo. According to Mazaheri (2010, 261), Hussein ramped up his anti-West rhetoric dramatically during this period. The Baʿth Party files also suggest efforts to promote anti-US sentiment among Iraqis. For example, one memorandum refers to efforts to encourage Iraqis to put signs in their shop and restaurant windows saying that Iraqis stand against the United States and do not want to deal with US weapons inspection teams. See BRCC Doc. No. 01-3807-0126-0094, 1997 for more details.

81. Bengio 2000, 97.

82. Sakai 2003, 144.

83. Davis 2005, 234.

Under the sanctions regime, Sunnis peripheral to Tikrit saw significant declines in quality of life and, despite the instrumental role they had played in putting down the uprisings, did not enjoy the same levels of access, employment, and privilege as Sunnis from in and around Tikrit. One cause was the downsizing of the Iraqi military which disproportionately affected western Sunnis who were prominently represented in these units.[84] At the same time, elite units—in which Sunnis from central Iraq were often over-represented—were paid in US dollars as a way to insulate those troops from the effects of inflation.[85] The Ba'thist regime was forced to limit the distribution of state largesse as a result of a tightening budget constraint.

To what extent would regional or tribal elites feel impacted by the negative economic shock suffered by non-elites in their home area? Elites, as a result of their privileged political and economic status, would seem to be insulated from the effect of sanctions. Tribal structures meant that elites were held responsible, to some degree, for the welfare of their tribal constituents and clansmen. As a tribal head, or leader within the tribal community, it would not be unusual to receive requests for assistance from less wealthy tribesmen, including for jobs and donations.

In sum, the economic embargo led to a narrowing of Hussein's support base over the course of the 1990s.[86] This narrowing "heralded a real change in Sunni opposition to the regime" and "a deepening cleavage" between groups within the Sunni population.[87]

Monopolizing Illicit Activity

A major source of illicit revenue during this time was derived from illegal oil trade. Jordan and Turkey were both engaged in illicit trade with Iraq and the US government protected this trade.[88] As state sector expenditures fell, Hussein and his immediate family sought to monopolize the forms of illicit economic opportunities that provided the only available avenue to wealth

---

84. Al-Marashi and Salama 2008, 186.
85. Graham-Brown 1999, 185.
86. Dawisha 1999, 563.
87. Zeidel 2010, 162.
88. Alahmad 2009, 100; Gordon 2010, 176–177. Smuggling took place under the guise of barter and bilateral trade agreements.

accumulation. It was during this period that the sons of Hussein, ʿUday and Qusay, emerged as key political and economic actors.[89] ʿUday and Qusay were known to be involved with the illicit oil trade, becoming "empowered" by the "lucrative black market."[90] According to Zeidel, power became increasingly concentrated in the hands of the extended Hussein family.[91]

Contractors and import-export merchants were two groups that benefited from sanctions.[92] Yet attempts to operate without connections to the regime were risky. In 1992, dozens of merchants, many of whom were associated with the Baghdad Chamber of Commerce, were executed for alleged profiteering; their assets were seized by the state.[93] In some cases, merchants were hanged for trying to charge higher-than-mandated prices for foodstuffs; tragically, it was sometimes the case that the individuals hanged were not the merchants setting the prices, but the hapless relative or store employee left to man the shop.[94] A series of executive decrees also worked to favor and protect the property of regime insiders while spurious charges were brought against independent businessmen as a strategy for confiscating their property or forcing the sale of their business.[95]

The Oil-for-Food program, initially put into place as a humanitarian project, soon became a massive moneymaking opportunity for the regime. The program did not result in growth of the local economy, but instead provided a gold mine for Hussein's close relatives, who enriched themselves with contracts for food, medicine, and other consumer products.[96] The method by which contracts were negotiated provided new rent-seeking opportunities which operated through the Iraqi state. International buyers paid kickbacks in the form of surcharges to access cut-price Iraqi oil, and this system was supported by a network of international lobbyists.[97] Regime insiders also accumulated revenue by selling food and provisions imported under

89. Davis 2005, 182.
90. Arnove 2002, 90.
91. Zeidel 2010, 162.
92. Graham-Brown 1999, 170.
93. Ibid., 171.
94. Bashir 2005, 139.
95. Sarah Graham-Brown, "Intervention, Sovereignty and Responsibility," *Middle East Report*, 193 (March/April 1995).
96. Bashir 2005, 208–215.
97. Alahmad 2009, 99–100.

Oil-for-Food to merchants on the black market.[98] According to Alahmad, the system that emerged "opened spaces for the Iraqi state to recast its power."[99]

The Duelfer Report, issued by the multinational, fact-finding Iraq Survey Group, provides summary insights into the position of the regime in the mid-1990s. The authors of the report consider 1996 as a turning point for the Baʿthists with the introduction of the Oil-for-Food program. Iraqi revenue went from $250 million in 1996 to $2.76 billion in 2001. Hussein—while opposed to "corruption" on the part of his underlings soliciting bribes or appropriating public assets—reserved the right to distribute the economic opportunities associated with the improving economic situation for himself. In the process, this eroded the impact of sanctions. In the words of the report, Oil-for-Food "rescued Baghdad's economy from a terminal decline created by sanctions."[100]

The United Nations eventually came to accuse Hussein of manipulating the program through kickbacks from thousands of companies and smuggling which allowed him to acquire billions of dollars.[101] The Volcker Report describes how the Iraqi regime used the Oil-for-Food program to derive illicit payments from companies that had received contracts for oil and humanitarian goods.[102] Under the program, Iraq—not the United Nations—chose its oil buyers, empowering the Baʿthist regime with forms of economic and political leverage. The report finds that the Baʿthist regime received more than $1.5 billion in income from kickbacks paid to the Iraqi government.

It is now generally accepted that despite the terrible damage suffered by the Iraqi population as a result of the economic embargo, Iraq's leadership found new political and economic opportunities during this period.[103] This has led some analysts to conclude that "elements of the core groups sustaining the regime like Hussein's extended family, various tribes, the commercial elite, and various segments of the security and armed forces ... actually prospered under embargo conditions, and the number of millionaires in Iraq grew far beyond

98. Sada 2006.

99. Alahmad 2009, 126.

100. *Final Report of the Iraq Survey Group* (the Duelfer Report), September 30, 2004.

101. Gordon 2010, 173.

102. *Manipulation of the Oil-for-Food Programme by the Iraqi Regime* (the Volcker Report), Independent Inquiry Committee into the United Nations Oil-for-Food Programme, October 27, 2005.

103. Graham-Brown 1999, 92.

the formerly limited number of elite families."[104] At the same time, those benefits were not widely enjoyed by the broader Sunni community or arguably any group of Iraqis outside of Hussein's inner circle of political cronies.[105]

While those closest to the leadership enjoyed opportunities under these conditions of austerity, the overall decline in public revenue available for distribution caused a narrowing of the regime's core coalition. This created opposition to Hussein's rule within the broader set of elites who had been beneficiaries of regime largesse in the pre-sanctions period. Economic exclusion took place on both ethnic and regional lines.[106]

CONCLUSIONS

Infrastructural damage associated with the Gulf War combined with United Nations-imposed sanctions to create a humanitarian disaster for the Iraqi people. Gordon describes the humanitarian situation in Iraq during the 1990s as similar to that of a nonstop "war or natural disaster."[107] It is thought that between 1990 and 2003, an estimated 500,000 children under five years of age perished due to the economic embargo,[108] relegating Iraq to what some have described as "pre-industrial" levels of development.[109]

Scholarly research suggests that personalist regimes and monarchies are more sensitive to the loss of external sources of revenue than single-party or

104. Rohde 2010, 66.

105. Corstange (2016) examines why the purported beneficiaries of ethnic favoritism often get only meager rewards in exchange for their loyalty. He finds that in an electoral setting, when a political constituency is dominated by a single vote-buying patron, voters in those areas enjoy only limited rewards from the vote-buying monopsonist (Ibid.). With regard to the Iraqi case, Sunni Arabs from outside of the regime's core geographic areas of support may have fared worse than other constituencies as a result of the monopsony power of the Ba'thist regime from the perspective of Sunni Iraqis.

106. Roessler (2011) raises the critically important question of why rulers would employ ethnic exclusion if it increased the risk of civil war? He finds that for sub-Saharan African cases, ethnic exclusion reduces the risk of a coup while increasing the risk of societal rebellion and civil war. In the Iraqi case, exclusion decreased the coup risk among Tikriti Sunnis, but left the regime vulnerable to insider threats from western Sunnis who no longer saw themselves as beneficiaries of the regime.

107. Gordon 2010, 102.

108. Ibid., 37.

109. Al-Jawaheri 2008, 2.

military regimes.[110] Iraq under Saddam Hussein had characteristics of both a personalist and single-party dictatorship, creating ambiguity in terms of a theoretical prediction for Hussein's vulnerability as a result of the economic embargo. The evidence that I have put forward suggests that the prolonged economic shock of sanctions seriously damaged the ability of the Iraqi regime to earn broad-based support through public goods provision. At the same time, however, the regime's competent management of a bare-bones rations system increased citizen dependence on the state in the face of severe food insecurity.

I also find that not all segments of the Iraqi population were equally hurt by the economic embargo. Sunnis from Iraq's western province of Anbar particularly suffered until the sanctions. In addition, the restrictive economic environment made political connections more important than before for entrepreneurial activity. An extensive network of illicit activities developed during the 1990s with the best opportunities restricted to those with close familial or other ties to Hussein.[111]

110. Wright 2010.
111. Mazaheri 2010, 263.

PART II

POLITICAL BEHAVIOR IN
IRAQ, 1979–2003

CHAPTER 6

COLLABORATION AND RESISTANCE IN IRAQI KURDISTAN

In April 1988, Baʿth Party officials received a letter from a long-time regime collaborator detailing his two decades of service to military intelligence in Iraqi Kurdistan.[1] In the letter, the collaborator claimed that he had never "cracked" under pressure and had fulfilled his many missions, including taking photographs of strategic areas; helping return defectors to the "national" side; collecting illicit weapons from villages; and even providing information about an operation against Hussein himself.[2] For his service, he had met Hussein and received a special commendation.[3] Despite this record of service, he complained that he had been insufficiently compensated and believed he was entitled to land on which to build a house and a mini-market. He also hoped to receive a Pepsi-Cola distribution license and a telephone line installed in his name.[4]

The letter tells us something about the transactional nature of the collaborator's relationship with the regime. Commitment and service to the party and the state could be signaled through costly action, providing an individual with a justifiable claim to payment. The information provided by collaborators was particularly valuable to the regime during times of conflict when Kurdish resistance had the potential to join with foreign enemies of the state to undermine regime security and stability. The exchange further suggests the limits on the regime's ability to satisfy the financial expectations of its collaborators.

1. Iraqi Secret Police Files Doc. No. 90071 to 90073, April 6, 1988.
2. Ibid.
3. The collaborator claims that he had even named his son Saddam and his daughter Hala (presumably after Hussein's daughter).
4. Ibid.

The letter also provides insights into the challenges associated with the regime's penetration of northern areas. The collaborator's photographic surveillance likely substituted for an on-the-ground presence, and local knowledge would have helped the collaborator determine the location of rebel weapons caches otherwise unknown to the regime. In this chapter, I argue that the relative illegibility of the Kurdish population to the Baghdad-based government led the regime to pursue suboptimal policies—particularly forms of collective punishment—toward the Kurdish population, at times of political and economic crisis. Although there had long been tension between Kurdish peoples and Arab-dominated governments in Baghdad, Kurds were not automatic enemies of the Iraqi state. Indeed, co-optation of Kurdish citizens and political groups was common and there existed meaningful forms of collaboration between the Iraqi regime and Kurdish constituencies. There is also evidence that the Iraqi regime in Baghdad understood that fair treatment of the Kurdish people would allow for greater forms of political cooperation.[5]

I argue that for Iraq's Kurdish population, broad-based cohesion as a nationalist group did not emerge until the end of the Iran-Iraq War. Scholars have long argued that factionalization within the Kurdish community has historically been so deep-seated that until that point there existed "virtually no sense of cohesive Kurdish nationality."[6] How, then, did Iraqi Kurds overcome factional differences to create the bonds of social cohesion and nationalist sentiment that made it possible to separate from the Baghdad-based government?[7] Or, as McDowall puts it, how did Kurds go from being a factionalized

5. How do nation-building policies impact citizen attitudes toward the state? Miguel (2004) finds that serious, long-run nation building reforms can encourage the successful bridging of social divisions in ethnically diverse societies. A state policy of high relevance relates to the equitable regional distribution of public investment. These intuitions apply to the Iraqi context as well. Widespread, largely equitable distribution of public goods invested Iraqi citizens in the state and regime. In my account, I argue that, in addition, the intensity and collective nature of punishment contribute to the structures of societal cleavage.

6. Lazier 1991, 82.

7. The literature on insurgent or nationalist resistance to incumbent regimes tends to focus on two broad categories. Structural accounts typically emphasize a series of slow-changing political, social, and economic forces. For example, Fearon and Laitin (2003) define the set of conditions—like rugged terrain and low levels of per capita GDP associated with weak state capacity—which make armed resistance most likely to occur. Cederman et al. (2011) find that structural economic inequalities are predictive of civil war onsets; Cederman et al. (2010) focus on the influence of ethnic power inequality where ethnic exclusion and competition tend to be associated with internal conflict. One alternative approach in the literature focuses on the

people to a coherent political community with the characteristics of nation-hood?[8] I argue that Kurdish nationalism was not a foregone conclusion but rather an outgrowth of Iraqi state policies related to governance challenges faced by the Baᶜthist regime. In particular, brutal and collective forms of state-imposed punishment against Kurdish Iraqis encouraged social cohesion at the level of the ethno-sectarian group.

My account contrasts with the conventional characterization of the relationship between Iraqi Kurds and the Iraqi state that describes the relationship as a colonial-era mismatch, ill-fated from the start. The typi-cal narrative suggests that Kurdish Iraqis—bound together by their shared peripheral nationalism—would eventually overcome the repressive tendencies of a Baghdad-based government.[9] The evidence that I provide in this chapter challenges the belief that Iraqi Kurds were characterized by an unconditional shared sense of national homogeneity that would inevitably result in political autonomy from the Iraqi state.

HISTORICAL OBSTACLES TO KURDISH NATIONALISM

A key marker of Kurdish identification is the use of the Kurdish language, of which there are two main dialects.[10] A second defining feature of Kurdistan relates to the fact that the Kurdish heartland is mountainous, centered on the Taurus and Zagros ranges, with peaks as high as 15,000 feet.[11] The relative

---

organization of protest movement itself. Staniland, for example, argues that the nature of the horizontal and vertical ties which make up their social bases determine the "ideational and social resources insurgent leaders can mobilize for war" (2014, 23). While Staniland does not go as far as to describe social ties as exogenous, he argues that "leaders embedded in social bases cannot fluidly reshape their social relations or political meanings" (2014, 24). The focus is squarely on the organizational, and to some degree cultural, history and constraints associated with particular rebel organizations. While groups can change, there is a greater focus on the structural conditions of the groups than the contingent outcomes associated with the actions of other actors.

8. McDowall 1996.

9. Hechter (2000, 17) defines peripheral nationalism as "when a culturally distinctive territory resists incorporation into an expanding state, or attempts to secede and set up its own government."

10. Aziz 2011, 49–50. The two main dialects are Surani and Kurmanji, though there is debate among Kurdish language specialists as to the existence of additional distinct dialects.

11. Bulloch and Morris 1992, 53.

inaccessibility of Kurdistan has meant that Kurdish regions have historically served as a natural frontier for various Middle Eastern empires, challenging imperial exercise of sovereignty over those areas.[12] Because states typically encounter difficulties when administering "marginal zones" of their territorial dominion, it is perhaps not surprising that governing Kurdish areas has posed a governance challenge for the states that border Kurdistan, like Iraq, Iran, Syria, and Turkey.[13]

The major "fault lines" within Iraqi Kurdistan have historically been based on linguistic, regional, and tribal lines.[14] Indeed, a variety of scholars of Kurdish society have argued that Kurds have traditionally preferred tribal interests over the interests of the Kurdish "nation."[15] Some scholars have gone as far as to argue that in Kurdish society, one's first duty has historically been to tribe and chief and that "the concept of a national duty towards fellow Kurds was practically non-existent."[16] McDowall, for example, finds no evidence of long-term feelings of nationalism despite the fact that the Kurdish "people" have existed as an identifiable group for over a thousand years.[17]

STATE-SOCIETY RELATIONS BEFORE THE ANFAL

In the early twentieth century, educated Kurdish elites sought to cultivate a more robust attachment to a Kurdish national identity within their community, encouraging a series of popular revolts based on nationalist demands.[18] Yet, Kurdish nationalism held little resonance outside of a narrow swath of urban intellectuals. Wimmer writes that "the idea of a national community of solidarity fighting for liberation from oppression by ethnic others" on the part of Iraqi Kurds had not been widespread, from a historical perspective.[19]

12. Van Bruinessen 1992, 13.
13. McDowall 1996, 15.
14. Graham-Brown 1999, 215.
15. Bulloch and Morris 1992, 74; Aziz 2011, 54.
16. Bulloch and Morris 1992, 75.
17. McDowall 1996. McDowall attributes the relative lack of nationalist sentiment among Kurds, at least when compared to Turks and Arabs, to the lack of a Kurdish "civic culture and an established literature" (2). An alternative, primordialist perspective would suggest that Kurdish nationalism is both ancient and inherent (Hassan 2013).
18. Aziz 2011, 62. Hassanpour (1992, 65) views Kurdish nationalism as part of an effort to resist incorporation into state structures during the early twentieth century.
19. Wimmer 2002, 185–186.

Hassan finds that the earliest forms of Kurdish nationalism did not extend to the middle or lower classes.[20]

Some scholars have suggested that efforts by urban-based Kurdish nationalists were largely thwarted by tribal interests[21] and that nationalist mobilization efforts were typically "isolated and uncoordinated."[22] Consequently, Kurdish nationalism has been in tension with tribal loyalties, which largely prevented Kurds from uniting with one another in common cause for a Kurdish nation.[23] Policies by the British to co-opt tribal chiefs may have further "stifled Kurdish nationalist potential" as these chiefs preferred to protect their economic interests rather than to mobilize against the state on behalf of Kurdish national interests.[24] In this way, the co-optation of tribal chiefs into the ruling elite may have helped to validate and strengthen chiefs in the eyes of the Kurdish people.[25]

The introduction of the Republican period, which began with the 1958 coup ending the monarchy, saw a change in the status of Kurds in Iraq. General ʿAbd al-Karim Qasim recognized the bi-national (Arab and Kurdish) character of Iraq, placing the Kurdish sun on the Iraqi flag, welcoming Kurdish leaders back from exile, legalizing the Kurdish Democratic Party, and releasing Kurdish political prisoners.[26] During this time, "territorial separation was not part of Kurdish claims because most Kurds did not see themselves as a separate political entity from Iraq."[27] Rather, claims for rights were made within the context of the Iraqi state. Qasim sought to cultivate a broad coalition of Arab nationalist, Communist, and Kurdish elements; while he courted the Kurds, Qasim remained wary of allowing Kurdish interests to become too powerful.[28] In 1961, after a dispute with Kurdish leader Mustafa Barzani, Qasim sent the Iraqi air force to bomb the village of Barzan.[29]

A series of coups in Baghdad followed and for each new leader in Baghdad, large segments of the Iraqi Kurdish population believed there would be an

20. Hassan 2013.
21. Aziz 2011, 62.
22. Bulloch and Morris 1992, 5.
23. Van Bruinessen 1992, 7.
24. Natali 2005, 32.
25. McDowall 1996, 15.
26. Natali 2005, 49.
27. Ibid., 51.
28. Van Bruinessen 1992, 27.
29. Bulloch and Morris 1992, 123.

opportunity for reconciliation. For example, after both the 1958 coup and the Ba'thist revolution of 1963 there was genuine optimism that regime change would usher in a period of Kurdish-Arab understanding.[30] According to Van Bruinessen, "Iraqi governments would first attempt to appease the Kurds, then be drawn into a war with them and be overthrown in a coup d'etat."[31] The result was that "inconsistent Kurdish management policies created a relationship between the Kurdish nationalist elite and central government that fluctuated between compromise and hostility."[32] And while there existed historical moments when Kurdish nationalist ideology moved toward greater or lesser degrees of "Iraqiness,"[33] throughout this period the goal was to support a Kurdish ethnic identity that would exist within the context of an Iraqi national identity.[34]

Conflict and Collaboration in the Early Ba'thist Period

In the wake of the 1968 Ba'thist coup, there were no early indications that the new Iraqi leadership would seek to thwart Kurdish interests. Like other Arab nationalist groups, the Iraqi Ba'thists recognized and made accommodation for non-Arab minority groups.[35] The Ba'th Party issued decrees that Kurdish be taught in Iraqi schools and universities, that a new university be built in the Kurdish city of Sulaymaniyya, that the Kurdish New Year be considered a national holiday, and that amnesty be offered to former Kurdish rebels.[36] A relatively conciliatory relationship seemed apparent, largely as a result of government efforts at fence mending.[37] Natali writes:

> [Iraqi President] Al-Bakr created a constitutional amendment stating that the Iraqi people consist of two main nationalities: Arabs and Kurds. High-ranking Ba'thist officials such as Brigadier General Sa'dun Ghaydun started taking symbolic tours of Kurdish provinces, promising to implement

30. Yildiz 2004, 16–17.
31. Van Bruinessen 1992, 28.
32. Natali 2005, 53.
33. Aziz 2011, 68.
34. Natali 2005, 55.
35. McDowall 1996, 323–324.
36. McDowall 1996, 325.
37. Natali 2005, 57. Even Hussein was seen as someone who had a relatively "amenable approach to the Kurdish question" (McDowall 1996, 324).

development programs for their Kurdish brothers. They also continued to negotiate with the Kurdish elite, ensuring its semi-legitimacy at the local and national levels.[38]

Jalal Talabani, a leading figure in the Patriotic Union of Kurdistan (PUK), felt at ease with the Baʿthists from an ideological perspective and argued that the Baʿth Party was the first to recognize the national rights of the Kurds.[39] Mustafa Barzani, the leader of the Kurdistan Democratic Party (KDP), was initially reluctant to cooperate closely with the Baʿth Party; this seemed to be a result of the Baʿth Party's association with his Kurdish enemies rather than any ideological or other impediment, however.[40] A peace accord in March 1970 paused the long-simmering "Barzani" rebellion.

At the time the agreement was made, there were no obvious grounds to suspect ill faith.[41] The accord represented the "best deal the Kurds of Iraq had been offered" and remained a foundation for negotiations with Baghdad into the future.[42] Terms of the agreement included establishing Kurdish as an official language of Iraq, alongside Arabic, to be taught as a second language throughout Iraq; Kurdish representation in senior and sensitive government positions; the right to create Kurdish civil society organizations; designated development funds for Kurdistan; and a guaranteed Kurdish Vice-President.[43]

While it is unclear if the agreement was negotiated in good faith on the part of Hussein, there were encouraging early steps regarding the implementation of the accord, including the appointment of KDP apparatchik in a number of key governorships.[44] In addition, after the signing, health care was extended to even the most remote Kurdish villages, new schools opened offering a Kurdish curriculum, and a new Kurdish academy of sciences was founded.[45] By the end of 1970, Baghdad was paying 6,000 peshmerga to serve as border guards and Mustafa Barzani enjoyed a generous monthly stipend.[46] In December 1970,

38. Natali 2005, 57.
39. McDowall 1996, 325.
40. Ibid.
41. Ibid., 327–328.
42. Ibid.
43. Ibid.
44. Yildiz 2004, 18–19.
45. Van Bruinessen 1992, 29.
46. McDowall 1996, 329.

Mustafa Barzani said that he was "optimistic" about the political future of Iraqi Kurds.[47]

Scholars have argued that the March 1970 agreement came close to succeeding as a political pact between Hussein and Iraqi Kurdish constituencies.[48] But the increasing salience of oil revenue in the early 1970s had two opposing effects on the relationship between Iraqi Kurdish constituencies and the state. On the one hand, increased oil revenue was a boon to the Iraqi economy, providing significant new opportunities for Iraqi Kurds. The construction sector expanded with new public works programs[49] and "many Kurds integrated into Iraqi society, taking advantage of the educational, commercial, and cultural opportunities that were tied to the country's new oil wealth."[50] Improved economic conditions and growing job opportunities also made it difficult for nationalist movements to recruit supporters as citizens became increasingly invested in the regime.

On the other hand, as oil became more important as a resource of the state, there was a greater desire on the part of Baghdad to control the northern city of Kirkuk and its environs as this area enjoyed the greatest geographic concentration of oil reserves.[51] The nationalization of fifty-five wells in the Kirkuk oil fields in 1972 was seen as an affront to Iraqi Kurds, who had hoped to lay a regional claim to those resources rather than transferring ownership to the Iraqi state.[52] McDowall writes that while "at the beginning of 1974 oil revenue was expected to be ten times higher than in 1972 ... a huge resource was now at stake."[53] A major strategy of the central government was to engage in a process of Arabization of Kirkuk and adjacent oil-rich areas, granting land deeds to Arabs and removing Kurds from these areas.[54] Large numbers of Iraqi Kurds were forced to move their residence during this time.[55]

47. Ibid.
48. McKiernan 2006, 57.
49. Bulloch and Morris 1992, 147.
50. Natali 2005, 62.
51. Natali 2005, 58.
52. Bengio 2012, 83. Yet at the same time, the Baʿth Party was working to mend fences with the KDP, describing the group in favorable terms and suggesting that it had a legitimate role in the representation of the Kurdish people (88). During this period, the regime also sought to increase the status of festivals that emphasized the history of ancient Iraq and the fraternity between Arabs and Kurds as a result of their shared land and history (Baram 1991, 54–55).
53. McDowall 1996, 335.
54. Natali 2005, 58; Razoux 2015, 55.
55. Aziz 2011, 8.

While the destruction of villages and depopulation of neighborhoods created new grievances, displaced Kurds were often moved to urban apartment blocs where they grew to be dependent on the state for either employment or handouts to the unemployed.[56] The petrol-fueled economy "placated Kurds by providing them with free monthly food rations, health care, and educational programs."[57] The net result was a depoliticization of many Kurdish Iraqis who were increasingly dependent on the state and state spending, even at a time when Arabization policies had the potential to increase the salience of their nationalist grievances.

Anti-regime activities by Kurdish Iraqis during the 1970s were intense, but also intermittent. The Ba'th Party sought to monitor the activities of Kurdish nationalist movements closely. Multiple regime and security service memoranda contained information on the names of the individuals who had congratulated Barzani on his safety after an assassination attempt; some of these documents also include employment information about those individuals.[58] Other documents list the names of all KDP supporters from a particular area.[59] Another file provides information about the names of individuals who had received weapons from the KDP.[60]

When Hussein was seen as reneging on aspects of the agreement and implementing policies with the goal of Arabizing the city of Kirkuk,[61] conflict broke out between the Kurdish nationalist movement and the Iraqi regime. At the same time, Iran encouraged Kurdish nationalist groups to launch a military campaign against the Iraqi regime.[62] Kurdish tribal chiefs took a variety of positions—while some joined the guerrilla war on the side of the nationalists, others attempted to remain neutral or even actively opposed conflict with the state.[63] According to one account, however, "the logic of opposing the (Kurdish) nationalist cause was not entirely mercenary ... victory for the nationalists would automatically have enhanced the standing of the tribes which led the rebellion, in this case the Barzanis ... rival tribes therefore

56. Natali 2005, 62–63.
57. Ibid.
58. See Iraqi Secret Police Files Doc. Nos. 20042 to 20045, October 3, 1971 and Doc Nos. 10003 to 10006, October 3, 1971.
59. Iraqi Secret Police Files Doc. Nos. 100031 to 100034, July 7, 1972.
60. Iraqi Secret Police Files Doc. No. 100008, June 22, 1973.
61. Yildiz 2004, 19; Razoux 2015, 55.
62. Van Bruinessen 1992, 31.
63. Ibid., 7.

had a sectarian interest in helping to ensure that victory was denied them."[64] In other words, rivalries within the Kurdish community worked against the pursuit of Kurdish nationalist aims.

Material support and encouragement from Iran were critical for the Kurdish insurgents. But when Iran signed the Algiers Agreement with Iraq in 1975 to end support for the movement in exchange for rights to a portion of the Shatt al-Arab waterway, the Kurdish resistance was largely brought to an end. This likely reflected a lack of commitment to open conflict with the Iraqi regime by the majority of Iraqi Kurds as well as important political divisions within the leadership of the Kurdish nationalist movement.

At the same time, Mustafa Barzani received criticism from a variety of groups for advocating the continuance of what was seen as a largely ineffective rebellion. McDowall writes that "the most bitter pill for Mulla Mustafa [Barzani] was the defection of his eldest son, Ubayd Allah, who claimed his father wanted to be an absolute ruler and did not want self rule even if he was given all of Kirkuk and its oil."[65] Coupled with the increased investment in Kurdistan by the Ba'thists, it seemed to many that there was little to gain from rebellion. In reference to Kurdish areas, McDowall writes:

> The Iraqi regime invested heavily in the area in order to provide a level of economic satisfaction … its collective village program created over 30,000 dwellings, at a cost of almost 90 million dinars. It also allocated 336 million dinars on developing the region, building up industry, laying metalled roads, building schools and clinics. Schools increased fourfold between 1974 and 1979; hospitals were built … and tourist facilities developed. Indeed, the Iraqi government probably spent more per head of population in Kurdistan than elsewhere in the country during the second half of the 1970s.[66]

Regime documents from this period point to considerable Kurdish collaboration with the Ba'thists as well as indications that Iraqi Kurdish citizens sometimes felt victimized by Kurdish nationalists. Village headmen often worked closely with the regime, providing information to party officials.[67]

64. Bulloch and Morris 1992, 75.
65. McDowall 1996, 337.
66. McDowall 1996, 340.
67. North Iraq Dataset Doc. No. 02477-101-55, February 3, 1977.

Some of this information related to the weapons and financial and technological capacity of anti-regime activists.[68] One memorandum discusses the grievances of locals when rebels entered their villages, demanding money, stealing livestock, and threatening non-combatants.[69] The headman of one village provided information to the regime about a driver who was suspected of moving rebels between villages; it was later determined that the driver was under duress to move the rebels and, as a result, the driver was released.[70]

State Management of Iraqi Kurdistan, 1980–1985

In the years and months leading up to the Iran-Iraq War, regime reporting from Iraqi Kurdistan stressed the importance of improving state-society relations. For example, the Ba'thist regime saw mutual intelligibility between Arabs and Kurds as an important goal. The teaching of Kurdish to Arabic-speaking students (and Arabic to Kurdish-speaking students) was described as an important step for reducing the linguistic barriers in the country.[71] One administrative report from the northern districts described the many needs of the local population as well as regime plans for addressing those needs.[72] This included finding employment and providing adequate compensation for Kurdish families which had been forced to relocate. Other local problems were discussed including the poor quality of roads to rural villages and attacks by rebels on those villages. The report highlighted the attempts made to improve the conditions of citizens in the North, including distributing gifts from Hussein as well as improving employment opportunities and greater government participation in public celebrations of happiness and mourning.[73]

The village headman is described in regime reports as an important intermediary, and regime officials were encouraged to meet with these village chiefs regularly so that the local leaders might raise public issues with authorities.[74] Disaffected northerners were invited to return to the national fold. It was also suggested that the public needed to become more aware of how Ba'th Party

---

68. North Iraq Dataset Doc. No. 02477-101-12, November 29, 1977.
69. North Iraq Dataset Doc. Nos. 00843-85-7 and 8, November 13, 1976.
70. Iraqi Secret Police Files Doc. No. 10245, August 14, 1980.
71. North Iraq Dataset Doc. No. 34589-312-909 to 914, c. 1978.
72. Iraqi Secret Police Files Doc. No. 10380 to 10397, July 17, 1980.
73. Ibid.
74. Ibid.

TABLE 6.1. Distribution of Baʿth Party participation across ranks in Erbil, April 1980.

Party Level	Number at Level
Active Members	34
Apprentice Members	16
Supporters	536
Sympathizers	10,437

rule was providing for the population both through mechanisms of reporting and accountability as well as through local literacy centers. The positive activities of the regime were contrasted in these reports with opposition groups who forced and threatened citizens into providing material support, in some cases using the mosque network to do this. The reporting emphasized the importance of reporting insurgent activity to the authorities, including urging parents to integrate their sons into state-building efforts.[75]

One document provides information on the number of individuals involved with the Baʿth Party in Erbil in April 1980, as well as their relative rank within the party.[76] This information is reported in table 6.1. The number of supporters and sympathizers far exceeds the number in the higher ranks of party participation, including "member" and "apprentice." This suggests that while party participation may have been quite broad, the Baʿth Party was hierarchical in Iraqi Kurdistan, with only very small percentages of individuals moving into the highest ranks.

Kurdish dissidents increased their operations in northern Iraq following the start of the Iran-Iraq War in the hope of "extracting political concessions from Baghdad."[77] Despite that, Hussein was confident about his political position in the North during the early years of the war.[78] Conflict between the KDP and PUK undermined nationalist efforts targeting the regime.[79] Hussein even boasted that Kurdish groups would never achieve anything because they were hopelessly divided against one another.[80] This assessment was shared by US intelligence. Reports from the time suggested that the Kurdish opposition

---

75. Ibid.

76. Ibid.

77. Declassified CIA National Foreign Assessment Center, Research Paper, "Iraq's Dissidents," July 1981.

78. Bulloch and Morris 1992, 157.

79. McDowall 1996, 346–347.

80. Ibid.

was so badly split—both ideologically and personally—that it was virtually impossible for it to pose a threat to the Baʿthist regime.[81] According to one assessment, the divisions went beyond the high-profile conflict between the PUK's Jalal Talabani and KDP's Mustafa Barzani to include a variety of groups that preferred to "rally to Baghdad's side and [were] serving as scouts and auxiliaries for Iraqi forces" rather than watch the rise of the Barzani clan.[82]

Baʿth Party officials also made efforts to co-opt large Kurdish clans and to administer the area in a way that reduced the potential for cooperation between Kurdish groups and Iran. Kurds were permitted to undertake their military service in Iraqi Kurdistan rather than on the southern front, deserters were frequently offered amnesty, and Hussein "took steps to ingratiate himself further with the local populace."[83] According to Hilterman, the Iraqi regime's key strategy in Kurdish areas during the Iran-Iraq War was to buy off tribal leaders who were then made responsible for recruiting members of the regime-aligned Kurdish militias (jash).[84] In some cases, Kurdish clans switched sides depending on the relationship between clan leaders and either the Iranian or the Iraqi regime.[85]

How much were ordinary individuals paid for their collaboration with the regime? Payment to police and security officers in northern Iraq in 1980 ranged from 10 to 30 Iraqi dinars per month depending on their rank; higher salaries went to the assistant general manager and lower salaries went to non-commissioned officers and account managers.[86] Salaries for village headmen in Iraqi Kurdistan in 1981 ranged from 20 to 30 Iraqi dinars per month.[87]

The regime also made efforts to appoint Kurds to high-ranking positions in the northern governorates. One set of memoranda from 1981 documents the top administrative leaders in Dohuk governorate—including the governor, directors of various units like the bureau of statistics, roads and bridges

81. Declassified CIA Directorate of Intelligence Assessment, "Iraqi Opposition: Status and Prospects," December 23, 1983.

82. Ibid.

83. McDowall 1996, 348.

84. Hilterman 2007, 87.

85. North Iraq Dataset Doc. No. 25181-101-58, December 7, 1981.

86. Iraqi Secret Police Files Doc. Nos. 30570 to 30571, July 14, 1980.

87. Iraqi Secret Police Files Doc. No. 100004, December 1981. While not a large sum, these salaries nonetheless represented a meaningful amount given then the prevailing exchange rate of about 0.3 Iraqi dinars to 1 US dollar. See Ofra Bengio, "Iraq," *Middle East Contemporary Survey*, 1982 for exchange rate information.

authority, as well as police chiefs of large municipalities, and bank and post office directors—by ethno-sectarian and other markers of identity. On the list of 135 individuals, only three were women. About 60 percent of these top administrative positions were held by Kurds, with Arabs holding about 30 percent and the rest distributed between Turkmen, Chaldean Christians, and one position held by a Shabak (ethnic Persian). The governor of Dohuk was described as being from an influential Kurdish family that was part of the Surchi clan of Ninawa. The governor was said to be a Baʿthist with a good reputation and no history of participating in sabotage activities. The memorandum further reports, however, that he operates within a very narrow circle and feels fearful when in unfamiliar crowds of people.[88] The information collected about these individual, administrative elites indicates the factors valued by the party and regime apparatus.

In addition, the Baʿthist regime sought to develop a positive reputation for itself in northern Iraq by demonstrating that regime officials were not above the law. In one case, an intelligence officer threatened citizens using his personal gun and citizens pushed back against this inappropriate behavior by engaging with bureaucratic channels.[89] In another case, a policeman was sentenced to death and his family was forced to pay 3,000 Iraqi dinars when he killed a citizen in Iraqi Kurdistan.[90] Abuse of power by state apparatchik worked against the regime's goal of cultivating a favorable public image and, as such, abuses were punished.

Despite the many examples of collaboration and cooperation that are found in the archival record, Kurdish resistance to Baʿthist rule was also common. One document reports that a policeman was supporting the insurgents by using his police car to acquire materials for their activities.[91] Another suggests that insurgents would regularly open fire on military petrol stations, the homes of military and security officers, as well as sometimes at civilian homes.[92] In one case, fifteen rebels entered a village and kidnapped the village headman, took him to the mountains and interrogated him.[93] Despite the fact that the Iraqi state had a larger and more sophisticated military, Bengio argues

88. Iraqi Secret Police Files Doc. Nos. 60023 to 60038, November 15, 1981.
89. North Iraq Dataset Doc. Nos. 22834-101-82 and 83, August 10, 1980.
90. North Iraq Dataset Doc. No. 21454-101-32, June 14, 1984.
91. North Iraq Dataset Doc. No. 38763-101-13, July 12, 1981.
92. North Iraq Dataset Doc. Nos. 19682-101-17 through 26.
93. Iraqi Secret Police Files Doc. No. 40188, August 19, 1983.

that "the army found it quite difficult to cope with the military challenge in Kurdistan, mainly because of the ruggedness of the region."[94]

The stakes associated with quelling protest behavior in northern Iraq increased with growing concern about cross-border cooperation between Kurdish militias and Iran. In July 1983, Iranian forces advanced on Iraqi Kurdistan. In retribution for Masud Barzani's support of Iran in the conflict, Hussein arrested 8,000 men who were wearing the red turban—a sign of membership in the Barzani clan—and subsequently killed them.[95] Barzani clan members who were members of the Ba'th Party were kicked out of the party shortly thereafter.[96] At the same time, the regime was careful to honor war dead who fought on the regime's side in the North. Party cadre were required to make visits to families affected by the war with the goal of fostering pride in the families of war martyrs.[97]

Iraqi Kurds who were believed to have participated in or provided material support to Kurdish guerrilla forces (i.e., peshmerga) were arrested and abused. Suspected association with the peshmerga led to prison terms in Abu Ghraib prison where individuals were subjected to physical and psychological torture, sometimes even being forced to donate blood to the Ba'th Party.[98] In some cases, a regime-allied government advisor (*mustashar*) quietly supported the insurgency while maintaining the appearance of loyalty to the regime.[99] Sometimes individual members of the pro-regime Kurdish militias were caught harboring peshmerga or providing intelligence assistance for the Kurdish nationalist cause.[100]

When attacks against regime interests occurred, how was repression meted out?[101] The testimony of individual Iraqis from northern regions suggests the blunt nature of state punishment. One informant said that his brother was arrested in 1980 after a major arrest campaign in his region; this was despite

94. Bengio 2012, 177.

95. Bulloch and Morris 1992, 217–218. Masud Barzani succeeded his father, Mustafa Barzani, as head of the KDP.

96. Iraqi Secret Police Files Doc. No. 10472, November 5, 1983.

97. Khoury 2013, 69.

98. Testimony of A. Muhammed, recorded in 2008.

99. Hilterman 2007, 93.

100. McDowall 1996, 356.

101. In some cases, the regime could show lenience toward an individual accused of anti-regime behavior. In one particular incident, a student was charged with demonstrating against the government. After signing a promise that she would not participate in future demonstrations, she was released (North Iraq Dataset Doc. No. 15518-63-45, April 27, 1982).

the fact that his brother was not involved with any political organization.[102] Another informant reported that his brother was killed in the early 1980s during a bombardment of Kurdish villages. The informant himself was still a preparatory student when he was arrested in 1982, accused of being part of a Kurdish nationalist organization.[103]

KURDISH ACTIVISM DURING THE ANFAL

The Anfal Campaign (1986–1989) against the Kurdish populations of Iraq has been described as perpetrating some of the most widespread and serious human rights abuses of the late twentieth century. The horrors inflicted on the Kurdish population of Iraq have been well-documented and included the collective punishment of villages believed to be harboring peshmerga fighters, forced resettlement of civilian populations, and conventional and chemical weapons attacks.

Scholars have argued that it was not until well into the Iran-Iraq War that feelings of Kurdish nationalism became common among ordinary Kurds.[104] In the early days of the Anfal, for example, there still existed extensive cooperation between the Baʿthist regime and Iraqi Kurdish populations. The Iraqi regime increased the size of the pro-regime Kurdish militia forces in the mid-1980s. Government advisors recruited Kurdish Iraqis who preferred participation in the pro-government militia over regular military service.[105] Some of these collaborators grew wealthy through payments they received for recruiting pro-regime militia members.[106] By the summer of 1986, these militias were estimated to be between 150,000 and 250,000 men strong, many times larger than the size of insurgent forces.[107] The regime was constrained,

102. Testimony of N. Salman, recorded March 2008.

103. Testimony of H. Ali, recorded December 2006.

104. Bulloch and Morris 1992, 6.

105. McDowall 1996, 355–356. Troops in the government-aligned battalions were quite well paid. Khoury (2013, 101) argues that these units deterred young Kurds from joining the rebels by providing them with gainful employment.

106. Lazier 1991, 97.

107. McDowall 1996, 354. For example, the difference in the number of fighters in the government-aligned national defense battalions to the peshmerga was 50,000 to 2,000 in one particular valley and, even, 200,000 to 2,600 in another locale (Hardi 2011, 28).

however, by decreases in public goods expenditures, which fell considerably between 1986 to 1988.[108]

Many Kurds held strong feelings of Iraqi patriotism and viewed the Iran-Iraq War as their own fight.[109] Collaboration was also common among tribal groups with rivalries to the Barzani clan. According to Makiya, Kurdish collaborators were often individuals who were distrustful of Kurdish opposition forces while at the same time accustomed to more comfortable lives as a result of an upbringing in cities and towns, rather than rural villages.[110] These anti-Barzani chiefs were "richly rewarded for their services, receiving lucrative factory licenses, land grants or export/import privileges ... some, for example, the leaders of the Surchi, Harki and Zibari tribes were already extremely wealthy ... they now became wealthier still."[111]

The Anfal Campaign required considerable logistical support and assistance from individuals who had specialized knowledge of the terrain and political circumstances of the area.[112] Kurdish troops were often also well-trained in guerilla fighting.[113] In 1987, Hussein ordered the establishment of a number of special detachments and brigades made up of such individuals. Four brigades were composed of Yezidi tribesmen. Other detachments were made up of men from Iraq's Kurdish population. For example, detachments formed in January 1987 drew heavily from the Kurdish Balak, Dizayi, and Khoshnaw tribes. In July 1987, additional detachments were organized, including units with large numbers of individuals from the Jaff tribe. Berzinji Kurdish tribe members were prominent in detachment No. 153. Fighters in these detachments were paid 85 Iraqi dinars for each fighter and 200 Iraqi dinars for each commander.[114]

At the same time, there continued to exist Kurdish insurgent groups who engaged in cross-border collaboration with the Iranian armed forces. The Iraqi

108. North Iraq Dataset Doc. No. 16409-101, 1989.
109. Jabar 1992.
110. Makiya 1993, 85.
111. McDowall 1996, 356.
112. At the same time, security agents, army officers, and party apparatchik working in Mosul and other "front-line" Kurdish regions were treated to new luxury cars (the black Mercedes Benz was a favorite) and opportunities to run racketeering schemes, drug rings, and brothels, according to one account (Tucker 2014, 259).
113. Bengio 2012, 177. See also van Bruinessen (1992, 40) who argues that the peshmerga feared the government-aligned battalions more than the regular army.
114. Iraqi Secret Police Files Doc. Nos. 30018 to 30124.

regime response to Kurdish collaboration with Iran was a military campaign to "cleanse" the Kurdish countryside of safe haven for peshmerga. Forced population movement was a major policy objective of the Anfal Campaign as it deprived the insurgents of this safe haven. Over the course of the Anfal, it is estimated that between 3,000 and 4,000 villages were destroyed, displacing 1.5 million people.[115] Wooded areas were burned down and rural Kurds came to be concentrated in three main cities—Erbil, Sulaymaniyya, and Dohuk.[116] Members of the pro-regime militias were not exempt from resettlement programs.[117] Often tribal groups were moved collectively to townships; the result was that "the absence of alternative employment reinforced their dependency on their chief and his dependency on government, and this began to replace territoriality as a defining basis for tribal solidarity."[118]

Despite attempts to deprive Kurdish nationalists safe haven and material support from local populations, anti-regime attacks in this period were common in the North and widely documented in the archival evidence. In June 1987, regime security forces were ambushed and killed, with insurgents succeeding in taking control of their headquarters and blowing up a bridge.[119] Around the same time, rebels were able to launch attacks on regime security forces in a mountainous region of northern Iraq.[120] In October 1987, rebels attacked a security base, killing one Iraqi soldier.[121] The same memorandum reports that an Iraqi military lieutenant escaped to Iran with his family, allegedly with the assistance of Iranian agents.[122] In another incident, insurgents forced their way into the home of a Ba'th Party comrade, but were repelled when the comrade fired shots.[123]

115. Graham-Brown 1999, 214; Yildiz 2004, 25.
116. Lazier 1991, 100. See also Kocher (2004) who argues that rural environments make policing more difficult for incumbent regimes. Forced population removal has commonly been used to deprive insurgents of a population base for support while also rendering previously rural populations more legible to the incumbent (Kalyvas 2006, 123). Kalyvas (133) argues that "incumbents tend to control cities, even when these cities happen to be the social, religious and ethnic strongholds of their opponents, whereas the insurgents' strongholds tend to be in inaccessible rural areas, even when rural populations are inimical to them."
117. McDowall 1996, 357.
118. Ibid.
119. North Iraq Dataset Doc. No. 34418-101-93, June 17, 1987.
120. North Iraq Dataset Doc. No. 34418-101-94, June 16, 1987.
121. North Iraq Dataset Doc. No. 34418-101-39, October 1, 1987.
122. Ibid.
123. North Iraq Dataset Doc. No. 34418-101-88, November 29, 1987. During this time,

TABLE 6.2. Number of attacks against Baʿth Party cadre and headquarters, 1987.

Location	Number of Attacks
Baghdad	3
South	18
Euphrates	17
Central	3
North	
—Mosul	1
—Ninawa	12
—Erbil	25
—Taʾmim	5
—Sulaymaniyya	17
—Dohuk	28

Resistance to Baʿthist rule in northern Iraq can be compared to resistance activity in other parts of the country. For example, the summary table of a 1987 report, which I reproduce in table 6.2, considers the number of attacks against Baʿth Party headquarters and party comrades. These incidents included the murder and kidnapping of party comrades as well as attacks on party headquarters, like bombings.[124] The number of attacks in the North is so relatively large that individual areas within the northern region are broken out to separately describe the full variation. It is notable that such attacks existed in southern Iraq (the Euphrates and South areas), but were rare in Baghdad and the Central areas.

Limited ability to "see" Iraqi Kurdistan during the Anfal Campaign meant that some areas were beyond the observational capacity of the state.[125] Indeed, procuring high-quality information in the northern areas continued to be a major area of concern for the regime. The regime conducted a census in 1987 in a bid to facilitate state control in Kurdish areas.[126] Participation in the census was supposed to be obligatory, but government orders did not reach some villagers in remote areas.[127] Faust argues that finding Baʿthists

---

Baʿth Party officials reflected on why individuals might turn away from the state to take up the "revolutionary banner." At least some segments of the Iraqi authorities believed that the goal of the insurgents was a new government that would be inclusive of all political parties and had a more democratic orientation. See Iraqi Secret Police Files Doc. No. 100003 to 100004, February 24, 1987.

124. See BRCC Doc. Nos. 01-2135-0004-1222 to 0129 for additional details.

125. Alahmad 2009, 68–69.

126. Alahmad 2009.

127. Ibid.

who spoke Kurdish well to fill staff positions in Kurdish territories continued to be a problem, leading the regime to offer shorter than normal assignment times and accelerated party promotions to those who agreed to serve in those areas.[128]

Effective collaborators were valued, but apparently hard to come by. In one case, a village head was removed for insufficient cooperation and not providing high-quality intelligence information.[129] Because of the challenges associated with identifying transgressors in northern areas, the regime engaged in a variety of collective punishment strategies. If an area was deemed to have rebel groups, an economic blockade was imposed through the closing of roads to the community.[130] This type of action was thought to lower the morale of villagers.[131] Under such directives, foodstuffs and other basic supplies were totally blocked.[132]

During the course of the Anfal, it was not unusual for army units to storm villages, arresting large numbers, including entire families, and making use of chemical and high-explosive bombardments that killed without discriminating between regime supporters and opponents.[133] Villages would be fired at in an indiscriminate way when Iraqi army units were unable to discern who had opened fire upon them.[134] According to Kurdish informants, "if an army patrol was fired on from a house or neighborhood, the entire area was held accountable."[135] Battles between peshmerga forces and the Iraqi army could last for days as military planes and helicopters would bomb homes, killing civilians and rebels alike.[136] Not even local advisors who were allied with the government could be guaranteed protection during episodes of indiscriminate, collective punishment.[137]

General Ali Hassan al-Majid (aka "Chemical Ali"), who had been appointed governor of the northern region, had been given power to do whatever was necessary to end cooperation between the peshmerga and Iran,

128. Faust 2015, 161.
129. North Iraqi Dataset Doc. No. 13458-101-52, February 18, 1987.
130. CRRC Doc. No. SH-PDWN-D-000-678, 1988.
131. Ibid.
132. Rabil 2002.
133. McDowall 1996, 359.
134. Lazier 1991, 101.
135. Makiya 1993, 99.
136. Testimony of A. Hussein, recorded in 2008.
137. Hilterman 2007, 95.

including the use of a "scorched earth" policy to deny civilian provision of food and shelter to the peshmerga.[138] Al-Majid attributed peshmerga successes to civilian material support but was poorly positioned to identify those who had assisted the rebels. Forced relocations of Iraqi Kurds to urban blocs continued in a bid to deprive the peshmerga of support. According to Bengio, Baghdad sought to "put the population of the border areas under close surveillance by moving them to more accessible locales."[139] Relocated individuals were often paid to evacuate their villages based on an appraisal committee that established a value for the confiscated property, but where families may actually have been paid more if they were believed to be sympathetic to the insurgents.[140] According to Makiya, "the regime was actually trying to bribe these people away from their political allegiances."[141]

The chemical weapons attack on Halabja in March 1988, in particular, was a turning point in the way many Kurdish Iraqis viewed their shared political fate. While chemical weapons attacks had taken place in multiple locations in Iraqi Kurdistan,[142] it was the attack on Halabja that resonated with greatest intensity for Iraqi Kurds. Halabja was targeted because of "assumed collaboration with Iran and Iranian-backed peshmerga."[143] In particular, Halabja had fallen into Iranian hands with the help of peshmerga forces the day before the chemical weapons attack. Baghdad "framed the Kurds' cooperation with Iran as high treason in Iraq's most critical hour."[144]

The Halabja incident stands out both for the intensity of the attack and the number of individuals killed.[145] Kurds came to call the Halabja incident

138. McDowall 1996, 353. How were the perpetrators of the repression compensated? Major financial rewards were given to eight high-ranking officers who participated in the planning and execution of the Anfal Campaign. See CRRC Doc. No. SH-AFGC-D-000-647, May 28, 1988.

139. Bengio 2012, 187.

140. Makiya 1993, 160.

141. Ibid.

142. Yildiz 2004, 26.

143. Bulloch and Morris 1992, 142–143.

144. Romano 2006, 199.

145. Valentino (2004) focuses on the instrumental aspect of mass killing, particularly the use of violence against those actors within society viewed as the most dangerous threats to the state. According to Valentino (2004, 4), "when perpetrators perceive the stakes to be high enough, and when less violent alternatives appear to be blocked or unworkable, however, the incentives to consider mass killing multiply. In this context, repression associated with guerilla conflict is the single most common motivation for mass killing. In Valentino's (2004) account

the Kurdish "Auschwitz" because the victims were "chosen merely because they were Kurds."[146] The perception that the Ba'thist regime killed Kurds as a result of their Kurdish identity is widespread among Anfal survivors.[147] Bulloch and Morris write that the attack on Halabja "more than any other single incident" reminded Iraqi Kurds "of their separate Kurdish identity... Halabja was a turning-point from which many nationalists mark the birth of a national consciousness."[148] Hiltermann concurs, arguing that the Kurdish "nation" was born out of the deeply emotional, national traumas of the Anfal.[149]

First-person testimony of the experiences of individuals living in northern Iraq at this time is illustrative. Kurdish informants reported fleeing to the mountains during aerial bombings of villages.[150] Despite the difficult conditions of the mountains where families would have little food to eat and poor shelter, the persecution in Kurdish towns and villages was often worse. Houses were burned, with families and children inside of them.[151] One informant— who was just ten years old when the Halabja attack took place—reports that his entire family was killed, including his mother, his four brothers, his grandmother, and the families of his aunt and his uncle. He recalls people vomiting and fainting from the chemical attack.[152] A teacher from Halabja reports that fourteen of his family members were killed in the attack and that he is still haunted by memories of people blinded by the chemical weapons trying to get away, and even mothers leaving their children behind to try to escape the chemical attack.[153]

Estimates of the number of Iraqi Kurds that perished in the Anfal run between 150,000 and 200,000 individuals.[154] As the Anfal Campaign intensified, the degree of cooperation between former adversaries within the Iraqi Kurdish community increased. In November 1986, Masud Barzani and Jalal

---

there is less focus on issues of legibility, in terms of distinguishing civilians from guerillas, and more of a focus on how to isolate guerillas from sources of civilian support.

146. Bulloch and Morris 1992, 142.
147. Tucker 2014.
148. Bulloch and Morris 1992, 142.
149. Hiltermann 2007, 226–227.
150. Testimony of A. Ahmed, recorded in 2008; Testimony of H. Abdallah, recorded in 2008.
151. Testimony of Abdallah, 2008.
152. Testimony of D. Hilmi, recorded in 2008.
153. Testimony of B. Ahmed, recorded in 2008.
154. McDowall 1996, 359; Yildiz 2004, 25.

Talabani met in Tehran with the goal of forming a coalition.[155] In 1987, the PUK and KDP normalized relations, despite some continued criticism of each other.[156] In June 1988, shortly after the Halabja attack, Iraqi Kurdish leaders "resolved to put aside sectarian differences within the nationalist movement and to form a unified Kurdistan Front to try to meet the challenge and to pursue their shared demands for autonomy... the parties which joined to form the front were Barzani's Kurdish Democratic Party (KDP) and the Patriotic Union of Kurdistan (PUK)."[157] This reconciliation extended to other groups as well, including the Kurdish Socialist Party, the Kurdish People's Democratic Party, and the Kurdish Branch of the Iraqi Communist Party.[158]

After the Halabja incident, the Iraqi regime continued its efforts to increase the legibility of the Kurdish countryside while simultaneously deploying official rhetoric which referenced the rights of Iraqi Kurds. In September 1988, the Iraqi government issued a general amnesty for all Iraqi Kurds (other than Jalal Talabani).[159] In 1989, Hussein paid multiple visits to Iraq's Kurdish areas, encouraging volunteers to move to new settlements by offering perks like free houses, agricultural land, and money for home construction.[160] Farmers who did remain in the countryside were asked to sign an oath swearing not to harbor rebels and to report any suspicious activity.[161] Insurgent groups at this time were believed by the regime to vary considerably in size and strength. One memorandum suggested that groups operating in the Harir mountains were relatively small, between twelve and ninety-three men, and dependent on villages for material support.[162]

Military convoys continued to clear villages with the goal of reducing the opportunities for insurgents to shelter there.[163] Families who had lived in the cleared villages would sometimes flee to neighboring villages or to the Turkish border, or would otherwise be moved to state-mandated residential

155. McDowall 1996, 351.
156. Bulloch and Morris 1992, 157.
157. Ibid., 6.
158. Both the KDP and the PUK continued to engage in insurgent activity, though from weak strategic positions; as one analyst described it, "in the wake of state genocide in 1988, there was little left for Kurdish leaders to lose" (McDowall 1996, 368).
159. See Bengio (2012, 185) on this point.
160. Bengio 2012, 188.
161. North Iraq Dataset Doc. No. 01967-101-70 to 76, 1988.
162. North Iraq Dataset Doc. No. 01884-61-26, June 8, 1988.
163. North Iraq Dataset Doc. No. 01884-61-32 to 46 and 01884-61-51 to 61, August 1988.

complexes.[164] Relocations were often accompanied by rhetoric about the importance of bringing modern amenities to Kurdish villagers.[165]

While the regime continued to fight the weak but determined insurgency, state discourse operated in a way that seemed to ignore the implications of the Anfal Campaign. For example, the Iraqi Ministry of Culture and Information sponsored a two-day seminar on the Kurdish poet Mewlewi in Sulaymaniyya and the Iraqi Ministry of Education continued to publish journals, books, and texts in the Kurdish language.[166] Studies were commissioned about how to improve relations between citizens and security services so that security officers would treat citizens properly and citizens would no longer fear the security services.[167] State directives ordered that Kurdish citizens be treated like other Iraqis and that no house was to be searched or person arrested without instructions from the General Security Directorate.[168] These orders also emphasized that Kurds continued to enjoy the right to nominate individuals for the National Council. The glaring disconnect between the official policies of the state and the reality of the regime's brutal repression invited dissension. During this time period, anti-regime slogans appeared on walls of local stores, homes, and schools in Kurdish areas; security services were quick to erase the slogans and investigate who was responsible.[169]

In a meeting with Ali Hassan al-Majid and the governors of Sulaymaniyya that took place just one year after the end of the Iran-Iraq War, Hussein discussed his concern for living conditions in Iraqi Kurdistan as well as his desire to improve economic development and particularly the tourism sector.[170] Hussein talked about the need to identify tourism projects that would improve the unemployment situation in Kurdistan with the goal of attracting Baghdad residents to the area in the summer and Basra residents in the winter. He also suggested the building of a watermelon jelly or tomato paste factory. Hussein expressed the belief that good employment opportunities would allow people to live honestly and avoid anti-regime incitement from nationalist groups.[171] Communications between Hussein and a security

164. North Iraq Dataset Doc. No. 01884-61-7 to 17, August 30, 1988.
165. Bengio 2012, 187.
166. Natali 2005, 59.
167. North Iraq Dataset Doc. Nos. 02532-101-69 through 73, October 12, 1987.
168. North Iraq Dataset Doc. No. 00049-101-8 to 11, November 21, 1988.
169. North Iraq Dataset Doc. No. 11339, 1988.
170. CRRC Doc. No. SH-SHTP-A-000-617, August 1, 1989.
171. Ibid.

director emphasized the importance of improving relations with the northern population.[172] Rather than completely writing off public development of Iraqi Kurdistan after the Anfal Campaign, the regime persisted in its efforts to improve the local economy, believing this would decrease support for Kurdish rebels.

The regime also took a keen interest in cultivating non-Kurdish minority groups to assist the Ba'thists in governance. For example, Hussein sought out briefings on the status of the Yezidi sect of northern Iraq, including their relations with local tribes.[173] According to this report, a number of Yezidis had volunteered to work with the Ba'th Party. The report suggested that only the most competent Ba'thist educators be deployed to Yezidi regions and that Ba'th Party sympathizers from within the sect should be recruited into the police and military academies. And party cadre thought that by increasing investment in development projects in Yezidi areas, Yezidi leaders might be able to influence the rank and file to resist the pull of Kurdish opposition forces. In a discussion of a dispute between members of the Yezidi sect and local tribesmen, it was suggested that the regime seek a speedy resolution of the conflict lest Kurdish groups make overtures to the Yezidis in a bid to win them over politically.[174]

In 1991, shortly after the eruption of popular uprisings in southern Iraq, Kurdish militias recognized that there was a unique opportunity to organize anti-regime protests in the Iraqi North. When government-affiliated militias turned against the regime, the protests gained even greater momentum. Masses gathered in streets, seizing the Ba'th Party headquarters, the secret police building, and a local prison.[175] A key factor in the success of the uprisings was the fact that the majority of government-aligned battalion forces (*jash*) switched sides.[176] In this move, formerly pro-regime militia leaders were "transformed from embarrassed collaborators with Baghdad into champions of the uprising."[177]

In many cases, the government advisors negotiated the departure of Iraqi forces who were unwilling to join the uprisings, offering regular forces safe

172. North Iraq Dataset 33229-101-97 through 101, March 22, 1990.
173. CRRC Doc. No. SH-MISC-D-000-098, March 1, 1992.
174. The report suggested that Masud Barzani had publicly stated that the Barzani clan were of Yezidi origin.
175. Yildiz 2004, 35.
176. Graham-Brown 1999, 154.
177. McDowall 1996, 371.

conduct to government lines if they laid down arms.[178] Indeed, the Kurdistan Front had a plan that there "should be no reprisals against army troops or ordinary members of the regime, nor indeed against the Popular Army, which played a vital role in the success of the rebellion."[179] While rank-and-file soldiers were not targeted for killings during the northern uprisings, Ba'th Party cadre, on the other hand, were killed in retribution for their abuses of the Kurdish population. Some party cadre were able to escape with the help of other citizens.[180] In Sulaymaniyya, it is estimated that about 900 members of the intelligence services were killed in one day of fighting, with a focus on targeting Ba'thists and torturers.[181] Fighting continued in the North until the United States agreed to send troops to northern Iraq; US and British troops arrived in Zakho on April 20, 1991, after which time Iraqi forces did not challenge coalition ground troops and were relatively cooperative.[182]

In the aftermath of the uprisings, the Baghdad-based government cut off salary payment to 300,000 civil servants working in Iraqi Kurdistan, demanding that they move immediately to government-controlled areas. Most civil servants refused. According to Bengio, "the readiness of the civil servants and the population as a whole to endure such hardships was indeed a barometer of the crystallization of Kurdish nationalism."[183] At the same time attempts at the collective punishment of Kurdish populations continued. In a conversation between Hussein and top officials, the Ba'thist elite suggested deploying air power to target the rebellious regions since they lacked the capacity to target individual rebels.[184] Eventually, an agreement was reached to establish an autonomous zone for the three main Kurdish governorates.

Even after the emergence of Kurdish autonomy in 1991, there continued to be a belief within the Ba'thist regime that the state needed to work for the political reintegration of northern governorates into the Iraqi state.[185]

178. Ibid.
179. Bulloch and Morris 1992, 18.
180. North Iraq Dataset Doc No. 38835-101-52, March 10, 1991.
181. Yildiz 2004, 35.
182. Graham-Brown 1999.
183. Bengio 2012, 201.
184. CRRC Doc. No. SH-SHTP-A-000-739, April 1991.
185. A document entitled "Kurdish Media Plan" from 2000 highlights the continued engagement by the Ba'thist regime with developments in the autonomous Kurdish region. This document was produced at the request of Hussein himself, who had asked that a 1997 Kurdish media plan be updated with new, proposed strategies. The document suggested Ba'thist

In 1993, the Mosul branch of the Baʿth Party wrote a report about how to respond to the Kurdish subversive groups and to encourage national unity with a focus on the reintegration of Iraqi Kurdistan. Recommendations included reaching out to Kurdish university students and union workers in order to foster better ties to the party; increasing the number of pro-regime, national unity slogans painted on walls in the semi-autonomous region; granting a general amnesty to deserters living in the Kurdish region; cultivating better ties with Kurdish tribes known to be neutral or pro-Baʿthist; reaching out to Kurdish groups previously associated with the Baʿth Party; and taking advantage of the general lack of security and of the instability in the area to show the Baʿth as a desirable alternative to life under the so-called Kurdish parties.[186]

Rumors related to the Kurdish question were also common in the files of the Baʿth Party during the 1990s. Many of these rumors focused on issues of Kurdish attacks on regime targets in the North, restrictions on Kurdish populations and, most commonly, reports about the possibility of regime attacks on Kurdish targets. For example, rumors about possible Baʿthist attempts to take back the Kurdish-controlled area continued to appear in the files in spring of 1997, the summer or early fall of 1999, and again in the summer of 2000.[187] A rumor circulating in Karbala in 2000 suggested that the "criminal" Talabani was undertaking preparations for an attack on Kirkuk.[188] In 2001, a rumor reported the intention of "sabotage groups" to block roads in Sulaymaniyya and Erbil in anticipation of the establishment of

monitoring of Kurdish-language publications and continuing collaboration with existing Iraqi Kurdish cultural leaders, media personalities, and religious figures to promulgate pro-Baʿthist ideas in the Kurdish media. This monitoring and communication was undertaken by various state intelligence and security agencies both within and outside of the autonomous zone, including in Salah al-Din governorate. The regime also published its own Kurdish-language publications (at a cost of more than 57 million Iraqi dinars), including newspapers, books, and pamphlets for children that promoted the idea of Kurdistan as an integral and indivisible part of Iraq (BRCC Doc. Nos. 01-3621-0000-0517 to 0523, 2000).

186. BRCC Doc. Nos. 01-3797-0001-0292 to 0301, 1993.

187. BRCC Doc. No. 148-4-5-0045, March 20, 1997; BRCC Doc. No. 148-4-5-0068, March 24, 1997; BRCC Doc. No. 133-5-7-0875, June 26, 1999; BRCC Doc. No. 133-5-7-0512, September 18, 1999; BRCC Doc. No. 133-5-7-0491, September 19, 1999; BRCC Doc. No. 01-2912-0004-0658 and 659, June 19, 2000; BRCC Doc. No. 01-2912-0004-0621, June 6, 2000.

188. BRCC Doc. No. 01-2912-0004-0452, September 12, 2000.

a Kurdish state.[189] The following year, just months before the US invasion, the branch leadership of Baghdad recorded a rumor that women from Ghazaliyya were discussing an impending Kurdish attack on Kirkuk with the goal of overthrowing regime control.[190]

CONCLUSIONS

In the 1960s, 60 percent of Iraqi Kurds had a strong tribal affiliation but, by the late 1980s, tribal affiliation had dropped to 20 percent.[191] Why did a society that had identified primarily based on tribal group come to increasingly exhibit an ethno-nationalist identity? This chapter provides an account for the rise of Kurdish nationalism that focuses less on cultural affinity and more on nationalism as a response to state repression.

Kurdish groups had historically alternated between fighting and negotiating with Iraq's Baghdad-based government.[192] And despite suffering forms of discrimination in political representation and rent distribution, the Kurdish regions of Iraq were long thought to be an integral part of the state by Iraqi Kurds and Arabs alike.[193] McDowall's assessment is that in the late 1970s, "a magnanimous and generous offer by Baghdad might have brought the Kurdish community into a productive and fulfilling relationship with the rest of the country."[194] Tripp provides a summary of this perspective, arguing that it would be a mistake to assume the existence of a single cohesive Kurdish community working together against Baghdad in the interest of Kurdish nationalism —"on the contrary, linguistic, tribal, geographical and political divisions have been as notoriously destructive of Kurdish unity... this gave the Iraqi government considerable respite in its dealing with the Kurds."[195]

189. BRCC Doc. No. 01-2912-0004-0056, June 9, 2001.
190. BRCC Doc. No. 040-4-2-0258, November 14, 2002.
191. Graham-Brown 1999, 216.
192. Ibid., 215.
193. Bengio 2012, 6–7. Indeed, from a historical perspective, Davis (2005) argues that there was a commitment on the part of all ethnic groups to Iraqi nationalism.
194. McDowall 1996, 368.
195. Tripp 1987, 68. Also, see Bengio (2012, 273) who argues that until quite a late date, Kurdish nationalism was more about establishing "Barzaniland" and "Talabaniland" than Kurdistan.

Prior to the Anfal Campaign, Kurdish collaboration with the Baʿthist regime was widespread, probably exceeding the number of individuals who supported Kurdish nationalist groups.[196] But collaboration on the part of some Iraqi Kurds with Iran during the context of war was considered a "severe violation of the basic principles of membership in Iraqi society," deserving of retribution.[197] During the Anfal Campaign, Baʿthist repression began to affect the entire Kurdish population.[198] My argument is that because Kurdish communities were subjected to brutal forms of collective punishment, this fostered high levels of social cohesion and Kurdish nationalism. This conclusion supports arguments by scholars like Aziz, who also suggests that Kurdish nationalism arose in reaction to state policies, including terror and ethnic cleansing.[199] Kurdish populations—buoyed by their increasingly nationalist outlook—took advantage of regime weakness following the Gulf War to establish an autonomous Kurdish zone in the North.

My interpretation of the Kurdish case differs, then, from Wimmer who argues that "the exclusion from access to the increasingly Arabised state gave rise to a strong and militant Kurdish nationalist movement."[200] While an ethnic grievance story provides a partial explanation for the nature of Kurdish grievance and mobilization, my reading of the historical and archival evidence suggests that the Baʿthist regime sought to incorporate Kurdish regions into state and party structures, particularly when financial resources allowed for

196. Bengio 2012, 86.
197. Al-Khafaji 2000, 278.
198. Graham-Brown 1999, 215.
199. Aziz 2011, 5. Two less direct streams of evidence also support this perspective. The first is that what it means to be a Kurd differs in relation to what it means to be a citizen of Iraq, Turkey, or Iran (Natali 2005, xviii). In particular, Natali (2005) argues that Kurdish movements differ hugely as a function of national policies of the countries in which they live. The result was a "tendency of Kurdish nationalists to see their own political future in terms of the non-Kurdish state in which they live" (Bulloch and Morris 1992, 232). A second form of evidence comes from an examination of what happened in Iraqi Kurdistan after 1991. While cooperation between Kurdish groups persisted initially through the elections of 1992, conflict between the PUK and KDP eventually broke out over disparities in economic resources associated with control of the border crossing to Turkey (Romano 2006, 209). According to Romano (210), "although the Kurdish population at large perceived the overarching need to unite in the face of the threat from Baghdad, KDP and PUK party elites were unable to put aside their differences." While Iraqi Kurdish populations continued to think of themselves in terms of their Kurdish national identity, the civil war between Kurdish factions suggests the context-specific nature of cooperation between groups.
200. Wimmer 2002, 11.

state-building efforts. Rather than ethnic exclusion and denial of distributive rewards, it was the nature of how Kurdish populations were punished in the context of the Iran-Iraq War that gave rise to a mass nationalist movement.

The punishment strategy employed was primarily the consequence of low bureaucratic capacity of the Baghdad-based regime in Iraqi Kurdistan.[201] My interpretation is in-line with Makiya, who writes that although "the Baʿth have killed more Kurds than anyone else in Iraq ... the Baʿth Party cannot be said to be ideologically anti-Kurdish, in the way, for instance, that the Nazis were ingrained anti-Semites."[202] This perspective is shared by Faust, who concludes that "ultimately, the Baʿth wanted the Kurds to accept the Arab nationalist narrative and assimilate into Iraqi Arab culture," but because these efforts were ultimately unsuccessful, the state began to take "more collective measures against the population."[203] The account I present also suggests that Kurdish nationalism was not an automatic result of processes related to modernization,[204] but rather a product of the modern state, and particularly of repression deployed in the face of challenges to state governance.

201. My interpretation is also consistent with Alahmad (2009), who argues that the brutality associated with the Baʿthist counterinsurgency reflected regime weakness and a state with limited ability to patrol its own territory. Alahmad argues that while the genocidal qualities of the Anfal Campaign have led some scholars to believe that the Iraqi state was all-powerful, in fact the way the Anfal Campaign was perpetuated actually suggests precisely the opposite. This is not to say that the events of the Anfal Campaign were not a genocide. Alahmad (2009, 33) argues, however, that focusing on the morality of the campaign (and the tendency to compare the events to the Holocaust) obscured a broader understanding of the politics of violence in the counterinsurgency context. For Alahmad, the use of chemical weapons against Kurdish populations was not a deliberate genocide against an ethnic group, but rather a miscalculated genocidal strategy of a weak state along a war front.

202. Makiya 1993, 218.

203. Faust 2015, 162.

204. Gellner 1983.

CHAPTER 7

POLITICAL ORIENTATION AND BAʿTH PARTY PARTICIPATION

Among the most robust findings in the empirical study of autocracy is the tendency for one-party regimes to be highly durable, resilient even to destabilizing shocks like prolonged economic crises.[1] Existing research has pointed to the functional benefits of authoritarian party rule. Brownlee emphasizes the role parties play in mediating elite disputes.[2] Magaloni argues that autocratic parties help to mitigate the commitment problem facing dictators who are hard pressed to credibly demonstrate their willingness to engage in power-sharing.[3] Blaydes describes how hegemonic parties can use elections to resolve distributive conflict within an authoritarian context.[4] Svolik suggests that regime parties strengthen autocratic control through their hierarchical assignment of service and benefits.[5] Boix and Svolik argue that parties, and other authoritarian institutions, alleviate monitoring problems that arise between a dictator and his allies as a result of the secrecy common in autocracies.[6]

Dictators also engage in mass mobilization of citizenries via party channels.[7] Party and state were often fused in Communist Party regimes where educational and employment opportunities were distributed by the state.[8] Clientelist infrastructures developed around non-Communist hegemonic parties

---

1. Geddes 1999.
2. Brownlee 2007.
3. Magaloni 2008.
4. Blaydes 2011.
5. Svolik 2012.
6. Boix and Svolik 2013.
7. Magaloni and Kricheli 2010.
8. Kornai 1992; Berend 1996; Grzymala-Busse 2002.

which have the potential to mobilize large numbers of voters.[9] Patronage relationships between regimes and their citizenries, in such a context, are often mediated by party brokers and elites.

This chapter explores both bargaining and mobilizing forms of citizen engagement for the case of Iraq's Ba'th Party. In chapter 2, I argued that material payoffs induce citizens to invest in autocratic regimes since such benefits lead them to positively assess the regime and come to believe that others may as well. Participation in the Ba'th Party provided Iraqis with a crucial avenue for access to regime-distributed benefits. Yet our understanding of empirical patterns in the distribution of these benefits is largely impressionistic.

In this chapter, I examine three measures of Ba'th Party participation which provide insight into the cross-sectional distribution of party benefits. In all three cases, the data are drawn from the mid-1990s and early 2000s. The first is official participation in the Ba'th Party, with a focus on the geographic distribution of Ba'th Party members at various levels within the party hierarchy. I find that while Ba'th Party membership varied considerably across Shi'i areas it tended, on the whole, to be lower than in Sunni-majority regions. In addition, membership in Shi'i areas tended to be skewed toward the lowest ranks of participation, suggesting smaller payoffs for the majority of Shi'a who did actively engage through party channels.

The Ba'th Party also created additional designations of distinction. For example, some individuals enjoyed "friend of the president" status with associated benefits.[10] I find that predominantly Sunni provinces in central Iraq tended to have the largest concentrations of "friend of the president" beneficiaries. Third, I analyze the distribution of the Ba'th Party "badge," which was given to a subset of individuals with long-standing service to the party. I find that party badges disproportionately went to individuals with tribal origins from areas regionally adjacent to Saddam Hussein's hometown of Tikrit.

In sum, the cross-sectional evidence on the distribution of party-based benefits during the last decade of Hussein's dictatorship suggests two key points. On the one hand, the incentives to affiliate with the Ba'th Party were sufficiently appealing to induce large swaths of the Iraqi citizenry—from

9. Magaloni 2006.
10. Technically, the designation was "friend of Mr. President Leader, Saddam Hussein," which I will shorten to "friend of the president" throughout.

across all ethno-sectarian groups—to participate in party structures. On the other hand, I show that higher-order benefits associated with the Ba'th Party disproportionately went to individuals who came from the geographic regions closest to Tikrit, as they served as the regime's loyal core.

One of the political implications associated with the uneven distribution of rewards was investment in the regime by various constituencies was also uneven. In chapter 5, I showed that sanctions differentially impacted segments of Iraq's Sunni community; Sunnis from Salah al-Din province tended to fare relatively well during the sanctions period compared to those from Anbar. How did differential provision of distributive benefits impact citizen behaviors? For individuals with a negative assessment of the regime, feeling compelled to show support for the Ba'th Party could be a source of personal anxiety and distress.

One way that dissatisfaction with the regime might be expressed was through withholding support for the Ba'th Party. The outcome variable on this subject for which I have the greatest temporal range is party identification for a particular subsection of the population—Iraqi high school students. Information was gathered about the political "orientation" of students beginning in the 1980s; in particular, students across Iraq were forced to state whether they were either Ba'thist in their orientation or political "independents." When the stakes for non-cooperation were relatively low, this indicator might be thought of as a barometer of citizen backing for the regime. For situations where the cost of non-cooperation was high or rising— in particular, for Shi'i communities after the 1991 Uprisings—the reluctance to eschew support for the Ba'th Party suggests a closing of political space for public dissent.

I find that during the 1987–88 academic year, at the height of the Iran-Iraq War, Iraqi students of a variety of ethno-sectarian backgrounds had the ability to abstain from identifying with the Ba'th Party. In that context, non-cooperation was highest in Iraqi Kurdish areas, which had been subject to the Anfal Campaign, and in the southern city of Basra, which had been particularly hard-hit in terms of war casualties. During the 1991–92 academic year, reluctance to identify as a Ba'thist was common across Iraq as the regime struggled to find its political footing in the wake of the 1991 Uprisings; indeed, many Iraqis believed that the Ba'thist regime would soon fall. Over time, however, the regime began to reconsolidate and reestablish its repressive capacity. By the 1995–96 academic year, the core districts of

Salah al-Din province, including Tikrit and al-Daur, saw large increases in Ba'thist political orientation, as did predominantly Shi'i districts in southern Iraq where increased scrutiny of Shi'i students raised the cost of expressing dissent. By the 2001–2002 academic year, the only Iraqi students who chose to avoid identifying with the Ba'th Party were from western provinces, like Anbar.

Taken together, the findings presented in this chapter speak to the conditions under which individuals identify to a greater or lesser extent with the hegemonic party in a one-party state. Cooperating with the Ba'th Party and its directives increased an individual's *intrinsic* utility as party participation provided economic benefits and opportunities.[11] Yet for some Iraqis, their overall assessment of the regime led them to wrestle with how to relate to the Ba'th Party. In particular, those with low levels of investment in the regime derived forms of *expressive* utility by withholding cooperation. This option was not available to all Iraqis at all times, however. Under highly repressive conditions, the costs of non-cooperation became so high that intrinsic utility concerns necessarily swamped the impulse for self-expression.

THE BA'THIFICATION OF IRAQ

The government under Hussein has been described as having three main pillars: the party, the military, and the bureaucracy where the party dominated the other pillars.[12] Faust argues that the "Ba'thification" of Iraqi society involved integrating Iraq's diverse population into a single Ba'thist nation while at the same time organizing the Iraqi state and society around party structures.[13] The Ba'th Party constituted a parallel government in many ways, and was the key institution through which the regime operated. Indeed, a dominant narrative in existing accounts of Iraqi politics focuses on the interweaving of the party and state machinery.[14]

---

11. Kuran (1995) describes intrinsic utility as the benefit an individual receives from taking an action. He contrasts this with expressive utility which comes from letting others know how one truly feels.

12. Sassoon 2012, 7.

13. Faust 2015, 70.

14. Hiro 1991, 20.

The Ba'th Party established cells in virtually every meaningful societal organization including government departments, professional syndicates, educational institutions, state-owned enterprises, and trade unions.[15] Success of the Ba'th Party has been attributed, to some degree, to its ability to expand and control aspects of the state, particularly the security apparatus.[16] Scholars specializing in the study of autocratic political parties have argued that important similarities exist between Iraq's Ba'th Party and Communist Party structures in Eastern European countries, like Bulgaria and the Soviet Union.[17]

Faust calls the Ba'th Party Hussein's "chief political instrument" and his "organ of meta-control."[18] Citizen experiences interacting with the party varied as a function of both their political identity and the broader political context. For some individuals, the Ba'th Party functioned as a "clearinghouse for counterinsurgency operations against rebellious populations"; for others, the primary role of the party appeared to be the monitoring of correct, and incorrect, political behavior.[19] The Ba'th Party was also instrumental in organizing the public,[20] as party activists worked to credibly signal their loyalty to the party and the president.[21]

Historical Trends in Party Development

After returning to power in July 1968, the Ba'th Party pursued a public strategy of downplaying the importance of preexisting social ties—like tribal, regional, and religious affinities—while, in private, relying on personal, tribal, and regional ties for the distribution of power and resources. An early party communique declared that the party was against sectarianism, racism, and

15. Ibid., 21.
16. Dimitrov and Sassoon 2014. See also Sassoon who describes the relationship between the party and the security agencies as one of "symbiosis" where information was shared by security agencies with the party (2012, 98).
17. Dimitrov and Sassoon 2014. The Ba'th Party in Iraq has been described as a "mono-organizational system" much like that which existed in the Soviet Union (Dimitrov and Sassoon 2014, 11). Soviet influence extended to a variety of areas beyond party structures—even the political artwork that appears on postage stamps demonstrated a Soviet influence (Reid 1993).
18. Faust 2015.
19. Khoury 2013, 7.
20. Ibid.
21. BRCC Doc. No. 008-4-6-45 to 46, December 6, 1997.

tribalism, which were all remnants of colonial rule.[22] During the late 1960s and early 1970s, anti-imperialist rhetoric was commonly expressed through Ba'th Party channels.[23] In 1976, its legislation criminalized the use of tribal names or names that would indicate family origin; Saddam Hussein al-Tikriti, for example, became Saddam Hussein. Cynical observers have suggested that the reason for this was to obscure the fact that so many Tikritis—Hussein's tribal and regional relations—were in government.

During the 1970s, the Ba'th Party grew its base considerably. The party sought to broaden support by working to indoctrinate large segments of the population, regardless of ethnicity, religious identification, or social class.[24] The oil-fueled growth of the state reinforced the strength of the party through expansion of the public sector. State employment increasingly became a lever that the regime could use to compel participation in the party. Al-Ali writes that "at some point, in the late 1970s, it became clear that certain career paths and professions were only available to people who had officially affirmed their loyalty to the party."[25] In particular, teachers and school principals were pressured to join the party. Students were also harassed to join the party, particularly if they were seen as influential within their social circle.[26] The net result was that between 1973 and 1979, the regime gained support among large segments of the population including Sunni Arabs, Chaldean Christians, and educated, secular Iraqi Shi'a.[27]

During the 1970s, upper-level party members were able to express opinions contrary to those of Saddam Hussein, but this became increasingly difficult over time.[28] In many cases, those individuals who held the strongest commitments to Ba'thist ideology and Arab socialism found themselves most at odds with the regime.[29] Suspicious car accidents among top Ba'th Party dissenters became common.[30] For ordinary citizens seeking economic or other opportunities in the growing public sector, it became increasingly costly to

22. Baram 1997, 1.
23. Davis 2005, 153–154.
24. Al-Ali 2007, 120.
25. Ibid.
26. Al-Ali 2007, 115.
27. Davis 2005, 149.
28. Ibid., 180.
29. Bashir 2005, 152.
30. Ibid., 153.

avoid the party. According to Al-Ali, "simply refusing to join the Baʿth Party became a political act in and of itself."[31]

Upon formal ascension to the presidency in 1979, Hussein sought to eliminate opposition to his rule from within the Baʿth Party.[32] To an even greater extent than before, Sunni Muslims from Tikrit came to control many of the most sensitive positions within the state apparatus, including the army, party, and cabinet.[33] Davis describes this as the point at which extended family rule in Iraq consolidated around Hussein's half-brothers, cousins, and others with kin ties.[34] Not surprisingly, during this period, party connections trumped expertise and experience as a criterion for advancement in a variety of domains. Baʿth Party members with fake doctoral degrees moved into high-ranking positions, for example.[35] The government also dismissed forty of Iraq's most prominent medical specialists to make room for party loyalists to be promoted.[36]

Party Development during and after the Iran-Iraq War

The Baʿth Party was crucial for managing the costs associated with Iraq's war with Iran.[37] In particular, "the party helped normalize the war in ways that would have been difficult to imagine had Iraq not been a one-party state."[38] During the same period, relatively less-educated Iraqis were recruited into the Baʿth Party, often finding work in state security. Baram argues that for these modest "country boys," the promise of economic security and privilege associated with their new party and employment opportunities led them to be loyal to the regime and Hussein.[39]

The party's relatively tepid response in the face of the 1991 Uprisings was disappointing for Hussein, however.[40] The party, which had been tasked

31. Al-Ali 2007, 119.
32. Davis 2005, 153–154.
33. Zeidel 2008, 89.
34. Davis 2005, 176.
35. Bashir 2005, 270.
36. Ibid., 275.
37. Khoury 2013, 49.
38. Ibid., 72.
39. Baram 2005, 7.
40. Graham-Brown 1999, 196.

with collecting information about unpatriotic elements,[41] not only failed to anticipate the protests, but party apparatchik appeared powerless in the face of the riots. Unsurprisingly, Ba'th Party membership in 1992 was down 40 percent compared to 1990, with the largest declines in Shi'i cities like Basra, Nasiriyya, Hilla, Najaf, and Karbala.[42] At the same time, the political alternatives to Ba'thism narrowed over time for Iraqis. Individuals paid a heavy price for advocacy of religious ideology and suspected involvement with the Da'wa Party, for example.

The Ba'th Party was weakened but continued to serve as an instrument for controlling dissent. In one meeting between Hussein and Revolutionary Command Council members, Izzat Ibrahim al-Duri discussed both the successes and failures of the Ba'th Party, particularly in southern areas.[43] In this meeting, Hussein suggested that the Ba'th Party needed more dedicated members who would be able to successfully cultivate social control.[44] There was an increasing consolidation of political power around those societal groups deemed most trustworthy. For example, just before the Gulf War, about 28 percent of the party's regional leadership were Tikritis. By the end of 1991, however, Tikritis and Duris made up 47 percent of regional leadership.[45]

YOUTH PARTY IDENTIFICATION

Youth mobilization in the service of the Ba'th Party was a long-standing priority for the Iraqi regime. In the 1970s, schools were seen as the key location for Ba'thist indoctrination. Teachers were investigated by the party to determine their compatibility with party doctrine, and school trips, even to sporting events or museums, were carefully monitored.[46] Schoolchildren were made to participate in morning rituals of saluting their teacher and a picture of Saddam Hussein as well as reciting Hussein's speeches and singing patriotic songs.[47]

41. Khoury 2013, 131.
42. Rohde 2010.
43. CRRC Doc. No. SH-SHTP-A-001-461, December 21, 1991.
44. Ibid.
45. Baram 2003, 105.
46. North Iraq Dataset Doc. No. 05007-103-92; North Iraq Dataset Doc. No. 05007-103.
47. Al-Ali 2007, 120.

Over time, the Ba'th Party continued to take a leading role in management of youth affairs. In conversations with his political advisors, Hussein conceded that the "youth issue" was both sensitive and difficult.[48] For these reasons, Hussein argued that youth affairs must be handled using Ba'thist methods. Promising young Iraqis were offered special classes in party ideology and the party was keen to cultivate young members.[49] According to Sassoon, the party sought to recruit students at an early age, even when they were in high school.[50]

School Registers

One aspect of this mobilization process involved the collection of an annual inventory of students (al-jard al-tullab al-sanawi), described in the Iraq Memory Foundation documents as the School Registers collection. The School Registers collection represents the official party records for each upper school student in Iraq.[51] Sassoon writes, "one main purpose of the School Register... was the potential recruitment of these students."[52] The desire to mobilize and recruit went hand-in-hand with the need to control and coerce. Schools were an important place of observation for the regime where teachers and students were being constantly monitored.[53] As a result, the School Registers include information about students and their families beyond name and address, also including data on political orientation, family reputation, and other information with political significance.

Information about how the School Registers were collected as well as the various uses for the Registers by the regime can be gleaned through a reading of associated memoranda. The Registers were collected for every academic year beginning in the mid-1980s and continuing until the overthrow of the regime. The content of the Registers changed in important ways following the 1991 Uprisings. While previously, information was only collected about

48. CRRC Doc. No. SH-SHTP-A-000-625, 1993.
49. Sassoon 2016, 44.
50. Sassoon 2012, 54.
51. This is an annual accounting of the nationwide student population by the party with a focus on boys from ages 12 to 18. The entire School Registers collection consists of 162,628 pages (1,036 volumes) for years 1983–2002.
52. Sassoon 2012, 55.
53. Ibid., 116.

the political orientation of the student and the reputation of his family (along with name, address, and other basics), the expanded format asked a series of additional questions.

One document details instructions for collection of the student inventory for the 2000–2001 academic year. The officer charged with collecting the data was to do his job undercover and to perform his duties secretly. The name of each student and school was to be documented and address confirmed. The information was to be indexed and then signed and stamped by the appropriate administrators.[54] Other documents describe the process by which the party comrade charged with ensuring that the Registers were finished and collected would receive a car (most often a Mitsubishi) and driver to travel to various schools.[55] Specific instructions were sent to party branch leaders about how to compile the information in the Registers, for example the need for each school to be put into its own file and to be signed by party officials.[56] Party officials required that information be carefully checked every year.[57] Meetings were held to assist party cadre in avoiding mistakes made in previous years.[58] Because information in the Registers reflected the child and family's security status, cooperation across various governmental units including the security services, party, and police was required.[59]

Party memoranda frequently stress the importance of receiving the information provided in the Registers in a timely manner.[60] A pressing concern was to provide information to the armed forces as well as military and police academies as they began screening individuals for government service suitability.[61] Determining the good standing of young men who might receive training and scholarships from the regime appears to have been a very important matter and the regime went to great lengths to ensure that no one with a politically

54. See BRCC Doc. Nos. 01-3025-0001-0098, 01-3025-0001-0099 and 01-3025-0001-0100.

55. BRCC Doc. No. 01-3025-0001-0104, February 26, 2001; BRCC Doc. No. 01-3025-0001-0039, August 10, 2001.

56. BRCC Doc. No. 01-2971-0001-0001.

57. BRCC Doc. No. 01-2496-0003-0200.

58. BRCC Doc. No. 01-3025-0001-0008, April 13, 2002.

59. BRCC Doc. No. 01-2496-0003-0037, 1996.

60. BRCC Doc. No. 01-3025-0001-0091, March 2001.

61. BRCC Doc. No. 01-3025-0001-0097, January 10, 2001.

questionable background might accidently be incorporated into the regime's security apparatus.[62]

To gain acceptance to a broad range of public educational opportunities, particularly those supported by Ministry of Defense funding, students had to pass a strict background investigation. Sassoon writes that in the 1970s and early 1980s, the military colleges sometimes accepted applicants who were political independents but deemed ripe for party indoctrination.[63] By the late 1980s, however, it appears that Baʿthists were strongly preferred.[64] Candidates for acceptance to such programs had to receive clearance from both the security apparatus and the local party branch, which provided additional details about the applicant and his family.[65]

A student registered by the regime as a political independent could be rejected from educational opportunities despite the student's merit as an applicant.[66] In one memorandum describing the 1993 selection process for Military Medical College students, instructions were given to automatically accept qualified Baʿthist students who had the "friend of the president" designation, whose father had such a designation, or who were the brothers of war martyrs. Secondary consideration was then given to 271 Baʿthist students for whom security and party information had been collected and were deemed otherwise acceptable but not exemplary. The remaining student applicants were thought to have unencouraging files and were rejected.[67] In another case, a student inquired as to why he had not been accepted for an educational opportunity; internal reports suggested he was refused for having an independent political orientation (i.e., non-Baʿthist).[68]

Student information in the School Registers took the following form: one row was recorded for each student, including his address and parents' names.

62. BRCC Doc. No. 01-3025-0001-0030, March 12, 2002.

63. Sassoon 2012, 135.

64. Ibid.

65. Ibid., 134. The Baʿth Party Regional Command files include dozens of letters and memoranda related to student applicant status at one of more than a dozen Ministry of Defense funded institutions of higher education. Students could be denied admission for any number of reasons, despite having high-level ties to the Baʿth Party—failing to submit graduation records on time, scoring low on the psychological portion of the interview, or even being unable to pronounce the letter *rāʾ* (i.e., having a lisp) (BRCC Doc. No. 01-3847-0003-0100, 1993).

66. BRCC Doc. No. 01-3847-0003-0100, 1993.

67. BRCC Doc. Nos. 01-3847-0003-0101 and 0102.

68. BRCC Doc. Nos. 3847-0199-0041 to 52, 1994.

The name of the school appeared at the top of each sheet of students. The basic format for the Registers consisted of the following ten questions and a narrow comments section:

1. Political orientation
2. Reputation of the student and his family
3. Nationality (i.e., Arab, Kurd, Turkman)
4. His and his family's position on the "Mother of All Battles"
5. His and his family's position in terms of treachery and treason
6. Does he have close ties to someone sentenced for hostility to the party or the revolution
7. Is he or his father among the "close friends" of the leader (God protect him)
8. Was a close relative (brother or father) martyred in either "Saddam's Qadisiyya" or the "Mother of All Battles"
9. Has he in the past or will he volunteer for Saddam's Fedayeen and, if so, what is his rotation number
10. Did he participate in the "Day of Pride" national training exercises

Political orientation in this context identified students as being either Baʿthists or politically independent (*mustaqill*). While the vast majority of students are identified in the Registers as Baʿthists, there do exist students who are identified as independent and the percentage of politically independent students varies over time and space. The vast majority of students have a "good" reputation in the School Registers. Nationality (*qawmiyya*) does not refer to Iraqi nationality, but rather whether the student is an Arab, Kurd or, much less frequently, Turkman or other group member. Sectarian identification in terms of the Sunni-Shiʿi designation does not appear at any point in official documentation.

For the fourth item, the "Mother of All Battles" refers to the student and his family's position on the Gulf War. There is very little variation on this measure. The fifth item describing treachery and treason (*ghadr wa khiyana*) is a reference to participation in the 1991 Uprisings.[69] Again, there is little variation on this outcome for the 2001–2002 academic year (as most individuals from treasonous backgrounds may have already been purged from

---

69. Regime reports often refer to the 1991 Uprisings as the "page of treason and treachery."

the school system). The next item refers to individuals with hostility to the Ba'th Party or the Ba'thist Revolution.

The seventh item refers to a student or his father's designation as a close friend of the leader, referred to by Sassoon as a "friend of the president." This was an official designation that emerged after the Gulf War that afforded "friend of the president" cardholders special privileges. These privileges included additional "points" added to his children's school applications, the honor of meeting the president once a year, special grants and holiday bonuses, priority over others Iraqis in meeting with government officials, and an annual gift of two summer suits and two winter suits, among other things.[70]

One main way that someone might receive a "friend of the president" card was if they had an immediate family member killed in either the "Mother of all Battles" or "Saddam's Qadisiyya"—information about casualties in the family were recorded as the eighth item on the list. "Saddam's Qadisiyya" was the regime's name for the Iran-Iraq War, referencing the 636 CE Arab Muslim defeat of the Sassanid Persian army. After the Gulf War, individuals who died in the Iran-Iraq War or the Gulf War were often posthumously awarded the "friend of the president" designation.[71]

The ninth question relates to whether the student volunteered to participate in Hussein's personal militia unit, "Saddam's Fedayeen" (*Fida'iyyu Saddam*).[72] Sassoon describes this group as a militia established after the disappointing performance of local Ba'th Party and army units in the wake of the 1991 Uprisings.[73] Results associated with question nine will be presented in chapter 10.

The final question that appears in the Registers relates to student participation in "Day of Pride" (*Yawm al-Nakhwa*) national training exercises sponsored by the Ba'th Party. Following the 1991 Uprisings, Saddam Hussein designated a day dedicated for national military training.[74] Students were expected to participate in these training activities and could suffer consequences

70. Sassoon 2012, 209.

71. Ibid., 157. See also Khoury (2013, 171) who writes that a December 24, 1993 RCC resolution declared the families of martyred soldiers would receive "friend of the president" status. For the purposes of this book, because of the close link between war deaths and "friend of the president" designation, I will use war martyrs as a covariate rather than as a dependent variable in this chapter.

72. Fedayeen are those who are willing to sacrifice, or martyr, themselves.

73. Sassoon 2012, 150.

74. Sassoon 2012, 148.

if they did not do so. According to one memorandum from 1998, students seeking acceptance to Iraqi military academies needed to provide a certificate of completion for the national training exercises.[75] Indeed, acceptance to these schools could be canceled if they could not prove their participation.[76] Participation rates across Iraq were very high.

Although the Baʿthists did not survey each school,[77] the School Registers represent the closest information akin to a census of political opinion and behavior across Iraq. The data that I have collected focus on sixth year secondary students, roughly equivalent to high school seniors. While summary statistics associated with question eight, on war martyrs, have already been presented in chapter 4, findings associated with two of the other questions— political orientation and "friend of the president" status —will be presented in this chapter. For questions two, four, five, six, and ten it is relatively rare to find students in the collection with a negative assessment.

Independent Political Orientation

Chapter 2 sets out a number of empirical expectations that might be evaluated using data on a student's willingness to state that he has a Baʿthist political orientation. I argue that investment in the regime depends on current and future reward streams, as well as expectations about the investment of others in the regime.

In addition, the decision to join the Baʿth Party could engender forms of psychological discomfort for individuals. While some students had personal or familial experience with the effects of regime repression, others felt as though their ethnic group, religious order, or tribe had been mistreated by the regime. Consequently, individual behavior was a function of both the repressive environment and one's investment in the regime. For individuals from groups outside of the regime coalition, any suggestion of disloyalty might bring scrutiny, reducing the incentive to express one's true feelings toward the Baʿth Party.

Figure 7.1 displays four maps of Iraq. The panel in the upper-left shows the distribution of politically independent students for the 1987–1988 academic

75. BRCC Doc. No. 01-2496-0003-0001, 1998.
76. BRCC Doc. No. 01-2496-0003-0003.
77. Khoury 2013, 45.

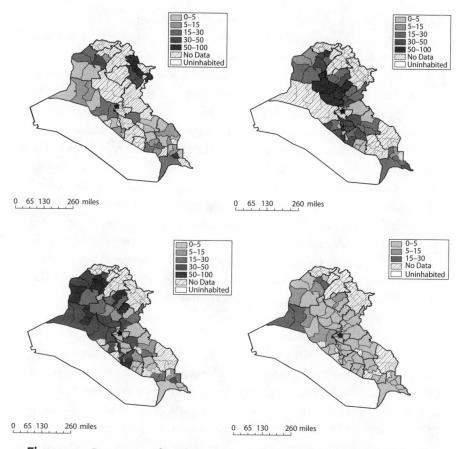

Figure 7.1. Percentage of students with an "independent" political orientation for academic years 1987–1988 (upper-left); 1991–1992 (upper-right); 1995–1996 (lower-left); 2001–2002 (lower-right).

year—the last year of the Iran-Iraq War. While data were either not collected or not available for Tikrit and adjacent districts, it is apparent that areas of northern districts around Sulaymaniyya and Mosul had large numbers of politically independent students, as did Basra. The relatively large numbers of politically independent students in Basra is not surprising given the concentration of Iran-Iraq War casualties there. Low levels of Ba῾th Party political identification in Iraqi Kurdistan is also unsurprising given the events associated with the Anfal. Across majority Sunni areas, there was variation in the percentage of politically independent students where Fallujah and

Ramadi appear to have witnessed larger numbers of students who eschewed Ba'th Party identification. During this period, to self-identify as a political independent was a choice available to individuals.

The 1991–1992 academic year represented a low point for the Ba'thist regime. Reeling from the loss of the Gulf War and the shock of the 1991 Uprisings, the regime faced a series of crises that, at the time, seemed insurmountable. Iraqis from a variety of backgrounds, including Sunnis from Saddam Hussein's home region, came to believe that public opposition to the regime was intense and that the United States would be able to enact regime change, should it desire to do so. In other words, investment in the regime was particularly low and Iraqis increasingly held the belief that their fellow Iraqis felt the same way. The upper-right quadrant provides information for the 1991–1992 academic year. Notice that data do not exist for many of the far northern districts. These areas were already autonomous in the wake of the 1991 Uprisings. The regime was highly vulnerable to overthrow at this point and levels of grievance were high. It may have also been unclear at this point in time if the regime had the capacity to crack down on political independents.

By 1995, the internal security situation had stabilized to a degree. The lower-left quadrant presents the percentage of politically independent students in the 1995–1996 academic year. This represented the worst period of the economic sanctions era, as the sanctions had been in effect for five years and the Oil-for-Food program had not yet been implemented. The Ba'th Party was reportedly so unpopular at this point that the regime had to pay officials to attend public ceremonies.[78] It is important to note, however, that even though Sunni areas show relatively large numbers of students who are identifying as non-Ba'thists, these figures were improving from the perspective of the regime in places like Tikrit and adjacent al-Daur. In addition, students in the predominantly Shi'i regions were increasingly identifying as having a Ba'thist political orientation, suggesting greater compliance with regime expectations.

By 2001–2002 (lower-right quadrant), we observe that the primarily Shi'i districts of the south have extremely low percentages of political independents. These results are consistent with scholars who argue that it was not until the late 1990s that the Ba'th Party was in a resurgent position again.[79]

78. Faust 2015, 5.
79. Rohde 2010.

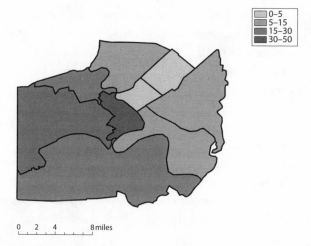

Figure 7.2. Percentage of Baghdad students with an "independent" political orientation for academic year 2001–2002.

Tikrit and some of its neighboring districts also observe very low numbers of students with an independent political orientation. Areas of Anbar governorate, including the districts of Qa'im, Ana, Fallujah, and Ramadi, maintained some political independents. Mosul and two surrounding districts in the Iraqi North also saw relatively large numbers of political independents. As an Iraqi Sunni, one way a person might show discontent was to avoid joining the Ba'th Party.[80] This option was too costly for some, however.

Figure 7.2 provides information about the percentage of students with an independent political orientation from across neighborhoods of Baghdad during the 2001–2002 academic year. The predominantly Shi'i neighborhood of Saddam City had among the lowest percentage of politically independent students. In contrast, the primarily Sunni Karkh neighborhood of central Baghdad had the highest percentage of politically independent high school students. Consistent with the cross-sectional, national variation in political orientation, non-cooperation was more possible for Sunnis than for Shi'a in the 2001–2002 academic year. This is despite the fact that support for the Ba'th Party among Shi'i students was almost certainly low for this period.

The behaviors summarized in the maps suggest that the Shi'a transition from first, an oppressed minority group where non-compliance was a costly,

80. Zeidel 2010, 164.

but not necessarily devastating act, to widespread (but not universal) resistance, finally to totalitarian conditions where severe punishment became the norm for even relatively small acts of non-compliance with the autocratic regime. One observable implication of this narrative would be that over time, levels of public non-compliance should decrease in Shiʿi areas of southern Iraq, replaced by more private acts of resistance. For Sunni Iraqis from the Tikrit region, preference for independent political status was high for 1991–1992 but low for other periods. This suggests that support for the Baʿth Party—even in areas of core loyalist support—was conditional. But Sunnis from other parts of Iraq—like Anbar—were much less likely to say that they were Baʿthists, even into the late period. This regularity is repeated when examining variation within Baghdad during the 2001–2002 academic year.

BAʿTH PARTY MEMBERSHIP AND MOBILIZATION

While much has been written about how Iraq's culture of fear induced political compliance,[81] relatively less emphasis has been placed on the material inducements associated with the party. Financial incentives for party participation are widely discussed in the literature on authoritarian political mobilization. Schnytzer and Sustersic consider the role rent distribution plays in party popularity.[82] Svolik suggests that dictatorial parties can extract considerable effort from citizens at relatively little cost since individuals view investment in party structures as an avenue for upward mobility.[83] In the Iraqi context, Sassoon enumerates the reward schemes and incentives offered to party members.[84] Dimitrov and Sassoon emphasize the importance of material interests in inducing compliance.[85]

This section elaborates on the incentives for joining the Baʿth Party before discussing some of the explicit mobilizational tools of the party. I also discuss membership trends using cross-sectional data with a particular focus on participation rates across various Iraqi governorates, as well as the relative rank of Baʿth Party participants.

81. Makiya 1988.
82. Schnytzer and Sustersic 1998.
83. Svolik 2012.
84. Sassoon 2012.
85. Dimitrov and Sassoon 2014, 11.

Benefits and Costs of Party Membership

Party membership was not mandated by law. As a result, Iraqis typically joined the party either because of their commitment to the ideology or for the perquisites.[86] Faust writes, for example, that while Iraqis affiliated with the party for a variety of reasons, it was particularly important that the party "controlled access to academic, professional, economic, and social opportunity."[87]

Some scholars have estimated that up to two-thirds of Ba'th Party members were government employees.[88] Prospective party members had to fill out extensive background questionnaires to confirm suitability; indeed, the Iraq Memory Foundation collection contains thousands of Ba'th Party membership applications. Employees of the state sector—like teachers and bureaucrats—were almost universally Ba'th Party members as the regime had strong incentives to ensure that young Iraqis were influenced by party stalwarts. And, all else equal, party membership helped people obtain promotions.[89] But joining the Ba'th Party was not a mere formality as it implied a long-term commitment. Party members were subjected to considerable training just to participate in it.[90]

In addition, privileges were taken away from individuals removed from the party. For example, one informant reported that he was a member of the Ba'th Party until he missed too many meetings and was forced out.[91] A variety of other circumstances could lead one to be removed from the party, including disloyalty to the Ba'th Party or the Ba'thist Revolution; evasion of compulsory military service (or irregular discharge from the military); failure to follow party directives; evasion of party responsibilities (like regular attendance at meetings); and attempts to seek political asylum outside of Iraq, including in Iran.[92] Ethical breaches could also justify discharge from the party, including providing false information on forms; providing incomplete information regarding the arrest or military service record of one's brother or nephew; and sexual harassment, including entering another's home with the

86. Sassoon 2012, 53.
87. Faust 2015, 171.
88. Heine 1993, 39–40.
89. Ibid.
90. Ibid.
91. Testimony of N. Hassan, recorded April 2007.
92. BRCC Doc. Nos. 01-3388-0001-0156 and 0157, July 26, 1983.

goal of peeping on his daughter. Finally, one could be dismissed from the party for attendance at the funeral of someone who opposed the government or for shooting at a fellow Ba'thist.[93]

One benefit of party membership that was widely sought by better-educated families was the five-point bonus on high school college admissions exams. Given the competitive nature of admissions to the most desirable faculties, like medicine or engineering, non-Ba'thist families were functionally excluded from admission.[94] Party membership offered individuals the power to intimidate others in society, including neighbors, colleagues, and teachers, should they have a lower party status.[95] Promotion in the party also conferred direct monetary transfers and in-kind payments, like vehicles, in exchange for participating in repressive operations and other party activities.[96]

While participating in the party conferred important benefits, complicity was not costless. Participation in party repression could foster contempt and hatred.[97] Reports from a 1995 file from the southern governorates of Basra and Dhi Qar provide some insight into the risks associated with party connections.[98] In one case, a group of "agents" burned down the *mudif*, or traditional communal house, of a shaykh who was reported to be a supporter of the party.[99] In another case, the house of a local shaykh who was a friend of the party was attacked; the sons and cousins of the shaykh fired back on the attackers.[100]

Examples of attacks on party facilities were also common in southern areas. One memorandum documents arrests associated with an anti-regime attack.[101] Agents had planned an attack against a local party headquarters, but a guard they had approached about helping them turned them in to the police. The agents had a gun, grenade, and a semi-automatic weapon. The guards responsible for raids on insurgents were praised in party memos, sometimes receiving awards or bonuses for their activities.[102] These types of incidents

93. Ibid.
94. David Baran, "Iraq: The Party in Power," *Le Monde Diplomatique* (English edition), December 2002.
95. Ibid.
96. Ibid.
97. Ibid.
98. BRCC Doc. No. 01-3874-0004-0017, 1995.
99. Ibid.
100. BRCC Doc. No. 01-3874-0004-0028, 1995.
101. BRCC Doc. No. 01-3237-0000-0061, 1993.
102. Ibid.

appear to have been quite common in the South, and a number of similar events can be identified in the collection.[103]

Breaking with the party could be costly, however. In one case, a party supporter was sentenced to seven years in prison for criticizing Hussein and an additional three years for covering up the activities of another individual.[104]

Party Recruitment and Mobilization

During the 1980s, the regime used the Ba'th Party to routinize war for the Iraqi population on what Khoury calls the "internal front."[105] Between 1985 and 1989, Ba'th Party offices extended to all parts of the country, including areas believed to be less supportive of state authority.[106] Within neighborhoods, direct and indirect pressures might be deployed to recruit new members. Monetary inducement and opportunities for advancement through the party ranks encouraged some individuals to join. In other cases, member recruitment relied on implicit threats to induce participation.[107] Within the Ba'th Party, individuals could move up the ranks from sympathizer to supporter, advanced supporter, apprentice member, active member, division member, section member, branch member, and secretary general.[108] To become even a sympathizer, one would need to reveal all past political affiliations (a failure to do so could result in one's execution); joining another political party after being a Ba'thist meant a seven-year prison sentence.[109] It could take years of training and service to reach the level of a prospective member.

Party cells and study circles held meetings for small groups of party participants to discuss recent events and party ideology; at these meetings, instructions might be issued and unusual activities documented in written reports.[110] Ba'th Party mobilizational efforts could also be deployed at critical political moments. A series of memoranda describes the public mobilization

103. BRCC Doc. Nos. 01-3874-0004-0106 and 01-3874-0004-0171.
104. BRCC Doc. No. 01-2117-0003-0399, April 7, 1986.
105. Khoury 2013, 48.
106. Ibid., 51.
107. David Baran, "Iraq: The Party in Power," *Le Monde Diplomatique* (English edition), December 2002.
108. Sassoon 2012, 46.
109. Ibid., 73.
110. Ibid.

TABLE 7.1. Mobilization activities c. January 1991, by region.

Location	# of Office Branches	Mobilizing Marches	Security Sessions (# Participants)	Party Sessions	Public Sessions
Baghdad	6	165	70 (19,021)	1,423	3,305
South	5	158	205 (24,698)	2,546	3,257
Euphrates	5	179	158 (14,274)	3,349	3,387
Central	3	79	151 (18,809)	4,527	3,985
North	6	229	179 (27,339)	10,273	6,602

(i.e., *ta'bi'a*) activities for the period before January 1991.[111] These events included mobilizing marches, party meetings, and special sessions focused on internal security. To get a sense of the scope of mobilizational activities in that period, table 7.1 reports details on the number of marches and meetings, as well as the number of participants at the security sessions. In addition to hundreds of mobilizing marches, thousands of public sessions were held to reach out to the Iraqi citizenry on behalf of the party and regime.

Table 7.2 provides information about the geographic distribution of party membership, across ranks. The columns provide information on the number of active members, apprentice members, supporters, and sympathizers as well as a population estimate for each governorate. The final column of table 7.2 provides the percentage of active members to supporters, a summary statistic which indicates the relative proportion of high-ranking party participants to low-ranking party participants, by governorate. Governorates in the Iraqi South, like Basra and Dhi Qar, are very low on this indicator, suggesting that although these areas have large numbers of supporters, very few individuals are willing or able to reach the higher echelons of the party apparatus. Salah al-Din, on the other hand, has a very large number of active members relative to supporters, as do Anbar and Diyala, the other governorates of the "central" administrative area of Iraq.

These observations are consistent with findings of scholars seeking to understand regional and sectarian representation in the leadership structure of the Baʿth Party. Baram writes, for example:

In the lower echelons, the number and percentage of Shiʿi party activists increases significantly, whereas Tikritis and other Sunni-Arab activists are

111. BRCC Doc. No. 024-5-2-0017 to 0123, February 13, 1991.

TABLE 7.2. Ba'th Party participation, by rank, across governorates, governorate population estimates, active members as a percentage of population and the proportion of active members to sympathizers, 2002.

Governorate	Active Members	Apprentice Members	Supporters	Sympathizers	Population (Est. 2007)	Members per 1,000	Members to Sympathizers
Baghdad	43,203	36,096	192,504	540,961	6,386,100	6.8	8:100
South							
Basra	12,016	12,463	196,117	290,409	1,761,000	6.8	4:100
Dhi Qar	14,098	11,072	136,077	166,258	1,427,200	9.9	8:100
Maysan	3,781	3,630	23,067	64,809	743,400	5.1	6:100
Wasit	9,957	6,462	48,895	113,624	941,800	10.6	9:100
Euphrates							
Muthanna	3,351	4,370	30,964	117,258	536,300	6.2	3:100
Najaf & Qadisiyya	7,073	12,543	56,723	116,938	1,813,000	3.9	6:100
Karbala	3,238	4,806	22,915	60,392	756,000	4.3	5:100
Babil	6,498	16,163	36,578	111,993	1,444,400	4.5	6:100
Central							
Anbar	14,474	8,315	45,872	80,096	1,280,000	11.3	18:100
Salah al-Din	19,090	23,383	50,436	73,617	1,077,800	17.7	26:100
Diyala	8,721	17,600	57,352	144,035	1,373,900	6.3	6:100
North							
Ninawa	17,798	16,690	71,014	125,113	2,473,700	7.2	14:100
Ta'mim (Kirkuk)	9,581	9,068	44,667	126,356	839,100	11.4	8:100

relatively few. By allowing Shi'i members to dominate the lower and middle levels of the party, where contact with the public is most extensive, it seems that the regime hopes to give the Shi'i majority a sense of participation and presence in running the party, while at the same time ensuring that the key positions of upper levels are dominated by Tikritis, Duris and other Sunnis.[112]

Davis argues that for Iraqi Shi'a, the only escape from allegations of ill-intent toward the regime was "to become more Ba'thist than the Ba'thists to prove their loyalty to Iraq."[113] And although many Shi'a were highly opposed to Hussein's regime, "pragmatism" prompted individuals to join the party "even though they would gladly burn down the party offices given a chance."[114]

"FRIEND OF THE PRESIDENT" STATUS

Hegemonic parties not only create multiple levels of commitment within a status hierarchy, but can also construct special designations that cut across party ranks and even extend to non-party members. In the Iraqi context, the "friend of the president" status served as a broad-based benefits designator. Although the benefits of "friend of the president" status were relatively modest, they could be meaningful particularly during the austerity of the sanctions period. In this section, I discuss regional variation in "friend of the president" status. I also investigate the relationship between "friend of the president" status and individual-level willingness to state an independent political identification.

Regional Variation in "Friend of the President" Status

According to Khoury, the "friend of the president" status "brought soldiers, clan leaders, martyrs, Ba'thists, and bureaucrats together under a category

---

112. Baram 2003, 105.
113. Davis 2005, 188.
114. David Baran, "Iraq: The Party in Power," *Le Monde Diplomatique* (English edition), December 2002.

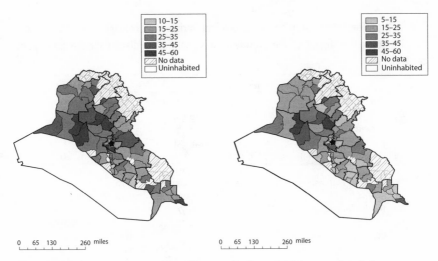

Figure 7.3. Left, percentage of students with "friend of the president" designation, 2001–2002; right, percentage with with "friend of the president" designation after controlling for war death in the family, 2001–2002.

of people who received periodic increases in entitlements."[115] According to Khoury's estimates, by 1998 this status covered about a fifth of the population. One of the conjectures common in the qualitative literature is that Sunnis from Tikrit received important benefits and privileges as a result of the regime's dependence on clan and family members to staff key positions in the bureaucracy and security apparatus. To what extent were those benefits enjoyed by the citizenry more broadly?

Figure 7.3 shows the percentage of Iraqi high school seniors or their fathers who were designated "friend of the president." Because a relatively large number of individuals and their families received that designation for having a war martyr in the family, I also map the percentage with a "friend of the president" designation after netting out the percentage of war martyrs. Lighter areas represent a smaller percentage with "friend of the president" designation, while darker areas represent a larger percentage with that designation. Southern, Shiʿi areas of the country see smaller percentages of the population with the "friend of the president" designation; those percentages become even lower after taking into account families with war martyrs. The Sunni areas of the country tend to have relatively high percentages of individuals with that

115. Khoury 2013, 150.

TABLE 7.3. Coefficient estimates for dependent variable, percentage of students whose families enjoy the "friend of the president" designation, by district for the 2001–2002 academic year.

	Model 7.1	Model 7.2	Model 7.3	Model 7.4
Percent Sunni	23.56	24.50	21.69	21.88
	(6.89)	(6.88)	(6.92)	(6.87)
Percent Kurdish	4.58	2.38	3.10	0.97
	(4.25)	(4.45)	(4.31)	(4.41)
Distance to Tikrit	0.001	0.004	−0.002	−0.000
	(0.011)	(0.011)	(0.011)	(0.010)
% Sunni*Distance to Tikrit	−0.074	−0.071	−0.070	−0.067
	(0.034)	(0.035)	(0.034)	(0.034)
Wealth Index		0.57		1.13
		(0.93)		(0.95)
Population Density			−0.003	−0.004
			(0.002)	(0.002)
Constant	15.61	10.62	17.84	9.27
	(4.27)	(8.00)	(4.55)	(7.86)
Observations	67	64	67	64
R^2	0.31	0.35	0.34	0.39

designation, with Tikrit and its neighboring district appearing at the highest levels, indicating a geographic concentration of privileged status.

Table 7.3 reports the coefficients associated with four models where the dependent variable analyzed is the percentage of a district with the "friend of the president" designation after subtracting the percentage of war martyrs for that area.[116] I consider the impact of an area's sectarian identity, its distance from Tikrit, the interaction between Tikrit and percentage Sunni, population density, as well as a covariate for wealth.[117] While the coefficient on the variable measuring wealth is positive in each of the two specifications where it is included, it is not statistically significant in either. Population density appears to be negatively associated with "friend of the president" designation.

For Sunnis living in Tikrit, the predicted probability for "friend of the president" designation is 38 percent, assuming mean levels of wealth and population density. For Sunnis living 200 miles from Tikrit, the prediction

116. I do this because having had a brother or father killed in one of the major wars was one route to receiving the designation yet not a channel that would reflect special privilege.

117. I include the variable for wealth in order to guard against the possibility of reverse causation (i.e., wealthy individuals are purchasing "friend of the president" status).

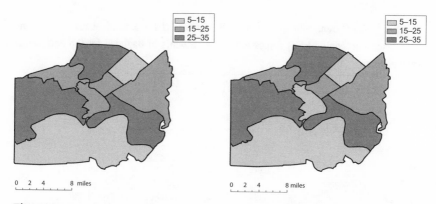

Figure 7.4. Left, percentage of Baghdad students with "friend of the president" designation, 2001–2002; right, percentage with with "friend of the president" designation after controlling for war death in the family, 2001–2002.

is only 25 percent. For Shi'i areas, the predicted probability is 17 percent. Kurdish districts have a predicted probability of 18 percent. Again, the Kurdish figure only reflects those Kurdish areas that remained governed by Iraq in the 2001–2002 academic year. As expected, Sunni areas in and around Tikrit had very high percentages of individuals with the "friend of the president" designation, even after controlling for wealth and population density. Sunni areas at some distance from Tikrit were, on average, more than 10 percentage points lower. Shi'i areas saw the lowest percentage of individuals with this designation.

Figure 7.4 maps the geographic variation in "friend of the president" status across Baghdad. Overall levels of "friend of the president" status tended to be lower in Baghdad than Sunni-majority areas of central Iraq. Within Baghdad, the area with the lowest percentage of "friend of the president" status was found in the Shi'i-predominant Saddam City neighborhood. The southern parts of the city—which are also Shi'i-majority—also tended to have low percentages of "friend of the president" status.

Within the sample of students in Baghdad, "friend of the president" status was enjoyed by about 17 percent of students and their families. Table 7.4 reports the results of three regressions which consider the factors associated with individual-level "friend of the president" status. The covariates that I include in the first regression are whether the student is Kurdish and his educational track (i.e., literature, science, or vocational—the omitted category

TABLE 7.4. Coefficient estimates from logit regressions for dependent variable, "friend of the president" status (0–1) across individual students in Baghdad for the 2001–2002 academic year.

	Model 7.5	Model 7.6	Model 7.7
Percent Sunni (district)	3.605	3.566	2.441
	(0.211)	(0.216)	(0.265)
Kurdish	−0.417	−0.405	−0.420
	(0.177)	(0.179)	(0.177)
Literature	−0.049	0.004	−0.038
	(0.047)	(0.048)	(0.047)
Science	0.094	0.134	0.072
	(0.043)	(0.044)	(0.043)
Martyr (father or brother)		1.576	
		(0.069)	
Wealth Index (district)			0.296
			(0.033)
Constant	−3.338	−3.462	−5.551
	(0.107)	(0.110)	(0.276)
Observations	22,682	22,520	22,682
Pseudo R^2	0.02	0.04	0.02

in the regression analysis).[118] Because the Ba'th Party did not maintain information about an individual's Sunni-Shi'i status, I apply the district-level estimate of percentage Sunni to each individual in that district. The regression results suggest that Kurds are less likely to enjoy "friend of the president" status, while this designation is increasing in the percentage Sunni. Both of these results are statistically significant. Science students are also statistically more likely to enjoy the "friend of the president" status.

The second model considers the same baseline regression but also includes a covariate for whether or not the student's first-degree relative (i.e., father or brother) was killed in either the Iran-Iraq War or Gulf War. In this specification, having a war martyr in the family is a highly significant predictor of "friend of the president" status; "friend of the president" designation is also increasing in percentage Sunni and for science students, while it is decreasing

118. In the Baghdad sample, about 1.6 percent of students are identified as Kurdish. The other minority groups identified in the Registers (including Assyrian, Chaldean Christian, and Armenian) were considerably smaller. Students in Baghdad were also fairly equally divided between students on the literature (31 percent), science (40 percent), and vocational (29 percent) tracks.

for Kurds. The third specification considers the correlates of "friend of the president" status with the inclusion of a district-level wealth index. District-level wealth is positively associated with "friend of the president" status; after controlling for wealth, Kurdish remains negatively associated with "friend of the president" status, while percentage Sunni and science track are positively associated with the designation.

Political Orientation and "Friend of the President" Status

What impact did "friend of the president" status have on political orientation? I was able to conduct analysis on the political orientation for high school students from Baghdad for the 2001–2002 academic year; in that sample, about 13 percent of high school students said that they were political independents.

Table 7.5 presents the results of a logistic regression where the outcome variable is coded as "1" if a student self-identified as politically independent. The results from Model 7.8 suggest that the percentage Sunni has a strong, positive association on being politically independent as does Kurdish identity. Literature and science students are also more likely to be politically independent relative to vocational students. Model 7.9 replicates the regression with the same set of covariates and adds the student's "friend of the president" status. The signs and substantive significance on the covariates remain largely unchanged from Model 7.8; "friend of the president" status is strongly negatively correlated with political independent orientation. In other words, individuals with this status were less likely to express an independent orientation, after controlling for other factors. This is perhaps not surprising since "friend of the president" status would have invested individuals in the regime.

I am also able to estimate how the proportion of other politically independent students within a school impacted the likelihood of a particular student declaring himself to be politically independent. In other words, this analysis allows me to see if there are agglomeration effects associated with political behaviors, like self-stated Ba'thist or independent political orientation. Model 7.10 suggests similar patterns as reported previously and adds the very strong correlation between a particular individual's political orientation and the percentage of students in one's school who also self-identify as independent. This result is consistent with the idea that one's assessment of the regime is conditional, to some degree, on the assessment of others.

TABLE 7.5. Coefficient estimates from logit regressions for dependent variable, political independent student (0–1) across individual students in Baghdad for the 2001–2002 academic year.

	Model 7.8	Model 7.9	Model 7.10
Percent Sunni (district)	2.993	3.149	3.006
	(0.215)	(0.215)	(0.365)
Kurdish	0.385	0.347	0.282
	(0.147)	(0.145)	(0.179)
Literature	0.333	0.314	0.259
	(0.052)	(0.053)	(0.066)
Science	0.548	0.555	0.260
	(0.048)	(0.048)	(0.060)
"Friend of the President"		−0.333	−0.443
		(0.055)	(0.063)
Percent Independents at School			7.390
			(0.119)
Constant	−3.552	−3.557	−5.067
	(0.111)	(0.111)	(0.190)
Observations	23,037	22,651	22,651
Pseudo R^2	0.02	0.02	0.32

PARTY BADGE RECIPIENTS

The "friend of the president" status provided one avenue by which benefits might be distributed. Yet there existed higher levels of distinction beyond "friend of the president" status. And because the benefits associated with receiving higher level awards were so critical to the life and well-being of an honoree and his family, receiving such a distinction "facilitated an Iraqi's decision to serve the regime.[119] According to Faust, "even if an Iraqi hated the Baʿth, the receipt of a medal gave him or her a stake in perpetuating the system in order to hold onto its concomitant benefits."[120] In other words, citizens invested in the party and the regime and through that investment, individuals and their families reaped rewards.

For example, the Baʿth Party "badge" in 1994 was given to all of those individuals who joined the party in 1969/1970 and enjoyed the "friend of the president" bureaucratic status.[121] Party badge holders were listed by their name, which typically included four parts (i.e., one's given name, father's given name, grandfather's given name, and a tribal or family name). The tribal name

119. Faust 2015, 178.
120. Ibid., 173.
121. The order to distribute this particular set of badges came on July 30, 1994.

TABLE 7.6. Number of 1994 Baʿth Party badge recipients for twenty most represented tribes as well as sectarian identification of the tribe and the distance of the "centroid" of the tribe's home region from Tikrit.

Tribe Name	Number of Badges	Predominantly Sunni	Tribal "Centroid" Close to Tikrit
Juburi	633	Yes	Yes
Dulaimi	222	Yes	No
ʿUbaydi	181	Yes	Yes
Janabi	151	Yes	No
ʿAzzawi	139	Yes	Yes
Taʿi	139	Yes	No
Bayati	106	Yes	Yes
Tamimi	104	Mixed	No
Shammari	101	Mixed	No
Khafaji	95	No	No
Duri	82	Yes	Yes
Zubaidi	80	Mixed	No
Mamouri	72	No	No
Hamdani	71	No	No
Rabiʿi	67	No	No
Jamili	64	Yes	No
Lahibi	60	Yes	No
Tikriti	60	Yes	Yes
Sabʿawi	58	Yes	No
Naʿimi	51	Yes	Yes

provides a particular kind of information about the patrilineal genealogy of the individual. The 1994 list of badge recipients includes hundreds of unique tribal names.[122]

Table 7.6 provides information about the tribes that are most represented on the list of party badge recipients, in descending order. I also provide some information about the majority-minority sectarian identification for each tribe. I have attempted to code for the predominant sectarian identity, where possible. One challenge is that we cannot know for the sectarian mixed tribes which individuals are party badge recipients (i.e., from the majority or minority sect).

122. This likely underestimates tribal names on the list, as those that I was not able to identify are coded as non-tribal. Hassan (2007, 1) finds that about 75 percent of the total Iraqi population are members of a tribe or have kinship to a tribe. Tribes in Iraq vary considerably in size. While the largest of Iraq's tribes numbers more than one million, the smallest have only thousands of members; there are approximately 150 major tribes in Iraq which are composed of about 2,000 smaller clans (Hassan 2007, 1). The most common non-tribal names from the list include Muhammad, Ali, Hussein, Abbas, Abdallah, and Ahmed, which indicate little about family origin.

There are over 600 individuals with the family name Juburi who appear on the list, for example. The Jubur tribe is a predominantly Sunni tribe with a strong presence in the area just north of Tikrit in central Iraq. One scholar who interviewed members of the Jubur tribe found that they were often recruited into intelligence agencies where they had the opportunity to go from relative poverty to lives of considerable influence in Baghdad with extensive opportunities for personal enrichment.[123] The results of my analysis suggest that tribesmen from the Jubur tribe were over-represented in the set of individuals who received special distinction by the Ba'th Party.

I also find overrepresentation of Sunni-majority relative to Shi'i-majority tribes in this list. In addition, of the predominantly Sunni tribes that do appear to be most represented, half of those tribes are geographically proximate to Tikrit.[124] This evidence supports the idea that Sunnis from the areas in and around Tikrit enjoyed high status and reward within the Ba'thist regime, even relative to other Sunnis, including those from western Iraq.

CONCLUSIONS

The Ba'th Party began as a small political party with its roots in a postcolonial wave of Arab nationalism and state-driven solutions to economic underdevelopment. Davis estimates that Ba'th Party membership reached one and a half million by 1981 and that "ties to the party remained important for anyone seeking to achieve important political or economic goals."[125]

The party eventually became a vehicle for regional, tribal, and personalist political interests organized around Saddam Hussein. Zubaida argues that after "having eliminated its rivals, the regime then turned upon itself, and, in a series of purges, progressively narrowed its ruling elites to particular clans and families."[126] The result was that, over time, "the Ba'th had become less a political party with an ideological core than a means of managing state security and Iraqis' social lives."[127] The failure of the party either to anticipate or

123. Abdullah 2006, 45.
124. The intelligence agencies were an important part of the regime's security apparatus and "recruited relatively large number from clans that owed total loyalty to Saddam Hussein" (Sassoon 2012, 11).
125. Davis 2005, 180.
126. Zubaida 1991, 208.
127. Khoury 2013, 53.

successfully head off the 1991 Uprisings led to a period of uncertainty. As citizens became less invested in the regime, which seemed highly vulnerable to overthrow, the party was relatively unsuccessful at enforcing compliance, particulary for young Iraqis. Over time, however, with increasing state reconsolidation, the Ba'th Party was able to reassert itself.

In this chapter, I have sought to demonstrate that support for the Ba'th Party was contextual, influenced by individual identity and status within the regime as well as broader changes over time in the political environment. Using data from a variety of archival sources, I am able to empirically identify the geographic regions with the greatest concentration of party-distributed benefits. One way to encourage greater investment in the regime was through the distribution of honorifics, which afforded distinction holders special privileges and perquisites. The "friend of the president" status—which provided privileges and handouts—was enjoyed by many Iraqis and particularly those from the central provinces of Iraq. Even higher-order benefits associated with the Ba'th Party disproportionately went to individuals who came from the geographic regions closest to Tikrit—the hometown of Saddam Hussein. These findings are broadly consistent with the evidence presented in chapter 5 which suggested that despite the conventional characterization of Ba'thist Iraq as a "Sunni" regime, there existed important distributional disparities both within the Sunni community as well as across ethno-sectarian communities.

The evidence presented in this chapter also speaks to the meaningful forms of public, political non-compliance undertaken by Iraqis. On the one hand, I show that large numbers of Iraqi students from across the country stated that they had a Ba'thist political orientation. Regional and temporal variation in self-stated Ba'thist political orientation must be understood in its political context, however. Before the 1991 Uprisings, Iraqis from a variety of backgrounds could withhold their support for the Ba'th Party; during that time, choosing to identify as a political independent might serve as a public signal of dissatisfaction with the regime. Ba'thist identification declined as citizens downgraded their assessment of the regime as well as their expectation that the regime would survive. By the late Ba'thist period, however, the regime was able to invest in a core of party supporters who were able to enforce public cooperation on large segments of the population; in the early 2000s, only western Sunnis had the ability and incentive to withdraw public support for the Ba'th Party.

CHAPTER 8

RUMORS AS RESISTANCE

Individuals living under the control of authoritarian regimes engage in a variety of survival strategies. Among those strategies are attempts to gather information which might provide one with an economic advantage or critical information to guide one's activities in an uncertain and fast-changing security situation. In other cases, information disseminated person-to-person offers critiques of political figures or allows individuals to coordinate forms of anti-regime political behavior. Yet central to the objectives of the most controlling political regimes is the desire to maintain a monopoly over information. This chapter describes a quietly subversive form of political behavior—the circulation of rumors.

The Iraqi regime collected and catalogued rumors that circulated, many of which were explicitly political in content. Yet even private communication that did not explicitly criticize the regime enjoyed a political quality because of the regime's desire to control information. A core argument of this chapter is that even rumors intended to assist an individual in day-to-day survival are regime-undermining because they break the regime's monopolistic control on relevant information. Hussein's regime had totalitarian aspirations, but never fully succeeded in totalizing forms of social control, as evidenced by the failure to quiet society's private communications.[1]

1. While this chapter focuses on rumors as collected by the Ba'thist regime, the regime also made strategic use of rumors. Khoury (2013, 66) writes about how party cadre were trained to disseminate some rumors and combat others during the Iran-Iraq War. Sassoon (2011, 84) also writes that the regime was known to spread rumors (and counter-rumors), particularly in northern Iraq. The analysis in this chapter focuses on the 1990s and early 2000s, a time during which there is less evidence for the instrumental use of rumors by the regime. Indeed, during this time, a major preoccupation of the region was with reading political trends within society rather than trying to influence those trends. See Sassoon and Dimitrov (2014) for more on how rumors were an important source of information to the regime about people's feelings on various issues.

I argue that under dictatorship, rumors can represent a narrow but relatively safe space for discourse. DiFonzo and Bordia define rumors as "unverified and instrumentally relevant information statements in circulation that arise in contexts of ambiguity, danger, or potential threat that function to help people make sense and manage risk."[2] For Kapferer, rumors are "the media of what goes unsaid: they allow one to bring up in public subjects that the political tradition forbids one to mention openly."[3] Private discourse about what would otherwise be publicly unspeakable depends on the existence of both interpersonal trust and social cohesion. Previous scholarly research suggests that rumors tend to move within existing social circles as individuals are only likely to share information of this type with those close to them.[4]

This interpretation of rumormongering as a political act connects to existing scholarly work which seeks to document the everyday forms of resistance available to those living under forms of political or economic subordination. For Scott, slander constitutes one of the weapons available as part of peasant resistance.[5] In authoritarian Syria, Wedeen argues that "resistance is made up primarily of mundane transgressions that do not aim to overthrow the existing order."[6] Given the increasing impossibility of direct political critique, the circulation of rumors, many of which worked against the regime's desired monopoly on information and discourse, served to undermine the objectives of the Iraqi regime.

This chapter has three key objectives. The first is to demonstrate the utility of looking at rumors as a manifestation of the "hidden transcript" of political resistance in autocratic regimes.[7] Second, using an original collection of over 2,000 rumors gathered from the Ba'thist files from the 1990s and early 2000s, I find that rumors appear to have been highly concentrated in Shiʻi areas. This finding is consistent with my theoretical expectation

2. DiFonzo and Bordia 2007, 13.
3. Kapferer 1990, 215.
4. Allport and Postman 1947, 35.
5. Scott 1985, 29.
6. Wedeen 1999, 87. Wedeen points to the popularity of political cartoons and jokes unfavorable to the ruling regime as evidence that "although Syrians may not challenge power directly, neither do they uncritically accept the regime's version of reality."
7. Iraq would seem to be a particularly good case for this argument. Davis (2005, 17) argues that even in the most oppressive regimes, subaltern groups can resist forms of authority through the use of "historical metaphor" in discourse that challenges power structures indirectly. In this context, circulation of rumors may provide a "safe" way to engage in political communication.

that during this period, Shiʿa of Iraq exhibited forms of group-level social capital that encouraged private communications of this type. I also find that rumors followed particular patterns of diffusion, commonly between the Euphrates region (home to the Shiʿi Shrine Cities of Najaf and Karbala) and Baghdad. Third, this chapter provides evidence that during periods of political uncertainty—often related to Iraq's external relations—rumors sought to coordinate forms of anti-regime sabotage and subversive political behavior. The vast majority of these anti-regime behaviors were rumored to have taken place or expected to occur in Shiʿi neighborhoods and regions.

RUMORS AND AUTHORITARIANISM

Rumors are often multi-functional for citizens of authoritarian regimes, providing critical forms of information to individuals seeking strategies for survival in high-risk political environments while simultaneously reflecting and encouraging forms of interpersonal trust between individuals through their safe transmission. Rumors often also reflect forms of political subversion and attempts to mobilize citizens collectively. If rumors serve different functions, their existence in a society also reflects multiple layers of political meaning. In this section, I discuss the existing literature on rumors, particularly as applied to the study of authoritarian regimes.

Defining Rumor

Rumors, particularly those circulating in advanced industrial democracies, have long been a subject of study in social psychology. Rosnow and Kimmel define a rumor as "an unverified proposition or belief that bears topical relevance for persons actively involved in its dissemination."[8] Slightly modified, Fine defines rumor as "an expression of a belief of topical relevance that is spread without secure standards of evidence, given norms for beliefs."[9] At their core, most definitions of rumor build upon the characteristics outlined by Knapp, who focuses on the relevant informational quality and word-of-mouth transmission of rumors.[10]

---

8. Rosnow and Kimmel 2000, 122.
9. Fine 2007, 5.
10. Knapp 1944.

Rumors—by their nature—are fleeting, often leaving no physical trace.[11] Word-of-mouth transmission also means that the information conveyed is short on details, with possible distortions in narrative. Rumors are often widely disseminated, but with no commonly known source.[12] Because of this, the speaker of the rumor is able to distance himself from the content, diverting responsibility from the reporter to the unknown source.[13] This allows for a degree of anonymity of attribution that is particularly important if a rumor conveys politically subversive or controversial themes.

How can rumors be differentiated from other forms of informal information transmission? As suggested, rumors relate to subjects of significance as opposed to gossip, which typically relates to subjects of limited significance.[14] Rumor might be further differentiated from myth or legend given the fact that it is topical in nature.[15] Rumors are also differentiated from news, in that news is (supposedly) verified.[16]

Rumors often arise when information is highly valued, but its quality tends to be poor. Perice argues that rumors are likely to emerge "in violent and dangerous situations."[17] Viola describes the case of the proliferation of rumors in Soviet peasant communities during Stalin's rule.[18] She finds that when confronted with the threat of major economic, political, and social change, rumors were "omnipresent" in the "propitious climate of fear and upheaval."[19] Information collected in such contexts not only has the potential to be actionable, but can also assist in reducing anxiety by helping individuals make sense of disruptive and uncertain situations.[20]

The most influential work on the social psychology of rumor emerged in response to the widespread circulation of rumors in western democracies, like the United States, during World War II. Knapp, for example, developed an influential, three-type classification scheme for rumors—(1) the wish, or pipe-dream rumor; (2) the fear, or bogey, rumor; and (3) the wedge-driving,

11. Bordia and DiFonzo, 2004.
12. Perice 1997.
13. Fine 2007, 6.
14. Bordia and DiFonzo 2004.
15. Knapp 1944.
16. Bordia and DiFonzo 2004.
17. Perice 1997, 1.
18. Viola 1996.
19. Ibid., 45.
20. Bordia and DiFonzo 2004.

or aggression, rumor. While wish rumors express the hopes of the people circulating the rumor ("there will be a revolution in Germany before the summer"), the fear rumor expresses citizen anxiety ("the entire Pacific Fleet was destroyed at Pearl Harbor").[21] Wedge-driving rumors seek to create disunity and to sow animosity across and between societal groups ("the Catholics in America are trying to evade the draft"). While Knapp's three-type classification provides a parsimonious and analytically useful scheme for categorizing rumors in the context of the United States during World War II, different social and political contexts require a reconsideration of the political role of rumors.[22]

Private Communication in Autocratic Regimes

Rumors play a special role under autocratic regimes that gives their circulation a political relevance perhaps even greater than during periods of war in democracies. While rumors can spread quickly and easily in free societies, rumors circulating in autocratic contexts tend to spread slowly, but often include more valuable information. As information repression increases, rumors become more valuable, in part, because the costs of their circulation are so high. In this section, I discuss the political relevance of rumor under conditions of autocracy with particular attention to issues of government information control, the relationship between rumor circulation and interpersonal trust, and rumor as a tool of political resistance.

Information Control

Rumors often serve to fill an informational void when other forms of information are not credible or available, as is commonly the case in authoritarian regimes.[23] In the context of a highly censored authoritarian regime, all "news" emanates from the state sector and is highly propagandistic in nature. As

21. Knapp 1944.
22. For example, Nkpa (1975) compares rumors in the United States in 1942 with those in Biafra from 1968 to 1970, during the Biafran Civil War. Nkpa (1975) finds that during the course of the civil war, the majority of circulating rumors were wish rumors, but that some rumors were more difficult to classify, requiring introduction of new conceptual categories.
23. Bordia and DiFonzo 2004, 33.

a result, rumor can serve to penetrate an autocratic regime's monopoly on information control. Private information is also often highly valuable in authoritarian contexts because an individual's political choices frequently reflect high-stakes calculations where one might be forced into action with only limited information.

Rumors can circulate even when levels of political repression are high. For example, in authoritarian Haiti, repression meant that open public debate was not possible, leading to a proliferation of "back-alley rumors."[24] Indeed, rumors pose particular challenges for authoritarian regimes, even when states enjoy a relatively high capacity for surveillance. Scott writes that "part of the relative immunity of the spoken word from surveillance springs from its low technological level."[25] Word-of-mouth communications are hard to link to a particular source and are more difficult to shut down than a printing press. Rumor, then, enjoys a kind of "double utility" as both an alternative public sphere to the one encouraged by the state while simultaneously serving as a form of discourse protected from the repressive force that may have destroyed the public sphere, in most cases a repressive authoritarian regime.[26]

In a study of Soviet life under Stalin, Bauer and Gleicher make extensive use of reports from refugee informants who state that much of their information about events and policies came from unofficial channels.[27] Indeed, word-of-mouth communication was highly important under Stalin, with 50 percent of subjects citing it as a regular source of information and 33 percent as their most important information source.[28] The importance of unofficial, word-of-mouth communications undermined the "essential premise of Soviet communications policy... the principle of monopoly."[29] Soviet media was organized and highly controlled; indeed, severe punishments were common for individuals who circulated prohibited material or anti-regime, political jokes. Yet, despite attempts to eliminate the circulation of rumors, there is little doubt that unofficial oral communications were important during the

24. Perice 1997.
25. Scott 1990, 162.
26. Fine 2007.
27. Bauer and Gleicher 1953.
28. In their study, Bauer and Gleicher (1953) find that while high-income individuals report more frequent exposure to rumors, low-income individuals describe rumors as being more important.
29. Bauer and Gleicher 1953, 297.

early Soviet period despite regime attempts to counter these communications through education and regime-sponsored radio broadcasts.

Rumor and Trust

The relationship between rumor and trust differs in democratic and authoritarian contexts. In this section, I will address three aspects of trust with respect to the concept in an authoritarian context: institutional trust, interpersonal trust, and trust within and between groups.

Rumors tend to proliferate in settings with low levels of institutional trust.[30] When organizations, particularly those that exert forms of political and social power, are not trusted by members of society, individuals turn to one another for vital information. The need for information may be intensified by the existence of poor-quality or politicized "facts" associated with regime propaganda efforts. When so-called authoritative sources—like state-run media—are "incomplete or inaccurate," rumor proliferates.[31] Yet even in settings where trust between individuals and institutions is low, if the cost of transmitting rumors becomes too high, individuals will be reluctant to engage in non-official forms of communication.[32]

The emergence of rumor does not just reflect a generalized breakdown in institutional trust, however, but also reflects and encourages the building of trust between individuals. According to Fine, "rumor both derives from and contributes to the social organization of trust."[33] In other words, breakdown in institutional trust can lead citizens to develop forms of interpersonal trust as part of efforts to seek out critical forms of information.

There are a number of reasons why interpersonal trust matters in rumor transmission. One is that in dictatorships, rumormongering is often criminalized, particularly if the information being transmitted hurts the regime or national reputation. A second reason is that judgments about information quality may be correlated with the level of trust one has in the individual transmitting the rumor. Third, individuals who transmit rumors often offer their interpretation and contextualization of the information.[34] Scott writes that "as a rumor travels it is altered in a fashion that brings it more closely

---

30. Fine 2007.
31. Fine 2007, 7.
32. Ibid., 12.
33. Ibid., 7.
34. Perice 1997; Bordia and DiFonzo 2004.

into line with the hopes, fears, and worldview of those who hear and retell it."[35] The nature of the relationship between the individual transmitting the rumor and the person hearing the rumor impacts the way the information is conveyed and interpreted.

Rumors also have the power to decrease levels of trust between groups. In particular, divisive or wedge-driving rumors can discourage trust between demographically distinct groups while, in some cases, helping to build solidarity within other groups. Within their communities, then, rumors represent an updating of the group's collective memory and beliefs.[36] Societies in which tension or mistrust between groups exists are more susceptible to divisive rumors.[37]

Guha's scholarly work on colonial India reflects all three aspects of the relationship between rumor and trust.[38] In particular, Guha writes about how rumors were instrumental in spurring the Sepoy Rebellion of 1857. Rumors regarding the British use of lard-greased cartridges triggered widespread panic by the largely Hindu, vegetarian population. Guha writes, "unfounded and unverifiable reports about greased cartridges, flour polluted by bone meal, and forcible conversion to Christianity... about issues touching on indigenous sentiment at profound depths merged into 'one gigantic rumour' and transformed the many disparate elements of popular grievance against the Raj into a war of sepoys and peasants."[39] In this setting, the impulse to pass on a rumor reflected an interpersonal bond where the communal quality of rumor transmission accounts for the rapid speed with which rumors spread. According to Guha, "rumour proved to be a powerful vehicle of the hopes and fears, or visions of doomsdays and golden ages, of secular objectives and religious longings, all of which made up the stuff that fired the minds of men."[40]

---

35. Scott 1990, 145.

36. Fine 2007, 15.

37. Ibid., 16. One might think that if a rumor does not turn out to be true that this might decrease an individual's trust in the person sharing information. It is important, however, to distinguish between trust in the quality of information being shared versus interpersonal trust. Rumors that are not realized as fact would decrease trust in the rumormonger as a credible source for information, but would not necessarily undermine interpersonal trust between the individuals.

38. Guha 1983.

39. Ibid., 255.

40. Guha 1983, 26.

Rumor as Resistance

Rumor assists forms of political resistance through a variety of channels. Fine describes rumor as a "form of political discourse" that "critiques the social order."[41] As a result, he suggests that analysis of rumor should be studied as part of the "sociology of action."[42] In addition, a rich literature on the "arts of resistance" suggests that rumor reflects the aspirations for political change felt by repressed groups.[43] Scott writes that "oppressed groups so often read in rumors promises of their imminent liberation ... a powerful and suppressed desire for relief from the burdens of subordination."[44] Rumor may also be a tool of political mobilization as "the autonomy and volatility of politically charged rumor can easily spark violent acts."[45] Guha goes as far as to argue that rumor is a "universal and necessary carrier of insurgency in any pre-industrial, pre-literate society."[46] And rumormongering itself, even on topics unrelated to political life, often entails forms of political risk that politicize the very act of private communication.

Viola's research on peasant rebellions under Stalin points to the use of rumor as facilitating resistance.[47] Rumors in Stalin's Russia served as "a form of underground news and dissident social expression."[48] Viola describes rumor as "intrinsically subversive" since political discussion of the state or its associated organs might create opportunities for anti-regime mobilization.[49] As a result, rumors in that setting served as much more than a survival strategy for the economically oppressed; they directly challenged the dictatorship while simultaneously encouraging forms of political mobilization. Viola discusses how "rumors spread fear, ensuring village cohesion in the face of danger from without ... rumors guaranteed village unity and mobilized the community against the state."[50]

41. Fine 2007, 5.
42. Ibid.
43. Scott 1990.
44. Ibid., 147.
45. Ibid., 144.
46. Guha 1983, 251.
47. Viola 1996.
48. Ibid., 45–46.
49. Viola 1996, 65.
50. Ibid., 46. The Soviet state thought rumors sufficiently important to develop a series of strategies for countering their circulation. Individuals who spread overtly political rumors were

IRAQI RUMORS

Regime attitudes toward information evolved over the course of Hussein's dictatorship, particularly as it became increasingly clear that some parts of society were less legible to the state and party apparatus. In 1987, Hussein, in a conversation with Ali Hassan al-Majid and other insiders, boasted that he did not need to rely on the intelligence services because the citizens of Iraq provided him with such good information about everything going on within Iraqi society.[51] By 1990, Hussein and top party cadre appeared to have grown more concerned about information control and the issue of societal rumors.[52] One regime insider suggested that the party had failed to do its job properly since rumors were rife and spreading rapidly both in Baghdad and elsewhere in the country. In response, party officials discussed implementing a more rigorous reporting regimen.[53]

The issue of how the regime should deal with rumors became particularly salient after the Iraqi invasion of Kuwait and in the run-up to the Gulf War. In another meeting, Hussein referenced a Ba'th Party manual on how to deal with rumors, suggesting the need to upgrade party protocols.[54] Speaking angrily, Hussein criticized his associates for their organizational failures in this regard. The need to refute rumors was also considered important as rumors were seen as a form of demoralizing sabotage that should be dealt with most seriously.[55]

Rumormongering was criminalized in Ba'thist Iraq given the regime's desire to control the spread of information. Individuals could be arrested and jailed if they were found to be spreading rumors.[56] Even small indiscretions could lead one to become the subject of regime repression. Iraqis accused of spreading rumors about the regime were imprisoned and, in some cases, killed.[57] Citizens

---

sentenced to prison or even killed; for relatively apolitical rumors, however, sentences of forced labor or fines might be imposed (62).

51. CRRC Doc. No. SH-SHTP-A-001-023, March 6, 1987.

52. CRRC Doc. No. SH-SHTP-A-001-230, c. 1990.

53. Ibid. The rumors that I analyze in this chapter were collected primarily after 1990, consistent with this report.

54. CRCC Record No. SH-SHTP-A-001-042, December 29, 1990.

55. Ibid.

56. Testimony of Q. Dandal, recorded February 2008.

57. Cameron Barr, "Iraq: Unsanctioned Voices," *Christian Science Monitor*, October 31, 2002 for one such story.

were expected to inform on one another and provide information about rumors circulating within society.[58] Informers would file a form detailing information about the rumor, including where and when the rumor began to spread, and an officer in charge would analyze the rumor and make a recommendation for how to deal with it.[59] The regime also commissioned studies focused on information control and cultivating pro-regime public attitudes.[60]

Why Collect Rumors?

Why might an authoritarian regime want to collect rumors? Rumors can be seen as an "index" of public morale,[61] revealing a great deal about the fears, hopes, and insecurities of people. In addition to serving as a general barometer of public sentiment, rumors serve as an important source of information about citizen attitudes toward the regime, in particular.[62] In addition, the Ba'thist regime had a strong incentive to receive early warning about communal violence or anti-regime political mobilization.[63]

Ba'th Party officials were concerned with the destabilizing effects of rumor-mongering as rumors could harm the objectives of the regime. But what do we know about the content of rumors circulating between citizens in autocratic Iraq? And to what extent does the content of the rumors speak to concerns of particular ethno-sectarian groups within Iraq? Rumors collected by the regime covered a diversity of subjects; despite the multiplicity of topics discussed, it is still possible to identify some high-frequency categories.

The vast majority of rumors circulating in Iraq during the 1990s and early 2000s relate to a series of high-relevance, substantive topics. This includes rumors on issues like protest behavior, targeted killings, and military

58. Sassoon 2011, 127.

59. Ibid.

60. For example, the Special Security Organization (SSO) commissioned a study on "How the Enemy Thinks." According to this report, enemies of the Iraqi state sought to change the loyalties of the Iraqi citizenry by exploiting weakness in mentality. One method by which this could happen was described as through rumormongering. See CRRC Doc. No. SH-SSOX-D-000-869, January 1992 to March 1993.

61. Knapp 1944.

62. Sassoon 2011.

63. Anthropologists, for example, have also written extensively about the way that rumors can mobilize communal violence, particularly in ethnically divided societies (Bubandt 2008).

mobilization in the face of impending or anticipated conflict. Rumors describing attacks against Baʿth Party members were common during the 1990s. For example, almost three dozen rumors report assassination attempts against high-level Baʿth Party and government officials. Information regarding military mobilizations, military service, and pardons as well as high-level defections remained important for large numbers of Iraqi citizens. As a result, it is perhaps not surprising that rumors about the military proliferated. Concerns about pending mobilizations and pardons for desertion would have been of particularly high salience for Shiʿa.

Perhaps more so than any other category of rumor, rumors about protest reflect a desire to coordinate political behavior. About 6 percent involved a specific call to action—half of which reflect explicitly anti-regime mobilization with the other half more ambiguous regarding the target of the coordinated political act. A relatively large percentage of these rumors relate to protests to take place in southern provinces and the Shiʿi slums of Baghdad. This trend is consistent with my empirical expectation that Shiʿa enjoyed interpersonal trust at the group level. Almost no rumors reflected pro-regime forms of mobilization.

In this section, I summarize some of the main subjects covered in the rumors and discuss their political implications. The rumors I discuss represent an illustrative set of topics circulating in Iraqi society.[64]

Military Mobilizations

Rumors about military mobilizations are one of the largest topics of discussion within the files. These topics are relevant for the entire Iraqi population but can be thought to have a particular salience for Iraq Shiʿa who have historically been drafted into military service at high rates and, during the course of service, are disproportionately injured or killed in conflict. In the fall of 1997, a number of rumors circulated about a call for all men born after 1959 to enter military service; a rumor the following month suggested that men born in 1962, 1968, 1969, and 1970 would all be called to military service in anticipation of a US attack on Iraq.[65] It was suggested around that time that

64. Some rumors also reflect forms of political confusion in Iraq's low information environment.

65. BRCC Doc. No. 162-2-2-0001, October 14, 1997; BRCC Doc. No. 01-3713-0000-0691, November 9, 1997.

service would be for two years and that conscription might be avoided for a payment of 400,000 Iraqi dinars.[66] Collecting information about these types of military mobilizations helped Iraqis plan for an uncertain future.

Many rumors that circulated were about impending military attacks and their consequences for regular citizens. For example, in 1999 rumors suggested that men born in the 1960s would be enlisted to counter an attack from Iran.[67] Preparatory and higher education students were expected to serve three years instead of the customary eighteen months, according to another rumor, with students moving through the following progression—one year in service to Saddam Hussein, the second year pursuing higher education, and the final year in mandatory military service.[68] Later that year, it was rumored that a war against Iran and against targets in the North would take place and that the Iraqi army was gathering on the country's eastern border.[69]

The previous examples place Iraq as the target of a rumored attack, requiring a defensive military mobilization. There also were a number of rumors suggesting that the Iraqi regime was initiating a military aggression itself. In January 1993, Hussein was rumored to have sent threatening messages to then-Emir of Kuwait Jaber al-Sabah, insinuating that Kuwait no long enjoyed the protection of foreign actors.[70] Around the same time, it was also rumored that Hussein would bomb Kuwait City and Israel.[71] In 1997, multiple rumors suggested that the Iraqi government had installed missiles near the border with Kuwait and that Iraq was prepared to attack Kuwait, Saudi Arabia, and Israel.[72] Hosni Mubarak was reported to be mediating between Iraq and Kuwait in order to solve the diplomatic crisis.[73] Shortly thereafter, it was reported that a large gathering of Iraqi forces was preparing to enter Kuwait, that the United States was searching for ten transcontinental missiles Iraq

66. BRCC Doc. No. 01-3713-0000-0678, November 9, 1997.
67. BRCC Doc. No. 133-5-7-0841, July 7, 1999; BRCC Doc. No. 133-5-7-0764, July 19, 1999.
68. BRCC Doc. No. 133-5-7-0694, August 1, 1999.
69. BRCC Doc. No. 133-5-7-0407, October 8, 1999; BRCC Doc. No. 133-5-7-0378, October 11, 1999.
70. BRCC Doc. No. 005-3-3-0799, January 15, 1993.
71. BRCC Doc. No.005-3-3-0752, January 19, 1993. The leaders of Kuwait were rumored to seek an improvement in relations with Iraq through the opening of new communication channels with Baghdad.
72. BRCC Doc. No. 01-3713-0000-0491, November 18, 1997.
73. BRCC Doc. No. 01-3713-0000-0584, November 18, 1997.

had stolen from Kuwait, and that Iraq was planning to hand over the stolen missiles to the Russians.[74]

Rumors about the capture and punishment of deserters were also common. In 1998, rumors circulated about deserters in Maysan being executed as part of a national campaign against military runaways.[75] In February 1999, clashes between party cadre and military deserters were reported in Dhi Qar.[76] Anticipated punishments were a particular concern. One rumor suggested that the right leg would be cut off of military deserters who failed to surrender themselves after the last pardon.[77] It was also rumored that runaways were being executed upon return to military service.[78] Another rumor speculated that soldiers were deserting because of poor conditions within the military, including the spread of drug and alcohol abuse and the existence of rebels within army ranks.[79]

Strategizing a response to the burden of military service was an issue of concern for virtually all Iraqi families and especially for Shiʿa, who made up a large part of the military rank-and-file. As a result, a great deal of attention was paid to rumors about pardons for desertion from military service or other blanket amnesties that might be offered. These rumors took many forms, including reports of a general pardon for all deserters, pardons for deserters and prisoners (due to the crisis with the United States), as well as a rumored "great pardon day" upon which the prisons would be emptied.[80] Such rumors were repeated in 2000 and 2002.[81]

Economic Conditions

Rumors about economic conditions were common and reflected the everyday anxieties of ordinary Iraqis. This is not surprising given the devastating

74. BRCC Doc. No. 01-3713-0000-0573, November 22, 1997; BRCC Doc. No. 01-3713-0000-0465, November 27, 1997; BRCC Doc. No. 01-3713-0000-0533, November 28, 1997.

75. BRCC Doc. No. 087-5-3-0917, November 11, 1998.

76. BRCC Doc. No. 087-5-3-0706, February 13, 1999.

77. BRCC Doc. No. 133-5-7-0329, November 2, 1999

78. BRCC Doc. No. 040-4-2-0583, October 18, 2001.

79. BRCC Doc. No. 040-4-2-0191, September 5, 2002.

80. BRCC Doc. No. 148-4-5-0692, October 5, 1996; BRCC Doc. No. 01-3713-0000-0485, November 10, 1997; BRCC Doc. No. 133-5-7-0603, August 30, 1999.

81. BRCC Doc. No. 01-2912-0004-0615, July 13, 2000; BRCC Doc. No. 01-2912-0004-0572, July 31, 2000; BRCC Doc. No. 040-4-2-0148, August 25, 2002.

economic effects of the international sanctions regime. For example, dozens of rumors discuss anticipated changes to the rations system or anticipated price increases.[82] Informational in quality, such rumors allowed individuals to take actions that might provide them with a small advantage in their commercial activities.

A number of rumors blamed the regime and relatives of Saddam Hussein for the country's bad circumstances. These rumors had a subversive quality in the sense that the president and his family were considered responsible—to at least some degree—for Iraq's economic misfortune. One rumor suggested that Hussein would nationalize farmlands and place agricultural lands under the control of his notoriously violent and corrupt son, 'Uday.[83] It was also rumored that the president's family had manufactured a tomato shortage in order to drive up the price of tomatoes they were selling.[84] Another rumor suggested that flour was of poor quality because 'Uday had been hoarding the higher quality wheat for his livestock.[85] In a similar vein, it was rumored that—at the height of the sanctions regime—'Uday demanded meat from Baghdad restaurants to feed a tiger he kept as a pet.[86] In 1997, it was rumored that Libya had sent 20 million chickens for the Iraqi people but that the Iraqi regime had sold the chickens to Jordan instead of distributing them to the population.[87]

Anti-regime Activities

Rumors about targeted assassinations were also commonplace in the Ba'th Party files. Victims of these reported acts of violence included regime actors as well as other citizens. In January 1997, a rumor suggested that an assassination attempt on the Irrigation Minister had led to the death of the Minister's driver.[88] Possibly associated rumors that circulated around the same time suggested that the wife of the Minister of the Interior had been assassinated;

82. See BRCC Doc. No. 01-3197-0001-0385 May 8, 1993 and BRCC Doc. No. 01-3197-0001-0463 May 10, 1993 for rumors about the plans to take certain denomination bills out of public circulation, for example.

83. BRCC Doc. No. 005-3-3-0141, April 16, 1993.

84. BRCC Doc. No. 005-3-3-0147, April 10, 1993.

85. BRCC Doc. No. 01-3197-0001-0070, June 26, 1993.

86. BRCC Doc. No. 148-4-5-0584, November 25, 1996.

87. BRCC Doc. No. 148-4-5-0128, March 15, 1997.

88. BRCC Doc. No. 148-4-5-0372, January 29, 1997.

the wife of the Minister of Agriculture had been killed; the Minister of Irrigation and his family had been killed; that there were plans to kidnap and kill the wife of the Minister of Commerce.[89] In other rumors, it was suggested that a committee to assassinate party and government officials had been formed in Anbar by the relatives of a military officer who had been executed by the government during the prior year.[90]

A number of rumors focused on the possibility of Shi'i-initiated acts of political subversion or popular protest, many of which were expected to take place in the south of Iraq. In June 1996, it was rumored that a protest would take place in honor of Hussein, son of Ali and grandson of the Muslim prophet.[91] In November 1997, there were multiple rumors about collective agitation. It was rumored that "traitors" had clashed with party cadre and police in Qadisiyya City,[92] that mobs in Ahwar were preparing to riot, and that Americans and others would intervene to take advantage of the situation.[93] In February 1998, it was reported that the Da'wa Party had moved to Kuwait but planned to enter Basra in order to engage in sabotage.[94] In the same month, it was reported that Kuwaiti leaders had been hiring agents from the Badr Forces for 1.3 billion US dollars in order to protect Kuwait in the event of a future crisis between Iraq and the United States.[95] As suggested by the diverse nature of these accounts, citizens were constantly concerned with the unstable nature of political life and the constant threat of violence and economic hardship.

Coding Rumors by Geographic Area

One of the observable implications of the theoretical argument put forward in chapter 2 is that punishment at the level of a communal group or clan,

89. BRCC Doc. No. 148-4-5-0257 February 18, 1997; BRCC Doc. No. 148-4-5-0218, February 20, 1997.
90. BRCC Doc. No. 148-4-5-0396, January 29, 1997.
91. BRCC Doc. No. 01-3536-0001-0491, June 30, 1996.
92. BRCC Doc. No. 01-3713-0000-0683, November 6, 1997.
93. BRCC Doc. No. 01-3713-0000-0604, November 13, 1997; BRCC Doc. No. 01-3713-0000-0573, November 22, 1997. One rumor circulating at this time even suggested that Saddam Hussein himself was an American agent creating chaos in Iraq. See BRCC Doc. No. 01-3713-0000-0553, November 25, 1997.
94. BRCC Doc. No. 01-3713-0000-0402, February 1, 1998.
95. BRCC Doc. No. 01-3713-0000-0314, February 26, 1998.

which became common in Shi'i parts of Iraq, encouraged forms of social cohesion within those communal or tribal units. At the same time, the increasing intensity of punishment meted out at Shi'i populations after the 1991 Uprisings encouraged individuals with grievances to engage in private rather than public forms of political non-compliance. Taken together, these arguments are associated with the empirical prediction that after 1991, Shi'a would be engaged in rumormongering to a greater extent than other Iraqis.

Figure 8.1 displays the geographic distribution of rumors taking into account the population of each region.[96] In the cross-section, a number of patterns emerge. First, the total number of rumors collected in the North and Central regions—which are primarily Sunni—was relatively small. Instead, areas with large or predominantly Shi'a populations, like the South and the Euphrates regions, tend to have large numbers of per capita rumors. Baghdad is also a major location of rumor circulation, perhaps not surprising given its density. The population of Baghdad has been estimated at two-thirds Shi'i and one-third Sunni during the period under study.[97]

I cannot rule out the possibility that rumormongering was always higher in Shi'i regions of Iraq compared to other parts of the country as I do not have data from the period before 1991. I am also not able to rule out that the Ba'th Party was more interested in collecting rumors in Shi'i areas compared to other areas of the country. Yet, the documentary evidence suggests that the Ba'th Party had a strong incentive to collect information from across Iraq. The patterns that I observe are consistent with my theoretical arguments and had I observed a different empirical pattern, my expectation could have been refuted.

Patterns of Rumors Circulation

A second, related implication is that rumors will circulate more easily with and across areas with higher levels of interpersonal trust. Of the more than 2,000

96. I report cross-sectional variation rather than over-time change in the number of rumors because I cannot be sure that all files on rumors have been included for all years. For example, for 1996 I am missing all rumors from the first half of the year. In addition, for 1998 I have no records for August, September, and the first part of October (the third reporting quarter).

97. What explains over-time variation in the distribution of rumors across regions? There is no obvious pattern to explain. While Baghdad rumors typically constitute between one-quarter and one-half of all reported rumors, the relative distribution between the Euphrates region and the south region varies considerably.

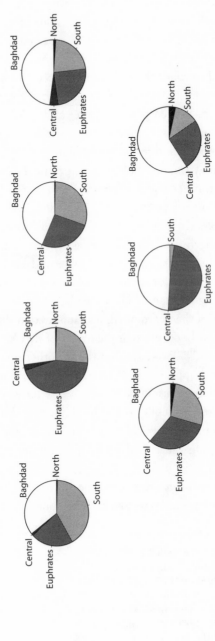

Figure 8.1. Rumors by region, 1996, 1997, 1998, and 1999 (top row) 2000, 2001, and 2002 (bottom row).

rumors in my dataset, about 150 occur more than once. What constitutes a repeated rumor? I draw on the literature associated with event history analysis to develop a coding strategy. In that literature, news headlines are parsed to include information about a subject, action, and object of the action. In analyzing the Iraqi rumors, I code a rumor as repeated if it meets two criteria—first, it shares either a subject-action, subject-object, or action-object with another rumor and, second, the two rumors occur within a span of three months. Because rumors are transmitted via private communications, I allowed the coding criteria to incorporate a degree of fluidity in the content of the information. In most cases, rumors that I code as repeated have considerable overlap in content and repeat multiple times.

What do these repeated rumors look like in practice? Consider three examples. In July 1999, a rumor circulated that the Baʿth Party released bags of diseased rats and mice in the predominantly Shiʿi Saddam City neighborhood of Baghdad to spread cholera in that area with the goal of encouraging people to move out of the neighborhood.[98] The following month, rumors about the disease-ridden rats in Saddam City continued.[99] A second example is drawn from May 2000 when it was rumored that the mythical "sword of Ali" had been seen in a Baghdad neighborhood.[100] Five days later it was rumored that a shining light in the shape of the sword of Ali had appeared in the garden of a house in that same neighborhood and that the owner of that house had been arrested by security officials.[101] Two days after that, another rumor suggested that the sword of Ali had appeared in that area.[102] A third example of a repeated rumor circulated in August 2000 when it was reported that the price of sugar would be increasing from 400 to 850 Iraqi dinars and that the share distributed in the rations program would be halved.[103] Four days later, it was rumored that the month's sugar share had not been distributed and this is why sugar prices were rising.[104]

The most common locations for the occurrence of repeated rumors were between (1) Baghdad, the Euphrates region, and the South; and (2) between

98. BRCC Doc. No. 133-5-7-0780, July 15, 1999.
99. BRCC Doc. No. 133-5-7-0783, July 21, 1999.
100. BRCC Doc. No. 01-2912-0004-0764, May 15, 2000.
101. BRCC Doc. No. 01-2912-0004-0744, May 20, 2000.
102. BRCC Doc. No. 01-2912-0004-0667, May 22, 2000.
103. BRCC Doc. No. 01-2912-0004-0536, August 14, 2000.
104. BRCC Doc. No. 01-2912-0004-0528, August 18, 2000.

Baghdad and the Euphrates region. Baghdad-South is the third most likely pattern for repeated rumors. Interestingly, Euphrates-South is less common, suggesting the centrality of Baghdad as a locus for rumor transmittal. It is not possible to rule out that these rumors were arising independently.

The "directionality" of the rumors, or what can be inferred about the geographic spread of the rumors based on when and where each rumor was reported, is another quantity of interest. For rumors circulating between the Euphrates region and Baghdad, the rumors were equally likely to have first been reported in either area. But for rumors that appeared in Baghdad, the Euphrates region, and the South, they are much more likely to have started in either Baghdad or the Euphrates region, later traveling to the South. Upon reviewing rumors that were repeated in the Euphrates region and the South, three-quarters began in the Euphrates area. What implications might we draw from these patterns? Urban, Shiʿi networks appear to be particularly dense locations for informal information transmissions.

Rumors and Political Crisis

Periods of heightened engagement with international actors were potentially vulnerable times for the Baʿthist regime. To what extent did anti-regime activists seek to undermine the state during these periods? And did Iraq's engagement with external actors create opportunities for coordinated action against regime interests? In this section, I explore the nature of rumormongering at different points in time with the goal of understanding how subversive activities may have been encouraged by periods of political crisis.

To do this, I examine the political circumstances and circulating rumors surrounding a handful of high-profile events, including confrontations with the United States in 1993, 1996, and 1998. I find that periods of political crisis tended to be accompanied by an increasing number of rumors that sought to coordinate acts of sabotage against the Baʿthist regime, suggesting the instrumental identification of such moments as an opportunity for anti-regime behaviors. The vast majority of rumored anti-regime activities are anticipated in Shiʿi majority areas.

Empirical analysis of these temporal trends is challenging, however, because of gaps in my ability to find files for all time periods as well as the fact that rumors both preview impending crises and reflect past events, influencing the number and content of rumors in any given period. While the pattern

I observe does not demonstrate a causal link between crises and anti-regime Shi'i mobilization, it is consistent with the intuition that crises of this sort were coordinating events for anti-regime activists. For periods of time where my data are more dense, I am able to offer comparisons in the intensity of rumors between periods with and without crises.

One period of crisis that offers a different empirical pattern is the one leading up to the US invasion of Iraq in 2003. During this period, the near inevitability of Hussein's forced removal by external actors decreased the incentive for anti-regime activists to engage in politically subversive behavior. Instead, rumors in the second half of 2002 focused on the distributive policies of the Ba'thist regime as it sought to shore up support among Iraqis in advance of the US invasion.

The Invasion of Kuwait and Wartime Uncertainty, 1990

A number of rumors cluster temporally around the time of the Gulf War. Some of these rumors reflected citizen uncertainty about anticipated events, while others suggested public attempts to coordinate behaviors that might make a US invasion less likely. In some cases, citizens sought to convince Saddam Hussein to withdraw from Kuwait before a foreign invasion would occur. The issue of the Iraqi presence in Kuwait, as well as cross-border tension with Kuwait, had large implications for all of Iraq's population; but because of the large number of Shi'i Iraqis in the armed forces as well as the proximity of Kuwait to the southern, predominately Shi'i parts of Iraq, Shi'a had a particularly high stake in a peaceful resolution to the crisis in Kuwait.

For example, in September 1990 rumors circulated about a possible Iraqi withdrawal from Kuwait.[105] The rumors suggested that government officials were asking Hussein to voluntarily depart Kuwait.[106] There were also rumors that a referendum would take place for Iraqi citizens to weigh in on whether Kuwait should remain part of Iraq or not.[107] One rumor stated that referendum forms had been distributed in Sulaymaniyya and that social pressure

105. BRCC Doc. No. 01-3868-0003-0041, September 9, 1990; BRCC Doc. No. 01-3868-0003-0043, September 9, 1990.
106. BRCC Doc. No. 01-3868-0003-0046, November 7, 1990; BRCC Doc. No. 01-3868-0003-0049, November 7, 1990.
107. BRCC Doc. No. 01-3868-0003-0044, October 25, 1990.

was being applied to citizens who wanted Iraq to withdraw from Kuwait.[108] Around the same time in Basra, rumors were circulating which suggested that Kuwait would soon be returned to the prewar status quo.[109] These rumors circulated despite the fact that spokesmen for the Baʿthist regime were continuing to maintain a tough stance, ruling out the possibility of a withdrawal, regardless of the consequences.[110]

A number of rumors in November 1990 reflected anticipation of a foreign attack on Iraq. One rumor suggested that the United States and other forces would attack Kuwait before the end of the month.[111] Other rumors suggested that the United States was planning an attack on Kuwait and that Iraqi artists were being arrested because of their connections to Kuwaiti intelligence.[112] Around the same time, a rumor spread that a terrorist organization which included American members would attempt to assassinate Saddam Hussein.[113] Shortly thereafter, rumors circulated that nefarious outside actors would be attacking Iraq imminently and that Basra would be the target of chemical attacks by the United States.[114] Around the same time, it was rumored that Hussein had a dream where he met one of God's prophets who asked him to return Kuwait its people and that he would do so.[115] By the end of November, US allies were committing to an increased troop presence in the Persian Gulf in anticipation of a multilateral military action. Britain sent an additional 14,000 troops, bringing the total British troop presence to 30,000, for example.[116] Spokesmen for the British Prime Minister suggested that Hussein would need to leave Kuwait peacefully or face being forced out.[117]

108. BRCC Doc. No. 01-3868-0003-0049, November 9, 1990.

109. BRCC Doc. No. 01-3868-0003-0048, November 8, 1990.

110. Reuters, November 4, 1990.

111. BRCC Doc. No. 01-3868-0003-0048, November 8, 1990.

112. See BRCC Doc. No. 01-3868-0003-0048, November 9, 1990; BRCC Doc. No. 01-3868-0003-0048, November 8, 1990; BRCC Doc. No. 01-3868-0003-0048, November 8, 1990, respectively.

113. BRCC Doc. No. 01-3868-0003-0048, November 8, 1990.

114. BRCC Doc. No. 01-3868-0003-0057, November 18, 1990.

115. BRCC Doc. No. 01-3868-0003-0057, November 18, 1990; see Wedeen (1999) for a discussion about how the retelling of dreams might serve as a way for citizens in autocracies to demonstrate their fluency in regime rhetoric while, in some cases, undermining the regime and its objectives.

116. Reuters, November 22, 1990.

117. Craig Whitney, "Major Plans to See Bush in December," New York Times, November 30, 1990.

In this context, nine distinct rumors report the same basic theme—that citizens would march under a slogan similar to "we don't want Kuwait, we want peace" or "we don't want Kuwait, we want the president (Saddam)."[118] These rumors appeared to be an attempt by Iraqi citizens to signal public support for an Iraqi withdrawal from Kuwait, most likely out of fear of an impending US attack. The use of a slogan suggesting Iraqis supported Saddam Hussein and that support for the president was not conditional on maintaining control of Kuwait may have been a bid to appeal to Hussein's ego and to give him a face-saving way to pull out of Kuwait. These rumors circulated at a time when some elites within Washington, DC—like Director of the Central Intelligence Agency, William Webster—were suggesting an immediate military attack should Hussein fail to withdraw from Kuwait while others—like Republican Senator Bob Dole—argued that restoring the Kuwaiti Emir to his throne was not worth the lives of American soldiers.[119] After the resolution of the 1990–1991 conflict, rumors about Kuwait persisted, particularly about the relationship between Kuwait and Iraq and often in association with discussion about the role of third-party actors, like the United States.

Showdown with the United States over Southern No-Fly Zone, 1993

The first half of 1993 saw the circulation of a number of rumors which reflected the extreme political uncertainty of that period. In early January, Iraq rejected an ultimatum to withdraw anti-aircraft batteries from the southern no-fly zone, sparking a political crisis with the United States and its allies.[120] Iraqi authorities sought to calm a jittery Iraqi populace fearful of renewed conflict.[121] Hussein vowed to recover Kuwait; shortly thereafter, allied warplanes

118. BRCC Doc. No. 01-3868-0003-0052, November 12, 1990; BRCC Doc. No. 01-3868-0003-0058, November 29, 1990; BRCC Doc. No. 01-3868-0003-0059, December 17, 1990; BRCC Doc. No. 01-3868-0003-0060, December 22, 1990; BRCC Doc. No. 01-3868-0003-0061, December 24, 1990; BRCC Doc. No. 01-3868-0003-0063, December 26, 1990; BRCC Doc. No. 01-3868-0003-0063, December 26, 1990; BRCC Doc. No. 01-3868-0003-0063, December 26, 1990; BRCC Doc. No. 01-3868-0003-0062, December 27, 1990.
119. See "Hussein Won't Order Pullout Unless Imperiled, CIA Says," New York Times, December 15, 1990 and "Dole Cautious on US Role in Gulf Combat," New York Times, December 31, 1990.
120. Agence France Presse, January 7, 1993.
121. Agence France Presse, January 12, 1993.

attacked anti-aircraft missile batteries in southern Iraq.[122] Activity in Baghdad slowed as Iraqis scanned the skies for new allied airstrikes. Hussein responded to the attacks with a promise of holy war against the United States and its allies.[123] When the Baʿthist regime failed to meet United Nations' demands, this set the stage for further possible strikes.[124]

In the wake of this renewed climate of hostilities, a number of rumors began circulating related to expected or pending troop mobilizations. One rumor suggested that men born between 1960 and 1966 would be called to military service and that men born in 1967 would be called to liberate the northern (i.e., autonomous Kurdish) areas.[125] Around the same time, rumors circulated suggesting that Kurdish attacks on regime targets were possible. It was reported that Kirkuk would be attacked on the night of January 25.[126] Rumors circulated that the United States would engage in a military strike in order to give support to a Kurdish military action.[127] Contradictory rumors about pending military demobilizations circulated during the same period. In February, rumors circulated about military downsizing.[128]

A number of rumors referenced calls for overthrow of the Baʿthist regime, likely in response to the sense that the regime was particularly vulnerable. Rumors circulated about assassination attempts against the sons of the president, ʿUday and Qusay, whose influence had grown over the course of the 1990s.[129] In March, it was suggested that protests would take place during Ramadan calling for regime overthrow.[130] Two rumors circulating around the same time suggested that anti-regime activists were spreading slogans calling for the assassination of Baʿth Party members.[131] Shortly thereafter, the head

122. Agence France Presse, January 13, 1993.
123. Agence France Presse, January 14, 1993.
124. Agence France Presse, January 17, 1993.
125. BRCC Doc. No. 005-3-3-0692, January 21, 1993; BRCC Doc. No. 005-3-3-0655, January 27, 1993.
126. BRCC Doc. No. 005-3-3-0641, January 20, 1993.
127. BRCC Doc. No. 005-3-3-0831, January 13, 1993; BRCC Doc. No. 005-3-3-0739, January 19, 1993; BRCC Doc. No. 005-3-3-0612, February 1, 1993.
128. BRCC Doc. No. 005-3-3-0320, February 23, 1993; BRCC Doc. No. 005-3-3-0326, February 28, 1993.
129. BRCC Doc. No. 005-3-3-0564, February 9, 1993.
130. BRCC Doc. No. 005-3-3-0308, March 1993; Ramadan took place between February 23 and March 24 in 1993.
131. BRCC Doc. No. 005-3-3-0265, March 16, 1993.

of General Security was rumored to have been shot.[132] In April, almost a dozen rumors suggested an assassination attempt against Interior Minister Watban Ibrahim Hassan (al-Tikriti), half-brother of Saddam Hussein.[133] According to some reports, he was shot in the predominantly Shiʿi Saddam City neighborhood of Baghdad by a fellow security service officer.[134] One associated rumor suggested the assassination attempt was accompanied by multiple, failed coup attempts.[135]

Former US President George Bush visited Kuwait April 14–16 to commemorate the allied victory in the Gulf War. During this visit, an Iraqi assassination attempt on Bush allegedly took place. Around this time, a number of rumors circulated about anti-regime attacks or activities, particularly in Shiʿi areas of Iraq. In Najaf, it was rumored that three thousand bearded Iranians would be entering Iraq.[136] The same document also suggests that there would be an uprising in the days to follow which the state would attempt to crush and that clashes would take place between security forces and bearded men.[137] The following Thursday was reported to be a date for resistance against the government in all cities, and that Karbala and Najaf would be surrounded by security in a bid to catch draft dodgers and deserters.[138] The government was also reported to be deporting residents of the Saddam City neighborhood.[139]

It was rumored that the Iraqi government was planning to gather all Kurds in southern Iraq in order to attack them with chemical weapons.[140] Also, a rumor suggested that the Iraqi government was preparing to attack northern Iraq (with the help of the Americans) in order to kill all Kurds; Arab Iraqis

132. BRCC Doc. No. 01-3197-0001-0727, March 24, 1993; BRCC Doc. No. 005-3-3-0223, March 29, 1993.

133. See BRCC Doc. No. 005-3-3-0106, April 18, 1993 for one example.

134. BRCC Doc. No. 005-3-3-0032, April 24, 1993; in 1995, Watban Ibrahim Hassan was shot and seriously wounded by ʿUday Hussein. See Youssef Ibrahim, "Hussein Family Dinner: Politics and Guns," New York Times, August 17, 1995 for more details.

135. BRCC Doc. No. 01-3197-0001-0655, April 27, 1993.

136. BRCC Doc. No. 005-3-3-0001, April 24, 1993. According to this rumor, state security forces would be harassing all bearded men as a result of the Iranian incursion. Around the same time, it was rumored that young Iraqi men would be compelled to shave their beards because ʿUday had shaved his facial hair, BRCC Doc. No. 005-3-3-0051, April 22, 1993.

137. Ibid.

138. Ibid.

139. BRCC Doc. No. 005-3-3-0081, April 19, 1993.

140. BRCC Doc. No. 01-3197-0001-0718, April 20, 1993.

living in northern areas would be notified to sell their homes and leave the area.[141] Protest riots were rumored to have taken place in Dhi Qar, Maysan City, and the Saddam City area of Baghdad.[142] Other rumors suggested protest riots to take place in the days to follow.[143] Rumors circulated about the killing of party members in both southern and northern parts of Iraq.[144] Military desertions were a major concern of the regime, and a number of rumors related to tracking down and punishing deserters. It was also rumored that the cities of Najaf and Karbala had been surrounded by regime forces in an effort to capture deserters.[145]

Saddam Hussein's birthday (April 28) served as a coordination date for many of the anticipated protest riots. For example, it was rumored that a military parade held in Baghdad on the occasion of Hussein's birthday would be bombed by a joint American–Israeli airstrike.[146] Rumors also claimed that protestors would use Hussein's birthday as the occasion for organizing riots.[147] In some of the rumors, Iranian infiltrators were thought to be entering Iraq as revolutionary agents to assist in the protests scheduled to take place on Hussein's birthday.[148] The Iraqi army was rumored to have launched an attack against Kurdish targets in Erbil and Sulaymaniyya.[149] In one case, it was rumored that a government offensive to "free" the North was described as a gift to Saddam Hussein on the occasion of his birthday.[150]

This was also a time of uncertainty about the economy and related impending political instability. It was rumored that a large protest against high prices would take place in Baghdad.[151] The Kuwaiti government was rumored to give "traitors" 500 million Iraqi dinars to buy dollars in the Iraqi market in order to harm the economy and make Iraqis complain about local economic

141. BRCC Doc. No. 01-3197-0001-0675, April 27, 1993.
142. BRCC Doc. No. 01-3197-0001-0327, April 23, 1993; BRCC Doc. No. 01-3197-0001-0704, April 25, 1993; BRCC Doc. No. 01-3197-0001-0561, April 25, 1993.
143. BRCC Doc. No. 005-3-3-0001, April 24, 1993.
144. BRCC Doc. No. 01-3197-0001-0704, April 25, 1993.
145. BRCC Doc. No. 005-3-3-0001, April 24, 1993.
146. BRCC Doc. No. 005-3-3-0039, April 22, 1993.
147. BRCC Doc. No. 01-3197-0001-0641, April 28, 1993; BRCC Doc. No. 01-3197-0001-0611, April 29, 1993.
148. BRCC Doc. No. 01-3197-0001-0375, April 27, 1993; BRCC Doc. No. 01-3197-0001-0669, April 27, 1993.
149. BRCC Doc. No. 01-3197-0001-0291, May 30, 1993.
150. BRCC Doc. No. 01-3197-0001-0375, April 27, 1993.
151. BRCC Doc. No. 01-3197-0001-0327, April 23, 1993.

conditions.[152] Reports of impending political unrest, especially in the South, suggested that citizens were stockpiling food and gasoline in anticipation of the crisis.[153] Information about compensation was also of interest to Iraqis who circulated rumors about salary and state payments. Rumors circulated about an impending 150 percent salary increase for military personnel who had fifteen years of service and a 100 percent increase for those with ten years of service.[154] Currency restrictions and concerns about currency circulation were also rumored.[155]

In May, Iraqi troops allegedly shot three farmers after crossing into Kurdish-controlled areas of northern Iraq.[156] Shortly thereafter, Kurdish officials reported that the Iraqi army had massed more than 100,000 men at the border with the autonomous Kurdish region.[157] These events set off a new set of rumors and uncertainty about additional, possible conflict. In the wake of these events, it was reported that protests had taken place in Dhi Qar and would take place in Maysan.[158] It was further suggested that riots would begin in Muharram—a sacred month of the Islamic calendar—and continue until the fall of regime.[159] Protests were anticipated in the Baghdad neighborhoods of Saddam City and Karrada.[160] A cruise missile attack by the United States hit intelligence locations in Baghdad on the evening of June 26; after that point, the political situation stabilized to a degree. The attack was launched in response to the alleged Iraqi assassination attempt against Bush.

152. BRCC Doc. No. 005-3-3-0081, April 19, 1993.

153. BRCC Doc. No. 01-3197-0001-0416, May 4, 1993. Rumors continued to circulate that protests and riots had taken place in Basra with agitators heading to Baghdad to foment further unrest. See BRCC Doc. No. 01-3197-0001-0451, May 11, 1993.

154. BRCC Doc. No. 01-3197-0001-0520, May 9, 1993.

155. See, for example, BRCC Doc. Nos. 01-3197-0001-0400, April 29, 1993 and 01-3197-0001-0539, May 6, 1993.

156. Agence France Presse, May 13, 1993.

157. Agence France Presse, May 25, 1993.

158. BRCC Doc. No. 01-3197-0001-0263, May 29, 1993.

159. BRCC Doc. No. 01-3197-0001-0118, June 16, 1993. Muharram was between June 21 and July 20 in 1993. It was also rumored that a group of Kurds had entered Baghdad with the intention to riot and that anti-Ba'th Party protests had taken place in Muthanna City which resulted in the arrest of over 500 individuals. See BRCC Doc. No. 01-3197-0001-0099, June 23, 1993 and BRCC Doc. No. 01-3197-0001-0082, June 27, 1993.

160. BRCC Doc. No. 01-3197-0001-0198, June 17, 1993.

Ba'thist Incursions into Kurdistan, 1996

Conflict between the PUK and KDP in Iraqi Kurdistan provided an opportunity for Hussein to reassert his security and intelligence presence in northern Iraq. On August 31, 1996, the Iraqi military—in what was its largest offensive since the Gulf War—crossed into the autonomous Kurdish region of Iraq and seized the city of Erbil. The Iraqi decision to occupy Erbil came just weeks after rumors circulated about conspiracies to kill Saddam Hussein or to unseat him in a coup.[161] Rumors about other forms of political instability were also circulating, including about the assassination of Ba'th Party members and protest uprisings in Basra and Dhi Qar, which allegedly required military intervention to contain. [162]

When the Iraqi military moved between 30 thousand and 40 thousand troops into Erbil, it did so against the strong warnings of the US government.[163] The Clinton administration immediately condemned the incursion and threatened to punish the Iraqi regime and military.[164] The next day, the United States launched a series of cruise missile attacks on military and command targets within Iraq with the goal of forcing Hussein to end his military action.[165] While most of the Iraqi forces were quickly withdrawn from the Kurdish enclave, US officials suggested that the regime left behind a "massive security presence" which would seek to intimidate opposition figures operating in the northern areas.[166] A number of rumors circulating at this time

161. See BRCC Doc. No. BRCC Doc. No. 148-4-5-0994, July 20, 1996; BRCC Doc. No. 148-4-5-1000, July 21, 1996; BRCC Doc. No. 148-4-5-0985, July 22, 1996; BRCC Doc. No. 148-4-5-1006, July 22, 1996.

162. BRCC Doc. No. 148-4-5-0835, August 26, 1996; BRCC Doc. No. 148-4-5-0773 September 15, 1996; BRCC Doc. No. 148-4-5-0739, September 18, 1996.

163. Steven Lee Myers, "US Calls Alert as Iraqis Strike a Kurd Enclave," *New York Times*, September 1, 1996.

164. Steven Lee Myers, "UN Halts Deal for Iraq Oil Sales as US Pledges Action on Attack," *New York Times*, September 2, 1996.

165. Steven Lee Myers, "US Attacks Military Targets in Iraq," *New York Times*, September 3, 1996; Alison Mitchell, "US Launches Further Strike Against Iraq After Clinton Vows He Will Extract 'Price'," *New York Times*, September 4, 1996.

166. Tim Weiner, "Iraq Pulling Out, but Leaving Spies Behind, US Says," *New York Times*, September 6, 1996. The question of how to sustain a regime presence in northern Iraq following the military withdrawal was the subject of rumors as well. One rumor suggested that the Ba'th Party leadership had promised party members that the government would give every family that moved to Erbil a house and 1 million Iraqi dinars. This speaks to the persistent challenge of ensuring party stalwarts would take up residence in predominantly Kurdish regions. See BRCC Doc. No. 148-4-5-0703, September 29, 1996.

224 • CHAPTER 8

were related to the role of Kurdish leaders, like Masud Barzani, regarding both prior and future military attacks.[167]

During and directly after the crisis, rumors suggested that enemies of the Ba'thists may have tried to take advantage of the circumstances to strike at the regime. Many of these rumors explicitly discuss the killing of Ba'thists in southern, predominantly Shi'i cities. For example, one rumor suggested that the southern city of Nasiriyya was under attack by opponents of the regime and was in danger of falling out of state control.[168] A related rumor suggested battles between party stalwarts and regime opponents in the nearby city of Suq al-Shuyukh.[169] Another rumor suggested an assassination attempt against Saddam Hussein by one of his bodyguards.[170] Opposition groups were reported to have killed regime officials in Basra and explosions were rumored to have taken place in Baghdad.[171] Rumors of this sort continued for the next few weeks.[172] The same July to September time frame in 1997—during which time there was no external crisis of this type—saw no rumors about collective popular or violent mobilization.

UN Weapons Inspections Crisis and Operation Desert Fox, 1998

The late 1990s were a period of conflict with the United Nations over the issue of weapons inspections. Political struggle over Iraqi disarmament culminated in Operation Desert Fox which was undertaken in response to Iraq's failure to comply with UN directives regarding inspection of weapons. The goal of the four-day US- and UK-led attacks was to hit Iraqi targets with the potential to develop and deliver weapons of mass destruction. Bombing targets included weapons research installations, air defense systems, weapons depots, and Republican Guard headquarters.

UN demands for access to disputed sites led to Iraqi objections which intensified beginning in the summer of 1998. A cluster of rumors about protests also emerged at that time as the crisis with the UN escalated. These

167. BRCC Doc. No. 148-4-5-0818, September 8, 1996; BRCC Doc. No. 148-4-5-0825, September 10, 1996.

168. BRCC Doc. No. 148-4-5-0850, September 1, 1996.

169. BRCC Doc. No. 148-4-5-0723, September 6, 1996.

170. Ibid.

171. BRCC Doc. No. 148-4-5-0773, September 15, 1996; BRCC Doc. No. 148-4-5-0739, September 18, 1996.

172. BRCC Doc. No. 148-4-5-0722, September 29, 1996.

rumors were particularly focused on Shi'i areas. It was rumored that the Republican Guard had been deployed to Dhi Qar City to end riots after the bombing of a party office; in order to pressure the city to give up the protestors, it was said that the state would cut off electricity and water.[173] It was rumored that Muhammad Muhammad Sadiq al-Sadr would come to Karbala from Najaf, where he would be killed by the state; rumors suggested that after his death, violent clashes would take place between the government and the people of Najaf and Karbala.[174] One rumor suggested that the government was going to kill any cleric who issued a religious edict and that the regime was responsible for poisoning clerics; the rumor went on to say that the people were ready for a revolution.[175] It was also rumored that the "page of treason and treachery" (i.e., the 1991 Uprisings) would be repeated in July.[176] Anti-regime activists were rumored to be planning to divide the Ba'thists with the goal of attacking their headquarters.[177] Attacks on party headquarters were anticipated in August, after which the Ba'thist leadership would remove Saddam Hussein from power.[178]

In October 1998, US President Bill Clinton signed HR 4655—the Iraq Liberation Act—which appropriated monies for Iraqi opposition groups with the goal of unseating Hussein from power.[179] In early November, the US Defense Secretary warned that military strikes would occur should Iraq thwart UN weapons inspections; Iraqi newspapers fired back that the weapons inspections teams had been infiltrated by US and Israeli spies.[180] The Ba'thist leadership remained defiant in the face of US and international pressure, insisting that Iraq had met its obligations to the UN.[181] With conflict likely, rumors about attacks on Ba'thist targets increased. In Nasiriyya, rumors suggested armed clashes targeting Ba'thists.[182] Anti-regime saboteurs in Maysan

173. BRCC Doc. No. 01-3713-0000-0117, June 30, 1998.
174. BRCC Doc. No. 01-3713-0000-0070, July 1, 1998.
175. Ibid.
176. BRCC Doc. No. 01-3713-0000-0006, July 7, 1998.
177. BRCC Doc. No. 01-3713-0000-0059, July 15, 1998.
178. Ibid.
179. See Philip Shenon, "House Votes $100 Million to Aid Foes of Baghdad," *New York Times*, October 7, 1998 for more details on the bill.
180. Agence France Presse, November 3, 1998.
181. Agence France Presse, November 9, 1998.
182. BRCC Doc. No. 087-5-3-0768, November 21, 1998.

were rumored to have gained control of some army bases, as well as weapons and soldiers.[183]

In the weeks leading up to the US attacks, there were rumors circulating about impending American strikes and potential Iranian attacks, with both military and civilian targets.[184] Some of these rumors said that the United States would strike with nuclear bombs, erasing Iraq from the map. One rumor suggested that Saddam Hussein would be forced out of Iraq within a month and that Iraq would transition to Ja'fari rule.[185] Rumors circulated that the Iraqi people were unhappy with their circumstances and afraid of the Ba'th Party.[186]

When the United States and Britain did unleash missile attacks on Iraq for the regime's failure to cooperate with UN weapons inspectors, witnesses suggested that many of these missiles landed on or around Saddam Hussein's palace in central Baghdad.[187] Concurrent with the US and British bombings were rumors which suggested that Iranian Badr Brigades would march on Basra and that foreign saboteurs had entered Iraq, leading to a tightened security situation.[188] Between December 25 and 30 there continued to be rumors about new, impending US attacks that would target party locations. In addition, clashes were rumored to take place between citizens and the party in Saddam City; it was further rumored that the army had moved to Basra in order to deal with clashes.[189] Around the same time, riots led by Shi'i religious clerics were predicted in Baghdad.[190] This period of intensified conflict with the United States can be compared to the first half of 1998, a period of time when there was no conflict with the United States. The first half of 1998 witnessed only two rumors about protest riots, while the second half witnessed many, suggesting an increase in attempts to mobilize collectively against the regime at a time of vulnerability.

183. BRCC Doc. No. 087-5-3-0911, November 21, 1998.

184. BRCC Doc. No. 087-5-3-0896 to 97, December 5, 1998.

185. Ja'fari rule suggests a shift to the school of Islamic jurisprudence common to most Shi'i Muslims. BRCC Doc. No. 087-5-3-0896 to 97, December 5, 1998; this rumor also suggested that these events would be accompanied by recognition of Israel.

186. BRCC Doc. No. 087-5-3-0896-97, December 5, 1998.

187. Agence France Presse, December 17, 1998.

188. BRCC Doc. No. 087-5-3-0890, December 18, 1998; BRCC Doc. No. 087-5-3-0873, December 22, 1998.

189. BRCC Doc. No. 087-5-3-0879, December 21, 1998; BRCC Doc. No. 087-5-3-0702, December 24, 1999.

190. BRCC Doc. No. 087-5-3-0820, December 28, 1998.

Clash with Clerics, 1999

The Iraqi regime's showdown with Shi'i clerics in the late 1990s created conditions ripe for rumor promulgation. Rumors about assassinations that targeted religious leaders were numerous. In some cases, no victim was named. In other cases, a particular cleric was reported as having been killed by the state. For example, in June 1998, multiple rumors referenced the assassination of Shi'i Grand Ayatollah Mirza Ali al-Gharawi, who was actually killed on June 18, 1998 according to news sources.[191] These rumors appeared after the killing and focused on attribution of blame or political implications of the assassination. One rumor reported that a jihad would be announced at Friday prayer as a response to the murder of clerics.[192] Another suggested that saboteurs would blow up dams and bridges in response to the killing.[193] Rumors alternately suggested that the Wahhabi movement was responsible for al-Gharawi's murder, the state was responsible for the killings, and authorities had arrested the two men responsible for the assassination.[194] It was also rumored that the government sought to eliminate any cleric who issued a fatwa.[195]

A large number of rumors related to the assassination of Shi'i cleric Muhammad Muhammad Sadiq al-Sadr, who was killed in February 1999. The rumors cover a variety of issues including speculation about the forces behind the killing, why Sadiq al-Sadr was targeted, and occurrences in the aftermath of the event. The majority of rumors that sought to attribute blame suggested that the government was responsible for the killing.[196] One rumor suggested that the government had killed Sadiq al-Sadr because he had publicly discussed controversial issues related to the release of prisoners.[197] An additional, related rumor suggested that Sadiq al-Sadr had asked Hussein to release imprisoned clerics, but that Hussein had not responded to this request.[198] The same rumor suggested that Sadiq al-Sadr was asked to mention Hussein in his

191. See "Obituary: Grand Ayatollah Sheikh Mirza Ali al-Gharawi," *The Independent,* June 24, 1998.

192. BRCC Doc. No. 01-3713-0000-0135, June 26, 1998.

193. BRCC Doc. No. 01-3713-0000-0001, July 8, 1998.

194. BRCC Doc. No. 01-3713-0000-0097, June 27, 1998; BRCC Doc. No. 01-3713-0000-0124, June 29, 1998, BRCC Doc. No. 01-3713-0000-0001, July 8, 1998.

195. BRCC Doc. No. 01-3713-0000-0070, July 1, 1998.

196. BRCC Doc. No. 087-5-3-0687, February 20, 1999; BRCC Doc. No. 087-5-3-0647, February 24, 1999.

197. BRCC Doc. No. 087-5-3-0601, February 24, 1999.

198. BRCC Doc. No. 087-5-3-0564, March 1, 1999.

sermons but did not do so; Sadiq al-Sadr reportedly told his fellow clerics that he would be killed and, as a result, kept his funeral shroud with him in the car in anticipation of the assassination.[199] A third rumor provided details regarding this theory, suggesting that, on the day of the assassination, a party comrade and another official had visited Sadiq al-Sadr, requesting that he stop asking to free the prisoners.[200] Sadiq al-Sadr reportedly refused and kicked the men out of his house.[201]

A number of rumors circulated about anti-regime collective action, particularly as related to Shi'i parts of the country. A clash between draft dodgers and party members was reported to have taken place in Dhi Qar.[202] Opposition agitators reportedly entered Zubayr and other areas of Basra governorate and destroyed government buildings; in response, the army supposedly isolated the districts in order to stop individuals from exiting or entering the area.[203] Protests and attacks on police were also rumored in Saddam City and other areas, leading to their encirclement by emergency forces.[204] It was even rumored that missiles would be directed at protesting areas.

Around the same time, rumors about anticipated riots encouraged individuals to coordinate their protest behavior. For example, one rumor suggested that at exactly 9 pm on Monday, "traitors" would engage in sabotage in order to fight the regime and the Ba'thist revolution.[205] In associated rumors, it was suggested that the Shi'a would protest against the regime or that protests would take place after the Friday prayer in the Musayyab district in response to a religious edict calling for jihad.[206] Shortly afterward, it was rumored that prayer sessions to honor the dead would take place in Saddam City and that these events would become an occasion for additional rioting and a march on central Baghdad.[207]

199. Ibid.

200. BRCC Doc. No. 087-5-3-0510, March 15, 1999.

201. It was also rumored that Hussein gave the orders to kill Sadiq al-Sadr because the cleric was issuing religious edicts that made citizens angry with the regime. See BRCC Doc. No. 087-5-3-0647, February 24, 1999.

202. BRCC Doc. No. 087-5-3-0706, February 13, 1999.

203. BRCC Doc. No. 087-5-3-0687, February 20, 1999.

204. BRCC Doc. No. 087-5-3-0251, February 23, 1999; BRCC Doc. No. 087-5-3-0647, Feburary 24, 1999; BRCC Doc. No. 087-5-3-0152, February 25, 1999.

205. BRCC Doc. No. 087-5-3-0154, February 25, 1999.

206. BRCC Doc. No. 087-5-3-0638, February 25, 1999; BRCC Doc. No. 087-5-3-0592, February 27, 1999; BRCC Doc. No. 087-5-3-0593, February 27, 1999.

207. BRCC Doc. No. 087-5-3-0510, March 15, 1999.

Dozens of rumors continued to suggest protests had occurred or were going to occur in the months to follow. For example, rumors circulated about an impending military rebellion in southern Iraq and that individuals who planned to protest at a particular event should wear black and carry white weaponry.[208] Another rumor suggested that a solar eclipse would serve as a signal for coordinated riots across a number of cities.[209]

Other rumors suggested that Qusay Hussein was responsible for the killing of Sadiq al-Sadr or that the assassination had been undertaken by agents of the Wahhabi movement.[210] One rumor suggested that Sadiq al-Sadr had been killed by American, British, and Zionist agents who were interested in stirring up sectarian conflict.[211] A similar report suggested that the CIA was behind the assassination of Sadiq al-Sadr with the goal of creating confusion within society.[212] Some rumors suggested that Sadiq al-Sadr had been killed because he issued a fatwa which stated that smoking during the holy month of Ramadan was banned, or that Sadiq al-Sadr had been killed by his fellow Shiʿa because he had supported the Iraqi regime.[213]

In the aftermath of the assassination, additional rumors circulated. One suggested that the killers of Sadiq al-Sadr who were executed were considered martyrs by the government and 6 million Iraqi dinars had been given to each family as a form of compensation.[214] It was also rumored that Sadiq al-Sadr was resurrected from his grave and gave a speech to a group of Iraqis telling them that World War III would be occurring shortly and that the Baʿthists would be killed.[215]

A significant cluster of rumors circulated in the spring of 1999 about an assassination attempt against Interior Minister Ali Hassan al-Majid. The rumors almost universally, and mistakenly, reported that he had been killed

208. BRCC Doc. No. 087-5-3-0451, March 16, 1999; BRCC Doc. No. 087-5-3-0108, April 28, 1999.
209. BRCC Doc. No. 133-5-7-0681, July 4, 1999.
210. BRCC Doc. No. 087-5-3-0622, February 26, 1999; BRCC Doc. No. 087-5-3-0152, February 25, 1999; BRCC Doc. No. 087-5-3-0607, March 2, 1999; BRCC Doc. No. 087-5-3-0571, March 7, 1999.
211. BRCC Doc. No. 087-5-3-0405, February 27, 1999.
212. BRCC Doc. No. 087-5-3-0541, March 2, 1999.
213. BRCC Doc. No. 087-5-3-0152, February 25, 1999; BRCC Doc. No. 087-5-3-0541, March 2, 1999.
214. BRCC Doc. No. 133-5-7-0704, June 5, 1999.
215. BRCC Doc. No. 133-5-7-0786, July 11, 1999.

in the attempt.[216] Multiple rumors also suggested third parties facilitated the killing of Ba'thists. In one rumor, it was reported that the United States distributed silencer pistols and money to encourage the killing of Ba'th Party members.[217]

How does this cluster of rumors compare to rumormongering during other periods of time? During the first six months of 2000, for example, rumors continued to spread about anti-regime collective mobilization, but far fewer than during the first half of 1999. When rumors about anti-regime activities did appear during the first half of 2000, they were focused on disruptions in Saddam City and Najaf, both predominantly Shi'i areas.[218]

In the Run-Up to War, 2002

In the years leading up to the US invasion of Iraq, political conditions were challenging for the regime, with threats emanating from a variety of different actors. Violence—both on the part of the regime as well as against the regime—was frequently rumored. In particular, rumors about the impending US invasion were common. As a US invasion became more and more of an inevitability, there appeared relatively few rumors about anti-regime collective mobilization. This empirical pattern is distinct from the other periods of political crisis that I have discussed. Rumors focused increasingly on payouts being offered by the Ba'thists to increase the regime's popularity in the face of the US military action. By late 2002, the probability of Hussein's removal from power seemed increasingly likely, reducing the incentive for individuals to mobilize before a US military action.

In June 2002, there did not yet exist a policy consensus within the Bush administration should options short of military invasion fail to dislodge Saddam Hussein from power.[219] At that point in time, US discussions focused

216. BRCC Doc. No. 087-5-3-0523, March 14, 1999; BRCC Doc. No. 087-5-3-0409, March 16, 1999; BRCC Doc. No. 087-5-3-0433, March 16, 1999; BRCC Doc. No. 087-5-3-0469, March 16, 1999; BRCC Doc. No. 087-5-3-0446, March 17, 1999; BRCC Doc. No. 087-5-3-0348, March 18, 1999; BRCC Doc. No. 087-5-3-0423, March 19, 1999; BRCC Doc. No. 087-5-3-0424, March 19, 1999.

217. BRCC Doc. No. 133-5-7-0836, July 10, 1999.

218. BRCC Doc. No. 133-5-7-0162, February 18, 2000; BRCC Doc. No. 133-5-7-0122, February 24, 2000; BRCC Doc. No. 133-5-7-0113, March 29, 2000.

219. Christopher Marquis, "Bush Officials Differ on Way to Force Out Iraqi Leader," *New York Times*, June 19, 2002.

on providing limited air and ground support for opposition groups as well as the possibility of an outright American invasion.[220] But by July, US President Bush was vowing to use all tools at his disposal to oust Hussein.[221] In response, the Iraqi parliament publicly offered its full support for Hussein.[222] Contemporaneously with these events, rumors circulating within Iraq suggested that thousands of American troops had already entered the Kurdish region.[223]

Rumors turned increasingly to the interplay between an impending US invasion and the economic fortunes of ordinary Iraqis. For example, one rumor suggested that if the Ba'thist regime failed to provide Iraqis with monthly allocations and a family car, then the United States would invade and overthrow the regime.[224] Other rumors focused on how the United Nations might assist in maintaining the value of the Iraqi dinar; it was also rumored that the UN Security Council resolution would authorize a modest monthly payment to every Iraqi.[225] It was even rumored that American planes would throw dinar bills over large areas of Iraq to distract people during a US invasion.[226]

By August, rhetoric about the likelihood of a US invasion began to escalate. US President Bush and his national security team were briefed on a "Baghdad First" military option, which would strike the capitol and its key command posts with the goal of killing or isolating Saddam Hussein and paralyzing Iraq's military capability.[227] Shortly thereafter, Vice President Cheney told Iraqi opposition figures that the Bush administration was committed to ousting Hussein and replacing him with a democratically elected government rather than another dictator.[228] The Pentagon also began sending weapons and supplies to the Middle East as part of preparation for the invasion.[229] During this period of escalating US rhetoric, the Ba'thist regime countered with

220. Ibid.
221. Agence France Presse, July 9, 2002.
222. Agence France Presse, July 15, 2002.
223. BRCC Doc. No. 040-4-2-0284, June 26, 2002.
224. BRCC Doc. No. 040-4-2-0270, July 3, 2002.
225. Ibid.; BRCC Doc. No. 040-4-2-0278, July 9, 2002.
226. BRCC Doc. No. 040-4-2-0249, August 3, 2002.
227. Thom Shanker, "Bush Hears Options Including Baghdad Strike," *New York Times,* August 7, 2002.
228. Michael Gordon, "Iraqi Opposition Gets US Pledge To Oust Hussein for a Democracy," *New York Times,* August 11, 2002.
229. Eric Schmitt and Thom Shanker, "American Arsenal in the Mideast Is Being Built Up to Confront Saddam Hussein," *New York Times,* August 19, 2002.

anti-US marches in the streets of Baghdad, the burning of Bush in effigy, and military parades of Saddam's Fedayeen.[230] In a bid to increase public support, Hussein declared an amnesty for prisoners.[231] A related rumor suggested a general pardon from army service for all deserters.[232]

Rumors circulating during this period focused on the anticipated particularities of the US invasion. Half a dozen rumors suggested that it would be accompanied by the use of an aerial spray that would put the Iraqi population to sleep. These rumors specified alternative durations for which the population would be impacted by the sleep "bombs" as well as different narratives about the accompanying attacks and troops.[233] Other rumors suggested that US forces would drop 50,000 paratroopers to surround Baghdad.[234] One rumor suggested that Iraqis living in the autonomous northern regions were taking vaccines to inoculate themselves against chemicals that the United States would use to kill the rest of Iraq's population.[235] Still other rumors focused on how the impending invasion would differ from the 1991 attack, including the belief that the invasion would be three-pronged, with forces come from the north and south as well as attacking Baghdad directly.[236]

Over the course of September, US officials escalated rhetoric about an invasion. A US attack on Iraq appeared inevitable. In an interview, Secretary of State Colin Powell defended the use of preemptive strikes against countries that threatened the United States and its interests.[237] Top Bush administrative officials increasingly consolidated their rhetoric around a common message that Hussein's time in power was limited and that the United States had no choice but to take decisive action to stem Iraq's weapons development.[238] US President Bush said that it was highly doubtful that Hussein

230. Agence France Presse, August 5, 2002; Agence France Presse, August 9, 2002.

231. Agence France Press, August 6, 2002; Prisoners had their death sentences commuted for crimes other than drug trafficking, spying, or premeditated murder.

232. BRCC Doc. No. 040-4-2-0148, August 25, 2002.

233. BRCC Doc. No. 040-4-2-0210, August 6, 2002; BRCC Doc. No. 040-4-2-0141, August 26, 2002; BRCC Doc. No. 040-4-2-0215, August 27, 2002; BRCC Doc. No. 040-4-2-0200, September 1, 2002; BRCC Doc. No. 040-4-2-0191, September 5, 2002.

234. BRCC Doc. No. 040-4-2-0223, August 15, 2002.

235. BRCC Doc. No. 040-4-2-0168, September 3, 2002

236. BRCC Doc. No. 040-4-2-0127, September 19, 2002.

237. James Dao, "Powell Defends a First Strike as Iraq Option," *New York Times*, September 8, 2002.

238. Todd Purdum, "Bush Officials Say the Time Has Come for Action on Iraq," *New York Times*, September 9, 2002.

would be able to meet UN demands to disarm.[239] And by September 20, Bush sought congressional approval to use force to disarm Iraq and dislodge Hussein from power.[240] Contemporaneously, rumors circulated in Iraq that Hussein was seeking a place to go into in exile; a related rumor suggested the family of Saddam Hussein would be sent to Morocco.[241]

On October 15, Hussein orchestrated a presidential referendum in a bid to show support for both himself and the Ba'thist regime.[242] According to Iraqi officials, Hussein earned a perfect 100 percent of votes in support of reelecting him to a new seven-year term; turnout was reported to be 100 percent.[243] Following the referendum, Hussein warned that a foreign military invasion would be met with popular resistance.[244] Invoking religious rhetoric, Hussein suggested that divine providence would ensure an Iraqi victory.[245]

Following the referendum, the content of rumors circulating within Iraq shifted. Increasingly, rumors began to spread about new regime policies which sought to curry favor with the population through various political concessions or payments for loyalty. In late October, it was rumored that there would be a reduction in the length of time required for mandatory military service, with just one year of service for college graduates and a year and half for others.[246] An associated rumor suggested that military service for party members might be reduced to nine months.[247]

239. David Sanger, "Bush Is Doubtful Iraq will Comply with UN Demands," *New York Times*, September 14, 2002.

240. Todd Purdum and Elisabeth Bumiller, "Bush Seeks Power to Use 'All Means' to Oust Hussein," *New York Times*, September 20, 2002.

241. BRCC Doc. No. 040-4-2-0133, September 19, 2002; BRCC Doc. No. 040-4-2-0122, September 22, 2002.

242. Although the referendum was intended to create the impression that the Iraqi people overwhelmingly supported Hussein, US attacks were rumored to be anticipated on the day of the referendum itself. See BRCC Doc. No. 040-4-2-0215, August 27, 2002 and BRCC Doc. No. 040-4-2-0119, September 22, 2002.

243. Agence France Presse, October 20, 2002.

244. John Burns, "11 Million Voters Say the Iraqi President Is Perfect," *New York Times*, October 17, 2002.

245. John Burns, "War Looms but God Is with Us, Hussein Tells Iraqis," *New York Times*, October 18, 2002.

246. BRCC Doc. No. 040-4-2-0047, October 31, 2002; BRCC Doc. No. 040-4-2-0038, November 6, 2002; BRCC Doc. No. 040-4-2-0034, November 16, 2002; BRCC Doc. No. 040-4-2-0015, November 21, 2002.

247. BRCC Doc. No. 040-4-2-0015, November 21, 2002.

Retirees were rumored to receive 1 million Iraqi dinars each.[248] A related rumor suggested that every Iraqi family with a ration card would get a 1 million Iraqi dinar gift from Saddam Hussein.[249] In other iterations of this rumor, funds would be distributed via the ration card system in varying amounts between 500,000 and 5 million Iraqi dinars.[250] Multiple rumors suggested that these cash grants would be offered in thanks from Saddam Hussein for the nation's support in the presidential referendum.[251] Different versions of this rumor suggested special gifts and support for students in addition to cash payments for the population via the ration card system.[252]

Regime stalwarts were rumored to receive even greater benefits. It was rumored that individuals with "friend of the president" status would receive cars; Jerusalem Army members were also rumored to receive special gifts.[253] A separate rumor also suggested those trained as part of the Jerusalem Army would receive cars.[254] Various rumors suggested gifts starting at 50,000 Iraqi dinars for Ba'th Party members with higher value payouts for individuals further up the command chain.[255] Other rumors suggested a more modest 25,000 Iraqi dinar gift from Hussein to party members.[256]

The period leading up to the US invasion, then, offers a different empirical setting for the circulation of rumors. With the escalation of war preparations in the United States, Iraqis did not discuss opportunities for organizing collective action against the Ba'thist regime but instead discussed particularities

248. BRCC Doc. No. 040-4-2-0046, October 31, 2002.

249. BRCC Doc. No. 040-4-2-0047, October 31, 2002.

250. BRCC Doc. No. 040-4-2-0023, November 2, 2002; BRCC Doc. No. 040-4-2-0049, November 2, 2002; BRCC Doc. No. 040-4-2-0012, November 20, 2002; BRCC Doc. No. 040-4-2-0030, November 30, 2002.

251. BRCC Doc. No. 040-4-2-0038, November 6, 2002; BRCC Doc. No. 040-4-2-0030, November 30, 2002.

252. BRCC Doc. No. 040-4-2-0015, November 21, 2002.

253. BRCC Doc. No. 040-4-2-0047, October 31, 2002.

254. BRCC Doc. No. 040-4-2-0015, November 21, 2002.

255. BRCC Doc. No. 040-4-2-0047, October 31, 2002.

256. BRCC Doc. No. 040-4-2-0012, November 20, 2002. The question of how to compensate the families of political prisoners was more complex. One rumor suggested that 500,000 Iraqi dinars would be given to each Iraqi family for which a political prisoner had not yet been released (BRCC Doc. No. 040-4-2-0048, November 2, 2002). Another rumor suggested that 3 million Iraqi dinars would go to each of the families of the executed (BRCC Doc. No. 040-4-2-0012, November 20, 2002). The idea that the regime sought to ingratiate itself with the families of political prisoners or those who had been executed suggests how widely the regime sought to gain support in the months before the US invasion.

of the impending invasion and opportunities for last-minute payoffs from the regime. Indeed, the rumors about promised benefits being offered probably signaled to the citizens of Iraq the regime's desperation as it sought to shore up support in advance of the US military attack.

CONCLUSIONS

This chapter elaborates on the idea of the "hidden transcript"[257] of subaltern societies, including the study of jokes, political cartoons, and other forms of subversive communication in authoritarian regimes. I have sought to define rumors as a substantively useful area of research for understanding forms of political resistance in Ba'thist Iraq. In particular, I have argued that the circulation of rumors in Iraq might be interpreted as a form of political non-compliance, even if those rumors did not directly criticize the Ba'thist regime. One reason for this is that the regime sought to maintain a monopoly on all forms of information—both political and non-political— thus rendering alternative communications a threat to this monopoly control.

This interpretation of the political role of rumors is in line with scholarly research which suggests that rumors can have important effects on a population even if they are not believed or it cannot be known that they were believed.[258] The content of the rumors themselves strongly challenges both the regime's narrative as well as restrictions on anti-regime communications. Rumors that sought to mobilize acts of sabotage against regime targets were common during periods of international strife or domestic turmoil, a finding which suggests that Iraqis may have sought to use crisis moments instrumentally to coordinate anti-regime behaviors. The uptick in rumors observed during moments of political crisis can be compared to non-crisis periods, which saw far fewer rumors seeking to mobilize activities against the regime. Whether or not rumored activities were true or attempts at coordination were acted upon, the rumors themselves provide evidence about attempts to subvert the regime. The period in the run-up to the US invasion of Iraq in 2003 serves as a noticeable exception to that trend. In late 2002, Iraqis

257. Scott 1990.
258. DiFonzo and Bordia 2007, 42.

probably thought Hussein would be deposed anyway, obviating the need for collective mobilization.

From an empirical perspective, I find that rumors were numerically most common in Shiʿi-majority parts of Iraq, including Shiʿi neighborhoods in Baghdad. This finding is consistent with my theoretical expectation that Iraqi Shiʿa enjoyed higher levels of interpersonal trust than Iraqi Sunnis and, as a result, were better able to engage in forms of private communication. I also find that rumors often traveled in particular ways, for example between Baghdad and the Shrine Cities of the Euphrates region, and between Baghdad, the Euphrates region, and the southern region. In an examination of the substantive topics discussed in the rumors, I find the greatest density of discussion around issues with high salience for Shiʿi communities, including those related to Iraq's southern border, impending military mobilizations, and assassination plots targeting Shiʿi clerical figures. Beyond the inferences I draw regarding the timing and geographic concentration of rumors, the content of the rumors themselves is deeply informative about the politics of everyday life in Iraq.

CHAPTER 9

RELIGION, IDENTITY, AND CONTENTIOUS POLITICS

John Nixon was the CIA's top senior leadership analyst on Iraq. His job was to identify Iraq's leading political and social actors and understand their personality traits and psychological motivations. According to Nixon, when Muhammad Muhammad Sadiq al-Sadr—a grand ayatollah and Iraq's leading Shiʿi cleric—was assassinated in February 1999, the CIA scarcely knew who he was, let alone anything about his emerging network of followers.[1] After the US invasion of Iraq in 2003, however, it became increasingly clear that a movement of Sadr followers was coalescing around his son—Muqtada al-Sadr. Although initially labeled a political lightweight, Muqtada al-Sadr's loyal following and control over the powerful Mahdi Army—a Shiʿi militia formed in the wake of the US invasion—made him an increasingly important player in a post-Saddam Hussein Iraq. In 2006, Nixon took the lead for the CIA on psychobiographical analysis of Muqtada al-Sadr. Nixon discovered that even three years into the war, the United States still barely knew anything about him or his political followers.[2]

In this chapter, I examine the roots of various religious groups, including the Sadr movement, which originated during the Baʿthist regime. I argue that particular characteristics common to Shiʿi religious organizations in Iraq made them relatively illegible to the Baʿthist regime and, in response, the Baʿthists turned to collective punishment of religious group members, which subsequently drove increased levels of group solidarity. The net result was the development of communal-level attachment organized around various clerical families within the Shiʿi community rather than the emergence of pan-Shiʿi solidarity. The followers of the Sadr family of clerics—first, Muhammad

1. Nixon 2016, 38.
2. Nixon 2016, 163.

Muhammad Sadiq al-Sadr and, later, Muqtada al-Sadr—represent one instance of sharpening religious group attachment that emerged under Ba'thist rule.

My arguments about identity and its relationship to the operation of state structures is fairly orthogonal to a large and growing literature on the policy preferences of the Ba'thist regime with regard to religion. Much of the existing literature on religion and politics during the Ba'thist regime focuses on Hussein's motivation beginning in the 1990s for undertaking the so-called faith campaign—the promotion of a more religious and socially conservative agenda.[3] My theoretical framework speaks to the issue of religious organization and citizen behavior from a different angle. I discuss how the Ba'thists sought to both punish and penetrate religious groups targeted for monitoring. I also report findings from a nationwide census of clerics that focused on evaluating their loyalty to the regime. While the vast majority of clerics were deemed to be operating within acceptable parameters, some were under a greater cloud of suspicion than others. Finally, I discuss how, despite a massive regime investment in neutralizing the political power of religious organizations, religious group members continued to engage in transgressive behavior with implications for the types of religious identity groups to emerge in Iraq after the US invasion.

RELIGIOUS ORGANIZATIONS

Shi'i religious organizations posed a particular legibility challenge for the Ba'thist regime. Thus far, I have argued that the preferences and political

3. Historically, the Ba'th Party had deployed mostly secular policies in the realms of criminal and family law. As a result, the policy shift in the 1990s has been deemed a change worth explaining. While some scholars have argued that Hussein himself was "in essence secular" and opposed politicization of religion by the state (Sassoon 2016, 56), others have suggested that Hussein had a personal religious epiphany that led him to change regime policies (Baram 2014). Nixon (2016) argues that Hussein was not hostile to religion itself but sought complete control over religious activity within Iraq. Helfont (2014) writes that although the Ba'th Party cooperated with Islamists abroad, this was only because this cooperation would be advantageous to the regime. There is no evidence that Hussein or the Ba'thist regime more generally displayed any sympathy for Islamism, Salafism, or Wahhabism; in fact, it appeared that Hussein had an aversion to any form of Islamization throughout his time in power, suggesting an instrumental regime motivation for the policy shift. See, for example, Samuel Helfont and Michael Brill, "Saddam's ISIS? The Terrorist Group's Real Origin Story," *Foreign Affairs*, January 12, 2016.

behaviors of Iraqi Shiʿa were—on average—less legible to the Baʿthist regime since the core leadership and bureaucratic cadre for the party drew heavily from the Sunni areas in and around Tikrit, a location physically and socially distant from Shiʿi population concentrations. In this section, I discuss two forms of religious organization and explicitly enumerate the core challenges associated with monitoring activities that took place within these groups. In the section that follows, I discuss the measures taken by the regime to counter these surveillance difficulties.

Centers for Shiʿi Learning

A hawza, or community for religious study, might best be understood as the location where Shiʿi clerics are trained. Litvak defines the hawza, more broadly, as "a communal whole which encompasses scholarship, interpersonal and social bonds, as well as organization and financial aspects."[4] For Litvak, the structure of the hawza tends to be amorphous, lacking a clear organizational structure or governing body to regulate the institution.[5] Prominent locations for religious training include the hawzas of cities like Qom and Isfahan in Iran, Beirut, Lebanon, and Lucknow, India. Within Iraq, the hawza in Najaf is particularly prestigious, and Karbala is another location for Shiʿi learning. Corboz describes the hawza itself as a source of "social capital."[6]

Several senior clerics serving as sources of religious authority, or *marajiʿ* typically constitute a hawza.[7] In any given hawza, there may be a handful of senior clerics at a time, with several dozen around the world. Within the Shrine Cities of Iraq—Najaf and Karbala—students tend to be linked to particular teachers, rather than to formal educational institutions, and patronage bonds are often strong between students and teachers.[8] There is no clear or singular route to becoming a *marjiʿ*, though it is generally understood that intelligence, piety, and scholarly and social capital all contribute.[9] There is intense competition within the international community of Shiʿi clerics to

4. Litvak 1998, 22.
5. Ibid.
6. Corboz 2015, 47.
7. In Iran, a *marjiʿ* would be similar to an *ayatollah*. A *marjiʿ* is considered a "source of emulation" for the community.
8. Litvak 1998.
9. Corboz 2015, 22–23.

become a senior religious authority for the global Shiʻi community.[10] Pious Shiʻa typically choose one of these senior clerics whose teachings would serve as a guide for different aspects of life.[11]

A particular cleric, then, operates within the hawza and has followers who see that individual as an exemplar of religious behavior.[12] He is also surrounded by a set of students from various countries who are at different stages of scholarly learning, as well as his own entourage responsible for management of his affairs. Part of the reason these networks historically have been dense is that the clerical establishment took actions to achieve their own transnational, professional objectives. Prominent clerics often operated in Farsi, or under strong influence from Iran, creating a barrier to regime penetration. Helfont argues that the transnational character of Iraqi Shiʻism was problematic for the regime as it was unable to monitor and control activities outside of its borders.[13]

Interpersonal ties within the community of religious scholars have also tended to be enduring.[14] Kinship ties might bind together followers both within and across different religious allegiances. And teacher-disciple relations may be formalized through marital ties to reinforce existing networks.[15] Shiʻi clerics also "closely guard" their independence and are willing to make material and other sacrifices to maintain it.[16] Strategies for funding clerical activities— through a system of tithing that exists separate from the state—limit the financial legibility of religious institutions from the perspective of the state.

---

10. Aziz 2001, 140. Disagreements between clerics—some of which might be doctrinal and others more personal in nature—lead groups to coalesce around particular clerical leaders (Fuller and Francke 1999, 107).

11. Cockburn 2008, 31.

12. What does it mean for a cleric to serve as a "source of emulation" for his community of followers? Clerics were responsible for providing guidance to members of the population during times of uncertainty. For example, in 1998 it was rumored that Muhammad Muhammad Sadiq al-Sadr had issued a fatwa that imported medicine capsules should be emptied into water (rather than swallowed whole) since the exterior capsule was made from pig's oil. In this instance, those individuals who viewed Sadiq al-Sadr as an exemplar of religious behavior would view his fatwa as providing appropriate guidance. See BRCC Doc. No. 087-5-3-0870, December 16, 1998 for a discussion about this incident.

13. Helfont 2015, 66.

14. Litvak 1998.

15. Corboz 2015, 30.

16. Helfont 2015, 81.

For all of these reasons, Shiʿi centers of religious learning have historically posed a legibility challenge for the Baʿthist regime despite the fact that the vast majority of clerics have sought to distance themselves from explicit political activism. From a historical perspective, Litvak argues that Shiʿi clerics have used "informal interpersonal ties… as the basis for social interaction" in the face of unfriendly state structures.[17] This tendency also appears to have been relevant during the Baʿthist period. State-clergy relations were strained when the Baʿth Party returned to power in 1968, particularly since Baʿthist policies threatened the relative autonomy of the religious establishment.[18]

Populist Islam and the Daʿwa Party

While centers for religious learning were focused primarily on the promotion of Islamic knowledge and the education of Shiʿi clerics, political Islamist groups provided a different message to a broader audience. The most prominent manifestation of this trend was the establishment of the Daʿwa Party, or the Islamic "Call" Party. Established in the late 1950s, the Daʿwa Party was created by a group of young Shiʿi clerics from Najaf as a response to fears about the growing popularity of both Arab nationalism and Communist ideology.[19] These Shiʿi clergy were disheartened by declining numbers of religious pilgrims and smaller cohorts of seminary students, as well as a more generalized weakening of the hawza.[20] Belonging to many of the prominent families that made up the Shiʿi clerical establishment, the founders sought to complement, rather than compete with, traditional religious authorities.[21]

Iraq's traditional religious class viewed the growing strength of the state as detracting from their influence.[22] Indeed, the Daʿwa Party was created with the goal of Islamizing society and the state, similar to the Muslim Brotherhood in Egypt. Daʿwa's discourse tended to be asectarian and nationalist,[23] a kind of

17. Litvak 1998, 4.
18. Corboz 2015, 128.
19. Louer 2012, 14.
20. Cockburn 2008, 38.
21. Ibid. Some of Iraq's most influential religious families were involved, including the Hakim, Bahr al-ʿUlum, Sadr, Shirazi, and ʿAskari (Jabar 2003a).
22. Jabar 2003a.
23. Cordesman and Baetjer 2006, 278.

populist Islam meant to appeal to Shiʿa and Sunnis alike.[24] Because the Daʿwa Party represented an alternative policy vision for Iraq, it emerged as a rival to the Baʿth Party.

The relationship between the traditional clerical elite and the Daʿwa Party was a complicated one. On the one hand, there existed meaningful ties between the Daʿwa Party leadership and Iraq's most influential clerical families. Louer, for example, argues that Shiʿi political Islam tended to be initiated and organized by clerics to a greater degree than Sunni movements.[25] On the other hand, the majority of traditional Shiʿi clerics sought to separate themselves from politics and political Islam movements entirely. Many Shiʿi clerics were apolitical and quietest, providing only weak or wavering support for the Daʿwa Party.[26] Further, for those who believed that Daʿwa served as an important bridge between the clerical class and the population, there existed disagreement over whether such a movement should be led by the traditional hierarchy or by the emerging class of clerical reformers.[27]

ISLAMIC ACTIVISM, IRAN, AND THE BAʿTH PARTY

Managing its relationship with the religious establishment and political Islamist movements was a major preoccupation of the regime. Relations between the Baʿth Party and the clerical elite were antagonistic when early attempts by the Baʿthists to co-opt senior clerics were rebuffed in the late 1960s.[28] Hussein was careful to acknowledge that religious "belief" was part of the Baʿth Party repertoire, but he likely made this statement out of concern that oppositional forces would use religious cover to drive a wedge between the Baʿth Party and the masses.[29]

In 1969, the regime attempted to bring the Shiʿi religious establishment and its educational system under state auspices, an effort that set off a series of confrontations.[30] Clashes took place following the state-imposed closure of

24. The Daʿwa Party also received the support of merchants who enjoyed a "political convergence" with junior clerics in terms of a desire to cultivate more modern modes of political mobilization (Jabar 2003a, 105–106).

25. Louer 2012, 5.

26. Jabar 2003a, 316–317.

27. Ibid.

28. Nakash 2006, 96; Saleh 2013, 66.

29. Hanna Batatu, "Iraq's Underground Shiʿi Movements," *Middle East Report*, 102 (January/February 1982).

30. Baram 1991, 18.

some religious institutions and the deportation of many religious students.[31] Protest riots among Shiʿa in 1974 and in 1977 led to the execution of some Islamist political activists. In response, the Baʿth Party began planning for a "systematic infiltration" of mosques by Baʿth Party cadre who would be charged with developing relationships with clerics in order to promote Baʿthism.[32] Regime officials were asked to create an inventory of clerics and their backgrounds, including family and social status,[33] a practice that was to continue into the 1990s.

Religious Activism and Muhammad Baqir al-Sadr

In the years leading up to the Iranian Revolution, religious rituals became a focal point for anti-regime activity. As a result, the Baʿthist regime sought to ban participation in religious ceremonies, which provoked a defiant backlash.[34] The leaderless riots that took place in 1974 and 1977 reflected a fusing of political dissent and pious sentiment.[35] Security forces opened fire on rioters, escalating the potential for conflict; clerics urged protestors to stop shouting anti-regime slogans in an attempt to diffuse the showdown.[36] One individual who took part in the 1977 riots reports that he was taken to a military prison as a result of his participation in the protest, charged with having given shelter to a Daʿwa Party member, and sentenced to a fifteen-year term in prison.[37]

Religious movements based in the Shrine Cities were increasingly seen as a major challenge to Baʿthist rule in Iraq.[38] In response, Hussein showed greater deference to Shiʿi clerics with the goal of bringing them into the regime's orbit.[39] Scholars have argued that the Baʿthists were, relatively speaking, lenient in their response to the demonstrations out of fear of generating a

31. Ibid.
32. Helfont 2015, 30–31.
33. Ibid., 38.
34. Aziz 1993, 213–214.
35. Cockburn 2008, 43–44.
36. Ibid., 46. In 1989, while discussing the events of 1977, Hussein referred to the armed demonstrations in Najaf and deliberations within the regime about how to handle the issue, whether to use the party, police, or military to end the demonstrations and signaled that the regime felt unprepared to deal with the challenge it faced at that time. See CRRC SH-SHTP-A-000-930, December 1989.
37. Testimony of H. Gheneim, recorded January 2008.
38. Mallat 1988.
39. Hanna Batatu, "Iraq's Underground Shi'i Movements" *Middle East Report*. 201 (January/February 1982).

backlash to heavy-handed repression. In 1977, Hussein made several high-profile visits to Karbala and Najaf, directing funds to the restoration of important mosques.[40] In 1979 alone, more than 24 million Iraqi dinars were spent on shrines, mosques, and other religious establishments.[41] Important Shi'i holy days were declared national holidays and more Shi'a were incorporated into high leadership positions.[42]

An important figure associated with both the clerical establishment and the founding of the Da'wa Party was Muhammad Baqir al-Sadr, a Shi'i cleric well known for his scholarly writing about pious living in a modern economic world. Baqir al-Sadr was a strong advocate for political activism on the part of the Shi'i clergy, a position that put him at odds with clerics who viewed such activism as dangerous for the future of the hawza.[43] Baqir al-Sadr's advocacy for activism was a source of tension with the Ba'thist regime, eventually forcing him to mask his public political activities and to sever his formal connection to the Da'wa Party.[44] Well aware of the strength of the security apparatus, Baqir al-Sadr and his followers realized that their resources were quite limited when it came to challenging the state.[45]

The Ba'thist regime sought to neutralize Baqir al-Sadr because of his growing political activism, but they were ultimately unsuccessful. Among Baqir al-Sadr's boldest acts of defiance was issuing a fatwa against Muslims joining the Ba'th Party,[46] but it was disagreement over how to handle the Iranian threat that ultimately hurt Baqir al-Sadr. Cockburn reports that a presidential envoy reached out and requested that Baqir al-Sadr criticize Iran or make a public show of support for the Ba'thist regime.[47] When that request was rejected, Baqir al-Sadr was put under house arrest and executed in April 1980. Because a Shi'i religious leader of his stature had not been executed by a contemporary political regime, Baqir al-Sadr may have believed that the government would not kill him for his political defiance.[48]

40. Jabar 2003a, 214.
41. Rohde 2010, 33.
42. Jabar 2003a, 214–215.
43. Cockburn 2008, 42–43. The traditional clergy focused, to a greater degree, on cultivating moral behavior on the part of individuals (48).
44. Ibid., 42–43.
45. Ibid., 34.
46. Aziz 1993, 215–216.
47. Cockburn 2008, 50.
48. Aziz 1993, 213.

The arrest and execution of Baqir al-Sadr occurred alongside more wide-spread repression against Daʿwa Party activists.[49] In 1980, membership in the Daʿwa Party was made punishable by death and the various crackdowns that took place damaged its organizational capacity.[50] Special instructions were issued regarding the security threat posed by relatives of sentenced anti-regime activists who were members of the "traitor" Daʿwa Party.[51] Relatives of Daʿwa Party members who had been executed were barred from employment in sensitive agencies.[52] Relatives of individuals who had been given lesser sentences could either stay or be transferred to other agencies, depending on their relationship with the convicted family member.[53] Importantly, being related to a Daʿwa Party activist did not result in immediate and severe repression. Instead, the goal was to reduce the regime's security vulnerabilities by shuffling those individuals into different government positions.

The regime made considerable effort to dampen the popularity of Islamist parties and identify Daʿwa Party members. Concern about the spread of dangerous ideas led the regime to buy all religious and political books on the market, for instance.[54] One Baghdad-born individual was arrested after being denounced by an informant. After a more thorough investigation, however, it could not be proven that he belonged to the Daʿwa Party and, as a result, he was released.[55] In other cases, it was more difficult to discern the guilt or innocence of the suspect. For example, a fifteen-year-old theology student from Basra was arrested on suspicion of belonging to a religious group, tortured, and imprisoned for ten years in Abu Ghraib prison.[56]

When searching for suspected Daʿwa Party members, the regime did not discriminate based on educational or wealth status.[57] One individual describes

49. Repression of the Daʿwa Party took place in the context of both the Iranian Revolution and the Iran-Iraq War.

50. Aziz 1993, 217; Jabar 2003a, 233.

51. CRRC SH-GMID-D-000-859, July 15, 1980.

52. Ibid.

53. Ibid.

54. North Iraq Dataset 02327-101-24, June 1, 1981.

55. CRRC Doc. No. SH-IDGS-D-000-311, 1981.

56. Testimony of M. al-Hassona, recorded September 2007.

57. Individuals who were accused of affiliation with the Daʿwa Party could also have their wealth confiscated. One investigative memo from 1984 describes the confiscation of transfer-able and non-transferable monies from 64 individuals accused of Daʿwa Party affiliation. These individuals lived in a variety of Baghdad neighborhoods including Kadhimiyya, Jamila, Habiba, ʿAmil, and Saddam City. See CRRC Doc. No. SH-IDGS-D-000-232, April 23, 1984.

himself as having been born into a very wealthy family. After having turned down the opportunity to join the Baᶜth Party in intermediate school, he was later suspected of being involved with someone who had joined the Daᶜwa Party.[58] The net result of the regime's repressive efforts was that Daᶜwa activities during the 1980s became sporadic, relatively ineffective, and tended to be carried out by individuals rather than through an organized effort.[59]

Regime Responses to Religious Activism

Hussein recognized that blunt, violent repression of suspected Daᶜwa Party activists was an imperfect strategy as it had the potential to undermine regime support among some segments of the population. According to Hiro, oppressive treatment of Daᶜwa Party activists was politically undesirable, encouraging Hussein to consider alternative approaches for managing the religious domain, including seeking out clerics sympathetic to the war cause while simultaneously "projecting himself as a pious Muslim."[60]

Government documents promulgated just prior to the start of the Iran-Iraq War suggest the Baᶜth Party's desire to engage more vigorously with religious elites, who were acknowledged as playing an influential societal role. Party officials believed that clerics could support regime interests, as long as they received appropriate direction from party cadre. It was suggested that monthly meetings take place between clerics and a special committee in order to discuss social and political topics.[61] At the same time, the regime increased its surveillance of dissident clerics.[62]

The regime's co-optation tactics sought to take advantage of a rift between quietest clergy focused on offering spiritual guidance to the community of believers and those clerics who concurred with Ayatollah Khomeini's advocacy of a more political role for Shiᶜi clerics. Indeed, these and other divisions within the Shiᶜi community meant that political elites were largely unsuccessful at uniting Iraqi Shiᶜa into a "self-conscious political community."[63] Financial incentives were deployed to buy off some religious leaders; in other

58. Testimony of M. al-Ghabban, recorded May 2007.
59. Jabar 2003a 233.
60. Hiro 1991, 61.
61. Iraqi Secret Police Files Doc. No. 10380 to 10397, July 17, 1980.
62. Hiro 1991, 61.
63. Chubin and Tripp 1988, 99.

cases, clerics sought out opportunities to cooperate with the regime, knowing this provided material and other benefits.[64] Hawza students were also approached for party indoctrination; after their party training they became assets for spying on their classmates both inside the classroom and in the dormitories.[65]

Yet, because the Ba'thists had only "limited experience working with religious actors," they felt the need to develop a more effective approach for engagement with clerics.[66] In the early 1980s, the regime began to develop systematic plans for dealing with the hawza.[67] At least two committees were tasked with investigating religious, educational institutions—the first to be chaired by Ali Hassan al-Majid and the second by Izzat Ibrahim al-Duri, both high-level party cadre.[68] Committee members met with religious leaders across the country and generated a lengthy set of recommendations that were eventually approved by Hussein and transformed into regime policy.[69] These recommendations included a strategy of constant surveillance and plans to reduce the absolute number of hawza students.[70] Rather than seeking to fight or destroy the religious establishment, the Ba'thists preferred to co-opt clerics instead. The goal would be to "feed off the authority and perceived authenticity of these institutions while employing them for the regime's purposes."[71]

Abu al-Qasim al-Khu'i—Iraq's preeminent Shi'i religious leader during the course of the conflict with Iran—displayed a consistently apolitical stance with regard to the state.[72] At the same time, al-Khu'i did not offer the type of vocal support for the Iraqi government that the Ba'thist regime had

64. Helfont 2015, 49.
65. Ibid., 83.
66. Ibid., 39.
67. Ibid., 79.
68. Ibid., 81.
69. Ibid., 80.
70. Kadhim 2013, 19.
71. Helfont 2015, 81. A recording from 1986 provides insight into Hussein's perceptions about the increase in piety among Iraqis. From Hussein's perspective, Islamist elites were not socially or politically innovative but had nonetheless benefited from a more general, generational shift toward religion. Hussein also suggested that the Ba'th Party had not been given sufficient credit for work it had done at the request of religious elites, including provision of funding for the mentally ill and the poor. See CRRC Record No. SH-SHTP-A-001-167, July 24, 1986.
72. Cockburn 2008, 61–62.

hoped to receive. For example, al-Khu'i refused to attend the Popular Islamic Conference held in Baghdad in 1983.[73] Chubin and Tripp write that al-Khu'i "persistently refused to submit to the government's demand that he make a pronouncement sanctioning the Iraqi war effort and condemning the Iranian regime ... he has paid for this by being placed under virtual house arrest."[74]

Hussein inferred dissent from within the clerical establishment when religious elites—like al-Khu'i—failed to make public statements in support of the war. Belonging to al-Khu'i's network was not a condemnable offense in itself, however; indeed, the Ba'th Party frequently sought to recruit and co-opt these individuals.[75] At the same time, uncertainty about the loyalties of individuals within al-Khu'i's circle meant that followers and students of the senior cleric were frequently arrested, or accused of supporting Iran, or the Da'wa Party.[76] Even being born into a pious family could lead to arrest on suspicion of anti-regime activity.[77] The regime was especially sensitive about reports that al-Khu'i was paying stipends to the families of students who failed to report to mandatory military service.[78]

At various points during the 1980s, Hussein considered expelling the hawza altogether, taking complete state control of religious education and closing all religious schools.[79] Such an action was rejected, however, in favor of a more measured approach. Arabization of the curriculum in Shi'i religious schools promoted the goal of reducing Persian influences[80] and, perhaps, also increasing the legibility of such institutions. Hussein also eventually required that all religious institutions in Iraq use Arabic in the classroom, including for discussion materials, sermons, and evaluations.[81]

Regime control over visas for entrance into Iraq provided an opportunity to cut the number of foreign seminary students while simultaneously gaining leverage over those students since they depended on visa renewals for their

73. Ibid., 63. Other members of the Shi'i religious establishment proved to be pliable, as evidenced by statements issued against Ayatollah Khomeini (Khoury 2013, 63).

74. Chubin and Tripp 1988, 100.

75. Helfont 2015, 78.

76. Helfont (2015, 78) reports on one regime study from 1985 that listed 65 clerics in the al-Khu'i network who were loyal to the regime. The Ba'th Party sought to distinguish between al-Khu'i followers who supported the regime and those who were believed to be disloyal.

77. Testimony of A. Al-Zubaydi, recorded May 2007.

78. Kadhim 2013, 23.

79. Ibid., 25; Helfont 2014, 358.

80. Helfont 2015, 83.

81. BRCC Doc. No. 01-3404-0002-0066, June 29, 1985.

continued study in Iraq.[82] During this time, the seminaries of Najaf were nearly emptied.[83] From 1985 to 1988, the number of religious schools in Najaf was reduced from twelve schools to two and religious schools in Karbala were also closed.[84]

A memorandum sent to Saddam Hussein in 1985 refers to the dearth of Arabic-Farsi translators working in intelligence circles and the fact that the regime was forced to rely on the recruitment of Farsi-speaking candidates from the Arabistan (i.e., Khuzestan) province in Iran.[85] The memorandum makes a number of recommendations for improving state capacity in this regard, including recruiting Iraqi graduates of Farsi literature programs; opening Ba'th Party language training institutes to train civil servants in Farsi; encouraging university programs to accept more students into Farsi studies programs; and identifying civilians who speak Farsi to join intelligence efforts as translators. These recommendations were agreed to by Hussein.[86]

MONITORING AND DISPLACEMENT OF SHI'I CLERICS

The hawza was long subject to regime scrutiny and the period of time associated with al-Khu'i's leadership was particularly challenging.[87] The end of the Iran-Iraq War failed to bring respite for the religious establishment as Ba'thist scrutiny of religious elites remained in place.[88] The 1991 Uprisings provided a new repressive context for religiously oriented actors. Al-Khu'i, despite being over ninety years old at the time of the uprisings, was placed under house arrest.[89] That same year, dozens of members of prominent religious families were "disappeared."[90] A UN human rights observer visiting

82. Helfont 2014, 358. Attempts to lure away Shi'i students to newly constructed religious schools under Ba'thist control were largely unsuccessful (Helfont 2015, 65).

83. Louer 2012, 11.

84. Kadhim 2013, 29.

85. BRCC Doc. Nos. 01-3404-0002-0649 to 0654, March 2, 1985. Reliance on translators from Khuzestan created a possible security threat to the Ba'thist regime. The shallow pool of Arabic-Farsi translators suggested that the regime's ability to penetrate Farsi-speaking communities was limited. Also see BRCC Doc. No. 01-3404-0002-0649, 1985.

86. Ibid.

87. Kadhim 2013, 17.

88. Helfont 2014.

89. Fuller and Francke 1999, 104.

90. Ibid., 99.

Iraq in January 1992 reported that the number of clergymen in Najaf had dropped from eight or nine thousand in the early 1970s to two thousand in the early 1980s and to just 800 by the early 1990s.[91]

At the same time, Da'wa Party activism continued to be monitored by the security services into the 1990s. Suspected Da'wa Party members—including elementary school teachers—were monitored and arrested in Saddam City.[92] Informant information was key to identifying a particular suspect while follow-up investigations assessed the extent of Da'wa Party complicity.[93]

A major military intelligence report on the Da'wa Party was circulated in 1995 discussing a variety of issues related to Islamic activism.[94] The report characterized the Da'wa Party as radical in both its thinking and methods, focused on waging a jihad against the regime with the goal of creating a sectarian, Shi'i state.[95] The specific strategies allegedly deployed included using religious occasions as opportunities to spark sectarian sentiment; circulating anti-regime rumors and praise for the Iranian regime; distributing Da'wa Party bulletins; generating anti-regime graffiti; encouraging armed confrontation with Ba'th Party cadre; assassinating Ba'thists, particularly security personnel; falsifying ID cards and other documents facilitating movement within and outside of Iraq; training female Da'wa Party agents for missions; passing Iraqi state information to the Iranian government; training in the use of weapons and explosives outside of Iraq; and using new forms of communication to avoid detection and surveillance.[96]

Despite repression of the Da'wa Party, the regime sought to suppress sectarianism within the Ba'th Party and worked against fostering religious resentments, more broadly.[97] Regime directives included a prohibition on

91. Cockburn 2008, 63.

92. BRCC Doc. No. 01-3787-0001-0336, March 24, 1990; BRCC Doc. No. 01-3787-0001-0343.

93. BRCC Doc. No. 01-3787-0001-0341, March 5, 1990; BRCC Doc. No. 01-3787-0001-0324, May 2, 1990.

94. CRRC Doc. No. SH-GMID-D-000-622, 1995.

95. Ibid. The regime believed that the Da'wa Party worked through a series of stages which included a focus on changing the cultural characteristics of society, a more overtly ideological political stage, a revolutionary period whereby the public would be incited with the goal of establishing a new state, and finally an outward looking phase which considered opportunities for regional expansion.

96. Ibid.

97. Helfont 2015, 160. The most notable exception to this trend were the anti-Shi'i editorials that ran in *Al-Thawra* immediately after the 1991 Uprisings.

discussion about religious sects in the army; intelligence service monitoring and punishment of those who violated such orders; new laws requiring prison sentences for insulting or destroying religious rituals, materials, or places of worship; and the overhaul of the intelligence services to add sections tasked with neutralizing sectarian sentiment.[98] The regime demanded absolute loyalty across sectarian groups but was aware that the distribution of attitudes toward the Ba'th Party and Hussein's leadership differed across communities.

The 1990s also witnessed Ba'th Party attempts at promotion and placement of loyalists into mosques.[99] The following section describes the two-pronged approach taken by the regime with regard to handling the issue of clerics in post-1991 Iraq. The first discusses regime efforts to replace the traditional clerical class with a new, party-loyal bureaucratic elite. The second related to new forms of monitoring that took place.

Replacing Religious Elites

A first step undertaken by the regime involved the attempt to replace existing religious elites with ones amenable to the regime. One plan of action suggested that advanced Ba'th Party members might agree to become clerics, assuming they were able to qualify for such a complex mission; the need for such individuals was deemed especially strong in the Euphrates region.[100] These Shi'i Ba'th Party members would be tasked with joining the hawza, disguised as new students, who would then pursue a normal course of study with the goal of training for leadership within the religious community.[101] One problem was that it was difficult to find volunteers among the party members who were willing to work as clerics.[102]

98. Helfont 2015, 161.

99. Sassoon (2012, 80) writes that Hussein's launch of the "faith campaign" (al-hamla al-'imaniyya) gave "greater prominence to religious occasions and pushed for greater piety in Iraq as an Islamic nation." For example, in February 1995, Ba'thists were required to begin religious training (al-Radi 2003, 94).

100. Kadhim 2013, 30.

101. Ibid., 31. After 1991, religious clerics became increasingly suspicious of new and strange students seeking to enter the hawza, believing they might be sent by the Iraqi intelligence agencies (Helfont 2015, 182). Sadiq al-Sadr is rumored to have subjected potential students to various "tests" in order to identify those sent by the intelligence apparatus; for example, he would ask the students to take off their turbans and then rewrap them, a task difficult for individuals posing as students (ibid.).

102. Ultimately they were able to place only a small number of informants in the hawza and coerce certain existing students to become informants (Kadhim 2013, 33).

An additional, complementary strategy was to establish Islamic institutions which existed under the control of the state and party. The most important of these was Saddam University for Islamic Studies, which was founded in 1988 and located in Baghdad.[103] Students at Saddam University for Islamic Studies were both Iraqi and foreign. According to Helfont and Brill, the establishment of this university and increasing engagement with religious groups and topics should not be seen as a religious turn by the regime; instead, they argue that Hussein continued to be "ruthlessly consistent" in his attacks on Islamist sympathizers who were not directly promoted by the regime.[104] By 2003, the regime seems to have successfully cultivated a "critical mass" of religious leaders who worked in the interest of the Baʿth Party.[105]

Party Evaluation of Islamic Clerics

In order to keep track of the political behaviors and Baʿth Party affiliation of religious leaders, the Baʿth Party created a national inventory of religious clerics in Iraq.[106] The regime's maintenance of this sort of information reflects a distrust of clerics and religious institutions. It also suggests that increasing the legibility of Iraq's clerical establishment and mosque network was a regime priority. Although the regime sought to create a more standardized method for assessing religious leaders, the execution of the information collection differed considerably across Iraqi regions.

Most of the clerics who were actively monitored by the party during this period were either a congregation leader (*imam*) or a person who served as both congregation leader and preacher (*khatib*).[107] While not all clerics were included (as suggested by the fact that some governorates have very few observations), thousands of clerics appear in the Baʿth Party surveillance files.

---

103. See Helfont (2014) for more on this subject.

104. Samuel Helfont and Michael Brill, "Saddam's ISIS? The Terrorist Group's Real Origin Story," *Foreign Affairs*, January 12, 2016.

105. Helfont 2015, 2.

106. Security reports also provided an inventory of major churches, their locations, and their sectarian affiliation (Chaldean, Assyrian Catholic, or Assyrian Orthodox) during the 1990s. See CRRC Doc. No. SH-MISC-D-001-090, July 1992.

107. The idea that authoritarian rulers seek to infiltrate a community of religious elites is not unique to this case. Nalepa and Pop-Eleches (2016) describe how Communist Party infiltration of the Catholic Church impacted social interactions in Eastern European contexts, like Poland.

Many are described as "good" (*jayyid*), meaning holding favorable—or at least acceptable—views toward the regime. Other individual clerics were described as "sound" (*salim*). Two clerics in the collection were described as prominent (*bariz*) and a small percentage were designated excellent (*mumtaz*). 148 individuals were explicitly described as being collaborators (*mut'awin*). Occasionally, individuals were described as nationalist (*watani*).

Given the lack of consistent coding criteria applied by the party apparatchik to the evaluations, I only report the percentage of clerics who were described in a negative way, for example as "not good." In Anbar, when clerics received a negative assessment, the terminology typically used was wavering or unsteady (*mudhabdhab*). Relatively few Anbari clerics were described as having a position in the party and those who did tended to be at a relatively low level of party advancement. While some clerics in Karbala were described as "good," a common clerical designation was "no negative observation can be made about him for the time being" (*la mulahaza salbiya 'alayhu fi al-waqt al-hadir*).[108] Occasionally, clerics would also be described as cunning or underhanded (*murawigh*). In Najaf, a number of clerics are described as malicious or rancorous (*'unsur haqid*).

Although the different governorates were asked to report on the same categories, not all governorates provided complete information. In most governorates, information was provided about the party affiliation of clerics. In Mosul, for example, this was reported in a complete and consistent way. Most Mosul clerics, almost 90 percent, were labeled as independent. The vast majority of Basra clerics were also labeled as political independents. Independent (i.e., having non-Ba'thist designation) should not be interpreted as harmful to regime interests, however. Assessments of clerics from Wasit are illuminating in this regard. While there were a large number of "independent" clerics in Wasit, extra details in their evaluations suggest that they were secret party collaborators.

Reporting about clerics from Baghdad also exhibited considerable variation. In some cases, clerics were suspected of Wahhabism.[109] In other cases, a cleric would be flagged if he had not successfully completed his military service. One Baghdad cleric was described as receiving suspicious visitors. Many were

108. I do not code this as a negative assessment when compiling statistics about cleric evaluation.

109. According to Nixon (2016, 4), Hussein became increasingly concerned with monitoring Wahhabism in Iraq during the 1990s.

TABLE 9.1. Evaluation of Muslim clerics across Iraqi governorates, 1995.

Location	# Clerics of Evaluated	% Negative Evaluation	% Sufi
Baghdad	990	0	2.8
South			
Basra	154	0	3.8
Dhi Qar	48	2.4	0
Maysan	21	0	0
Wasit	18	0	0
Euphrates			
Muthanna	2	0	0
Qadisiyya	10	0	0
Najaf	69	7.7	0
Karbala	117	1.5	0
Babil	45	0	
Central			
Anbar	375	3.1	68.9
Salah al-Din	275	0	4.2
Diyala	178	0	21.3
North			
Mosul	151	0	
Ninawa	222	2.0	4.0
Ta'mim	120	0	0
Erbil	5	0	

described as not religiously extremist. Only one was described as banned from giving sermons. Many were described as active party collaborators. While some were under suspicion, none who were evaluated received an explicitly negative evaluation and about one-third of the clerics did not receive any mark in the evaluation category.[110]

Table 9.1 summarizes the percentage of clerics who received negative evaluations in 1995.[111] The absence of dissident clerics in Baghdad is surprising, particularly given the challenges the regime faced in managing predominantly Shi'i neighborhoods like Saddam City. Less surprising are the relatively large

110. A positive assessment by the Ba'th Party allowed individual clerics more leeway in terms of the opinions they could profess (Kadhim 2013). As a result, public statements by clerics did not necessarily suggest a loss of regime control (Helfont 2015, 228). Rather, some Shi'i scholars issued edicts based on secret requests of the regime (Ibid., 182–183).

111. BRCC Doc. No. 01-2753-0000-0657, 1995.

percentage of Najaf-based clerics who received a negative evaluation. The table also reports on whether the cleric received a "traditional" (*taqlidi*) or Sufi designation.[112] This information was indicated in a fairly thorough way for most locations.[113] Sufi clerics were much more likely to be found in predominantly Sunni governorates than other parts of Iraq. They appear to have been particularly common in Anbar province, a region that was increasingly shut out of Ba'thist redistributive networks during the 1990s.[114]

The Ba'thists also sought to collect information on whether or not a cleric prayed for the president as part of a public sermon. Where this information was indicated, like in Diyala governorate, most clerics did pray for the president. In one case, the cleric in question not only prayed for the president but called for his success and victory, as well. A cleric in Wasit used the pulpit to pray for the longevity of the president and victory over the enemies of Islam. Other sermons asked for luck and long life for the president.

SADIQ AL-SADR AND THE GROWTH OF THE SADRIST MOVEMENT

Abu al-Qasim al-Khu'i died of natural causes in 1992 at the age of ninety-three. His death created an opportunity for Hussein to encourage the promotion of a high cleric of Arab, rather than Persian, descent and one who he hoped would be more amenable to Ba'th Party directives.[115] Despite the regime's contentious history with the Sadr clerical family, Muhammad Muhammad Sadiq al-Sadr—first cousin to Muhammad Baqir al-Sadr—emerged as a potential candidate. From the perspective of the regime, Sadiq al-Sadr seemed a good choice as he was believed to be "relatively malleable."[116]

112. Based on the fact that only two designations were possible here, I assume that a label of traditional should be interpreted as non-Sufi here.

113. In Baghdad, however, only about one-fifth of the clerics received an evaluation as to whether they were Sufi or traditional. About 2.8 percent of the total clerics listed (including those that received no designation) received a Sufi designation. As a result, this might be seen as a lower bound on the percentage of Sufi clerics in Baghdad.

114. The growing proclivity for Sufi clerics in these areas may have been a precursor to the rise of Sufi-led Sunni insurgent groups like the Army of the Men of the Naqshbandi Order (JRTN) after 2006.

115. Cockburn 2008, 97–98.

116. Louer 2012, 91.

Sadiq al-Sadr had been subject to regime repression in the 1970s during the early years of his career. One of Sadiq al-Sadr's biographers speculated that during the cleric's time under house arrest, he developed the belief that a quietist stance was insufficient for dealing with a dictator like Saddam Hussein.[117] Yet Sadiq al-Sadr, at least initially, deployed what appeared to be a quietest stratagem. Sadiq al-Sadr appeared to be apolitical, operating within the regime's guidelines for pious activity.[118] Whereas Muhammad Baqir al-Sadr had engaged in direct forms of confrontation and engagement with the regime, Muhammad Muhammad Sadiq al-Sadr appeared to be working to create a mass cultural movement, leaving politics to the Ba'th Party.[119] But in the end, Sadiq al-Sadr proved difficult to control.

Sadiq al-Sadr was an appealing figure for many Iraqis. He was a populist, Islamic revivalist, and Iraqi nationalist who came from an eminent family.[120] After the 1991 Uprisings, Hussein was concerned about future protests and sought to relax forms of persecution against Iraqi Shi'a.[121] Sadiq al-Sadr "used the breathing space this gave him" to revive his core of supporters.[122] Sadiq al-Sadr established an apparatus around himself in the form of a new cadre of seminarians, responsible for the functions of the infrastructure surrounding his activities.[123]

Sadiq al-Sadr was able to gain followers among the Shi'i masses through his attempts to address the problems of their daily lives while also "undermining the propaganda of the regime."[124] His concern with everyday issues was especially appealing to Iraqis impoverished by economic sanctions.[125]

Rise of the Sadrists

While the origins of the Sadr movement can be found in the writings and political activism of Baqir al-Sadr,[126] it was the repression of Sadiq al-Sadr

117. Cockburn 2008, 102.
118. Jabar 2003a.
119. Cockburn 2008, 99–103.
120. Ibid., 98.
121. Cockburn 2008; Ismael and Fuller 2008.
122. Cockburn 2008, 98.
123. Jabar 2003a, 273; Cockburn 2008, 109.
124. Cockburn 2008, 99.
125. Ibid., 107.
126. Ismael and Fuller 2008.

and his followers that eventually encouraged high levels of solidarity within the group. During the early period of Sadiq al-Sadr's clerical leadership, it was believed that he "feigned cooperation with the regime," inferred from the fact that he avoided politics and focused instead on social and economic issues.[127] Indeed, relations between Sadiq al-Sadr and the regime were stable until 1997.[128] Eventually, however, transgressions committed by Sadiq al-Sadr and his followers opened the door to regime repression in a way that encouraged the merging of political Islam and clerical authority.

Showdown over Increasing Activism

A turning point in the relationship between Sadiq al-Sadr and the Ba'thist regime came with the cleric's introduction of Friday prayers in April 1998—delivered in colloquial language at the Kufa Mosque—as a way to link the hawza with a broader community of his followers.[129] The introduction of Friday prayers was unusual for Shi'a, as this was more traditionally a feature of Sunni Islamic communities.[130] Indeed, Kadhim says this was the first major example of a weekly Shi'i prayer of this type taking place.[131] The event drew an attendance of more than 10,000 worshippers who listened to sermons that were not controlled by or supportive of the regime.[132] Louer suggests that with this act, Sadiq al-Sadr turned against the Ba'thists as these sermons provided an opportunity for public mobilization against the regime.[133] From that point on, the regime viewed Sadiq al-Sadr with increased suspicion.[134]

Tens of thousands of adherents attended the prayers at the Kufa Mosque, overwhelming the monitoring capacity of the regime and creating a sense of

127. Cockburn 2008, 109. The question of whether there was ever a truly cooperative relationship between Sadiq al-Sadr and the Ba'th Party regime is difficult to know. Kadhim (2013, 39) reviews captured documents looking specifically for such evidence and does not find any for this claim.

128. Cockburn 2008, 110.

129. Nakash 2006, 95.

130. Cockburn 2008, 111.

131. Kadhim 2013, 10.

132. Cockburn (2008, 124–125) suggests less prominent examples of Friday sermons first appeared in Kut beginning in 1996 and that Sadiq al-Sadr issued a fatwa inaugurating these sermons in 1997. The timing of the April 1998 sermon was the occasion of a religious holiday, increasing the temporal salience of religious sentiment (Kadhim 2013, 37).

133. Louer 2012, 91.

134. Cockburn 2008, 124.

panic among the Baʿthists.[135] Eventually, worshippers were attending Friday sermons offered by various clerics at up to seventy locales.[136] Attempts were made by the regime to monitor the Friday prayers through the use of informants.[137] Reports included information about the number of worshippers (including female attendees) as well as the name of the cleric giving the sermon and details about references to the United States and Israel.[138] Thousands of people attended Sadiq al-Sadr's sermons, which grew increasingly critical of the Baʿthist regime.[139] Iraqis were particularly attuned to identifying situations when Sadiq al-Sadr's discourse did not match up with regime discourse, as this reflected a form of resistance to Hussein.[140]

From Saddam City to Sadr City

Sadiq al-Sadr supporters emerged as particularly prominent in urban slums which have traditionally posed a challenge to legibility due to their density and limited accessibility. For some parts of Baghdad's slums, public transportation did not exist; potholes and sewer-filled streets could also make movement difficult.[141] Helfont reports on the regime response to its discovery of a number of unsanctioned mosques in a poor Baghdad neighborhood in 1996.[142] The party ordered local Baʿthists to bring all of these mosques under the control of the Ministry of Endowments and Religious Affairs and to also limit the number of mosques that might operate in the area.[143]

The most important Shiʿi slum in Baghdad had a population of over two million and went from being called Revolution City (*Madinat al-Thawra*) to Saddam City to, after 2003, Sadr City.[144] Saddam City was historically a major migration destination for rural residents; these individuals often came from areas like Maysan and Dhi Qar provinces, including from the marsh areas.[145]

---

135. Kadhim 2013, 37.
136. Nakash 2006, 96.
137. BRRC Doc. No. 01-3759-0002-0844, January 9, 1999.
138. BRRC Doc. No. 01-3759-0002-0792, February 4, 1999.
139. Jabar 2003a, 273.
140. Ismael and Fuller 2008.
141. Harling 2012, 77.
142. Helfont 2015, 213.
143. Ibid.
144. Cockburn 2008, 114.
145. Harling 2012, 65.

The regime collected information about all of the mosques and religious congregation halls in Saddam City.[146] The regime also paid careful attention to the number of war martyrs from the neighborhood.[147]

Tribal leaders had an important political role in Saddam City as a result of the rural background of many of the migrants. In a meeting between Hussein and tribal leaders from Saddam City after the 1991 Uprisings, the Baʿthists sought to use these local power brokers to gain greater control over the area.[148] The tribal leaders went to great lengths to show their allegiance and loyalty to Hussein, saying that it was an honor to have their neighborhood named after him and reminding Hussein that they had been instrumental in turning over thousands of soldiers who had deserted from military service and were hiding in Saddam City.[149]

The 1999 Protests

Although general directives existed about the handling of Sadiq al-Sadr's activities, the Baʿth Party soon became overwhelmed by the cleric's activities and the growing number of followers across Shiʿi areas of Iraq.[150] Sadiq al-Sadr was ordered to praise the regime during Friday prayers and to limit the size of his congregation, two things he was loathe to do.[151] On January 29, 1999, Sadiq al-Sadr denounced the arrest of some of his deputies, demanded their immediate release, and condemned future arrests of his followers.[152] Baʿthists in Najaf were increasingly concerned about the number of Friday prayer attendees—reported in January and February of 1999 as at least 10,000.[153] According to Kadhim, the regime began an offensive against Sadiq al-Sadr and his followers, arresting his representatives and initiating a

146. BRCC Doc. No. 01-3404-0002-0062, August 1985.
147. BRCC Doc. Nos. 01-3404-0002-0053 to 0061, July 1985.
148. CRRC Doc. No. SH-SHTP-A-000-891, 1991.
149. Ibid. Another tribal leader appealed to Hussein to spare the neighborhood his anger, as any anti-regime rioting that had taken place there was undertaken by homosexuals and not the bulk of the citizens. Hussein encouraged forms of retaliatory in-group policing by suggesting that any murder of the homosexuals responsible for instigating the riots would not be considered a crime by the regime.
150. Kadhim 2013, 13.
151. Cockburn 2008, 129.
152. Kadhim 2013, 48.
153. Ibid., 47–48.

propaganda campaign against him in collaboration with the assistance of some of his clerical rivals.[154] On February 19, Sadiq al-Sadr and two of his sons were assassinated in their car. His youngest son, Muqtada al-Sadr, was not killed.

Spontaneous, unorganized public demonstrations broke out in response immediately after the deaths despite the fact that doing so was criminalized by the regime.[155] Protesters deployed anti-Hussein and anti-Baʿthist slogans in what the regime reports describe as a rapidly evolving and violent situation.[156] A variety of protest activities continued for the month to follow.[157]

The regime undertook a multifaceted response to the protests. In Saddam City, security forces opened fire on crowds, killing dozens of people.[158] The Baʿthists also sought to activate their networks of co-opted clerics to sow confusion about the identity of the assailants; most Iraqis, however, believed that the regime was responsible for the killings.[159]

The Baʿth Party records also provide details on the internal regime discussions that took place in the wake of the assassination. As soon as the assassination occurred, the Saddam City branch of the party received the directive to tighten regulations, double the number of security guards at the party headquarters, and pay attention to any suspicious activity. During emergency meetings, the leadership coordinated to try to create a unified plan of action.[160] One memorandum discussed citizen responses to Sadiq al-Sadr's assassination in Saddam City and elsewhere. The memo emphasized the need to end demonstrations through the strength of the party apparatus.[161] Other reports emphasized the courage and commitment of party cadre who opposed the protesters, including detailed casualty reports with the number and medical status of injured comrades as well as estimates of material losses, including cars.[162]

Anti-regime activities continued in the weeks and months that followed. On February 25, it was reported that a party member was stabbed by a

154. Ibid.
155. Cockburn 2008, 132.
156. BRCC Doc. No. 01-3759-0002-0766, 1999.
157. Cockburn 2008, 133.
158. Ibid., 132.
159. Helfont 2015, 184.
160. BRCC Doc. No. 01-3759-0002-0765, February 22, 1999.
161. BRCC Doc. No. 01-3759-0002-0767, February 22, 1999.
162. BRCC Doc. No. 01-3759-0002-0766, 1999.

Sadr supporter.[163] On February 26, it was reported that pro-Sadr cassette tapes and opposition flyers were circulating in Saddam City; the afternoon prayer, however, was reported to be normal, calling for calm and avoidance of bloodshed.[164] Reports of Ba'th Party member injuries during disturbances in Saddam City continued into March.[165] Party members killed were to be considered by the state to be "martyrs" with the associated compensatory benefits for their families.[166] Oppositional writing continued to be discovered in Saddam City.[167] One detailed report focused on Friday sermons in the mosques of Saddam City, providing information about the number of worshippers and their general disposition.[168]

Some of the most intense rioting took place in Basra on March 17. Human rights reports suggest that heavily armed Ba'th Party members began rounding up suspects the next morning, continuing for several days.[169] Entire families were arrested.[170] The Iraqi government also routinely demolished the houses of those they suspected of involvement in the uprising.[171] Individuals who were suspected of involvement, or were worried about arrest, often stayed with friends, moving locations repeatedly.[172] This suggests not only that punishment undertaken in the wake of the events of Basra was collective and indiscriminate at the "family" level, but also that individuals bound by trust relations provided shelter for suspected agitators despite the considerable risk families took to hide targets of arrest.

Although some additional disturbances continued to take place into April, the regime became increasingly invested in intelligence sector investigations into the identity of the rioters.[173] Monitoring of suspects continued in Saddam City, where individuals were followed both to Friday prayers and to their visits of Najafi clerics in the area.[174] Other suspects were thought to have

163. BRCC Doc. No. 01-3759-0002-0730, February 25, 1999.
164. BRCC Doc. No. 01-3759-0002-0723, February 28, 1999.
165. BRCC Doc. No. 01-3759-0002-0641, March 21, 1999.
166. BRCC Doc. No. 01-3759-0002-0644, March 23, 1999.
167. BRCC Doc. No. 01-3759-0002-0640, March 25, 1999.
168. BRCC Doc. No. 01-3759-0002-0628, April 3, 1999.
169. "Ali Hassan al-Majid and the Basra Massacre of 1999," Human Rights Watch Iraq, February 17, 2005.
170. Ibid.
171. Ibid.
172. Ibid.
173. BRCC Doc. No. 01-3759-0002-0504, April 23, 1999.
174. BRCC Doc. No. 01-3759-0002-0510, April 25, 1999.

fled Saddam City for Najaf, where they were in hiding.[175] Locating and monitoring suspects was a top priority.[176] Individuals were sometimes mistakenly caught up in the regime dragnet that followed. According to one informant, a group of policemen raided his house in the wake of the 1999 protests to arrest his brother, who was charged with participating in the demonstrations; the informant was mistakenly arrested instead, and eventually released.[177]

In April, the regime sought to shift blame from themselves and executed four men convicted of the Sadr assassinations in a closed trial; these events took place over the objections of Shiʿi religious leaders.[178] One of the accused, a Shiʿi prayer leader from Najaf, was reportedly in prison at the time of the assassination; the other three accused were also religious scholars.[179] Arrests of theological students continued and nineteen additional followers of Sadiq al-Sadr were executed by the end of 1999.[180]

Politically transgressive activities took place into the summer. One memorandum reported an assassination attempt on a top Baʿthist security official that occurred in Saddam City.[181] According to that report, the perpetrator was under the influence of senior cleric Muhammad Baqir al-Hakim, who was believed to have issued a fatwa to kill party, military, and police officials. The report also mentioned the need for continued monitoring and the persistent worry of reprisals and future planned attacks against regime representatives.[182]

Surveillance of the Sadr family and followers continued as well.[183] Despite this, underground forms of political subversion continued to take place by Sadiq al-Sadr supporters. Photos of Sadiq al-Sadr reportedly were secretly available for sale in Saddam City and the Jamila neighborhood.[184] Flyers produced by Sadr supporters also circulated in Saddam City.[185] The regime continued to be concerned with the illegal sale of Shiʿi sectarian posters

175. Ibid.
176. BRCC Doc. No. 01-3759-0002-0505, April 25, 1999.
177. Testimony of M. Hussein, recorded April 2007.
178. *Annual Report on International Religious Freedoms*, US Department of State, 2000.
179. Ibid.
180. Ibid.
181. BRCC Doc. No. 01-3759-0002-0367, May 31, 1999.
182. Ibid.
183. BRCC Doc. No. 01-3219-0000-0093, June 3, 1999.
184. BRCC Doc. No. 01-3759-0002-0232, June 28, 1999; BRCC Doc. No. 01-3219-0000-0097, July 10, 1999.
185. BRCC Doc. No. 01-3759-0002-0143, July 22, 1999.

and publications across Baghdad.[186] One report suggested that a cleric gave a Friday sermon in a mosque that had pictures of Sadiq al-Sadr hanging on the walls.[187] In response, the regime continued its efforts to minimize opportunities for political agitation in Sadrist mosques.[188] In particular, the memorandum spoke to the important role the Ba'th Party apparatus should play in minimizing the possibility for transgressive incidents and to maintain the peace.

A major study on opposition groups, their publications, and Friday prayers was conducted by the office of Saddam's Fedayeen.[189] Friday prayers and other religious occasions continued to be emphasized as periods of vulnerability for the regime since clerics had the ability to attract youth who might be called upon to become political agitators. The Euphrates region, southern governorates, and the Saddam City neighborhood of Baghdad were all described as potentially vulnerable areas. Hussein's militia sought to acquire better quality intelligence regarding religious institutions. Intelligence officers were to be selected according to a variety of criteria, including mental flexibility, faithfulness, and the ability to act quickly in critical situations. It was also suggested that such individuals should not have tribal problems or personal enemies. The intelligence officer would be responsible for cultivating sources who could acquire accurate information about the intentions of subversives before they had a chance to actualize their plans. This would allow time to coordinate with security organizations and the Ba'th Party.

A number of techniques and procedures were considered for how to handle potential problems.[190] It was suggested that Hussein's militia should form small security detachments where three to four detachments would be deployed in suspect areas. These small groups would be responsible for immediate intervention to suppress agitators and to provide early information to centralized authorities. The detachments were to select a suitable and close location as a safe "base" and starting location for activities. The detachments should include active Ba'th Party members and they should be armed. Financial bonuses would be offered to individuals assigned with the tasks of both gathering information and dealing with these difficult security challenges.

186. BRCC Doc. No. 01-2129-0000-0555, July 24, 1999.
187. BRCC Doc. No. 01-2129-0000-0557, July 29, 1999.
188. BRCC Doc. No. 01-2129-0000-0589, July 4, 1999.
189. CRRC Doc. No. SH-FSDM-D-001-093, 1999.
190. Ibid.

CONCLUSIONS

Religious organizations associated with pious beliefs and practices are among the most robust and significant civil society networks in the late twentieth century and early twenty-first century Middle East. It is perhaps unsurprising that the Baʿthist regime, with its strong secular leanings, clashed with religious activists in Iraq. Baʿth Party elite recognized the mobilizational power of religion and continually sought to monitor and neutralize religious influence. Hussein worked defensively to manage the political threat posed by religious mobilization with the goal of doing so "before it turned completely against his Baʿthist regime."[191] In the face of a strong and repressive state, the Shiʿi clergy typically acquiesced to the system, preferring to focus on spiritual life.[192] Reluctant to engage in direct forms of political contestation, most clerics created their "own domain of schools, students, followers, and charities."[193]

Quietism was not the choice of all clerics, however, and where political transgressions by religious activists did occur, the regime sought to punish those activists. Daʿwa Party members were ruthlessly persecuted during the Baʿthist regime. And between 1970 and 1985, at least forty-one Muslim clerics—many of whom were associated with the Daʿwa Party—were executed.[194] Gathering accurate intelligence about the activities of religious activists, however, held special challenges for the regime. Religious groups tended to be insular, made up of individuals with family ties and marriage connections. Each major cleric had his students, followers, and mechanisms for the distribution of club goods. Shiʿi religious seminaries were difficult for Baʿthists to penetrate compared to other civil society groups as they sometimes operated in Farsi, rather than Arabic. Within those networks, it was difficult for the Baʿthist regime to identify political transgressors even if they knew the general locus of the transgression. Ultimately, the Baʿth Party regime lacked the manpower and resources to manage the religious domain effectively and, as a result, chose to repress problematic religious activists.[195]

In the wake of the 1991 Uprisings, Muhammad Muhammad Sadiq al-Sadr emerged as a major religious figure. Initially tolerated and even encouraged

191. Helfont 2015, 28.
192. Visser 2008, 31.
193. Zubaida 2002, 208.
194. Fuller and Francke 1999, 101.
195. Helfont 2015, 43.

by the Baʿthists, Sadiq al-Sadr successfully connected his religious seminary with a following in rural, southern communities and Baghdad's Shiʿi slums.[196] Sadiq al-Sadr institutionalized his following during the international sanctions period.[197] Following his 1999 assassination, protests by his followers led to repression of the "Sadrists." The group to emerge became a political movement with a "genuine social base" that could "rely on the consistent support of a core group of the population."[198] This chapter argues that the group-level repression that was meted out against Shiʿi clerical groups by the Baʿthist regime during the 1990s encouraged the cementing of boundaries between factions within the Shiʿi community while simultaneously increasing forms of social trust within them.

196. Nakash 2006, 95.
197. Jabar 2003a, 273.
198. Al-Ali 2014, 44.

CHAPTER 10

MILITARY SERVICE, MILITIAS, AND COUP ATTEMPTS

In December 1997, regional officials from the southern provinces of Basra and Dhi Qar penned a letter to their Baʿth Party counterparts praising the citizens of their region for their exemplary commitment to volunteerism in the service of Saddam Hussein. In the letter, the officials extolled the citizens of Basra and Dhi Qar for their willingness to give up their possessions, their lives, and even the lives of their children to serve the regime. To document this commitment, the officials provided various forms of evidence including that high percentages of residents had volunteered for regime militias; that tribal leaders were assisting in the defense of borders with Iran and Kuwait and had promised to avoid fighting with each other so that they might better protect the country from foreign attack; that women, teenagers, the disabled, and the elderly were participating in fedayeen training camps; and that local leaders would transport participants to fedayeen training at their own personal expense.[1] The officials also reported that a large number of these militia volunteers had signed blood oaths and had dedicated their worldly possessions to the regime.[2]

A letter of this sort raises a number of important questions. Why did officials from Basra and Dhi Qar seek to signal the commitment of their constituents in this way? And what value did the Baʿthist regime see in militia volunteers who were poorly positioned to actually engage in militia activities? Finally, why would individuals seek to volunteer for this type of military service?

1. BRCC Doc. Nos. 008-4-6-28 and 29, December 11, 1997.
2. Ibid.

A core problem of civil-military relations relates to how civilian authorities, like hegemonic parties, can curb the power of the military establishment.[3] Kamrava argues that Middle Eastern autocracies are especially worried about internal challengers, particularly from the military.[4] One reason for heightened concern is that Middle Eastern leaders have sought to professionalize their armies in a bid to survive in a competitive regional environment and tend to be highly reliant on their military establishments. In the extreme, a civilian ruler can be overthrown in a military-initiated coup d'etat.[5] Autocrats are particularly worried about such a possibility as coups are the most common form of irregular leadership change in dictatorships.[6] Indeed, Faust argues that internal coups and assassination plots were the single most dangerous threat to the Ba'thist regime.[7]

To prevent coups, dictators often engage in efforts to subordinate the armed forces, both ideologically and politically.[8] Regimes also engage in processes of "coup-proofing." Quinlivan writes, "the essence of coup-proofing is the creation of structures that minimize the possibilities of small groups leveraging the system to such ends."[9] This includes exploitation of family, ethnic, and religious identity as a way to restrict high-level service as well as the cultivation of multiple, internal armies and intelligence agencies that might counter and monitor each other.[10]

Saddam Hussein was deeply concerned with the possibility that his regime would become dominated by the military. It was Hussein's belief that by investing in the institutional strength of the Ba'th Party, it would make it difficult, if not impossible, for military interests to overthrow the government.[11] At the same time, Hussein pursued a "dual armies" model where

3. Bland 1999.
4. Kamrava 2000, 67.
5. Singh defines a coup attempt as an "explicit action, involving some portion of the state military, police or security forces, undertaken with the intent to overthrow the government." While generals can be successful in launching coups because they possess forms of "soft" power over the military, colonels control actual troops because they directly command. Coups launched from the bottom rungs of the military hierarchy are akin to mutinies and tend to be violent, confused, and unlikely to succeed (Singh 2014, 10).
6. Singh 2014, 3.
7. Faust 2015, 157.
8. Belkin and Schofer 2003.
9. Quinlivan 1999, 133.
10. Quinlivan 1999.
11. Dodge 2003, 62.

fear of the military encouraged the creation of alternative, ideological military forces to keep the regular army in check.[12] For the Baʿthist regime, the creation of paramilitary units, even those that did not serve any obvious military purpose, was seen as a counterbalancing, mobilizational organization for regime stalwarts.

Greitens argues that in countries where coup threats are perceived as high, autocrats create a more fragmented and less inclusive security apparatus and that this harms the regime's monitoring capability.[13] The Iraq case suggests a slightly different set of circumstances. Despite the relatively fragmented nature of the security apparatus, Hussein himself served as a key coordinating and centralizing authority. In addition, security agencies served to check one another to ensure that no organization reported false information. For example, multiple security organizations produced biannual reports on the activities of hostile political movements within Iraq.[14]

This chapter explores the relationship between the Baʿthist regime and the Iraqi military, broadly defined. A first empirical focus relates to the question of draft dodging. I address what this phenomenon meant for regime stability, but also what draft evasion suggested about Iraqi society and societal attempts at political defiance. A next empirical section takes up the question of how and why the regime created a series of ancillary military units, in particular, state- and party-sponsored militias. I discuss the units created, which segments of Iraqi society were mobilized for participation in those units, and how such units assisted in efforts at safeguarding the regime. Finally, I consider regime vulnerability to coup attempts, most of which were initiated by elements from within the Iraqi military. While the regime became increasingly vulnerable to internal military threats during the international sanctions period, none of these coups was successful. I attribute the failure to overthrow Hussein during this period, at least in part, to the high degree of security service penetration of the predominantly Sunni military officer corps.

MILITARY-BAʿTH PARTY RELATIONS

The Iraqi military became increasingly subordinated to the Baʿth Party during Hussein's period of political power. Yet despite the "Baʿthification" of the military, given the size and diversity of the armed forces, it was impossible to

12. Kamrava 2000.
13. Greitens 2016.
14. Helfont 2015, 93–94.

exercise totalizing forms of political control over either elites or rank-and-file soldiers.[15]

Historical Development of the Iraqi Military

From its origins as a national armed force upon Iraqi independence, the Iraqi military has served a domestic role, enforcing internal security by putting down sectarian, tribal, and other revolts or resistance to central government rule.[16] In contrast to conventional militaries that focus on external security threats, the Iraqi military has historically served as a "central institution of domestic politics and instrument of repression."[17]

As a result of the Ottoman preference for training Sunni, rather than Shiʿi, military officers, the early twentieth-century Iraqi officer corps was primarily made up of "lower-middle class Sunni Arab and Kurdish families."[18] And while the military college was open to all Iraqis regardless of their ethnic or sectarian identity, the majority of instructors and cadets were Arab Sunnis.[19] Beginning in the 1930s, officers from Tikrit rose in prominence and number; it is speculated that a decline in Tikrit's main industry—traditional boat making from animal hides—made the military a more desirable option for young Tikritis.[20] In addition to over-representation of people from certain regions in the military, for rural parts of Iraq tribal structures were favorably "oriented towards the military role."[21]

By the late 1960s, a major effort was initiated with the goal of bringing the military under civilian political control.[22] The party sought to penetrate the army, making it a capital offense for members of the armed forces to engage in political activity other than participation in the Baʿth Party.[23] In addition, hundreds of Iraqi military officers—particularly those who were

15. According to Heller (1993, 42), there were three challenges facing the Baʿthist regime from the army: the need to ensure the army's willingness to suppress communal challenges by creating an officer corps made up of Sunni Arabs, the desire to ensure political loyalty by purging potentially disloyal officers, and limiting the opportunities for dissident unit commanders to act independently with the goal of organizing a coup.

16. Heller 1993, 39.

17. Al-Marashi and Salama 2008, 3.

18. Ibid., 14.

19. Ibid., 28.

20. Baram 2003, 94.

21. Batatu 1978, 10.

22. Al-Marashi and Salama 2008, 8.

23. Heller, 44.

high competence—were exiled, forcibly retired, imprisoned, or killed if they were perceived as disloyal.[24] During this time, the preponderance of military officers came from provincial Sunni Arab towns from areas north and west of Baghdad, including Tikrit, Rawa, and Fallujah.[25]

During the 1970s, the Baʿthists enjoyed some success at subordinating both the Ministry of Defense and the Republican Guard to party interests.[26] The party also created an ideologically oriented paramilitary unit called the Popular Army (*al-Jaysh al-Shaʿbi*), which was controlled not by the Ministry of Defense but by the Baʿth Party.[27] Confident that threats from within the army could be contained by the creation of alternative "anti-armies," like the Republican Guard and Popular Army, the size of Iraq's military grew enormously over the course of the 1970s. With only six divisions in the mid-1960s, the Iraqi Army eventually grew to forty-four divisions during the Iran-Iraq War.[28] Estimates of troop size suggest an increase from 50,000 in 1968 to 140,000 in 1977 to 430,000 in 1980 and eventually to almost one million by 1988.[29]

As Hussein's personal power grew during the same period, key posts within the military increasingly came to be occupied by clansmen from his home region.[30] According to one account:

> The highest ranks in the armed forces and in the Guard were staffed by members of Hussein's Tikriti Al-Bu Nasir tribe … the exploitation of special loyalties formed a "community of trust" among those privileged officers from Tikrit, as well as the surrounding Sunni Arab areas that staffed the state's central administration, the security organizations and the top echelons of the officer corps.[31]

In this way, the Tikriti elite became the regime's "decisive core" with high levels of investment in interlocking political and kinship ties as well as shared economic interests.[32]

24. Dodge 2003, 61.
25. Al-Marashi and Salama 2008, 115.
26. Ibid., 8.
27. Bashir 2005, 60; Al-Marashi and Salama 2008, 125.
28. Al-Khafaji 2000, 267.
29. Jabar 1992; Jabar 2003a, 118.
30. Jabar 1992.
31. Al-Marashi and Salama 2008, 144.
32. Jabar 1992.

Civil-Military Relations under Hussein

Although not trained in military affairs, Hussein viewed himself as a visionary battlefield strategist, a belief that eventually drove a wedge between himself and Iraq's professional officer corps. During the course of the Iran-Iraq War it became increasingly clear that Hussein's tactical decisions were reckless and unsuccessful.[33] Indeed, the military setbacks had a destabilizing political effect as his battlefield failures led Hussein's popularity to decline.[34]

To eliminate opposition within the military, Hussein undertook a number of strategies including "the intensification of the use of informants and security services to monitor the military, and the use of rotations, arrests, and executions to eliminate seditious and subversive soldiers and officers... in other words, the state created a pervasive sense of internal fear by penetrating the Iraqi military at every level."[35] The military was transformed by Hussein into an "organ" of the Baʿth Party where military orders were routinely cleared by party headquarters before implementation.[36]

Eventually it became clear that the Baʿthist regime would need to utilize a wider array of military expertise to gain a tactical advantage in the conflict, but also to handle management of the domestic implications of the war. The net result of this was a dilution of Tikriti political power.[37] Officers from the so-called Sunni triangle, including towns like Ana, Bayji, Dur, Sharqat, Samarra, and Ramadi, became increasingly important, with a high degree of representation from tribal networks including the Dulaimi, Juburi, ʿAzzawi, and ʿUbaydi.[38]

Immediately after the cessation of fighting in the Iran-Iraq War, it became clear that maintenance of such a large standing army was beyond the economic capability of the regime. The Iraqi government also feared that the army might turn into an "uncontrolled leviathan" at its full mobilizational capacity.[39] At the same time, given the breadth of the army's popular base, downsizing it would be politically costly.[40] The Iraqi invasion of Kuwait in

33. Al-Marashi and Salama 2008, 129.
34. Bengio 1988, 363–364.
35. Al-Marashi Salama 2008, 129.
36. Hiro 1991, 20.
37. Jabar 1992.
38. Davis 2005, 32; Al-Marashi and Salama 2008, 144–145.
39. Jabar 2003a; Al-Marashi and Salama 2008, 176.
40. Jabar 1992.

August 1990 provided a renewed purpose for the army. The invasion initially went smoothly for Iraqi forces, with most Kuwaiti units surrendering almost immediately.[41] Yet the pillaging of Kuwaiti wealth and valuables suggested a "lawlessness and unpredictability" of the military that acted like an organized crime syndicate.[42] The entrance of the US-led coalition into the conflict forced the Iraq Army's withdrawal from Kuwait.

Soldiers returning from Kuwait incurred massive casualties as they retreated.[43] Many of these troops were already disgruntled because they had been poorly fed and paid and inadequately armed for battle.[44] The coalition air campaign was devastating for Iraqi soldiers, as it "ultimately wiped out the bulk of these angry and retreating forces."[45] The popular uprisings that followed spread from southern city to city. According to Jabar, "the popular explosion, building since 1988, was detonated by the retreating soldiers and officers who had survived the horrors" associated with the chaotic and deadly withdrawal from Kuwait.[46]

Despite the scope and intensity of the 1991 Uprisings, other units within the broader armed forces apparatus mobilized effectively to regain social and political control over southern Iraq. Republican Guard units—equipped with better training and weaponry—remained loyal to the regime and were effective at putting down the insurrections.[47] There was also a relevant ethno-sectarian element to the management of the domestic conflict—"the predominantly Arab Sunni soldiers were defending their privileged status in the Iraqi state, understandably expecting that Hussein's fall would be a tremendous loss for them as well … their success demonstrated how at least one element of the Iraqi armed forces excelled in its traditional role of suppressing internal insurrections."[48] The result was that, despite massive and widespread anger and losses in the wake of the military withdrawal, "the very section of the armed forces left intact by the [George H. W.] Bush administration … carried out their domestic security tasks almost to perfection."[49]

41. Jabar 2003a, 119.
42. Davis 2005, 182.
43. Al-Marashi and Salama 2008, 183.
44. Ibid.
45. Jabar 2003a, 120.
46. Jabar 1992.
47. Al-Marashi and Salama 2008, 184.
48. Ibid.
49. Jabar 2003a, 121.

Following the end of the Gulf War, the military was reduced in size considerably, with the army shrinking from ten to five corps and from forty-six to fifteen infantry divisions.[50] Estimates suggest that the armed forces, once a million in number, were reduced to less than 500,000 and that the ability to restock armaments also declined dramatically.[51] There is little doubt that the reduced purchasing power of the regime had a major impact on the size and treatment of the military in the early 1990s. According to one story circulating at the time, the Iraqi Army Chief of Staff visited the kitchen of one brigade and found the men barely surviving on little more than bread.[52]

Beyond the challenges associated with the budget constraint, Dodge also articulates a political logic associated with reducing the size of the military—"by shrinking the size of the army, the ruling elite has strengthened its coherence and removed all those it considered to be disloyal ... the idea was to create a smaller, more disciplined force that would be ideologically committed to defending the regime."[53] Those regional and kinship groups that had been stretched thin in a million-man force would enjoy greater density in a smaller military.[54]

This type of downsizing particularly hurt western Sunnis who were prominently represented in eliminated or downsized units. Jabar argues that Sunnis from Anbar had historically been well represented in the security apparatus.[55] But eventually there came to be an increasing stratification within the Sunni community where those immediately surrounding Hussein and his family were "understood as 'royal,' while the Duri, Rawi, Dulaimi, Juburi and others assumed positions equivalent to 'Earls,' 'Lords' and 'Sirs,' respectively."[56] The main beneficiaries of the regime's reorientation were individuals from the areas south of Mosul to Tikrit.[57] The increasingly narrow geographical origins of the officer corps privileged loyalty over competence, hurting Iraq's military readiness. On the other hand, recruitment and promotion patterns of this type were effective at countering the regime's internal enemies.

50. Al-Marashi and Salama 2008, 186.
51. Dodge 2003, 64; Jabar 2003d, 122.
52. Pasha 2003, 100.
53. Dodge 2003, 64.
54. Jabar 2003d, 122.
55. Jabar 2003a, 133.
56. Jabar 2003a, 116. In addition, other than a single, prominent general from Mosul, virtually no high-level political officials were drawn from major Iraqi urban centers (al-Khafaji 2000, 279–280).
57. Al-Khafaji 2000, 279–280.

AVOIDING MILITARY OBLIGATIONS

The question of when and why individuals meet obligations associated with compulsory military service is a core substantive issue in the social sciences. Levi, for example, considers issues of political consent in the context of military service requirements as imposed by democratic regimes in the nineteenth and twentieth centuries.[58] I consider the conditions under which individuals avoid service obligations in an autocracy where issues of shared social obligation and quasi-voluntary action take on a different meaning. Iraqi citizens were long cynical about military conscription.[59] Military conscription, however, was an important part of the nation-building project where service in the military was a strategy "to cement the public's loyalty to a patriotic and professional army that would incorporate Iraqis of all sects and ethnicities, as well as urban, rural and tribal elements into a cohesive, national institution."[60]

The Baʿthist regime was highly concerned with the issue of deserters and, indeed, spent considerable resources trying to locate individuals who failed to complete their compulsory military service. Why was the issue of draft evasion so important to the regime? Not only did draft evasion have serious implications for military readiness, it was during compulsory military service that the regime was able to exercise control over the lives of cohorts of young Iraqi men.

The failure to complete military obligations to the state had important political and social implications. Draft evaders were often forced into marginal or illegal economic activities, like black marketeering, that worked against state attempts to fix prices and control markets. The party worked to educate the public that desertion was a treasonous act that created an "atmosphere of crime and lawlessness and undermined public safety."[61] War deserters sometimes formed their own gangs in cities like Baghdad, contributing to urban crime.[62] High levels of military desertion also challenged the regime narrative of a "heroic national struggle" against external enemies, like Iran.[63]

Draft dodging represented an unusual political space since it created a fundamental information problem for the regime. While the identity of the

58. Levi 1997.
59. Al-Marashi and Salama 2008, 29.
60. Ibid., 24–25.
61. Khoury 2013, 76.
62. Rohde 2010, 35.
63. Khoury 2013, 73.

deserter is known with certainty, there continued to exist some ambiguity about the political orientation of the deserter—the private information dimension of relevance. Because individuals avoid the draft for a variety of reasons, including fear of injury or death during the course of military service, evasion of military service was not an exclusive marker of political opposition. Yet while there existed compelling, apolitical incentives to avoid compulsory military service, draft evasion could be viewed as a form of political defiance.[64] Khoury writes that because outright resistance to the Baʿth Party was difficult to organize, such resistance "manifested itself most clearly with significant resistance to the war and took the form of desertion, dereliction of duty, or surrender to the enemy."[65]

To what extent did draft evasion rely on the complicity of others? Draft evasion was an act often only possible with the existence of social cohesion where extended family networks might provide financial or other forms of support for the draft dodger while in hiding. Because draft dodgers navigated the line between "criminality, political dissent and rebellion," there existed real risks to supporting individuals in hiding.[66] Individuals who sheltered deserters were seen as politically dangerous and deserving of punishment.[67] The regime sought to reward situations where family members turned in relatives who were deserters, as these were seen as the highest examples of loyalty to the nation.[68]

Draft Evasion during the Iran-Iraq War

A major problem for the Iraqi regime during the Iran-Iraq War related to the relatively large numbers of young men who either deserted from the army or

64. Khoury 2013.
65. Khoury 2013, 8.
66. Khoury 2013, 74.
67. Khoury 2013, 73.
68. Khoury 2013, 76. While rewards associated with exemplary service or martyrdom in war were offered to the martyr's family, punishment for desertion was also applied to the extended family. According to Khoury, punishment for desertion involved sanctions levied against extended family and second-degree kin (173). The overall effect of this form of policing and repression was that an individual's behavior was tied to the rights of his kin with the effect of "augmenting the regulatory power of kin and entrenching clan loyalties" (174). Collective punishment of the families of deserters intensified in 1994 when it was ordered that if someone in the family was a deserter, the family would have to give up its ration card (154).

engaged in forms of draft evasion by being slow to report for their military service.[69] Able-bodied men between the ages of eighteen and forty-five were conscripted into the armed forces or militias—a military necessity given the population advantage Iran enjoyed over Iraq.[70] Desertion was punishable by death, though a variety of documents suggest that this directive was not strictly enforced.

Most deserters and draft dodgers in the early 1980s were Kurds who could find refuge in mountain areas controlled by Kurdish guerillas.[71] Many Kurdish Iraqis were exempted from military service if they volunteered for pro-regime militias, like the *jash*, which helped to control the Kurdish North.[72] But the regime continued to issue arrest orders for deserters and stragglers in northern districts as well as directives to take control of financial resources belonging to these individuals should they fail to complete some form of military service.[73]

By the mid- to late 1980s, the problem of desertions was common in the south as well. This is probably not surprising given the large numbers of Iraqi soldiers from southern governorates who were being killed or taken prisoner during the course of combat. Chubb and Tripp argue that desertion often served as a substitute for political militancy; and because deserter groups were physically isolated and fragmented, the regime developed strategies for handling the situation.[74]

Hussein himself was deeply troubled by draft evasion. He believed that Iraqis failed to understand the difficult situation facing the country, or the sacrifices required. During a meeting with advisors he asked a rhetorical question to those hiding deserters—would they accept the occupation of Baghdad or Basra?[75] Hussein also related stories about Iraqis who check to

69. These individuals are described in the memos as *mutakhallifin*, literally the stragglers (or absentees), and refers to those who failed to report for their required military service in a timely way. Absenteeism was defined as failure to report to military or reserve duty for five days after an assigned date, while desertion was failure to report to duty after thirty days (Khoury 2013, 73).

70. Front-line soldiers during the war typically fell into one of four categories, according to Khoury (2013, 95): professional volunteers trained at military academies, reservists with multiple years of training, soldiers from the party militias, or paramilitary units or conscripts with virtually no training at all.

71. Sassoon 2012, 152.

72. Rohde 2010, 35.

73. Iraqi Secret Police Files Doc. Nos. 10031 to 10044, March 17, 1984.

74. Chubb and Tripp 1988, 103.

75. CRRC Doc. No. SH-SHTP-A-001-023, March 6, 1987.

make sure their martyred sons were not shot in the back (suggesting they had run away in battle) as well as families who spit on a son who had been executed for retreating.[76] Hussein further argued that a son would not commit treason unless the man's family was politically ill-motivated, thus placing responsibility for acts of desertion on the deserter's family.[77]

One part of the regime's strategy for reducing the number of deserters related to increasing the legibility of the marsh areas where deserters often fled. Bounded by Amara in the North, Nasiriyya in the West, and Basra in the East, the Iraqi marshes were among the largest wetland ecosystems in Western Asia. Some estimates suggest that by October 1986, 30,000 deserters were hiding in the southern marshes.[78] The existence of large numbers of deserters in the marshes constituted a security problem for the regime.

A 1987 report provided recommendations from a committee regarding operational implementation of a plan for the marsh areas.[79] The report acknowledged that the marshes had become a haven for deserters, outlaws, and members of hostile parties who sought to launch sabotage operations. Recommendations included renewed security operations in the marshes. It was also suggested that deserters hiding in the marshes might be turned into informants in exchange for amnesty for deserting military service. Villages were collectively punished through a variety of channels including economic seige, the banning of the sale of fish, and refusing to give marsh dwellers their food rations.[80] According to Fuller and Francke, a classified report entitled "Plan of Action for the Marshes" discussed imposition of economic sanctions and other forms of collective punishment against marsh communities.[81]

Reports from the spring and summer of 1987 provide information on draft dodging for the Euphrates region, which encompasses governorates including the holy cities of Najaf and Karbala as well as Babil, Qadisiyya, and Muthanna.[82] For the period between May 27 and June 26, 1987, the total number of deserters arrested in the Euphrates region was 374, and another 2,216 deserters surrendered themselves to authorities. The largest numbers

76. Ibid.
77. Ibid.
78. Rohde 2010, 35.
79. CRRC Number SH-RVCC-D-000-218, May–September 1987.
80. Ibid.
81. Fuller and Francke 1999, 103.
82. I was unable to find documents that showed the relative rates of desertion across the country for this time period.

of these individuals were from Najaf and Qadisiyya; despite having only a slightly larger population than Karbala, Najaf had almost three times as many arrested deserters and deserters who had turned themselves in.[83] The number of individuals executed for deserting during this same period was 146. The Baʿth Party led 848 meetings on the subject of draft evasion with community leaders during this period, the largest numbers of which took place in Babil and Karbala.

Draft Evasion after 1990

The Gulf War and 1991 Uprisings intensified the problem of desertions.[84] Jabar relates the story of Ahmad, an Iraqi corporal exhausted by years of warfare:

> I forged an ID identifying me as a peasant to evade being recruited again. But after two months the order to exempt peasants from military service was rescinded … Hope came when a conscript from the Albu Hijam tribe whispered that he was going to desert and seek shelter in the Hawr al-Hammar marsh, as he had done before. He invited me to go with him on the condition that I tell no one.[85]

Individual experiences of draft evasion like the one described above were repeated by thousands of Iraqi conscripts and soldiers during the course of the 1990s. In 1994—after offering a short window for clemency if they rejoined their assigned units—the Baʿth Party began to offer financial inducements for anyone who provided information about the whereabouts of a deserter.[86] Also in 1994, Hussein ordered that deserters would be punished with ear amputations.[87] Evading service more than once would lead to both ears being cut off and the possibility that a "minus" sign would be etched on the forehead.[88] An additional decree outlawed medical treatment to repair an amputated ear.[89] In December 1994, it was reported that medical students

---

83. BRCC Doc. Nos. 01-2135-0004-0020 to 0022, 1987.
84. Sassoon 2012, 152.
85. Jabar 1992.
86. Sassoon 2012, 153.
87. Associated Press, "Saddam Orders End to Ear Amputations for Deserters," March 17, 1996.
88. Sassoon 2012, 153.
89. Khoury 2013, 155.

TABLE 10.1. The number of draft dodgers and deserters arrested by area and the number of these individuals who had an ear cut off, from a report dated January 1995.

Location	Deserters Arrested	Ears Amputated	Percent Amputated
Baghdad – Khalid (bin al-Walid)	484	38	8
Baghdad – Hamza (Sayyid al-Shuhada)	1,015	35	3
Baghdad – Abu Jaʿfar (al-Mansur)	527	26	5
Baghdad – Saddam	2,336	172	7
Baghdad – Saʿd (bin Abi Waqas)	476	58	12
Baghdad – al-Rashid	833	86	10
Baghdad – Adhamiyya	837	39	5
Basra & Dhi Qar – Basra	1,899	312	16
Basra & Dhi Qar – Dhi Qar	1,651	72	4
Maysan & Wasit – Maysan	533	20	4
Maysan & Wasit – Wasit	412	3	1
Babil, Karbala & Najaf – Babil	420	68	16
Babil, Karbala & Najaf – Karbala	583	12	2
Babil, Karbala & Najaf – Najaf	351	11	3
Qadisiyya & Muthanna – Qadisiyya	391	5	1
Qadisiyya & Muthanna – Muthanna	183	5	3
Salah al-Din & Anbar – Salah al-Din	110	12	11
Salah al-Din & Anbar – Muʿtasim	63	7	11
Salah al-Din & Anbar – Anbar	68	11	16
Salah al-Din & Anbar – Jazira	12	3	25
Diyala – Diyala	280	16	6
Ninawa, Mosul, Dohuk & Erbil – Ninawa	87	48	55
Ninawa, Mosul, Dohuk & Erbil – Mosul	58	27	47
Ninawa, Mosul, Dohuk & Erbil – Dohuk			
Ninawa, Mosul, Dohuk & Erbil – Erbil			
Ta'mim & Sulaymaniyya – Ta'mim	252	25	10
Ta'mim & Sulaymaniyya – Sulaymaniyya			

from Basra were arrested for refusing to carry out amputations; they were threatened with having their own ears removed if they failed to comply.[90] Doctors were, in some cases, executed for refusing to carry out ear cutting and amputations for other crimes, like thievery.[91]

Table 10.1 provides information from a 1995 report about the number of deserters caught.[92] These data are at the level of administrative security units; while I do not have population data to create a per capita estimate of

90. Graham-Brown 1999, 195.

91. "Iraq's Brutal Decrees Amputation: Branding and the Death Penalty," *Human Rights Watch*, June 1995.

92. BRCC Doc Nos. 01-3874-0004-0502 to 0529, January 9, 1995.

desertions, these geographic units were created to have roughly comparably sized populations. Areas with the largest number of deserters are the Saddam City neighborhood of Baghdad and the southern governorates of Basra and Dhi Qar. The number of deserters from Sunni areas like Salah al-Din and Anbar is small. These data are consistent with my theoretical expectation that after 1991, forms of "underground" transgression that relied on the cooperation of trusted others would be highest for Shi'i communities within Iraq. Table 10.1 also provides information about the degree to which local authorities complied with the demand to amputate the ears of deserters. There exists considerable variation on this measure. Notably, northern areas saw the largest percentage of ears amputated as a percentage of draft dodgers and deserters.

PARTICIPATION IN MILITIA ORGANIZATIONS

The regime, led by the Ba'th Party, took a number of steps to depoliticize the Iraqi military while simultaneously creating a series of ancillary military units—state- and party-sponsored militias—that could serve as counterarmies should there ever be a move by the military against the regime. Indeed, the regime was especially concerned about controlling risks associated with attempts at military overthrow.[93] These new organizations included the Special Republican Guard—formed after the 1991 Uprisings to provide a potential balance to existing Republic Guard forces—and various militia units, like Saddam's Fedayeen. Graham-Brown has suggested that Saddam's Fedayeen was formed in 1995 out of fear of regional and tribal interests from Sunnis living in Anbar and Mosul.[94]

Fedayeen units were meant to represent the organization of individuals willing to make the highest level of sacrifice for the regime. The idea of organizing units of individuals who were willing to sacrifice themselves for the president, party, and Ba'thist revolution likely drew inspiration from militant Palestinian nationalists who were willing to risk their lives for the Palestinian cause. A speech given by Hussein at al-Bakr University in 1978 emphasizes the importance of self-sacrifice. In that address, Hussein states that

93. Rohde 2010, 55.
94. Graham-Brown 1999, 193.

the most effective approach for countering Iraq's enemies would be through self-sacrifice, or martyrdom.[95]

The theme of personal sacrifice for the Ba'thist regime became particularly salient in the wake of the 1991 Uprisings. In the months and years following the demonstrations, hundreds of Iraqis sent personal letters volunteering themselves, and sometimes their relatives, for "suicide" or "sacrifice" operations (*'amaliyyat fida'iyya*). One boxfile within the Ba'th Party Regional Command files is a collection of these letters. Most of the volunteers promised to defend the nation and the revolution at any cost. In one letter, the head of the Kartan tribe offered more than two dozen tribesmen from across the country for service to Hussein and the regime.[96] Volunteers from the western province of Anbar are also found in the file.[97]

Most volunteers, however, were individuals living in the heavily Shi'i provinces of southern Iraq. A September 1991 letter from two female volunteers from Wasit promised to defend Iraq and the revolution to the death, with a signature of bloody thumbprints as a token of their commitment.[98] Volunteers from Wasit and multiple individuals from Qadisiyya appear as volunteers in the files.[99] Dozens of individuals from Basra and other southern areas also offered themselves for such operations.[100] Why would individuals from a community that was subjected to serious political and social repression volunteer to sacrifice themselves for Hussein, the Ba'th Party, and Ba'thist revolution? Even more so than members of the Sunni community, Iraqi Shi'a needed to find costly ways to signal their commitment to the regime if they were to be viewed as compliant. One way that an individual might signal this commitment was to volunteer for a "suicide" militia of this sort.

Volunteerism, particularly the decision to volunteer for a dangerous or costly activity like "self-sacrifice," is puzzling. Even more puzzling is the

95. CRRC Record No. SH-PDWN-D-000-341, June 3, 1978.
96. BRCC Doc. No. 01 3032 0001 0016-0017, January 1993.
97. BRCC Doc. No. 01-3032-0001-0009, January 1993, and BRCC Doc. No. 01-3032-0001-0012, January 20, 1993.
98. BRCC Doc. No. 01-3032-0001-0093, September 1991.
99. See BRCC Doc. No. 01-3032-0001-0038, September 28, 1992 and BRCC Doc. No. 01-3032-0001-0014, January 20, 1992.
100. See BRCC Doc. No. 01-3032-0001-0020, October 12, 1992, BRCC Doc. No. 01-3032-0001-0029, October 13, 1992, BRCC Doc. Nos. 01-3032-0001-0030 and 0031 and BRCC Doc. Nos. 01-3032-0001-0040 and 0041.

TABLE 10.2. Number of fedayeen volunteers trained or in training by geographic location or unit, 1991.

Location	Branches	# Trained	# in Training
Baghdad	6	195	200
South	5	1,270	1,355
Euphrates	5	3,282	2,500
Central	3	902	300
North	6	787	1,261
Republican Guard			245
State Security		62	94
Military Intelligence			24
General Security		654	173
Heet (Anbar) Training Camp			993
Total	25	7,152	7,145

decision to volunteer explicitly for the purpose of sacrificing oneself for a regime that was unpopular, even despised, by a large percentage of its citizens. Yet recruitment for fedayeen units was robust across Iraq around the time of the Gulf War. Table 10.2 provides information on the number of individuals trained or in training for such units across Iraq.[101] While the records do not provide details about the recruitment process for these training sessions, there are large numbers of individuals from southern, northern, and Euphrates regions who had been trained or were in training for fedayeen units.

Over time, the recruitment and training of militia volunteers became institutionalized in the form of Saddam's Fedayeen.[102] Sassoon calls the group Hussein's personal paramilitary.[103] Al-Marashi and Salama find that Saddam's Fedayeen grew to 15,000 to 25,000 men following its establishment

101. BRCC Document No. 024-5-2-0121, 1991.

102. The militias were a major subject of rumors circulating in Iraq during the late 1990s and early 2000s, reflecting the growing importance of such institutions in the final years of the Ba'thist regime. In November 1997, it was rumored that night school students would be taken into Saddam's Fedayeen; a related rumor suggested that students who registered for vocational school would be withdrawn and, instead, enrolled in Saddam's Fedayeen (BRCC Doc. No. 01-3713-0000-0618, November 10, 1997; BRCC Doc. No. 01-3713-0000-0559, November 22, 1997). In February 2000, rumors circulated that volunteers for Saddam's Fedayeen would be sent to Saudi Arabia, Kuwait, and northern areas (BRCC Doc. No. 01-2912-0004-0500, February 21, 2000). Another rumor suggested that any individual killed during their service as part of Saddam's Fedayeen would receive 25,000 US dollars in compensation for their families from Saudi Arabia (BRCC Doc. No. 01-2912-0004-0473 September 6, 2000).

103. Sassoon 2016, 202.

in 1995.[104] The group was headed by 'Uday Hussein and differed from other state-sponsored militias as its officers were permanent and came from the Republican Guard or Iraqi Army.[105]

What incentive did individuals have to join Saddam's Fedayeen? Al-Marashi and Salama have suggested that recruits to these units were often very loyal to the regime elite and enjoyed benefits like higher salaries compared to other military units.[106] For example, in 1998, fedayeen fighters were reported to receive a salary of 30,000 Iraqi dinars per month, a large salary for that time, especially during the embargo.[107] Saddam's Fedayeen came to develop a reputation for being a kind of criminal gang responsible for acts of extreme violence.[108]

Yet the costs for poor performance in the group were potentially severe. One memorandum issued by the head of Saddam's Fedayeen to the commanders of various lower level units provided guidance on when unit leaders should be executed for poor performance.[109] For example, the memorandum states that if two or more sections of a platoon commander are defeated, he would be executed; similarly, if a regiment commander had two of his companies defeated, he would be executed, and so on. There also existed a standing execution order for fedayeen fighters who hesitated in carrying out an order; cooperated with the enemy; damaged equipment; or hid information from the party, country, or leader.

In addition to Saddam's Fedayeen, the Ba'th Party recruited individuals for its own fedayeen unit. A series of documents from the early 2000s provide information about the names of individuals who volunteered for the party fedayeen, among other paramilitary groups. These lists often include hundreds of names and many of the individuals have names that indicate a tribal affiliation. For example, a document listing volunteers for the party fedayeen provides the names of 338 individuals. About half of these individuals had names that indicated a tribal affiliation with over eighty unique tribes represented, suggesting the breadth of the volunteer base for militias of this type.

104. Al-Marashi and Salama 2008, 187.
105. Sassoon 2012, 150. Some have speculated that Saddam's Fedayeen also may have been established as a counterweight to the Special Republican Guard over which Hussein's younger son, Qusay, enjoyed considerable influence (Al-Marashi and Salama 2008, 187).
106. Ibid.
107. CRRC SH-FSDM-D-000-364, January 15, 1998.
108. Bashir 2005.
109. Ibid.

The largest tribal groups represented included the Shammari, Juburi, Asdi, Tamimi, and ʿUbaydi as well as individuals from the Bani Hassan and Bani Rakib tribes.

Fedayeen Recruitment for the Palestinian Cause

Beginning in the late 1990s and early 2000s, emphasis turned increasingly to mobilizing Iraqi fedayeen volunteers in solidarity with the Palestinian nationalist cause.[110] A number of militias were organized on behalf of Palestine including volunteers for missions and training sessions named in honor of Muhammad al-Durra, the Palestinian child who was allegedly shot by the Israel Defense Forces during the early days of the Second Intifada in 2000.[111] Other memoranda suggest that party members were also interested in participating in sacrifice operations targeting an American or Israeli embassy anywhere in the world.[112]

In February 2001, the Jerusalem Army was created. According to one journalistic account, the Jerusalem Army was launched after a meeting during which Hussein ordered the creation of military training camps for Iraqis committed to the Palestinian cause.[113] The militia immediately began attracting volunteers. Financial and careerist incentives seemed to be a major driver of recruitment. Retired military personnel who suffered near economic ruin as a result of international sanctions were able to supplement their government pensions in exchange for training volunteers; farmers could expect access to agricultural programs for their participation; and university staff who volunteered had opportunities for foreign teaching assignments.[114] Rumors circulated that individuals who volunteered as part of a paramilitary to "free" Jerusalem would be given one million Iraqi dinars.[115] Baʿth Party memoranda

---

110. There existed precedent for discussing Baʿthist mobilization through the lens of the Arab-Israeli conflict. A conversation between Baʿth Party officials in 1989 discussed how associating the nationalist struggle with the fight against the "Zionist" enemy may be seen as a useful strategy for politically mobilizing young Iraqis. See CRRC Doc. No. SH-SHTP-A-001-396, May 3, 1989.

111. See BRCC Doc. No. 004-4-1-0560, July 18, 2001, for example.

112. BRCC Doc. No. 01-2739-0000-0364, November 22, 2000.

113. David Baran, "Iraq: The Party in Power," *Le Monde Diplomatique* (English edition), December 2002.

114. Ibid.

115. BRCC Doc. No. 01-2912-0004-0348, November 14, 2000.

indicate that by June 2001, the Jerusalem Army had received too many applicants.[116]

Fear of sanction may have also induced some individuals to participate in the Jerusalem Army. For example, it was rumored that those who failed to volunteer in support of the Palestinian Intifada would lose their rations.[117] Another rumor suggested that the Baʿth Party was forcing young men into the Jerusalem Army, including prisoners who had completed half of their prison terms.[118]

The Jerusalem Army did not actually fight in Palestine, though at times it was rumored that forces would be deployed should Iraq be attacked by external actors.[119] So what did its members actually do? One rumor circulating in April 2000 suggested that when a high-ranking military official tried to defect and flee for the border, paramilitary units—like the Jerusalem Army— were deployed in the streets to maintain order.[120] Members of militias might also serve as a public signal of strength for the Baʿthists. In August 2002, 15,000 uniform-wearing, gun-wielding Jerusalem Army members staged a military parade in Baghdad.[121] According to press reports published at the time, public mobilization efforts were undertaken as a show of national solidarity in anticipation of a US military campaign to topple Hussein.[122]

Over time, Jerusalem Army participation became increasingly institution-alized. The form for entry into the Jerusalem Army suggested eligibility for individuals eighteen to fifty-five years old.[123] In December 2001, Hussein ordered that volunteers who trained with the militia more than once would receive a monthly reward for at least six months.[124] In March 2002, it was decided that the regime would begin issuing a "Jerusalem Badge" for the volunteers with benefits similar to the "Mother of all Battles Badge."[125] A Revolutionary Command Council decision in April 2002 specified precisely

116. BRCC Doc. No. 01-3025-0001-0079, June 3, 2001.
117. BRCC Doc. No. 01-2912-0004-0335, November 19, 2000; BRCC Doc. No. 040-4-2-0434, January 24, 2002.
118. BRCC Doc. No. 040-4-2-0458, January 13, 2002; BRCC Doc. No. 040-4-2-0434, January 24, 2002.
119. BRCC Doc. No. 040-4-2-0599, October 1, 2001.
120. BRCC Doc. No. 01-2912-0004-0810, April 14, 2000.
121. Agence France Presse, August 9, 2002.
122. Ibid.
123. BRCC Doc. Nos. 004-4-1-0367 to 0368, February 27, 2002.
124. BRCC Doc. No. 004-4-1-0432, December 2, 2001.
125. BRCC Doc. No. 004-4-1-0357, March 2, 2002.

TABLE 10.3. Number of fedayeen volunteers for Palestine missions from the ten most represented tribes.

Tribe Name	Number of Volunteers	Predominantly Sunni	Tribal "Centroid" Close to Tikrit
Juburi	182	Yes	Yes
ʿUbaydi	32	Yes	Yes
Hamdani	28	No	No
Bayati	22	Yes	Yes
Naʿimi	20	Yes	Yes
Jamili	16	Yes	No
Ta'i	14	Yes	No
Salhi	13	No	No
ʿAzzawi	11	Yes	Yes
Bajari	10	No	No

TABLE 10.4. Jerusalem Army leaders and male and female volunteers, for most represented tribes.

Leaders		Male		Female	
Tribe Name	Number of Leaders	Tribe Name	Number of Volunteers	Tribe Name	Number of Volunteers
Juburi	5	Juburi	29	Zubaydi	13
ʿUbaydi	3	ʿUbaydi	27	ʿUbaydi	13
		Dulaimi	23	ʿAzzawi	10
		ʿAni	22	ʿAti	8
		Zubaydi	18	Bayati	7
		Shammari	17	Juburi	7
		Taʿi	16	Rabiʿi	7
		Hadithi	15	Mashhadani	7
		Rabiʿi	15	Samarrai	6
		Mashhadani	14	ʿAni	6
		Khafaji	14	Khafaji	6
		Samarrai	13		
		ʿAzzawi	13		

who was eligible for the Jerusalem Badge.[126] Later that year, orders were given regarding the role certain Jerusalem Army teams would take to lead in fighting American and Zionist enemies.[127]

Tables 10.3 and 10.4 provide information pertaining to the tribal composition of both the fedayeen volunteers for Palestine missions and the Jerusalem Army, respectively. For the former, party documentation suggests 705

126. BRCC Doc. No. 004-4-1-0183, April 14, 2002.
127. BRCC Doc. No. 003-5-5-0192, July 23, 2002.

volunteers of individuals willing to undertake missions of self-sacrifice inside Palestinian territories or anywhere the leadership saw fit.[128] Of the volunteers for this militia, 69 percent had names that indicated a tribal background with 54 different tribes represented on that list. Most of the tribes listed were predominantly Sunni tribes, and the most represented tribes were located near Tikrit. There is no evidence to suggest that any of these units actually undertook missions in Israel or Palestine.

Table 10.4 provides information about volunteers for the Jerusalem Army and includes three separate categories—Jerusalem Army leaders (30), male volunteers (1,021), and female volunteers (578). Of the thirty Jerusalem Army leaders listed, 23 had a name that indicated a tribal background. Of those 23, the most represented were the Juburi (5) and the ʿUbaydi (3) with fifteen other tribes represented by one individual each. For the male Jerusalem Army volunteers, almost 60 percent had a name that indicated a particular tribal connection with over 160 unique tribal names represented on the list. Juburi, ʿUbaydi, and Dulaimi tribesmen were the most common. For the female Jerusalem Army volunteers, out of 578 individuals, about half had names that indicated a tribal connection. The most represented tribes were a smaller percentage of the overall list, suggesting a relatively dispersed set of tribal affiliates. Over 100 unique tribal names were represented on this list.

Youth Mobilization for Militias and Military Training

The Baʿthist regime was particularly keen to have young Iraqis participate in paramilitary organizations like Saddam's Fedayeen. Indeed, Hussein ordered that student volunteers for the fedayeen should receive priority when applying to the police academy and the military.[129] The variation in volunteer rates across Iraqi districts is mapped in figure 10.1, based on data from the 2001–2002 School Registers. The map shows that there existed considerable geographic variation in the level of volunteerism for the militia. Tikrit and the area just north of Tikrit—known to be home to the Jubur tribe—had a relatively large number of volunteers. Yet, rates of volunteerism in predominantly Shiʿi regions around Basra, like Abu al-Khasib, also show high participation rates.

128. BRCC Doc. Nos. 01-2739-0000-0455 to 465, December 30, 2000.
129. BRCC Doc. No. 020-3-6-18, May 18, 1995.

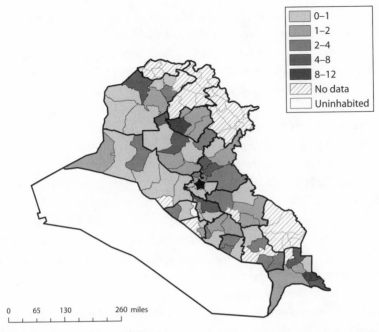

Figure 10.1. Percentage of high school students who volunteered for Saddam's Fedayeen, 2001–2002.

Table 10.5 reports the results of a series of regressions where the percentage of students who volunteered for Saddam's Fedayeen is the dependent variable. Volunteerism is statistically significantly higher in Sunni areas for all four specifications (Models 10.1 through 10.4), controlling for other factors. Wealth and population density are not significant predictors in any specification. I use Model 10.4 to calculate predicted probabilities associated with the results; holding wealth and population density at their means, for Sunnis from Tikrit, the predicted probability is 5 percent. For Sunnis living 200 miles from Tikrit, however, it is only 2 percent. For Shiʿa living 200 miles from Tikrit it is less than 1 percent, but for Shiʿa living 400 miles from Tikrit it is 2 percent. This suggests that by 2001–2002, Sunni students from in and around Tikrit were most likely to join Saddam's Fedayeen, controlling for other factors, but that Sunnis living some distance from Tikrit were statistically less likely to do so. Within the Shiʿi community, areas most peripheral, measured in distance from Tikrit, had higher volunteer rates than Shiʿi areas closer to Tikrit.

TABLE 10.5. Coefficient estimates for dependent variable, percentage of students who had volunteered for Saddam's Fedayeen, by district for the 2001–2002 academic year.

	Model 10.1	Model 10.2	Model 10.3	Model 10.4
Percent Sunni	4.91	5.13	4.94	5.25
	(1.08)	(1.85)	(1.85)	(1.90)
Percent Kurdish	1.08	0.91	1.11	0.97
	(1.12)	(1.12)	(1.15)	(1.22)
Distance to Tikrit	0.007	0.007	0.007	0.007
	(0.003)	(0.003)	(0.003)	(0.003)
% Sunni*Distance to Tikrit	−0.021	−0.018	−0.021	−0.019
	(0.009)	(0.009)	(0.009)	(0.009)
Wealth Index		−0.195		−0.219
		(0.248)		(0.264)
Population Density			0.000	0.000
			(0.001)	(0.001)
Constant	−0.31	0.948	−0.351	1.01
	(1.15)	(2.15)	(1.22)	(2.17)
Observations	67	64	67	64
R^2	0.12	0.14	0.12	0.14

It is also possible to examine the individual determinants of volunteering for Saddam's Fedayeen within the Baghdad sample. About 2.3 percent of Baghdad students volunteered in 2001–2002 to be in Saddam's Fedayeen. Table 10.6 reports the results of a series of logistic regressions where the individual student is the unit of analysis and the outcome variable is whether or not the student volunteered for Saddam's Fedayeen. Model 10.5 reports the results with the inclusion of variables meant to capture ethnicity and educational track. In this model, Kurdish students are less likely to volunteer than Arab students, and students living in Sunni districts are more likely to volunteer than those in non-Sunni districts. Science-track students are also statistically less likely to volunteer than others. Model 10.6 takes into account whether the student or his family enjoyed "friend of the president" status. I find that "friend of the president" status is highly correlated with propensity to volunteer for Saddam's Fedayeen. Model 10.7 takes into account agglomeration effects. I find that the larger the percentage of students in the school who are volunteering, the more likely an individual student is to volunteer. In this model specification, the effect of Kurdish ethnicity is no longer statistically significant. Conditional on agglomeration effects, literature-track students are more likely than other types of students to volunteer and Sunni districts see a reduced probability of volunteering.

TABLE 10.6. Coefficient estimates from logit regressions for dependent variable, volunteering for Saddam's Fedayeen across individual students in Baghdad for the 2001–2002 academic year.

	Model 10.5	Model 10.6	Model 10.7
Percent Sunni (district)	1.437	1.316	−1.179
	(0.523)	(0.527)	(0.663)
Kurdish	−1.741	−1.714	−0.968
	(1.003)	(1.003)	(1.007)
Literature	−0.094	−0.102	1.006
	(0.105)	(0.105)	(0.167)
Science	−1.227	−1.229	−0.040
	(0.134)	(0.134)	(0.208)
"Friend of the President"		0.350	0.553
		(0.116)	(0.150)
Percent Participation at School			15.720
			(0.765)
Constant	−4.181	−4.178	−4.809
	(0.260)	(0.261)	(0.329)
Observations	22,898	22,589	22,589
Pseudo R^2	0.03	0.03	0.46

Another avenue toward upward mobility for Iraqi youth could be found through educational opportunities funded by the military and security services. Higher education institutions supported by the military and state security took on a number of forms, including the College of Military Engineering, the Police Academy, and the Police Preparatory School, in addition to the First Military College, Naval Academy, and Air Force Academy, including pilot training. It was also possible for students to have their medical studies paid for by the Ministry of Defense, and special positions were reserved for both men and women to receive these opportunities. Finally, there were specialized training opportunities including for officers of the interior security forces and courses for law enforcement officials and judges. While some of these programs had a very high acceptance rate, others were more selective, like acceptance into the College of Military Engineering and applications for Ministry of Defense–sponsored medical training.[130]

With the goal of creating a loyal and ideologically oriented military, it became increasingly important to make sure that the military academy was

130. See BRCC Doc. No. 01-3847-0003-0039, 1994 for one example providing information on how many students applied and were accepted to various military colleges, academies, and training sessions.

reserved for students who were likely to be Baʿth Party loyalists in the future.[131] Indeed, Sassoon suggests that controlling all military educational establishments was a high priority for the regime.[132] Thousands of documents within the collection deal with the issue of vetting students for higher education opportunities associated with the military and security services. Typically schedules of applicants would include information on the student, his family reputation, nationality (i.e., Arab, Kurd, Turkman), address, place of birth, as well as father's (and sometimes grandfather's) name and place of birth. One memorandum from 1992 suggested the importance of also collecting information on tribal affiliation and party rank, in some cases.[133]

A call for applicants to military academies issued in 1992 asked for students who were Iraqis by birth aged 17–21, with loyalty to the country, people, and military of Iraq; a diploma; sound mental and physical condition; a good reputation and moral character; and no background of political crimes.[134] Indeed, in assessing the student files, political considerations were key. A 1993 memorandum about students seeking admission for military medical training suggests that first priority was offered to students with a Baʿthist political orientation who were a "friend of the president," the sons of "friends of the president," and the sons or brothers of war martyrs. Next, other students with a Baʿthist political orientation were considered. Others were considered to have information that was unencouraging and, thus, not suitable for admission.[135]

Another document considered the case of a student who had a relative who was on the Baʿth Party Regional Command.[136] The well-connected relative called to find out why the student had been rejected; apparently all of his information was fine except the fact that he was listed as having an independent political orientation. A handwritten note on the memorandum suggested clear instructions to avoid engaging in favoritism as a result of interventions of this type.[137]

Regime officials deliberated about military academy admissions seriously, as mistakenly accepting a student with an inappropriate background could

131. Dodge 2003, 61.
132. Sassoon 2012, 133.
133. BRCC Doc No. 01-3847-0003-0145, 1992.
134. BRCC Doc No. 01-3847-0003-0106, 1992.
135. BRCC Doc No. 01-3847-0003-0101 and 0102, 1993.
136. BRCC Doc No. 01-38-3847-0003-0091, September 27, 1993.
137. Ibid.

be highly problematic for the regime. Another set of memoranda discuss students seeking admission into the First Military College in 1993. In one case, a Baʿthist who had otherwise encouraging information was discovered to have had a maternal cousin who had been executed during the Iran-Iraq War for feebleness, or cowardice, in combat. Another cousin was serving a prison term for thievery and his aunt's husband was under suspicion for pro-Iranian political inclinations. A handwritten note on the memorandum suggests a person with such a family background should be disqualified from consideration.

A second Baʿthist individual under consideration was hurt by his failure to actively participate in party activities. He did not have the support of the local party organization and, as a result, was considered a poor candidate. A third candidate had a favorable file, but a cousin had been executed for desertion. He was not admitted but added to a "reserve" pool of individuals who might be considered at a later time. A fourth candidate with the tribal name Juburi had a favorable file except that his father's cousin had been sentenced to twenty years in prison for conspiracy against the regime in 1990 (though he was later pardoned). A handwritten note on the file suggests that he should be rejected. A final candidate discussed had an acceptable file except that his father's cousin was formerly a Communist, though no longer at odds with the regime. He was also added to the "reserve" pool.[138]

Iraqi students were also encouraged to participate in various party-sponsored youth camps.[139] To prepare for these camps, local organizers set up meetings with the school board and held seminars about the program.[140] To incentivize participation, youth camp attendees were offered priority acceptance to military and police academies.[141] Further, youth camp participants who were the sons of martyrs received cash rewards.[142] Local Baʿth Party

138. BRCC Doc. Nos. 01-3847-0003-0094 to 0098, January 12, 1993.

139. A publication on youth camps details the procedures and tasks of different governmental units, including schools, for how resources should be devoted to these activities. For each camp of 750 children, there was a requirement of three supervisors and thirty teachers; for 500 campers, three supervisors and only twenty teachers were required. Students eligible for these programs were between the ages of 12 and 17 and healthy, responsible students. In 2001, the report suggests that 22,952 young people participated in these camps across the country. See BRCC Doc. No. 125-3-2-114 to 131, 2002.

140. BRCC Doc. No. 125-3-2-72, May 2, 2002.

141. BRCC Doc. No. 125-3-2-87, December 26, 2001.

142. BRCC Doc. Nos. 125-3-2-36 to 44, 2002.

leaders made visits to these camps, bringing gifts for the youth participants.[143] Great care was taken to maintain clean and appealing camp sites, as youth camps were viewed as an important location for Ba'th Party recruitment and indoctrination.

ATTEMPTS AT SEIZING POWER

The "Tikriti" nature of Ba'thist rule meant that Sunni regional and tribal interests of non-Tikriti groups were significantly underrepresented in high military posts relative to individuals who shared Hussein's family, clan, and regional background.[144] When Iraq's budgetary situation was favorable, "practically all tribes in the Sunni Arab areas were accorded benefits," including the Juburi, 'Ubaydi, Dulaimi, and others.[145] But when confronting the challenges of a prolonged war against Iran, resentment on the part of officers increased when "relatives and clansmen of Hussein were promoted more rapidly and in many cases without enduring the fighting on the front."[146] Conditions of economic scarcity, like during the sanctions regime, intensified rivalry over limited regime resources.

As a result, Hussein was constantly worried about coup attempts[147] and most feared threats from his fellow Sunnis, despite the fact that they formed the backbone of his support.[148] To guard against this, he tried to surrounded himself with individuals who could not create an independent base of power.[149] Since the early days of Hussein's rule, the regime showed a preference for placing family members and geographically based tribesmen from Tikrit and its environs in sensitive positions of government, including the military, bureaucracy, intelligence, and security services. The most sensitive jobs in the military and security sectors were given to direct blood relatives of Hussein, as it would be difficult for those individuals to plot against

143. BRCC Doc. Nos. 125-3-2-28 to 35, 2002.
144. Davis 2005, 177.
145. Baram 2003, 99.
146. Al-Marashi and Salama 2008, 144.
147. Sassoon 2012, 138.
148. Nixon 2016, 109.
149. Sassoon 2012, 230. Hussein also sought to provide good salaries, especially for officers, to help guard against discontent (Sassoon 2016, 101).

him.[150] The Al-bu Nasir tribe, a Sunni tribe geographically centered in Tikrit, controlled the regime's most feared and important internal security agency—the Special Security Organization (*jihaz al-amn al-khass*)—as well as the Special Republican Guard units tasked with security around Baghdad.[151]

The preference for regional and kin loyalists intensified over time to the detriment of Sunnis from outside of the Tikriti heartland. Under the sanctions regime, Sunnis peripheral to Tikrit saw significant declines in quality of life and, despite the instrumental role they had played in putting down the uprisings, did not enjoy the same levels of access, employment, and privilege as Sunnis from in and around Tikrit. According to one well-placed military source, by the end of the 1990s over 80 percent of officers came from Salah al-Din governorate, particularly Tikrit, while only 10 percent were from Mosul and less than 10 percent from Anbar governorate.[152]

Publicly Reported Assassination and Coup Attempts

Coup attempts were a common feature of Iraqi political life during Hussein's presidency. Despite the many coup attempts documented in both the media and scholarly sources, none were successful in unseating Hussein. A key reason for their failure relates to the fact that the institution best positioned to overthrow the regime—the Sunni-controlled military—was also highly legible to the Ba'th Party regime. Dodge concurs, arguing that "coup plots were continually uncovered, but their discovery pointed to the inability of mutinous officers to conspire with more than a handful of others before being betrayed."[153] In this section, I discuss documented coup attempts and, where possible, the reason for coup failures.[154]

150. Dodge 2003, 65.

151. Baram 2003, 97. The organization of the secret police and strategies for discouraging elite defection have received both empirical elaboration and theorization in the study of autocratic politics (Quinlivan 1999; Bellin 2004; Dimitrov and Sassoon 2014).

152. Baram 2003, 104.

153. Dodge 2003, 61.

154. A well-known assassination attempt took place in 1982. In that incident, Hussein's motorcade was attacked as it passed through the small town of Dujayl, north of Baghdad. Although Dujayl is located in the predominantly Sunni governorate of Salah al-Din, the inhabitants of the town were mostly Shi'a. Following a speech by Hussein in the town, his motorcade was attacked by gunmen hiding in date orchards adjacent to the road. Eventually more than 100 townspeople were executed for the attempt, which was thought to have been organized by Da'wa Party activists.

Many of the documented coup attempts against Hussein took place following the end of the Iran-Iraq War. In the aftermath of the conflict, Hussein's status was threatened by the growing stature of generals who emerged from the conflict as national war heroes. As Hussein sought to sideline these individuals, some moved against him. Scores of officers were arrested and accused of belonging to a secret organization attempting to bring down the government; other officers were forced into retirement.[155] Assassination plots against Hussein were uncovered in 1988 and early 1989 and military purges followed.[156] According to Al-Marashi and Salama:

> The removal of the generals convinced some officers to plan a coup before further purges would affect them. A plot within the military to assassinate Hussein unfolded in late 1988 and later resulted in the execution of dozens of complicit Republican Guard officers. In November 1988 a plan was discovered to shoot down Saddam Hussein's plane on his way to Egypt. A third coup attempt within the armed forces was discovered in September 1989.[157]

One of the likely victims of these purges was the Iraqi Minister of Defense Adnan Khayrallah—cousin and brother-in-law of Hussein—who was killed in a suspicious helicopter crash.

In January 1990, the Special Security Organization successfully pre-empted a coup by military officers of the Juburi tribe who sought to assassinate Hussein.[158] The Juburi had been important contributors of troops during the Iran-Iraq War and, in exchange, public money and jobs were channeled to the group; yet Hussein was suspicious that Juburi were becoming too powerful within the regime so he fired two Juburi ministers, effectively cutting the benefits to the community.[159] The attempted coup was seen as a reaction to Hussein's efforts to weaken Juburi influence. While some Juburi officers were killed for their participation in anti-regime plots, other Juburi were quickly pensioned off.[160]

---

155. Gause 2002.
156. Khoury 2013, 33–34.
157. Al-Marashi and Salama 2008, 175.
158. Baram 2002, 222.
159. Martin Walker, "Buying the Tribes from Saddam," *United Press International*, April 3, 2003.
160. Baram 2003, 99.

Military officers had a mixed response to Iraqi plans to invade Kuwait in 1990. Those who supported the idea of an invasion were concerned about the timing of the attacks while others opposed the invasion outright, but could only voice their concerns in the most cautious ways.[161] Some officers feared that a failed attempt at invasion would provide an opening for exploitation by regional rivals, including Iran, Turkey, and Israel.[162] While Hussein initially encouraged an open discussion on the part of military commanders, hundreds of officers were reportedly killed by November 1990, presumably for angering Hussein.[163]

The international sanctions period also witnessed a series of attempted military coups, emanating particularly from tribes with a basis in the so-called Sunni Triangle. The Special Republican Guard supposedly thwarted a coup attempt from within the Republican Guard in the summer of 1992.[164] In 1993, officers associated with the 'Ubaydi tribe were suspected of coup plotting and were singled out as "would-be revolutionaries."[165] A prominent military doctor from Hussein's own Tikrit region was arrested and executed for either having information about or participation in this plot. According to one account, he was executed (death by wild dogs) for not revealing the existence of a plot against the regime.[166] Other accounts suggest that he either made a joke about Hussein in the presence of informants or was actually involved in the plot itself.[167]

In 1993, there was an additional Juburi-led coup attempt.[168] Apparently, after a purge of disloyal Juburi officers, Hussein reached an agreement with an emerging tribal leader within the Juburis.[169] Importantly, for tribes like the Juburis and 'Ubaydis whose areas of influence are located near Tikrit, even past periods of disloyalty would not automatically disqualify all tribesmen from high rank within the regime. Baram points out that until the final days

161. Jabar 1992.
162. Ibid.
163. Ibid.
164. Al-Marashi and Salama 2008, 188; Gordon 2010, 13.
165. Baram 2003, 99.
166. See Cameron Barr, "Iraq: Unsanctioned Voices," *Christian Science Monitor*, October 31, 2002.
167. Al-Marashi and Salama 2008, 188.
168. Martin Walker, "Buying the Tribes from Saddam," *United Press International*, April 3, 2003.
169. Ibid.

of the regime, loyal Juburis and 'Ubaydis remained prominent within the government.[170]

Perhaps the most serious threat to the regime came from members of the Dulaimi tribe, who hailed primarily from western Iraq and, particularly, the province of Anbar. Dulaimi tribesmen—who had been critical in putting down the 1991 Uprisings—revolted against the regime in 1995 after the execution of General Muhammad al-Dulaimi and a number of other Dulaimi officers. Muhammad al-Dulaimi was suspected of plotting a coup against Hussein. A number of other tribes, including the Jumailat, Anis, Rawis, and Kubaysis—were reported to sympathize with the Dulaimis. Press reports from that period suggest that the rebellion was also linked to a shrinking of Hussein's power base.[171] It was reported that as many as 1,000 soldiers and officers from a Republican Guard unit were involved in the protests.[172] A battalion led by General Turki al-Dulaimi is reported to have attacked a radio transmitter and helicopter base at Abu Ghraib, on the outskirts of Baghdad.[173]

In 1996, officers associated with the al-Duri tribe—also from Anbar province—were accused of attempting a coup. According to Al-Marashi and Salama, "since trusted tribes like the Dur and Dulaim were involved in these coups," Hussein promoted officers from other tribes as a way to balance his vulnerability.[174]

While knowledge or even strong suspicion of disloyalty meant the end of an individual's life, it did not mean that entire tribes were dislocated from the patronage structure, particularly for Sunni Arab tribes that tended to be the most legible to the regime. The existence of a "black sheep" within the broader tribal group did not spell the end of political life for all fellow tribesmen.[175] Even after the Dulaimis participated in a tribal revolt, the tribe was able, to a considerable degree, to rehabilitate themselves in the eyes of Hussein.[176]

170. Baram 2003, 99.
171. Ed Blanche, "Iraqi Rebels Claim Sunni Clans Gathering Against Saddam," *Associated Press*, June 18, 1995.
172. Youssef Ibrahim, "Iraq Reportedly Cracks Down on Clan that Tried a Coup," *New York Times*, June 20, 1995.
173. Ed Blanche, "Iraqi Rebels Claim Sunni Clans Gathering Against Saddam," *Associated Press*, June 18, 1995.
174. Al-Marashi and Salama 2008, 188.
175. Ibid., 191.
176. Ibid.

Rumored Assassination and Coup Plots

Ideally, I would validate public reports of coup plots with internal Ba'th Party documents about attempted takeovers. Unfortunately, I was not able to clearly identify such documents. This is perhaps not surprising as a paper trail of these events could be a vulnerability to the regime down the line. As an alternative to identifying regime documentation of coup attempts, I instead highlight the insider threats to Hussein and his regime through an examination of twenty rumors about anticipated or attempted coups and high-level assassination plots that appeared in the Ba'th Party files.[177] These coup and assassination attempts were reported as rumors and not as verified incidents.[178] Yet if we think that high-stakes incidents of this sort would be discussed within private communications networks, rumors of such events would seem to provide an alternative measure of the events themselves.

For example, in March 1991, an army officer reported that the commander of the second legion had plans to advance six teams toward Baghdad in order to undertake a coup.[179] Around the same time, it was reported that anti-party and anti-revolution graffiti was found in the al-Dura neighborhood of Baghdad. In January 1993, a rumor suggested that a coup led by a military officer would take place on the 19th of the month.[180] In early February 1993, another rumor reported that participants in the attempted coup had been military officers from the Abedi and Juburi tribes.[181] Juburi participation in this attempt was later confirmed by other sources and may have been the follow-up to an unsuccessful coup attempt in 1990.

In April 1993, a number of rumors circulated regarding failed coup attempts. It was rumored that Samir al-Shaykhli—a former mayor of Baghdad

---

177. Provoking a military coup undertaken by Iraqi security officials was long considered the preferred outcome by US intelligence officials who sought to dislodge Hussein. Press reports suggest that in the summer of 1996, several dozen Iraqis working with US intelligence inside Iraq were arrested and executed in the wake of a failed coup attempt. See Tim Weiner, "For 3rd Time in 21 Years, Saddam Hussein's Foes Pay Price for a Foiled US Plot," *New York Times*, September 9, 1996 for more on the US role in Iraqi coup-making. By 2002, however, CIA officials viewed a successful coup as unlikely. See Christopher Marquis, "Bush Officials Differ on Way to Force Out Iraqi Leader," *New York Times*, June 19, 2002.

178. All of the rumors are reported in the 1990s with no rumors about coup attempts in the 2000s.

179. BRCC Doc. Nos. 035-4-4-0015 to 0021, March 5, 1991.

180. BRCC Doc. No. 005-3-3-0752, January 19, 1993.

181. BRCC Doc. No. 005-3-3-0564, February 9, 1993.

and Minister of Interior—had led a failed coup attempt.[182] Shortly thereafter, it was rumored that Watban Ibrahim Hassan al-Tikriti, Interior Minister and half-brother to Saddam Hussein, had been shot and injured and that there had been multiple coup attempts.[183] Two additional rumors suggested that a military coup would take place on April 28, Saddam Hussein's birthday.[184]

Rumors of attempted coups reemerged in 1996 and continued to be reported through 1999. In July 1996, it was reported that high-ranking army officers had been conspiring to kill Hussein, but that the plot was discovered by the security apparatus and the conspirators arrested.[185] Later that month a rumor suggested that a high-ranking military commander who was a cousin of Wafiq al-Samarrai—a senior intelligence officer who had defected to the Kurdish autonomous areas in 1994—had attempted a coup ten days prior.[186] According to one rumor circulating in 1996, the people of Anbar—specifically the Jumailat clan—received the body of a high-ranking military officer who had been executed by the authorities and this event was highly upsetting to the Anbari population.[187] A rumor in July 1997 reported an aborted coup plot organized by leading military officers.[188] In June 1998, a failed conspiracy involving senior army officers was rumored and a coup was predicted for August 2 including attacks on party bases.[189] Failed coups were also rumored in March, May, and July 1999.[190] In the case of the rumored July coup attempt, seventy-three military officers of a variety of ranks were reported to have been involved.[191]

182. BRCC Doc. No. 01-3197-0001-0491, April 21, 1993.

183. BRCC Doc. No. 01-3197-0001-0655, April 27, 1993; BRCC Doc. No. 01-3197-0001-0443, May 11, 1993.

184. BRCC Doc. No. 01-3197-0001-0663, April 27, 1993; BRCC doc. No. 01-3197-0001-0641, April 28, 1993.

185. BRCC Doc. No. 148-4-5-0994, July 20, 1996.

186. BRCC Doc. No. 148-4-5-1006, July 22, 1996.

187. BRCC Doc. No. 148-4-5-0793, September 12, 1996.

188. BRCC Doc. No. 162-2-2-0291, July 24, 1997.

189. BRCC Doc. No. 01-3713-0000-0107, June 27, 1998; BRCC Doc. No. 01-3713-0000-0059, July 15, 1998.

190. BRCC Doc. No. 087-5-3-0470 March 16, 1999; BRCC Doc. No. 087-5-3-0421, March 17, 1999; BRCC Doc. Nos. 087-5-3-0163 to 0165 May 20, 1999; BRCC Doc. Nos. 133-5-7-0742 to 0743, July 21, 1999.

191. BRCC Doc. Nos. 133-5-7-0742 to 0743, July 21, 1999.

Rumors about targeted killings were also common.[192] Frequently these rumors discussed impending assassination attempts, or wrongly reported the assassination of someone who had not in fact been killed. The individuals targeted in these rumored assassination attempts ranged from government ministers to anti-regime activists to Saddam Hussein himself. Assassination attempts against Hussein's sons—'Uday and Qusay Hussein—were also frequently rumored to have occurred. Many of these rumors also included information about the likely perpetrators of the attack.

More than a dozen rumors suggested assassination attempts against Saddam Hussein. In November 1990, it was rumored that a terrorist team with American members would seek to assassinate the president.[193] In July 1996, it was rumored that high-ranking security and military officers, including Watban Ibrahim Hassan al-Tikriti, had conspired to kill the president.[194] Two rumors circulating the following month suggested household threats to the president. One rumor suggested that the cook in Hussein's home had poisoned his food, but that the plot had been exposed and perpetrators executed.[195] Another, somewhat similar, rumor reported that Hussein had asked a housekeeper to drink the cup of tea she had carried to him and then she dropped dead. The rumor was that it was Hussein's wife (described as "Umm 'Uday," mother of 'Uday) who poisoned the tea and that she herself was then killed by Hussein.[196] In September 1996, two rumors reported assassination

192. Military defections were also politically problematic for the regime, as exemplified by the defections of Hussein and Saddam Kamel, sons-in-law to Saddam Hussein. A handful of reported rumors focus on the subject of high-level defections. While less threatening than a coup or assassination attempt against Hussein or his sons, the defection of senior military officials could politically damage the regime. All four rumors of this type appeared over a five-month period in 2000; each rumor was also reported by the Ba'th Party branch leadership in southern Iraq. One rumor suggested a plan by Iyad Fatih Khalifa al-Rawi to escape to Syria after an attempted plot against the regime (BRCC Doc. No. 133-5-7-0063, March 25, 2000). Two rumors point to the escape from Iraq of Hamid Sha'ban, a major figure in the Iraqi Air Force, with one rumor suggesting ten officers fled with him (BRCC Doc. No. 01-2912-0004-0792, April 22, 2000; BRCC Doc. No. 01-2912-0004-0630, July 9, 2000). In May, a rumor circulated that the general commander of Saddam's Fedayeen absconded with fedayeen monies and fled the country; 'Uday Hussein supposedly issued an arrest warrant for him (BRCC Doc. No. 01-2912-0004-0770, May 9, 2000).
193. BRCC Doc. No. 01-3868-0003-0048, November 8, 1990.
194. BRCC Doc. No. 148-4-5-0994, July 20, 1996; BRCC Doc. No. 148-4-5-1000, July 21, 1996.
195. BRCC Doc. No. 148-4-5-0937, August 9, 1996.
196. BRCC Doc. No. 148-4-5-0886, August 28, 1996.

attempts on Hussein, with one being reported to have been perpetrated by his bodyguards.[197]

In March 1997, the Minister of Finance and his nephew were rumored to be planning to kill Hussein.[198] In May 1998, a rumor circulated that a group of women would approach Hussein to shoot him in his car.[199] The following month, it was rumored that the party had mobilized as a result of an assassination attempt against Hussein.[200] In January 1999, it was rumored that the uncles of Hussein Kamal—Hussein's son-in-law—had tried to assassinate Hussein.[201] In June of that same year, it was rumored that someone close to Hussein would try to kill him.[202] A group of security officials were rumored to have failed in an assassination attempt against the president.[203]

More than two dozen rumors described attempts to kill the sons of Saddam Hussein. The corruption and moral depravity displayed by ʿUday, in particular, was so politically problematic that one regime insider wrote that delegation of power to Hussein's sons "destroyed any trust in Saddam and his regime."[204] In February 1993, there was a rumor of an assassination attempt against both ʿUday and Qusay Hussein; the following month, it was rumored that an assassination attempt had taken place against ʿUday Hussein upon leaving a meeting of the Olympic Committee.[205] The largest number of rumors circulated around the time of an actual assassination attempt against ʿUday Hussein.[206] On December 16, 1996, one rumor suggested that the state announcement about the attack on ʿUday had not been true and had instead been an attempt to distract Iraqis from increasing market prices.[207] On the same day, one rumor suggested that ʿUday had been killed and another

197. See BRCC Doc. No. 148-4-5-0723, September 6, 1996 and BRCC Doc. No. 148-4-5-0703, September 29, 1996, respectively.

198. BRCC Doc. No. 148-4-5-0157, March 6, 1997.

199. BRCC Doc. No. 01-3713-0000-0229, May 5, 1998.

200. BRCC Doc. No. 01-3713-0000-0144, July 23, 1998.

201. BRCC Doc. No. 087-5-3-0812, January 3, 1999.

202. BRCC Doc. No. 133-5-7-0704, June 5, 1999.

203. BRCC Doc. No. 133-5-7-0695, July 22, 1999.

204. Bashir 2005, 151.

205. BRCC Doc. No. 005-3-3-0564, February 9, 1993; BRCC Doc. No. 005-3-3-0380, March 3, 1993.

206. International media sources reported ʿUday shot and wounded on December 12, 1996, following an announcement on Iraqi Youth Television. See "Saddam Hussein's Son Shot and Wounded," *CNN World News*, December 12, 1996.

207. BRCC Doc. No. 148-4-5-0518, December 16, 1996.

suggested that the attempt against ʿUday had not been by strangers, but instead by ʿUday's relatives.[208]

A flurry of rumors the following week suggested a variety of parties who might have been responsible for the assassination attempt, including the Daʿwa Party, tribal interests (in particular, the Watbani and Sabawi families and the family of Hussein Kamal), as well as merchants.[209] The rumors also suggested additional details about the attempt including that the attack had taken place in the Mansur district by either one or more people waiting for ʿUday outside of his car who then approached and shot him; it was also suggested that electricity was shut off in the Mansur district at the time of the attack.[210] Large rewards were actually offered by the regime to those with information about the attempt.[211]

In January 1997, a series of rumors circulated about another assassination attempt against a son of Hussein. In one report, Qusay Hussein was trapped in his car, which exploded minutes after he exited the vehicle; as a precaution, his driver and bodyguard would be switched every three days.[212] Separate rumors also suggested that Qusay had been attacked, but not harmed.[213] Other rumors circulating in that same month suggested the attack had not been against Qusay, but instead, ʿUday. One rumor suggested seven thousand people had been arrested for attempting to kill ʿUday and that food rations would not be distributed as collective punishment for the attack.[214] A rumor circulating in June 1999 suggested that Hussein had killed ʿUday because ʿUday was interested in taking power for himself.[215] Additional rumors about assassination attempts against Qusay circulated in August 1999 and September 2002.[216]

208. BRCC Doc. No. 148-4-5-0524, December 16, 1996.

209. BRCC Doc. No. 148-4-5-0346, December 21, 1996; BRCC Doc. No. 148-4-5-0486, December 22, 1996.

210. BRCC Doc. No. 148-4-5-0346, December 21, 1996; BRCC Doc. No. 148-4-5-0486, December 22, 1996.

211. BRCC Doc. No. 148-4-5-0346, December 21, 1996.

212. BRCC Doc. No. 148-4-5-0378, January 2, 1997.

213. BRCC. Doc. No. 148-4-5-0324, February 3, 1997; BRCC Doc. No. 148-4-5-0257, February 19, 1997.

214. BRCC Doc. No. 148-4-5-0426, January 20, 1997; BRCC Doc. No. 148-4-5-0396, January 29, 1997.

215. BRCC Doc. No. 133-5-7-0858, June 19, 1999.

216. BRCC Doc. No. 133-5-7-0624, August 24, 1999; BRCC Doc. No. 040-4-2-0195, September 1, 2002; BRCC Doc. No. 040-4-2-0089, September 12, 2002; BRCC Doc. No. 01-2454-0002-0049, September 24, 2002.

CONCLUSIONS

The Ba'thist regime in Iraq built what was, at one time, the largest army in the Arab world, and it fought one of the longest and deadliest conventional wars of the late twentieth century. Saddam Hussein long recognized the potential threat posed by the military. Dominated by a party-oriented civilian leadership, the regime was highly vulnerable to overthrow by generals who controlled troops and weapons. As a result, civil-military cooperation was seen as dangerous. The Ba'thists believed that the only way to reduce vulnerability to the military was by subordinating it completely.[217] According to Sassoon, the regime was "intent on infiltrating the army and monitoring its movements... a plethora of intelligence and security services had the sole function of being alert to any sign of mutiny or dissension."[218]

In addition to the challenge of coup plots by members of the military elite, Hussein was simultaneously concerned with popular revolt by ordinary Iraqi soldiers and a near epidemic of military desertion that threatened the capabilities and legitimacy of his regime. Failure to effectively manage conscripted soldiers had the potential to damage military effectiveness, claims of regime legitimacy, and even social stability. As a result, the regime was preoccupied with management of both elite and rank-and-file concerns associated with the military.

Because Iraq was almost continually at war between 1980 and 1991, the country was in a "hypermilitarized" state where war preparation and war making were integrated into multiple aspects of governance.[219] While enormous financial resources were directed into the expansion of Iraqi military capacity, "the Ba'thist regime skillfully worked to neutralize that huge institution politically."[220] This took place in a number of ways, particularly the "Ba'thification" of the army and use of the party bureaucracy to screen military recruits.[221]

Downsizing of the military began in earnest starting in 1991 and, combined with the economic impact of the trade embargo, created a uniquely difficult situation for the regime. Some elements of the Sunni Arab community,

217. Chartouni-Dubarry 1993, 30.
218. Sassoon 2016, 95.
219. Al-Khafaji 2000, 259; Khoury 2013.
220. Al-Khafaji 2000, 267.
221. Khoury 2013, 84.

like Anbari Sunnis, believed that they had been instrumental in putting down the 1991 Uprisings but felt shut out by military downsizing. A key observable implication of those changes were the regime-threatening coup and assassination attempts that took place during the 1990s. To try to counter those threats, the regime created multiple paramilitary organizations to serve as effective counterweights to the regular army. By creating these multiple internal security groups, the collective identity of the military was damaged, but it became increasingly difficult for any single military or militia unit to move against the regime.[222] The multiple, failed coup attempts that took place in Iraq during the 1990s simultaneously reflected the deep dissatisfaction of many non-Tikriti Sunnis with Ba'thist rule but also the complete security sector penetration of those networks that sought to unseat Hussein.

222. Dodge 2003, 59.

CHAPTER 11

CONCLUSION

The 2003 US intervention in Iraq unseated a dictatorship that had persisted through decades of internal and external challenges that few other autocrats would have been capable of surviving. And some have speculated that in the absence of the US invasion of Iraq in 2003, the Ba'thists would have continued in power for years to come.[1]

A first-order question might be "why Iraq?" In other words, why did Ba'thist Iraq have such oppressive, and ultimately dysfunctional, governance when compared to other Middle Eastern states? Although neighboring states were not particularly free, few developed the apparatus for coercion and the will to repress found in Iraq under Hussein. My argument suggests that challenging structural constraints combined with external shocks to undermine state-building. In particular, the regime's inability to monitor and accurately punish dissent in Iraq's diverse population contributed to the use and impact of state violence. I develop an account for how variation in societal legibility can lead states to engage in repressive behaviors that ultimately undermine their state-building efforts.

The external challenges facing the Ba'thist regime, while in no way unique, may have been more intense than those confronting otherwise similar autocratic regimes. A large endowment of oil resources meant that by the late 1970s, Iraq was among the most wealthy, modern, and sophisticated countries in the Middle East. But if oil wealth facilitated state- and nation-building in the 1970s, it also contributed to the curse of raised societal expectations, a heightening of regime hubris vis-à-vis other regional actors,

1. Dimitrov and Sassoon 2014. Given the staggering costs of the war—estimated by some at over $1 trillion—few Americans would say that the US intervention was worth what was paid in lives and money, not to mention the negative, downstream impact of regional instability in the wake of the American withdrawal from Iraq. When one speaks to Iraqis, however, many see the war as an act of liberation, freeing millions from political oppression.

and a profound vulnerability to shocks in the world market for oil. The unanticipated resilience of Iran in the face of the Iran-Iraq War, combined with the 1986 collapse in the world price of oil, left the Baʿthist regime politically exposed and susceptible to popular unrest. Political decisions were made under conditions of wartime stress. In this context, Hussein found himself increasingly confronting a set of regime-threatening circumstances that seemed outside of his control.

In addition to the vulnerability to external shocks, the regime's limited ability to effectively monitor Iraq's diverse populations represented a second fundamental challenge. Effective monitoring of a population most directly relates to issues of state capacity. Herbst writes about how physical geography and low population density make it difficult for African states to exert control over their territories.[2] To that, I would suggest that cultural distance can decrease legibility of a state's citizenry. In Baʿthist Iraq, there was considerable unevenness in the state's ability to penetrate society, at least in part because of language differences and geographic inaccessibility. This is not to say that the state-building enterprise is doomed to fail in plural societies but, rather, that diverse societies face particular challenges that are most effectively overcome with extensive bureaucratic investment and public goods provision. Plural societies also require a commitment to an equitable distribution of state burdens and restraint on the part of the regime when faced with the impulse to punish under conditions of limited information.

Even if we are unable to answer definitively the question of why Iraq emerged as among the most repressive autocratic countries of the twentieth century, examining individual and community responses to growing autocracy in Iraq provides a window into how forms of resistance and compliance emerge under such regimes.[3] Scholars who seek to characterize compliance

2. Herbst 2000.

3. Despite a rich and growing theoretical and empirical literature on a range of citizen behaviors under conditions of social, political, and economic repression, I was not able to identify a single theoretical framework for understanding behavioral outcomes across the full spectrum of potential behaviors, from collaboration to rebellion. Petersen (2001) comes closest by both identifying the full spectrum of behaviors and then explaining, with great care, the conditions under which individuals and communities might move from one position on the spectrum to the next. My account differs from Petersen (2001) in a number of ways, including more focused attention on behaviors beyond resistance and rebellion, and by adopting a view that individuals and communities might move discontinuously (i.e., not sequentially) across behaviors under conditions of political repression.

with and resistance to onerous political and economic demands suggest that individual behavior reflects a complex set of material and cognitive considerations. On a most basic level, the need for survival often serves as a motivator for compliant behavior in high-stakes political environments. Citizens of dictatorships are required to make constant, tacit choices regarding whether to do what is expected of them or deviate from regime expectations of behavior. Authoritarian regimes cannot survive without groups of individuals who are active and willing cooperators with the dictator. Often such cooperation affords individuals, and sometimes their families, forms of physical security that cannot be achieved in other ways. Yet the degree of support and collaboration observed often exceeds expectations given the mental stress and discomfort we might expect when in close cooperation with a political oppressor.

Despite the considerable personal vulnerability to which one is exposed as a result of non-compliant behavior, individuals living in dictatorships do sometimes engage in highly dangerous acts of protest and resistance that put themselves, and often those with whom they are associated, at considerable risk. When citizens choose to break with regime expectations of appropriate behavior, regimes respond with punishments that are contingent upon a number of factors, including the type of behavior, the political position of the transgressor, and the regime's ability to accurately identify the transgressor. Totalitarian regimes are characterized—to a greater degree than their authoritarian counterparts—by increasing intensity of punishment for political transgressions. That said, Iraq under Saddam Hussein was situational in its totalitarianism.

Influential studies have sought to endogenize citizen behavior—like participation in a revolutionary social movement—as a function of state action. Goodwin argues that "people do not tend to join or support revolutionary movements when they believe that the central state has little if anything to do with their everyday problems, however severe those problems may be."[4] In this context, states construct the revolutionary movements that challenge them through a series of channels—including protection of particular social, economic, or cultural arrangements, or exclusion of state power or resource-sharing—that are causally cumulative.[5] Staniland argues, on the

4. Goodwin 2001, 25.
5. Goodwin 2001, 45–49.

other hand, that a focus on state-centric variables in the study of insurgency has "overpromised and underdelivered" because such an approach fails to take into account the historical social and political pillars of social movements and groups.[6] My objective is not to describe citizens as mere reflections of state power, but to encourage an examination of the roots of the social and political foundations of societal interaction. Ignoring the hugely influential impact of state action on citizen beliefs misses the incentives and behaviors of the most important political actor in most autocratic contexts—the state itself.

SUMMARY OF ARGUMENTS

A major argument of this book is that when states punish their citizens for dissent, the way that punishment is implemented influences forms of political identity that become salient within the population. States are key actors in this narrative. This is not because states and their leaders, like Saddam Hussein, invent the ethno-national, religious, or tribal cleavages that exist within their societies, but rather because dictators make ugly and destructive policy choices, particularly when faced with financial limitations and governance constraints, and these choices influence the political beliefs and behaviors of their citizens.

In my narrative of Iraqi political development, the 1970s stand out as a period of intense state-building in terms of the capacity and reach of the formal structures of power, but also a period of nation-building in terms of the cultivation of Iraqi nationalist sentiment that emerged in response to the distributive ability of the state. The Ba'thist regime's success in the 1970s was not a reflection of Hussein's genius but, rather, a function of the regime's willingness to spend the country's oil windfall on public goods and state employment in ways that helped large segments of the population. During that period, Iraqis from across a variety of sectors—state bureaucrats, teachers, businessmen, and artisans—experienced upward mobility and with it strengthened their allegiance to the Iraqi state and the Ba'th Party.[7] Inter-marriage across ethno-sectarian groups was common and business partner-ships often included Iraqis of different religious and ethnic backgrounds.[8]

6. Staniland 2014, 223.
7. Rohde 2010, 26.
8. Fuller and Francke 1999, 99.

Where identity-based challenges to the state did exist, they tended to be limited in scope and the Baʿthist regime was largely successful at repressing transgressions in a manner that did not provoke widespread public outrage.

Hechter and Kabiri argue that Hussein and the Baʿthists sought to govern through a form of direct rule where the state imposed top-down, centralized authority, and legal uniformity on the Iraqi population.[9] The downside of direct rule in this account, however, is that the regime assumes the costs of policing while simultaneously providing the bulk of society's collective goods.[10] In the Iraqi case, a tightening budget constraint over the course of the 1980s decreased public support for the regime, pushing more individuals toward anti-regime activities. When the regime sought to punish individuals for their transgressions, the often collective nature of punishment impacted identity in ways that undercut the state-building efforts of the 1970s. For example, collective punishment of Kurdish populations as a result of cross-border collaboration between Iran and peshmerga units during the Iran-Iraq War contributed to Kurdish feelings of nationalism. Indiscriminate punishment of Iraqi Kurds served as a shared experience for northern populations and created a common belief about the linked nature of their future survival. Memory of shared trauma served as a catalyst for the cultivation of group identity.[11]

Ayoob has argued that a ruling elite can choose to balance the demands of competing groups by seeking to assimilate or annihilate these groups.[12] My argument suggests that assimilationist policies are not always feasible in the short term and, further, that states can enter into spirals of attack and punishment with devastating consequences. Kurdish Iraqis were not predestined or predetermined enemies of the Iraqi state. Rather, Kurdish nationalism was inadvertently fostered by the Iraqi state as a result of the actions the state took against Kurdish populations during a period of fiscal and military crisis.

My interpretation of the Kurdish case contrasts with scholars who make culturally based arguments about the historical roots of social and political movements. One problem with those arguments is that they tend to do a poor job of explaining relatively rapid changes in citizen beliefs and

9. Hechter and Kabiri 2009.
10. Ibid.
11. Haddad 2011. Collective traumatic experiences—like the legacy of slavery for African Americans—serve as important drivers of collective identity (Eyerman 2001).
12. Ayoob 1995, 169.

behaviors. It is true that Kurdish social and political movements—like the KDP and the PUK—have historical roots and traditional bases of support, but those legacies do not explain the rapid strengthening of Kurdish national-ist sentiment during the 1980s. Kurdish political behavior reflected choices made in reaction to state action. Previously, cooperation between Kurdish groups had been infrequent and opportunistic, clearly not a result of undying cultural affinity within the community of Iraqi Kurds.

At the opposite extreme, where high levels of regime penetration into a community were possible, the regime could impose punishments for trans-gressing regime norms in more surgical, precise ways targeted at individuals, not collective groups. The social networks that emerged in such a context were weak, discouraging societal policing of in-group transgressors while simultane-ously increasing the probability of within-group denunciations.[13] In addition, the ease with which information could be gathered on opposition to the regime meant that sharing feelings of anti-regime sentiment with anyone— even trusted confidants—was tantamount to a public act. As a result, forms of public defiance were more common among Iraqi Sunnis than non-Sunnis. The reliance on Iraqis from Tikrit and neighboring areas also represented a decrease in political importance for those from Upper Euphrates towns, like Ana and Ramadi, in Anbar governorate.[14] For example, Dodge, describing the Baʿthist period, writes that "the Sunnis who are not Tikritis feel discriminated against."[15]

This sense of discrimination within the Sunni community became exacer-bated over the course of the sanctions period, manifesting itself in public forms of political discontent by non-Tikriti Sunnis, including a reluctance to iden-tify with the party and increasing prevalence of coup attempts. Interpersonal rivalries between high-level elites—like those that existed between Hussein's sons and his sons-in-law—were well-known and a "lack of trust" prevailed among the military leadership in Iraq.[16] Among non-elites a similar pattern is apparent. Inglehart, Moaddel, and Tessler investigate the issue of intra-ethnic trust in Iraq just after the US invasion in 2003.[17] In the survey that they

13. It is probably not surprising to think that people feel more comfortable snitching on neighbors when group ties are weak.
14. Sakai 2003, 144.
15. Dodge 2003, 66.
16. Sassoon 2016, 109-110.
17. Inglehart, Moaddel, and Tessler 2006.

conduct, intra-ethnic trust was highest for Kurds (96 percent), middling for Shiʿa (86 percent), and lowest for Iraq's Sunni community (68 percent).

For Iraqi Shiʿa, the Baʿthist regime was largely successful in its assimilationist policies, at least through the first half of the Iran-Iraq War. As they bore the disproportionate burden of war "tax" for Iraqi society, however, many Shiʿa increasingly came to resent the Baʿthist regime. But despite the hardship of war and economic austerity imposed on Shiʿa, these communities did not seek to "separate from the state" and instead sought "political power and representation in the government in proportion to their weight among the population."[18]

When transgressive political acts took place in predominantly Shiʿi areas like Saddam City in Baghdad, the Shrine Cities of Najaf and Karbala, and rural and urban areas of southern Iraq, the Baʿthist regime struggled to ascertain the transgressors with precision. As a result, the Baʿthists meted out punishment based on available intelligence. Since the regime's penetration of Shiʿi communities was imperfect, punishment for political transgression was blunt, often at the level of the communal group. These communal groups might include clans or tribes, but also collectives based on the followers of a particular religious leader. As a result, regime dragnets led to the arrest of individuals with only a loosely shared identity affiliation with the bad actor. Yet punishment of individuals based on this shared group identity had the effect of actually encouraging further identification at the group level. From an empirical perspective, increasing interpersonal trust at the group level was associated with rumormongering and draft evasion—political activities only possible within socially cohesive communities.

RELATIONSHIP TO EXISTING WORK ON BAʿTHIST IRAQ

While the narrative I have put forward is out-of-step with journalistic accounts of Iraqi politics, how do my findings speak to the extensive existing literature on Saddam Hussein and Baʿthist Iraq? Given the size and scope of this literature, I will focus on four core points.

First, recent scholarly work on the Baʿthist regime has been sensitive to the diversity of political behaviors both across and within ethnic groups. For

18. Nakash 1994b, 277.

example, like Jabar I recognize the heterogenous nature of identity ties in Iraq as well as the complex internal differences within various ascriptive groups.[19] Baram argues that under the Baʿth Party, "Iraq's Sunni-Shiʿi-Kurdish cleavage was not absolute, nor was it always the most important fault line in Iraqi society."[20] Sassoon finds that Iraqis from a variety of backgrounds—including Shiʿa and Kurds—served at the highest levels of Iraqi security and governmental agencies until the 2003 invasion.[21] Zeidel argues that Sunni identity did not exist in Baʿthist Iraq in terms of a "normative communal identity."[22] Visser points to the long history of co-existence between Sunnis and Shiʿa in Iraq—a norm that was only rarely and generally unsuccessfully challenged.[23] I hope that this project, along with this previous work, can help definitively put to rest the idea that Iraqi politics should be viewed through a strictly Sunni-Shiʿi-Kurdish prism.

Second, I build upon the work of existing scholars who focus on the use of rewards and punishments in Iraq under Hussein.[24] With regard to the use of rewards and other incentives as a strategy of statecraft, my main contribution is to provide empirical evidence about the ways that different regional and tribal groups were privileged. For example, within the category of Iraqi Sunnis, individuals and families from central Iraq were disproportionate beneficiaries of regime largesse relative to those from western Iraq; and within central Iraq, certain tribes from in and around Hussein's region of origin—for example, members of the Juburi tribe—were favored over others. While observers of Iraqi politics had long identified such patterns, the empirical evidence that I provide documents the extent of those disparities. I also report on the disproportionate harships suffered within Iraq's populations as a result of war and sanctions, contributing to our understanding of the political implications of the asymmetric distribution of rewards and burdens.

With regard to the use of repression, my contributions are more theoretical and extend existing work. Khoury discusses the complex and, often, contradictory use of punishment against individuals and families during Iraq's wars; while the regime rewarded people as individuals, punishment often took place

19. Jabar 2003a.
20. Baram 2014, 81.
21. Sassoon 2016, 124.
22. Zeidel 2010, 165.
23. Visser 2012a.
24. Sassoon 2012; Khoury 2013; Faust 2015.

against family units.[25] Sassoon finds that collective punishment—like the blocking of employment or educational opportunities and the confiscation of assets—against family members might be used against members of opposition parties and those involved in assassination plots.[26] While these scholars point to the intentional use of collective punishment as a strategy of statecraft, I provide a different logic for how and why punishment was meted out at the collective in a way that relates not to punishment's deterrent effect, but rather to issues of legibility and state capacity. Dimitrov and Sassoon argue that, in contrast to intelligence-gathering capabilities in Communist Bulgaria, Iraqi intelligence gathering was never sufficiently sophisticated to engage only in fine-grain, targeted repression, forcing a continued reliance on mass repression instead.[27] I agree with their assessment and extend their insight by spelling out the effects of punishment for identity formation and related political behaviors. I also elaborate on forms of quiet resistance to repression that receive only passing discussion in most scholarly works.

Finally, my arguments speak to how and why certain sectarian or other identities become activated in the Iraqi case. Haddad focuses on four factors which influence the creation of sectarian cleavage in Iraq—external influence, economic competition, competing myth-symbols, and contested cultural ownership of the nation.[28] I add the identity-creating impact of collective repression to his insights. My conclusions also build on and provide a specific logic for scholars who argue that the Ba'thists actually achieved the opposite of what they set out to achieve politically. Rather than succeeding in homogenizing the nation, regime actions actually deepened forms of ethnic, religious, and cultural cleavages, to the detriment of Iraqi nationalist sentiment.[29]

CREATING A SECTARIAN IRAQ

A key theme of this book relates to the conditions under which potentially relevant political cleavages become more or less salient for citizens living

25. Khoury 2013, 173–174.
26. Sassoon 2012.
27. Dimitrov and Sassoon 2014.
28. Haddad 2011, 10.
29. Al-Khafaji 2000, 282; Jabar 2003, 15.

under conditions of dictatorship.[30] Scholars have argued that the Baʿthist regime sought to impart a sense of national identity that would supersede other identities.[31] And in even the most private of regime correspondence, Baʿthist officials depicted problems within the country in nationalist—not sectarian—terms.[32] According to Khoury, the regime was primarily concerned with obedience and security and, as a result, power was not allocated on explicitly sectarian lines.[33] Alahmed suggests that despite political dominance by Iraqi Sunnis since the establishment of the Iraqi state, Sunnis never acted as a unified sect with a mission to dominate during the many years of political control.[34] Indeed, Makiya suggests that "the Baʿth never built a Sunni confessional state in Iraq … nor did they build one ideologically opposed to Shiʿism."[35]

How then did Iraq—a country with a historical legacy of intercommunal cooperation—become embroiled in sectarian violence so intense we label it ethnic cleansing and civil war? In this section, I discuss the process by which ethno-sectarian identity became increasingly salient in Iraq after 2003.

US Policy and Encouragement of Sectarian Identity

The form of sectarianism that emerged after the 2003 American invasion was new to Iraq.[36] Ismael and Fuller argue that the growth in political sectarianism was, in large part, a result of the destruction of the Iraqi state and American-imposed policies, like de-Baʿthification.[37] Anyone who had belonged to the Baʿth Party—including school teachers, who were almost universally Baʿthists—was deemed unsuitable for government service. The Iraqi army was disbanded. These US policy decisions did not account for the

---

30. Scholars of Iraqi politics have long identified the choice set of potentially salient cleavages. Davis (2005, 5) suggests ethnic and class cleavages associated with social equity have been key dimensions of differentiation in Iraqi society as well as societal differentiation regarding political stability. Others have emphasized social cleavages based on regional identities (Visser 2008). Tribal interests have also been described as a major source of political cleavage within Iraqi society (Baram 1997).
31. Ismael and Fuller 2008.
32. Helfont 2015.
33. Khoury 2010.
34. Alahmed 2009, 208.
35. Makiya 1993, 218.
36. Khoury 2010.
37. Ismael and Fuller 2008.

reality that the vast majority of party members at the time of the invasion were simply individuals seeking apolitical government employment and who were not true or dedicated party loyalists. De-Ba'thification was endorsed by political entrepreneurs, like Ahmed Chalabi, who sought to control state employment opportunities in a post-2003 Iraq.[38]

De-Ba'thification has been described by some as among the worst transitional justice processes ever undertaken by a Western power.[39] By the end of the process, the Iraqi state was little more than a hollow carapace with limited capacity to project political power or exercise effective governance.

Perhaps as destructive as the dismantling of Iraq's administrative structure was the creation of a governing council where council members were selected based on their sectarian ethnic affiliation. In particular, the Coalition Provisional Authority and the Iraqi leadership council agreed to the formation of the 25-member Iraqi Governing Council (IGC), which was inaugurated in July 2003. Ethno-sectarian apportionment was a defining, structural feature of the council. Such a selection strategy was based on a stylized conventional wisdom about the "tripartite" nature of Iraqi society, but the net effect was to increase the salience of ethnic divides in Iraq. In the end, the desire to make the council's composition mirror Iraq's ethno-sectarian demographics deepened these societal rifts.[40]

The International Crisis Group was prescient in its analysis in 2003. According to one group report:

> The principle behind the Interim Governing Council's composition also sets a troubling precedent. Its members were chosen so as to mirror Iraq's sectarian and ethnic makeup; for the first time in the country's history, the guiding assumption is that political representation must be apportioned according to such quotas. This decision reflects how the Council's creators, not the Iraqi people, view Iraqi society and politics, but it will not be without consequence. Ethnic and religious conflict, for the most part absent from Iraq's modern history, is likely to be exacerbated as its people increasingly organise along these divisive lines.[41]

38. It was thought that de-Ba'thification would create new employment opportunities for non-Sunnis (Harling 2012, 64).

39. Al-Ali 2014, 69.

40. Osman 2014, 158.

41. International Crisis Group, "Governing Iraq," *Middle East and North Africa Report, 17*, August 25, 2003.

With the move to competitive parliamentary elections in 2005, ballots came to be associated with sectarian power.[42] In the throes of electoral competition, shared ethnic and sectarian bonds were privileged in voter mobilization at the expense of more universalizing principles of Iraqi nationalism and civic equality.[43] According to an influential report on the transitional period, the "flawed" January 2005 elections and subsequent drafting and ratification of a highly sectarian Iraqi constitution in October 2005 created a critical juncture in the hardening of sectarian identities.[44] Iraqis increasingly came to see the United States and its state-building efforts as part of a strategy to instigate sectarian strife.[45]

How was it that the US government created a set of policies that strongly enhanced ethnic identification? US intelligence reports had promoted assumptions about the ethno-sectarian nature of political cleavages in Iraq since at least the early 1980s. Similarly, the dominant discourse in the global media long suggested that political attitudes in Iraq were uniquely determined by ethno-religious affiliation.[46] US and coalition forces believed that ethno-sectarian identification was "natural" to Iraq.[47] In the eyes of Paul Bremer and members of his team, Iraq was populated by people who hated other sectarian groups.[48] But, according to Al-Ali, "just about any Iraqi could have told Bremer and his associates that blind ethno-sectarian hatred was actually quite rare in Iraq."[49]

Davis argues, more generally, that Western observers frequently assume Middle Eastern societies suffer a structural defect in their political culture where citizens identify with their ethnic or sectarian group over their national identity.[50] For Davis, when Western policymakers adopt this type of logic, policy interventions reflect these reductionist approaches.[51] Campbell

42. Osman 2014, 159.

43. Ibid.

44. International Crisis Group, "The Next Iraqi War? Sectarianism and Civil Conflict," *Middle East and North Africa Report*, 52, February 2006.

45. Roel Meijer. 2005. "Association of Muslim Scholars in Iraq." *Middle East Report*. 237 (Winter 2005).

46. Ibid.

47. Harling 2012, 10.

48. Al-Ali 2014, 70.

49. Ibid.

50. Davis 2008. In line with this false premise, Middle Eastern countries are inherently vulnerable to forms of ethnically driven political instability that only an authoritarian ruler who enforces pluralism and inter-communal tolerance can control (Davis 2008).

51. Ibid.

provides a compelling account about what happens to international discourse and policy action when a conflict becomes labeled an ethnic struggle.[52] In his exploration of the Bosnian War, he argues that conventional representations of the conflict had the tendency to "deploy an ethnically structured way of seeing" that denied the "radical contingency" of political identity.[53] The result was an "impoverished discourse of identity politics" that crippled the ability of the international community to respond adequately to the violence.[54]

Terrorist Organizations and Activation of Sunni Identity

Into the governance void created by de-Baʿthification, regional and international actors sought to influence Iraqi political life. In particular, radical Islamists—like al-Qaeda—invested in Sunni provinces, including Anbar.[55] Iraqi Sunnis, at the time, were leaderless and divided. According to Patel, Sunni Arabs did not exist as a coherent group nor did they adopt a common bargaining position or electoral strategy in the wake of the US invasion; further, no unifying institutions or leaders emerged at this time from within the Sunni community.[56] Gerges characterizes the political scene in Iraq after Hussein as highly fragmented.[57]

Extremists like Abu Musab al-Zarqawi attacked Shiʿi targets with the explicit goal of unifying Sunni interests in the face of Shiʿi counterattacks.[58] Radical Islamists made "strategic use of sectarian clashes."[59] For example, in correspondence between al-Zarqawi and Osama bin Laden, al-Zarqawi argued in favor of targeting Iraqi Shiʿa in terror attacks:

> What I mean is that targeting and striking [Shiʿa] at the religious, political and military levels will provoke them to show their dog to the Sunnis

52. Campbell 1998.
53. Ibid., 14.
54. Ibid. Assumptions about the nature of identity politics limited the menu of possible approaches for international actors. According to Campbell, "the international community's structural solutions for Bosnia produced the very ethnicization of politics they later criticized, furthered the nationalist project they ostensibly wanted to contest, and provided no space for the non-nationalist formations they professed to support" (225).
55. Totten 2011.
56. Patel 2016.
57. Gerges 2016, 7.
58. Warrick 2015.
59. Gerges 2016, 6.

and have it snarl at them, revealing the hidden envy boiling deep in their hearts... if we are successful in dragging them into the sectarian war, it will be possible to awaken the sleeping Sunnis when they feel the imminent danger and annihilation at the hands of these Sabaeans [i.e., the Shiʿa].[60]

According to Gerges, "from the beginning, Zarqawi's strategic goal was to trigger all-out Sunni-Shiʿi Islamic war and mobilize and co-opt Sunni opinion ... [Zarqawi] pledged to savagely attack civilian and religious targets, thus provoking the Shiʿa to retaliate against the Sunnis."[61] Attacks against Shiʿi targets spurred retaliation. By late 2006, violence against Sunnis increased to the point that leading figures in the Sunni community began to argue publicly that Iranian-sponsored Shiʿi militias were engaged in a genocidal campaign against Sunnis.[62] In this way, Iraqi Sunni identity was activated, or reactivated, after many years of what might be considered family or regional (i.e., Tikriti) rule. By November 2006, the Islamic State's Ministry of Media in Anbar province called upon Sunni communities around the world to stand beside their sectarian brethren and support the Islamic State.[63]

Shiʿi Activism after 2003

Prior to 2003, most Iraqi Shiʿa did not think of themselves primarily in sectarian terms.[64] Yet, in the immediate aftermath of the US invasion, religious leaders from within the Shiʿi community emerged as brokers of political power.[65] Why were religious elites particulary influential at this time? I have argued that collective punishment of religious communities during the Baʿthist period increased social capital for religious groups.[66] This made religious groups and their leaders relatively well-positioned to emerge with influence after the US invasion.

60. CRRC Doc. No. AQ-MCOP-D-001-785.
61. Gerges 2016, 82.
62. Al-Ali 2014, 114–15.
63. CRRC Doc. No. AQ-MCOP-D-001-858, November 7, 2006.
64. Patel 2016.
65. Juan Cole, "Shiite Religious Parties Fill Vacuum in Southern Iraq," *Middle East Report Online*, April 22, 2003.
66. In addition, mosques served as focal locations for social organization in the wake of the collapse of the Iraqi state (Patel 2016).

Muqtada al-Sadr, son of assassinated Muhammad Muhammad Sadiq al-Sadr, and his supporters took advantage of the Iraqi security vacuum.[67] After US troops entered Baghdad, Muqtada al-Sadr reportedly reached out to a number of his father's former students and lieutenants as part of an initial mobilization.[68] The vision he put forward was "plebian, nationalistic, anti-American, and anti-Iranian," reflecting cross-cutting political cleavages within Shi'i society.[69] Some have argued that the Sadrist movement was among the most "enigmatic forces" to have emerged in post-invasion Iraq.[70] Indeed, a conventional narrative suggests Muqtada al-Sadr "came out of nowhere" since US officials seemed consistently surprised by the strength of his support.[71]

As I have argued, however, the Sadr movement finds its roots in the Ba'thist dictatorship. Sadr supporters were strongly concentrated in areas that had been "brutalized by Ba'th Party goons."[72] Loyalists to Muqtada al-Sadr began to develop their own medical, educational, judicial, and other services after the American invasion and also recruited for the Mahdi Army, his militia.[73] The Sadrist movement dispensed charity to the local needy,[74] while at the same time forcefully taking over mosques, issuing death threats, and paving the way for the creation of a Shi'i Islamic state.[75] Muqtada al-Sadr emerged as an ascendant leader in the wake of the US invasion, exploiting divisions within the Shi'i community.[76]

The Sadr movement was not the only faction offering a route to social order and organization, however, as a number of different groups sought to assert authority in the highly fractured political environment. Sadrist militants and cadre tended to be younger and scarred by the economic embargo, but there existed tremendous diversity within the Shi'i community on a

67. Visser 2005, 170.
68. Patel 2016.
69. Harling 2012, 78–79.
70. Ismael and Fuller 2008.
71. Dan Murphy, "Sadr the Agitator: Like Father, like Son," *Christian Science Monitor*, April 27, 2004.
72. Juan Cole, "Shiite Religious Parties Fill Vacuum in Southern Iraq," *Middle East Report Online*, April 22, 2003.
73. Raphaeli 2004.
74. Ismael and Fuller 2008.
75. Juan Cole, "Shiite Religious Parties Fill Vacuum in Southern Iraq," *Middle East Report Online*, April 22, 2003.
76. Cordesman and Baetjer 2006, 279.

variety of dimensions, including the rightful role of the formal Shiʿi religious establishment.[77] The Supreme Council for the Islamic Revolution in Iraq (i.e., SCIRI) sought to assert itself in Kut; Nasiriyya came under the control of the Daʿwa Party; and a council of clerics and tribal leaders were organizing institutions of self-rule in Karbala.[78]

Intra-Shiʿi conflict became intense in the wake of the US invasion. In April 2003, ʿAbd al-Majid al-Khuʾi—the 40-year-old son of former Grand Ayatollah Abu al-Qasim al-Khuʾi—returned to Iraq and shortly thereafter was murdered along with two of his supporters at a Shiʿi holy shrine. Following the al-Khuʾi assassination, Sadrists demonstrated outside of the home of Grand Ayatollah Ali al-Sistani—the hawza's most senior cleric—demanding his return to Iran.[79] It was not until al-Sistani mobilized over one thousand tribesmen from nearby areas that the crowd was dispersed.[80] Another prominent Shiʿi figure, known as the "keeper of the key" to the tomb of Imam Ali, was murdered at the hands of Muqtada al-Sadr's supporters.[81] According to one observer, western audiences were quickly discovering that Iraqi Shiʿa were not unified in their vision for a postwar Iraq.[82]

SCIRI, a main rival to the Sadr movement, had strong ties to the Najafi religious establishment and the elite al-Hakim clerical family. According to Mallat, the Iranian regime believed that with the downfall of Hussein, SCIRI would be able to come to power in Baghdad.[83] US and Iranian interests came into rare alignment as SCIRI endorsed America's sectarian vision for a federal and decentralized Iraqi state.[84]

Despite the existence of intense divisions within the Shiʿi community, an increasing number of bombings and assassinations against Shiʿi targets by Sunni radicals in 2005 increased the salience of Shiʿi identity. According

77. Harling 2012.
78. Juan Cole, "Shiite Religious Parties Fill Vacuum in Southern Iraq," *Middle East Report Online*, April 22, 2003.
79. Raphaeli 2004.
80. Ibid. An investigation by the hawza into al-Khuʾi's murder named Muqtada al-Sadr's supporters responsible for the killing (Raphaeli 2004). According to Raphaeli (2004), the report of the findings was presented to US Marine Corps officials, but no action was taken.
81. Ibid.
82. Juan Cole, "Shiite Religious Parties Fill Vacuum in Southern Iraq," *Middle East Report Online*, April 22, 2003.
83. Mallat 1988.
84. Ismael and Fuller 2008.

to one report, a "dirty war" waged by a relatively small group of Sunni insurgents was fomenting sectarian strife through the killing of Shiʿa.[85] This period of intense violence was seen as the point at which "latent sectarianism took wings, permeating the political discourse and precipitating incidents of appalling violence and sectarian 'cleansing.'"[86] Shiʿa increasingly sought to close ranks in the face of indiscriminate, anti-Shiʿi violence.[87]

In a letter written from SCIRI to its militia—branches of the Badr Corps—it was suggested that the Badr forces, likewise, make every effort to encourage sedition among the armed Sunni factions.[88] This would be accomplished by attacking Iraqi army and police, assassinating Sunni officers, clerics, and tribal leaders, and destroying telecommunications and other infrastructure in Sunni areas so they would become abandoned.[89] SCIRI believed that these actions would help to create discord among the armed Sunni factions, undermining stability and slowing the formation of a Sunni Islamic state.[90] In February 2006, the Askari Mosque in Samarra was bombed. Reprisals undertaken against Sunni targets in the aftermath of the Samarra bombing unleashed a new wave of sectarian tension.[91] Within a year, the conflict in Iraq was being labeled a "civil war."[92]

The Reconstruction of Iraq?

The postcolonial states of the Arab world have faced a series of structural challenges to state- and nation-building. Relatively low-capacity states with diverse populations sought to impose control over territories that operated with considerable autonomy during the Ottoman period. A plague of coups d'etat in the 1950s and 1960s were eventually overcome by the development

---

85. International Crisis Group, "The Next Iraqi War? Sectarianism and Civil Conflict," *Middle East and North Africa Report 52*, February 2006.

86. Ibid.

87. Al-Ali 2014, 101.

88. CRRC Number AQ-MCOP-D-001-736, January 5, 2005.

89. Ibid.

90. Ibid.

91. International Crisis Group, "The Next Iraqi War? Sectarianism and Civil Conflict," *Middle East and North Africa Report 52*, February 2006.

92. James Fearon, "Iraq's Civil War," *Foreign Affairs*, March/April 2007.

of authoritarian political institutions. At the same time, the postcolonial states of the Arab world also enjoyed some meaningful advantages and opportunities. Memories of anti-colonial struggle often encouraged a sense of social cohesion. Ideological trends, including pan-Arabism and, later, Islamism, were influential in mobilizing popular support and allegiance. And after 1973, natural resource wealth meant that state-building could be undertaken in a robust manner.

For decades, political elites sought to lay the foundations of a modern Iraqi state built on a shared national identity.[93] The state enacted policies with the goals of political unification, educational uniformity, and homogenization of identity.[94] These goals continued under Ba'th Party rule. This project has described the un-making of national identity through an examination of the Iraqi state in the late twentieth and early twenty-first centuries. There is no reason to believe, however, that the Iraqi state and identity could not be reconstructed.

How might this occur? The victory of the Iraqi Army over the Islamic State in Mosul in July 2017 was viewed by many as a key victory for the Iraqi state. Yet the retaking of the city came at a high cost, with thousands of civilian casualties in addition to utter devastation of Mosul's Old City.[95] Restoring essential public services and rebuilding infrastructure will undoubtedly require a massive financial investment.

Yet blindly throwing money at the challenge of nation-building is clearly not the answer. The approximately $60 billion the United States spent to reconstruct Iraq after the 2003 invasion failed to achieve the desired state-building results; rather, the manner by which funds were distributed seems to have increased rent-seeking and corruption.[96] Indeed, as of 2016, Iraq was ranked the 166th most corrupt country (out of a total of 176 countries) in the world by Transparency International.[97] Likewise, electoral institutions alone have been insufficient to generate desired state-building outcomes.

93. Osman 2015.

94. Ibid.

95. Tim Arango and Michael Gordon, "Iraqi Prime Minister Arrives in Mosul to Declare Victory Over ISIS," *New York Times*, July 9, 2017.

96. See "Learning from Iraq," *Final Report from the Special Inspector General for Iraq Reconstruction*, March 2013 for how the US government came to view fraud, waste, and resource abuse during the Iraqi reconstruction effort.

97. See Transparency International's Corruption Perceptions Index 2016 at https:// www.transparency.org/.

Elections without basic state capacity have the potential to introduce political instability.[98] The lessons from this book would suggest that the effective and equitable distribution of state resources (and burdens) can build states while indiscriminate forms of state repression exacerbate ethnic boundary-making and sectarian polarization, working against the construction of a state and nation.

CAUSES AND EFFECTS OF REPRESSION OUTSIDE OF IRAQ

My core contributions to our understanding of repression are twofold. First, I have sought to create a better understanding of how resources and constraints underlie the use of repression. Second, I have tried to provide a clearer idea of the citizen responses repression prompts.

The ideas and evidence that I have presented in this book are plausibly general even if my application has been focused on the Iraqi case. There are at least two ways that we might think about the generalizability of the arguments and empirical documentation that I have put forward. The first is to consider how my theoretical arguments relate to other literatures on the causes and effects of collective and particularistic political interactions. For example, some of the ideas that I have presented with regard to repression have parallels in the literature on public and private benefits in the distributive politics literature.

The second strategy involves investigating two empirical associations suggested by my arguments for a larger sample of cases. One relates to the predicted positive empirical relationship between group legibility and collective punishment. If groups are highly legible to political regimes, they should be subject to fewer instances of collective punishment, all else equal. Another relates to an anticipated positive correlation between a regime's use of collective punishment and a group's resistance activities. An exploratory analysis of data from the Minorities at Risk (MAR) project provides an opportunity to consider these two empirical relationships using cross-sectional data across a wide variety of groups. While these analyses cannot adequately address inferential concerns about how and why some groups are more or less legible

98. Monten 2014. Similarly, for Feldman (2004) elections should be later in a state-building process, after the establishment of basic security.

to political regimes to begin with, they provide one form of evidence for the empirical plausibility of my core arguments.

Parallels with the Literature on Collective versus Targeted Benefits

A number of influential models investigate the allocation of collective and targeted goods to voters in elections. For example, Cox and Lizzeri and Persico ask why political parties in Britain switch from a strategy of individual bribery of voters to one of programmatic policy benefits.[99] This literature follows a number of similar logical steps to the mechanisms that I have described in my discussion of punishment and repression. First, in both the repression and the rewards cases, it is costly to monitor individuals. Monitoring voters and their behaviors is a non-trivial task that is subsequently associated with the delivery of benefits. Although models represent these monitoring costs in a variety of ways, Cox and Lizzeri and Persico share an implicit assumption that costs are increasing in the number of voters to be rewarded.[100] Since the number of voters changed during the period they study via reforms associated with the expansion of suffrage, Cox and Lizzeri and Persico argue that British parties' switch from individualized to collective rewards was driven by the increasing number of voters (with monitoring costs held constant). My investigation considers when political regimes might switch from individualized to collective punishment. In my analysis, numbers are held constant but monitoring costs differ across groups. Thus, in both cases, collective strategies are adopted when the monitoring costs associated with an individualized strategy become too great.

Other segments of the distributive politics literature, while not focused on the choice between individualized and collective targeting, share my assumption that groups are differentially legible to different political actors. In an influential model of distributive politics, Dixit and Londregan allow transfers between parties and voters to occur via a "leaky bucket"—of the dollars offered by the party to each member of the group, only a fraction

---

99. See Cox (1987) and Lizzeri and Persico (2003).

100. As a result of large and, potentially, increasing monitoring costs, members of the elite may wish to reform the political system since a growing electorate increases the electoral value of policies with diffuse, rather than particularistic, benefits.

may get through.[101] Importantly, the fraction depends on the identity of the group, a consideration that allows for the possibility that each party has core support groups that it understands well and, as a result, can efficiently deliver benefits to group members. For the case of repression, I argue that monitoring of transgressive behaviors is costly and these costs vary as a result of variation in how legible group populations are to political regimes.

Empirical Implications

Collective punishment has long been used as a way to retaliate against groups when regimes are hard pressed to identify individual rebellious actors. For example, communities might be held collectively responsible when political regimes believe that the collective has been tolerating or harboring subversives. Is retribution always necessary, especially considering the potential negative externalities associated with collective punishment? Regimes prefer that citizens never transgress—either because of citizen acquiescence or through successful policing of behavior within the group—but often have to punish since doing nothing generates a positive probability of future rebellion. Indeed, Davenport has called the "law of coercive responsiveness" a core finding in the study of repression. When challenges to the status quo take place, authorities are compelled to employ repressive action to counter or eliminate the behavioral threat.[102]

There exist a number of historical and contemporary cases that resemble the core empirical expectations of this project. Similar to the Iraqi case, collective punishment is common during periods of war. For example during the First World War, German invasions of Western Europe were marked by numerous acts of collective punishment in response to either real or perceived acts of resistance. During the Second World War, the Nazis were notorious for punishing entire villages—in Poland, Serbia, France, Ukraine and elsewhere—for the assassination of a single Nazi soldier.

Even in peacetime, however, political regimes engage in forms of collective punishment despite their best efforts to increase the successful monitoring of

101. See Dixit and Londregan (1996).
102. Davenport (2007) defines the "law of coercive responsiveness" as the idea that governing authorities should respond with repression to behavior that threatens the political system, government personnel, the economy, or the lives, beliefs, and livelihoods of those within their territorial jurisdiction.

subject populations. In China's western Xinjiang province, ethnic Uyghurs claim that they are often considered "guilty by association" as a result of their racial and religious background.[103] When terrorist attacks have occurred, the Chinese government has been quick to blame the Uyghur minority.[104] For example, in the wake of a 2013 terrorist attack that killed five and injured an additional forty people, Chinese state media said that the state would be increasing its intelligence gathering capacity after detaining one hundred individuals in a police roundup.[105] According to one observer of the political situation, all Uyghurs are suspects in what amounts to a form of collective punishment.[106]

The Chinese regime's preferred strategy has been to facilitate in-group policing of communities to reduce the costs of surveillance to the state. Villagers in remote parts of Xinjiang province are incentivized by local authorities to spy on their neighbors.[107] Chinese officials claim that attempts to institutionalize forms of community policing through "joint responsibility contracts" have been successful.[108] Subsequently, however, the Chinese government has engaged in additional, alternative forms of collective punishment. For example, in 2016 the Chinese government issued blanket recalls on passports for residents of Xinjiang as part of a "collective management" strategy.[109]

To what extent might one consider the broader generalizability of the arguments that I have put forward? Using the Minorities at Risk Project (MAR) dataset it is possible to see if empirical correlations exist between repression of a group's civilian population (i.e., those not engaging in violent or nonviolent collective action) and characteristics of the different groups.[110] This variable captures the idea of collective punishment and is measured

103. CBS News, "China's Uighur Problem Rooted in Terrorism or Racism?" November 11, 2014.

104. Ibid.

105. Nathan Vanderklippe, "In Wake of Tiananmen Explosion, China Cracks Down on Uyghur Minority," *Globe and Mail*, November 5, 2013.

106. Ibid.

107. Radio Free Asia, "Uyghur Villagers Forced by 'Contract' to Spy on Neighbors," April 29, 2016.

108. Ibid.

109. Human Rights Watch, "Passports Arbitrarily Recalled in Xinjiang—Heightened Control Over Travel for Residents of Uighur Muslim Region," November 21, 2016.

110. The current release of the MAR dataset includes data for the period 2004-2006 and information about over 800 groups across dozens of countries. Only groups that might potentially be at risk are included in the dataset. For multiethnic societies, major identity groups

as a 0-5 scale that goes from no repression (0) to surveillance (1), harassment/containment (2), non-violent coercion (3), violent coercion short of killing (4) and violent coercion including killing (5). This coding includes tactics used by any government agency including the military, police and special security services.

Three variables included in the MAR dataset capture what the coding team describes as "measures of distinctiveness" where the relevant comparison is between the group at risk and the largest (i.e., plurality or majority) ethnic group in the state. These "measures of distinctiveness" might serve as a proxy for the relative legibility of different minority groups. The first measure considers if there is a different language group where groups can either be characterized by linguistic assimilation with the plurality group (0), multiple group languages, at least one of which is different from the plurality group (1), or the group's use of one language that is different from the plurality group (2). The theoretical expectation would be that increasing language difference should be associated with a higher level of collective punishment of that group. The second variable I consider relates to cultural difference where there are different group customs related to marriage, family, and other societal practices, like dress. For this variable, the coding considers if the group has the same social customs as the plurality group (0) compared to groups with different social customs from the plurality group (1). The third variable which might influence the political regime's ability to render a societal group "legible" relates to religious difference where a group is coded as either having the same religion as the plurality group (0), being a different sect within the same religion as the plurality group (1), or as a different religion (2).

For each of the three variables—language, custom, and religious belief—there is a positive, statistically significant correlation with repression of a group's civilian population, the measure which I take as a proxy for collective punishment. Going from low to high on each of the measures of distinctiveness leads groups to move from a predicted probability of no repression of the civilian population to something between harassment and non-violent

---

are all included in the MAR dataset. For example, in Iraq, this would include Kurds, Shiʿa and Sunnis. In Lebanon, Druze, Sunnis, Shiʿa, Maronite Christians, and Palestinians are included in the MAR dataset. In Egypt, Coptic Christians (but not Sunnis) are considered a minority at risk population. As a result, I am only looking at that set of cases for which minorities are potentially vulnerable and then I examine variation within that set of cases. Birnir et al. (2015) discuss how to extend the Minorities at Risk data to avoid issues of selection bias.

coercion. The effect size is smallest for religious difference and larger for differences in language and customs. These results suggest that collective punishments are visited most often upon less legible groups.

The MAR dataset also reports information on group organization for "joint political action," a variable that proxies for some of the non-compliance behaviors that I have sought to measure in this project. The scale's low value is the case where there is no political movement or organization which represents group interests (0) whereas the high value on this scale is measured as group interests promoted by militant organizations (5). To what extent is group organization for "joint political action" increasing with higher levels of repression against civilians? While a naive correlational analysis cannot speak to the ways that these two variables endogenously affect each other, it is nonetheless worth reporting that there is a positive and substantively large, statistically significant correlation between these two variables. For a group with no civilian repression, group organization for "joint political action" is predicted to go from promotion of group interests through conventional political parties and movements to a prediction of conventional and militant strategies with high levels of civilian repression.

An alternative measure of non-compliance worth investigating is rebellious activity. In particular, is rebellious activity associated with repression against civilians? Again, using the MAR data I find that there is a positive, statistically significant correlation between repression of civilians and rebellion. With no civilian repression, the predicted probability of rebellion is very low but as civilian repression goes from its lowest level to the highest level, the predicted probability increases to an expectation of terrorism and local rebellions.

Toward a More General Understanding of State Repression

Despite important advancements in the study of repression, Davenport and Inman have argued that scholars know comparatively little about the impact of repression on social and political phenomena.[111] Indeed, researchers have paid more attention to rebel attacks on governments than state repression against those within their territorial jurisdiction.[112]

111. Davenport and Inman 2012.
112. Davenport 2007.

In recent years, scholarly research has focused to a greater extent on puzzles associated with the allocation of government goods and services—distributive politics—than the allocation of government punishments and oppressions—the politics of repression.[113] This has left a number of core puzzles about the politics of repression neglected. Davenport argues that a more elaborate theoretical explanation for why repression takes place would be a welcome contribution to the literature, as well as for the inclusion of the study of repression as a core area of interest to political science rather than as the exclusive domain of studies of law, human rights and political theory.[114] This project has sought to address some of these shortcomings in the literature, and in a way that engages directly with core concepts within the field of comparative politics, including constructivist ideas of identity formation.

113. See Golden and Min (2013) for a review of the recent literature on distributive politics within the subfield of comparative politics.

114. See Davenport (2007). For example, discussions of collective punishment have mostly existed within the study of international law. Scholars have discussed the conditions under which it might be justified to impose burdens on individuals by virtue of the fact that someone from their group has caused a harm (Pasternak 2011). May (2011) has theorized about the various forms of collective punishment and considers the normative implications of collective punishment.

BIBLIOGRAPHY

Abdullah, Thabit. 2006. *Dictatorship, Imperialism and Chaos: Iraq since 1989*. London: Zed Books.

Ahram, Ariel. 2011. *Proxy Warriors: The Rise and Fall of State-Sponsored Militias*. Stanford, CA: Stanford University Press.

Ahram, Ariel. 2015. "Development, Counterinsurgency and the Destruction of the Iraqi Marshes." *International Journal of Middle East Studies*. 47(3): 447–466.

Ahram, Ariel. 2016. "The Rise and Fall of Iraq in the Social Sciences." *Social Science Quarterly*. 97(4): 850–861.

Alahmad, Nida. 2009. "State Power in Iraq, 1988–2005." Doctoral dissertation, New School for Social Research.

al-Ali, Nadje Sadig. 2007. *Iraqi Women: Untold Stories from 1948 to the Present*. London: Zed Books.

al-Ali, Zaid. 2014. *The Struggle for Iraq's Future: How Corruption, Incompetence and Sectarianism have Undermined Democracy*. New Haven, CT: Yale University Press.

Albrisem, Qasim. 2013. *Flight from Saddam*. London: Sketchnews.

Alkazaz, Aziz. 1993. "The Distribution of National Income in Iraq." *Iraq: Power and Society*. Editors, Derek Hopwood, Habib Ishow and Thomas Koszinowski. Reading: Ithaca Press.

Allport, Gordon and Leo Postman. 1947. *The Psychology of Rumor*. New York, NY: Holt, Rinehart & Winston.

Alnasrawi, Abbas. 1994. *The Economy of Iraq: Oil, War, Destruction of Development and Prospects, 1950–2010*. Westport, CT: Greenwood Press.

Altemeyer, Bob. 1998. "The Other 'Authoritarian' Personality." *Advances in Experimental Social Psychology, Volume 30*. San Diego, CA: Academic Press.

Anderson, Benedict. 1983. *Imagined Communities: Reflections on the Origin and Spread of Nationalism*. London: Verso.

Arendt, Hannah. 1968. *The Origins of Totalitarianism*. New York, NY: Harvest Book.

Arnove, Anthony. 2002. *Iraq under Seige: The Deadly Impact of Sanctions and War*. Cambridge, MA: South End Press.

Ayoob, Mohammed. 1995. *The Third World Security Predicament: State Making, Regional Conflict, and the International System*. Boulder, CO: Lynne Rienner.

Ayubi, Nazhi. 1995. *Over-stating the Arab State: Politics and Society in the Middle East*. London: I.B. Tauris.

Aziz, Mahir. 2011. *The Kurds of Iraq: Nationalism and Identity in Iraqi Kurdistan*. London: I.B. Tauris.

Aziz, Talib. 2001. "Baqir al-Sadr's Quest for the Marja'iya." *The Most Learned of the Shi'a: The Institution of the Marja' Taqlid*. Editor, Linda Walbridge. Oxford: Oxford University Press.

Aziz, T. M. 1993. "The Role of Muhammad Baqir al-Sadr in Shi'i Political Activism from 1958 to 1980." *International Journal of Middle East Studies*. 25(2): 207–222.

Bakke, Kristin, Xun Cao, John O'Loughlin and Michael Ward. 2009. "Social Distance in Bosnia-Herzegovina and the North Caucasus Region of Russia: Inter and Intra-ethnic Attitudes and Identities." *Nations and Nationalism*. 15(2): 227–253.

Balcells, Laia. 2011. "The Consequences of Victimization on Political Identities: Evidence from Spain." *Politics and Society*. 40(3): 311–347.

Baram, Amatzia. 1991. *Culture, History and Ideology in the Formation of Ba'thist Iraq, 1968–89*. New York, NY: St. Martin's Press.

Baram, Amatzia. 1997. "Neo-Tribalism in Iraq: Saddam Hussein's Tribal Policies 1991–96." *International Journal of Middle East Studies*. 29(1): 1–31.

Baram, Amatzia. 2003. "Saddam's Power Structure: The Tikritis Before, During and After the War." *Iraq at the Crossroads: State and Society in the Shadow of Regime Change*. Editors, Toby Dodge and Steven Simon. International Institute for Strategic Studies. Adelphi Paper 354.

Baram, Amatzia. 2005. *Who Are the Insurgents? Sunni Arab Rebels in Iraq*. Washington, DC: U.S. Institute of Peace.

Baram, Amatzia. 2014. *Saddam Husayn and Islam, 1968–2003. Ba'thi Iraq from Secularism to Faith*. Baltimore, MD: Johns Hopkins University Press.

Baram, Amatzia and Barry Rubin. 1993. *Iraq's Road to War*. New York, NY: St. Martin's Press.

Bashir, Ala. 2005. *The Insider: Trapped in Saddam's Brutal Regime*. London: Abacus Press.

Batatu, Hanna. 1978. *The Old Social Classes and the Revolutionary Movements of Iraq: A Study of Iraq's Old Landed and Commercial Classes and of Its Communists, Ba'thists, and Free Officers*. Princeton, NJ: Princeton University Press.

Batatu, Hanna. 1986. "Shi'i Organizations in Iraq: Al-Da'wah al-Islamiyah and al-Mujahidin." *Shi'ism and Social Protest*. Editors, Juan Cole and Nikki Keddie. New Haven, CT: Yale University Press.

Bates, Robert. 1983. "Modernization, Ethnic Competition, and the Rationality of Politics in Contemporary Africa." *State versus Ethnic Claims: African Policy Dilemmas*. Editors, Donald Rothchild and Victor Olunsorola. Boulder, CO: Westview Press. 152–171.

Bauer, Raymond A. and David B. Gleicher. 1953. "Word of Mouth Communication in the Soviet Union." *Public Opinion Quarterly*. 17(3): 297–310.

Belkin, Aaron and Evan Schofer. 2003. "Towards a Structural Understanding of Coup Risk." *Journal of Conflict Resolution*. 47(5): 594–620.

Bellin, Eva. 2004. "The Robustness of Authoritarianism in the Middle East: Exceptionalism in Comparative Perspective." *Comparative Politics*. 36(2): 139–157.

Benabou, Roland and Jean Tirole. 2006. "Incentives and Prosocial Behavior." *American Economic Review*. 96(5): 1652–1678.

Bengio, Ofra. 1988. "Iraq." *Middle East Contemporary Survey*. Editors, Itamar Rabinovich and Haim Shaked. Boulder, CO: Westview Press.

Bengio, Ofra. 1993. "Iraq's Shiʿa and Kurdish Communities: From Resentment to Revolt." *Iraq's Road to War*. Editors, Amatzia Baram and Barry Rubin. New York, NY: St. Martin's Press.

Bengio, Ofra. 2000. "How Does Saddam Hold On?" *Foreign Affairs*. 79(4): 90–103.

Bengio, Ofra. 2010. "On the Brink: State and Nation in Iraqi Kurdistan." *Iraq Between Occupations: Perspectives from 1920 to the Present*. Editors, Amatzia Baram, Achim Rohde and Ronen Zeidel. New York, NY: Palgrave MacMillan.

Bengio, Ofra. 2012. *The Kurds of Iraq: Building a State within a State*. Boulder, CO: Lynne Rienner.

Berend, Ivan. 1996. *Central and Eastern Europe, 1944–1993*. New York, NY: Cambridge University Press.

Bernhardt, Florian. 2012. "Firm Conviction or Forced Belief? The Islamic Dawah Party's Response to Khomeini's Theory of Wilayat al-Faqih." *International Journal of Contemporary Iraqi Studies*. 6(3): 299–314.

Bhavnani, Ravi, Karsten Donnay, Dan Miodownik, Maayan Mor, and Dirk Helbing. 2014. "Group Segregation and Urban Violence." *American Journal of Political Science*. 58(1): 226–245.

Birnir, Johanna. 2007. *Ethnicity and Electoral Politics*. Cambridge: Cambridge University Press.

Birnir, Johanna, Jonathan Wilkenfeld, James Fearon, David Laitin, Ted Robert Gurr, Dawn Brancati, Stephen M Saideman, Amy Pate and Agatha Hultquist. 2015. "Socially Relevant Ethnic Groups, Ethnic Structure and AMAR." *Journal of Peace Research*. 52(1): 110–115.

Bland, Douglas. 1999. "A Unified Theory of Civil-Military Relations." *Armed Forces & Society*. 26(1): 7–25.

Blaydes, Lisa. 2011. *Elections and Distributive Politics in Mubarak's Egypt*. New York, NY: Cambridge University Press.

Blaydes, Lisa and Justin Grimmer. 2017. "Political Cultures." Working paper, Department of Political Science, Stanford University.

Boix, Carles and Milan Svolik. 2013. "The Foundations of Limited Authoritarian Government: Institutions, Commitment, and Power-Sharing in Dictatorships." *Journal of Politics*. 75(2): 300–316.

Bordia, Prashant and Nicholas DiFonzo. 2004. "Problem Solving in Social Interactions on the Internet: Rumor as Social Cognition," *Social Psychology Quarterly*. 67: 33–49.

Brooks, Risa. 1998. *Political-military Relations and the Stability of Arab Regimes*. Adelphi Paper No. 324. New York, NY: Oxford University Press.

Brownlee, Jason. 2007. *Authoritarianism in an Age of Democratization*. New York, NY: Cambridge University Press.

Brubaker, Rogers. 2004. *Ethnicity without Groups*. Cambridge, MA: Harvard University Press.

Bubandt, Nils. 2008. "Rumors, Pamphlets, and the Politics of Paranoia in Indonesia". *Journal of Asian Studies*. 67(3): 789–817.

Bueno de Mesquita, Bruce, Alastair Smith, Randolph Siverson, and James D. Morrow. 2003. *The Logic of Political Survival*. Cambridge, MA: MIT Press.

Bulloch, John and Harvey Morris. 1992. *No Friends but the Mountains: The Tragic History of the Kurds*. London: Viking.

Cammett, Melani. 2015. "Sectarianism and the Ambiguities of Welfare in Lebanon." *Current Anthropology*. 56(11): 76–87.

Cammett, Melani and Sukriti Issar. 2010. "Bricks and Mortar Clientelism: Sectarianism and the Logics of Welfare Allocation in Lebanon." *World Politics*. 62(3): 381–421.

Campbell, Davis. 1998. *National Deconstruction: Violence, Identity and Justice in Bosnia*. Minneapolis, MN: University of Minnesota Press.

Cederman, Lars-Erik, Nils Weidmann and Kristian Gleditch. 2011. "Horizontal Inequalities and Ethnonationalist Civil War: A Global Comparison." *American Political Science Review*. 105(3): 478–495.

Cederman, Lars-Erik, Andreas Wimmer, and Brian Min. 2010. "Why Do Ethnic Groups Rebel? New Data and Analysis." *World Politics*. 62(1): 87–119.

Cetinsaya, Gokhan. 2006. *Ottoman Administration of Iraq, 1890–1908*. London: Routledge.

Chartouni-Dubarry, May. 1993. "The Development of Internal Politics in Iraq from 1958 to the Present Day." *Iraq: Power and Society*. Editors, Derek Hopwood, Habib Ishow, and Thomas Koszinowski. Reading: Ithaca Press.

Chaudhry, Kiren Aziz. 1991. "Power, Poverty and Petrodollars." *Middle East Report.* 170: 14–23.

Christia, Fotini. 2012. *Alliance Formation in Civil Wars.* New York, NY: Cambridge University Press.

Christia, Fotini. 2008. "Following the Money. Muslim versus Muslim in Bosnia's Civil War." *Comparative Politics.* 40(4): 461–480.

Chubin, Shahram. 1988. "Iran and the War: From Stalemate to Ceasefire." *Iran and Iraq at War.* Editors, Shahram Chubin and Charles Tripp. London: I.B. Tauris.

Chubin, Shahram and Charles Tripp. 1988. *Iran and Iraq at War.* London: I.B. Tauris.

Clark, Janine and Bassel Salloukh. 2013. "Elite Strategies, Civil Society, and Sectarian Identities in Postwar Lebanon." *International Journal of Middle Eastern Studies.* 45(4): 731–749.

Cockburn, Patrick. 2008. *Muqtada al-Sadr and the Shia Insurgency in Iraq.* London: Faber and Faber.

Cole, Juan. 2002. *Sacred Space and Holy War: The Politics, Culture and History of Shiʿite Islam.* London: I.B. Tauris.

Condra, Luke and Jacob Shapiro. 2012. "Who Takes the Blame? The Strategic Effects of Collateral Damage." *American Journal of Political Science.* 56(1): 167–187.

Corboz, Elvire. 2015. *Guardians of Shiʿism: Sacred Authority and Transnational Family Networks.* Edinburgh: Edinburgh University Press.

Cordesman, Anthony and Patrick Baetjer. 2006. *Iraqi Security Forces: A Strategy for Success.* Westport, CT: Praeger.

Corstange, Daniel. 2016. *The Price of a Vote in the Middle East: Clientelism and Communal Politics in Lebanon and Yemen.* New York, NY: Cambridge University Press.

Coughlin, Con. 2002. *Saddam: His Rise and Fall.* New York, NY: Harper Perennial.

Dari-Mattiacci, Giuseppe and Gerrit de Geest. 2010. "Carrots, Sticks and the Multiplication Effect." *Journal of Law, Economics, & Organization.* 26(2): 365–384.

Davenport, Christian. 2007. "State Repression and Political Order." *Annual Review of Political Science.* 10: 1–23.

Davenport, Christian and Molly Inman. 2012. "The State of State Repression Research since the 1990s." *Terrorism and Political Violence.* 24(4): 619–634.

Davenport, Christian. 2015. *How Social Movements Die: Repression and Demobilization of the Republic of New Africa.* New York: Cambridge University Press.

Davis, Eric. 2005. *Memories of State: Politics, History and Collective Identity in Modern Iraq.* Berkeley, CA: University of California Press.

Davis, Eric. 2008. "A Sectarian Middle East?" *International Journal of Middle East Studies*. 40(4): 555–558.

Dawisha, Adeed. 1999. "'Identity' and Political Survival in Saddam's Iraq." *Middle East Journal*. 53(4): 553–567.

Dawisha, Adeed. 2008. "The Unraveling of Iraq: Ethnosectarian Preferences and State Performance in Historical Perspective." *Middle East Journal*. 62(2): 219–230.

Dawisha, Adeed. 2009. *Iraq: A Political History from Independence to Occupation*. Princeton, NJ: Princeton University Press.

Dawood, Hosham. 2003. "The 'State-ization' of the Tribe and Tribalization of the State: The Case of Iraq." *Tribes and Power: Nationalism and Ethnicity in the Middle East*. Editors, Faleh Abdul-Jabar and Hosham Dawod. London: Saqi.

Dawson, Michael. 1994. *Behind the Mule: Race and Class in African-American Politics*. Princeton, NJ: Princeton University Press.

della Porta, Donatella. 2013. *Clandestine Political Violence*. New York, NY: Cambridge University Press.

Diamond, Larry. 2005. *Squandered Victory: The American Occupation and the Bungled Effort to Bring Democracy to Iraq*. New York, NY: Henry Holt and Company.

DiFonzo, Nicholas and Prashant Bordia. 2007. "Rumor Psychology: Social and Organizational Approaches." Washington, DC: American Psychological Association.

Dimitrov, Martin and Joseph Sassoon. 2014. "State Security, Information and Repression: A Comparison of Communist Bulgaria and Ba'thist Iraq." *Journal of Cold War Studies*. 16(2): 3–31.

Dixit, Avinash and John Londregan. 1996. "The Determinants of Success of Special Interests in Redistributive Politics." *Journal of Politics*. 58(4): 1132–1155.

Dodge, Toby. 2003. "Cake Walk, Coup or Urban Warfare: The Battle for Iraq." *Iraq at the Crossroads: State and Society in the Shadow of Regime Change*. Editors, Toby Dodge and Steven Simon. International Institute for Strategic Studies. Adelphi Paper 354.

Downes, Alexander. 2007. "Draining the Sea by Filling the Graves: Investigating the Effectiveness of Indiscriminate Violence as a Counterinsurgency Strategy." *Civil Wars*. 9(4): 420–444.

Dreze, Jean and Gazdar, Haris. 1992. "Hunger and Poverty in Iraq." *World Development*. 20(7): 921–945.

Drezner, Daniel. 1999. *The Sanctions Paradox: Economic Statecraft and International Relations*. New York, NY: Cambridge University Press.

Ehteshami, Anoushivaran. 2013. *Dynamics of Change in the Persian Gulf: Political Economy, War and Revolution*. New York, NY: Routledge.

Elster, Jon. 2015. *Explaining Social Behavior: More Nuts and Bolts for the Social Sciences*. New York, NY: Cambridge University Press.

Ermakoff, Ivan. 2008. *Ruling Oneself Out: A Theory of Collective Abdication*. Durham, NC: Duke University Press.

Erskine, Toni. 2011. "Kicking Bodies and Damning Souls: The Danger of Harming 'Innocent' Individuals While Punishing 'Delinquent' States." *Accountability for Collective Wrongdoing*. Editors, Tracy Isaacs and Richard Vernon. New York, NY: Cambridge University Press.

Escriba-Folch, Abel and Joseph Wright. 2010. "Dealing with Tyranny: International Sanctions and the Survival of Authoritarian Rulers." *International Studies Quarterly*. 54(2): 335–359.

Eyerman, Ron. 2001. *Cultural Trauma: Slavery and the Formation of African American Identity*. New York, NY: Cambridge University Press.

Farouk-Sluglett, Marion and Peter Sluglett. 1990. *Iraq since 1958: From Revolution to Dictatorship*. London: I.B. Tauris.

Faust, Aaron. 2015. *The Baʿthification of Iraq: Saddam Hussein's Totalitarianism*. Austin, TX: University of Texas Press.

Fearon, James. 2003. "Ethnic and Cultural Diversity by Country." *Journal of Economic Growth*. 8(2): 195–222.

Fearon, James. 2006. "Ethnic Mobilization and Ethnic Violence." *Oxford Handbook of Political Economy*. Editors, Barry Weingast and Donald Wittman. Oxford: Oxford University Press. 852–868.

Fearon, James and David Laitin. 1996. "Explaining Interethnic Cooperation." *American Political Science Review*. 90(4): 715–735.

Fearon, James and David Laitin. 2003. "Ethnicity, Insurgency, and Civil War." *American Political Science Review*. 97(1): 75–90.

Feldman, Noah. 2004. *What We Owe Iraq: War and the Ethics of Nation Building*. Princeton, NJ: Princeton University Press.

Ferejohn, John. 1986. "Incumbent Performance and Electoral Control." *Public Choice*. 50: 5–25.

Ferree, Karen. 2011. *Framing the Race in South Africa: The Political Origins of Racial Census Elections*. New York, NY: Cambridge University Press.

Fine, Gary Alan. 2007. "Rumor, Trust and Civil Society: Collective Memory and Cultures of Judgement." *Diogenes* 54(1): 5–18.

Fuller, Graham and Rend Rahim Francke. 1999. *The Arab Shiʿa: The Forgotten Muslims*. London: Macmillan.

Gandhi, Jennifer and Adam Przeworski. 2006. "Cooperation, Cooptation, and Rebellion under Dictatorship." *Economics and Politics*. 18(1): 1–26.

Gause, Greg. 2002. "Iraq's Decisions to Go to War, 1980 and 1990." *Middle East Journal*. 56(1): 47–70.

Gay, Claudine. 2004. "Putting Race in Context: Identifying the Environmental Determinants of Black Racial Attitudes." *American Political Science Review*. 98(4): 547–562.

Geddes, Barbara. 1999. "What Do We Know about Democratization after Twenty Years?" *Annual Review of Political Science*. 2: 115–144.

Geddes, Barbara. 2003. *Paradigms and Sand Castles: Research Design in Comparative Politics*. Ann Arbor, MI: University of Michigan Press.

Gellner, Ernest. 1983. *Nations and Nationalism*. Ithaca, NY: Cornell University Press.

Gerges, Fawaz. 2016. *ISIS: A History*. Princeton, NJ: Princeton University Press.

Golden, Miriam and Brian Min. 2013. "Distributive Politics Around the World." *Annual Review of Political Science*. 16: 73–99.

Goldhagen, Daniel Jonah. 1996. *Hilter's Willing Executioners: Ordinary Germans and the Holocaust*. New York, NY: Alfred Knopf.

Goodwin, Jeffrey. 2001. *No Other Way Out: States and Revolutionary Movements, 1945–1991*. New York, NY: Cambridge University Press.

Gordon, Joy. 2010. *Invisible War: The United States and the Iraq Sanctions*. Cambridge, MA: Harvard University Press.

Graham-Brown, Sarah. 1999. *Sanctioning Saddam: The Intervention Politics in Iraq*. London: I.B. Taurus.

Grant, Ruth. 2006. "Ethics and Incentives: A Political Approach." *American Political Science Review*. 100(1): 29–39.

Greitens, Sheena Chestnut. 2016. *Dictators and their Secret Police: Coercive Institutions and State Violence*. New York, NY: Cambridge University Press.

Grzymala-Busse, Anna. 2002. *Redeeming the Communist Past: The Regeneration of Communist Parties in East Central Europe*. New York, NY: Cambridge University Press.

Guha, Ranajit. 1983. *Elementary Aspects of Peasant Insurgency in Colonial India*. Oxford: Oxford University Press.

Gurr, Ted Robert. 1970. *Why Men Rebel*. Princeton, NJ: Princeton University Press.

Habyarimana, James, Macartan Humphreys, Daniel Posner, and Jeremy Weinstein. 2009. *Coethnicity: Diversity and the Dilemmas of Collective Action*. New York, NY: Russell Sage Foundation.

Haddad, Fanar. 2011. *Sectarianism in Iraq: Antagonistic Visions of Unity*. London: Hurst & Company.

Hadenius, Axel and Jan Teorell. 2007. "Pathways from Authoritarianism." *Journal of Democracy*. 18(1): 143–156.

Hardi, Choman. 2011. *Gendered Experiences of Genocide: Anfal Survivors in Kurdistan-Iraq*. Burlington, VT: Ashgate.

Harling, Peter. 2012. "Beyond Political Ruptures: Towards a Historiography of Social Continuity in Iraq." *Writing the Modern History of Iraq: Historiographical and Political Challenges*. Editors, Riccardo Bocco, Hamit Bozarslan, Peter Sluglett, and Jordi Tejel. London: World Scientific.

Harris, Kevan. 2013. "A Martyr's Welfare State." *Middle East Authoritarianisms: Governance, Contestation, and Regime Resilience in Syria and Iran.* Editors, Steve Heydemann and Reinoud Leenders. Stanford, CA: Stanford University Press.

Harris, Kevan. 2016. "Social Welfare Policies and the Dynamics of Elite and Popular Contention." *Power and Change in Iran: Politics of Contention and Concilia-tion.* Editors, Daniel Brumberg and Farideh Farhi. Bloomington, IN: Indiana University Press.

Hassan, Hussein. 2007. *Iraq: Tribal Structure, Social and Political Activities.* Washington, DC: Library of Congress, Congressional Research Service.

Hassan, Zheger. 2013. "Kurdish Nationalism: What are Its Origins?" *International Journal of Contemporary Iraqi Studies.* 7(2): 75–89.

Hechter, Michael. 1987. *Principles of Group Solidarity.* Berkeley, CA: University of California Press.

Hechter, Michael. 2000. *Containing Nationalism.* New York, NY: Oxford University Press.

Hechter, Michael. 2013. *Alien Rule.* New York, NY: Cambridge University Press.

Hechter, Michael and Nika Kabiri. 2009. "The Dilemma of Social Order in Iraq." *Social Computing and Behavioral Modeling.* Editors, Huan Liu, John Salerno, and Michael Young. New York, NY: Springer.

Heimer, Carol. 2001. "Solving the Problem of Trust." *Trust in Society.* Editor, Karen Cook. New York, NY: Russell Sage Foundation.

Heine, Peter. 1993. "Political Parties, Institutions and Administrative Structures." *Iraq: Power and Society.* Editors, Derek Hopwood, Habib Ishow, and Thomas Koszinowski. Reading: Ithaca Press.

Helfont, Samuel. 2014. "Saddam and the Islamists: The Ba'thist Regime's Instrumen-talization of Religion in Foreign Affairs." *Middle East Journal.* 68(3).

Helfont, Samuel. 2015. *Compulsion in Religion: The Authoritarian Roots of Saddam Hussein's Islam.* Dissertation, Princeton University.

Heller, Mark. 1993. "Iraq's Army: Military Weakness, Political Unity." *Iraq's Road to War.* Editors, Amatzia Baram and Barry Rubin. New York, NY: St. Martin's Press.

Herb, Michael. 2009. "A Nation of Bureaucrats: Political Participation and Economic Diversification in Kuwait and the United Arab Emirates." *International Journal of Middle East Studies.* 41(3): 375–395.

Herbst, Jeffrey. 2000. *States and Power in Africa: Comparative Lessons in Authority and Control.* Princeton, NJ: Princeton University Press.

Hertog, Steffan. 2016. "Back to the Seventies?" *Oil States in the New Middle East: Uprisings and Stability.* Editors, Kjetil Selvik and Bjorn Olav Utvik. New York, NY: Routledge.

Hiltermann, Joost. 2007. *A Poisonous Affair: America, Iraq and the Gassing of Halabja.* New York, NY: Cambridge University Press.

Hiro, Dilip. 1991. *The Longest War: The Iran-Iraq Military Conflict*. New York, NY: Routledge.

Horowitz, Donald. 2000. *Ethnic Groups in Conflict*. Berkeley, CA: University of California Press.

Human Rights Watch. 1993. "Genocide in Iraq: The Anfal Campaign Against the Kurds." *Middle East Watch Report*.

Humphreys, Macartan and Jeremy Weinstein. 2006. "Handling and Manhandling Civilians in Civil War." *American Political Science Review*. 100(3): 429–447.

Imad, Amal. 2012. "Citizenship and Identity: A Case Study of Shiʿi Muslims in Samarra and Wider Iraq." *The Shiʿa of Samarra: The Heritage and Politics of a Community in Iraq*. Editor, Imranali Panjwani. London: I.B. Tauris.

Inglehart, Ronald, Mansoor Moaddel, and Mark Tessler. 2006. "Xenophobia and In-Group Solidarity in Iraq: A Natural Experiment on the Impact of Insecurity." *Perspectives on Politics*. 4(3): 495–505.

Ismael, Jacqueline and Shereen Ismael. 2007. "Iraqi Women under Occupation: From Tribalism to Neo-feudalism." *International Journal of Contemporary Iraqi Studies*. 1(2): 247–268.

Ismael, Jacqueline and Shereen Ismael. 2008. "Living through War, Sanctions and Occupation: The Voices of Iraqi Women." *International Journal of Contemporary Iraqi Studies*. 2(3): 409–424.

Ismael, Tareq. 2008. *The Rise and Fall of the Communist Party of Iraq*. New York, NY: Cambridge University Press.

Ismael, Tareq and Max Fuller. 2008. "The Disintegration of Iraq: The Manufacturing and Politicization of Sectarianism." *International Journal of Contemporary Iraqi Studies*. 2(3): 443–473.

Jabar, Faleh. 1992. "Why the Uprisings Failed." *Middle East Report*. 22.

Jabar, Faleh. 2003a. *The Shiʿite Movement in Iraq*. London: Saqi.

Jabar, Faleh. 2003b. "Clerics, Tribes, Ideologues and Urban Dwellers in the South of Iraq: The Potential for Rebellion." *Iraq at the Crossroads: State and Society in the Shadow of Regime Change*. Editors, Toby Dodge and Steven Simon. International Institute for Strategic Studies. Adelphi Paper 354.

Jabar, Faleh. 2003c. "Sheikhs and Ideologues: Deconstruction and Reconstruction of Tribes under Patrimonial Totalitarianism in Iraq, 1968–1998." *Tribes and Power: Nationalism and Ethnicity in the Middle East*. Editors, Faleh Abdul-Jabar and Hosham Dawod. London: Saqi.

Jabar, Faleh. 2003d. "The Iraqi Army and the Anti-Army: Some Reflections on the Role of the Military." *Iraq at the Crossroads: State and Society in the Shadow of Regime Change*. Editors, Toby Dodge and Steven Simon. International Institute for Strategic Studies. Adelphi Paper 354.

al-Jawaheri, Yasmin Husein. 2008. *Women in Iraq: The Gender Impact of International Sanctions*. Boulder, CO: Lynne Rienner.

Johnson, Rob. 2011. *The Iran-Iraq War*. London: Palgrave Macmillan.

Kadhim, Abbas. 2013. "The Hawza under Siege: A Study in the Baʿth Party Archive." IISBU Occassional Paper, Institute for Iraqi Studies, Boston University.

Kaempfer, William, Anton Lowenberg, and William Mertens. 2004. "International Economic Sanctions Against a Dictator." *Economics and Politics*. 16(1): 29–51.

Kalyvas, Stathis. 2006. *The Logic of Violence in Civil Wars*. New York, NY: Cambridge University Press.

Kamrava, Mehran. 2000. "Military Professionalization and Civil-Military Relations in the Middle East." *Political Science Quarterly*. 115(1): 67–87.

Kapferer, Jean-Noël. 1990. *Rumors: Uses, Interpretations, and Images*. New Brunswick, NJ: Transaction.

Karakayali, Nedim. 2009. "Social Distance and Affective Orientations." *Sociological Forum*. 24(3): 538–562.

Karklins, Rasma and Roger Petersen. 1993. "Decision Calculus of Protesters and Regimes: Eastern Europe 1989." *Journal of Politics*. 55(3): 588–614.

Kelley, Stephanie. 2004. "Rumors in Iraq: A Guide to Winning Hearts and Minds." Masters Thesis, Naval Postgraduate School.

Kerry, Mark. 2008. *Tigers of the Tigris: An American Advisor's Journey Through Culture, Religion and Intrigue in Building the Iraqi Army*. Indianapolis, IN: Dog Ear Publishing.

Khadduri, Majid and Edmund Ghareeb. 1997. *War in the Gulf, 1990–91: The Iraq-Kuwait Conflict and Its Implications*. Oxford: Oxford University Press.

al-Khafaji, Isam. 1992. "State Terror and the Degradation of Politics in Iraq." *Middle East Report*. 22.

al-Khafaji, Isam. 2000. "War as a Vehicle for the Rise and Demise of a State-Controlled Society: The Case of Baʿthist Iraq." *War, Institutions, and Social Change in the Middle East*. Editor, Steven Heydemann. Berkeley, CA: University of California Press.

al-Khafaji, Isam. 2003. "A Few Days After: State and Society in a Post-Saddam Iraq." *Iraq at the Crossroads: State and Society in the Shadow of Regime Change*. Editors, Toby Dodge and Steven Simon. International Institute for Strategic Studies. Adelphi Paper 354.

Khoury, Dina Rizk. 2010. "The Security State and the Practice and Rhetoric of Sectarianism in Iraq." *International Journal of Contemporary Iraqi Studies*. 4(3): 325–337.

Khoury, Dina Rizk. 2012. "The 1991 Intifada in Three Keys: Writing the History of Violence." *Writing the Modern History of Iraq: Historiographical and Political Challenges*. Editors, Riccardo Bocco, Hamit Bozarslan, Peter Sluglett, and Jordi Tejel. London: World Scientific.

Khoury, Dina Rizk. 2013. *Iraq in Wartime: Soldiering, Martyrdom, and Remembrance*. New York, NY: Cambridge University Press.

Kimmel, Allan J. 2004. *Rumor and Rumor Control: A Manager's Guide to Understanding and Combatting Rumors*. Mahwah, NJ: Lawrence Erlbaum.

Kirdar, Nemir. 2009. *Saving Iraq: Rebuilding a Broken Nation*. London: Weidenfeld and Nicolson.

Kirmanj, Sherko. 2013. *Identity and Nation in Iraq*. Boulder, CO: Lynne Rienner.

Knapp, Robert H. 1944. "A Psychology of Rumor." *Public Opinion Quarterly*. 8: 22–27.

Kocher, Matthew. 2004. *Human Ecology and Civil War*. PhD dissertation, Department of Political Science, University of Chicago.

Kocher, Matthew, Thomas Pepinsky, and Stathis Kalyvas. 2011. "Aerial Bombing and Counterinsurgency in the Vietnam War." *American Journal of Political Science*. 55(2): 201–218.

Koehler, Kevin. 2008. "Authoritarian Elections in Egypt: Formal Institutions and Informal Mechanisms of Rule." *Democratization*. 15(5): 974–990.

Kornai, Janos. 1992. *The Socialist System*. Princeton, NJ: Princeton University Press.

Kricheli, Ruth, Yair Livne, and Beatriz Magaloni. 2011. "Taking to the Streets: Theory and Evidence on Protests under Authoritarianism." Working paper, Department of Political Science, Stanford University.

Kubba, Laith. 1993. "The War's Impact on Iraq." *The Iran-Iraq War: The Politics of Aggression*. Editor, Farhang Rajaee. Gainesville, FL: University of Florida Press.

Kuran, Timur. 1991. "Now Out of Never: The Element of Surprise in the East European Revolution of 1989." *World Politics*. 44(1): 7–48.

Kuran, Timur. 1995. *Private Truths, Public Lies*. Cambridge MA: Harvard University Press.

Kurzman, Charles. 2013. "Death Tolls of the Iran-Iraq War." Retrieved from `http://kurzman.unc.edu`.

Lawrence, Adria. 2013. *Imperial Rule and the Politics of Nationalism: Anti-Colonial Protest in the French Empire*. New York, NY: Cambridge University Press.

Lazier, Sheri. 1991. *Into Kurdistan: Frontiers under Fire*. London: Zed Books.

Lazier, Sheri. 1996. *Martyrs, Traitors and Patriots: Kurdistan after the Gulf War*. London: Zed Books.

Levi, Margaret. 1988. *Of Rule and Revenue*. Berkeley, CA: University of California Press.

Levi, Margaret. 1997. *Consent, Dissent and Patriotism*. New York: Cambridge University Press.

Levi, Margaret and David Olson. 2000. "The Battles in Seattle." *Politics and Society*. 28(3): 309–329.

Lifton, Robert Jay. 2000 [1986]. *The Nazi Doctors: Medical Killing and the Psychology of Genocide*. New York, NY: Basic Books.

Linz, Juan. 2000. *Totalitarian and Authoritarian Regimes*. Boulder, CO: Lynne Rienner.

Lipset, Seymour Martin and Stein Rokkan. 1967. *Party Systems and Voter Alignments: Cross-national Perspectives*. Toronto: Free Press.

Litvak, Meir. 1998. *Shiʿi Scholars of Nineteenth-Century Iraq: The ʿUlama of Najaf and Karbala*. New York, NY: Cambridge University Press.

Lizzeri, Alessandro and Nicola Persico. 2004. "Why did the Elites Extend the Suffrage? Democracy and the Scope of Government, with an Application to Britain's 'Age of Reform'." *Quarterly Journal of Economics*. 119(2): 707–765.

Lohmann, Susanne. 1994. "Dynamics of Informational Cascades: The Monday Demonstrations in Leipzig, East Germany, 1989–91." *World Politics*. 47(1): 42–101.

Long, Jerry. 2004. *Saddam's War of Words: Politics, Religion and the Iraqi Invasion of Kuwait*. Austin, TX: University of Texas Press.

Louer, Laurence. 2012. *Shiism and Politics in the Middle East*. New York, NY: Columbia University Press.

Lupu, Noam and Leonid Peisakhin. 2017. "The Legacy of Political Violence across Generations." *American Journal of Political Science*. 61(4): 836–851.

Lust, Ellen. 2009. "Competitive Clientelism in the Middle East." *Journal of Democracy*. 20(3): 122–135.

Lyall, Jason. 2006. "Pocket Protests: Rhetorical Coercion and the Micropolitics of Collective Action in Semi-authoritarian Regimes." *World Politics*. 58: 378–412.

Lyall, Jason. 2009. "Does Indiscriminate Violence Incite Insurgent Attacks? Evidence from Chechnya." *Journal of Conflict Resolution*. 53(3): 331–362.

Lyall, Jason. 2010. "Are Co-ethnics More Effective Counterinsurgents? Evidence from the Second Chechen War." *American Political Science Review*. 104(1): 1–20.

Lyall, Jason and Isaiah Wilson. 2009. "Rage Against the Machines: Explaining Outcomes in Counterinsurgency Wars." *International Organization*. 63.

Machain, Carla Martinez, T. Clifton Morgan and Patrick Regan. 2011. "Deterring Rebellion." *Foreign Policy Analysis*. 7(3): 295–315.

Mackey, Sandra. 2002. *The Reckoning: Iraq and the Legacy of Saddam Hussein*. New York, NY: W. W. Norton & Co.

Magaloni, Beatriz. 2006. *Voting for Autocracy: Hegemonic Party Survival and its Demise in Mexico*. New York, NY: Cambridge University Press.

Magaloni, Beatriz. 2008. "Credible Powersharing and the Longevity of Authoritarian Rule." *Comparative Political Studies*. 41(4–5).

Magaloni, Beatriz and Ruth Kricheli. 2010. "Political Order and One-Party Rule." *Annual Review of Political Science*. 13: 123–143.

Mahdi, Kamil. 2007. "Iraq's Economic Reforms in Perspective: Public Sector, Private Sector and Sanctions." *International Journal of Contemporary Iraqi Studies*. 1(2): 213–231.

Makdisi, Ussama. 2000. *The Culture of Sectarianism: Community, History and Violence in Nineteenth-Century Ottoman Lebanon*. Berkeley, CA: University of California Press.

Makiya, Kanan. 1993. *Cruelty and Silence: War, Tyranny, Uprising and the Arab World*. New York, NY: W.W. Norton & Company.

Makiya, Kanan. 1998. *Republic of Fear: The Politics of Modern Iraq* (updated edition). Berkeley, CA: University of California Press.

Mallat, Chibli. 1988. "Religious Militancy in Contemporary Iraq: Muhammad Baqer as-Sadr and the Sunni-Shia Paradigm." *Third World Quarterly*. 10(2): 699–729.

al-Marashi, Ibrahim and Sammy Salama. 2008. *Iraq's Armed Forces: An Analytical History*. London: Routledge.

Marr, Phebe. 2004. *The Modern History of Iraq* (second edition). Boulder, CO: Westview Press.

Marx, Anthony. 1998. Making Race and Nation: A Comparison of South Africa, the United States, and Brazil. New York, NY : Cambridge University Press.

Masoud, Tarek. 2014. *Counting Islam: Religion, Class, and Elections in Egypt*. New York, NY: Cambridge University Press.

May, Larry. 2011. "Collective Punishment and Mass Confinement." *Accountability for Collective Wrongdoing*. Editors, Tracy Isaacs and Richard Vernon. New York, NY: Cambridge University Press.

Mazaheri, Nimah. 2010. "Iraq and the Domestic Political Effects of Economic Sanctions." *Middle East Journal*. 64(2): 254–268.

McDowall, David. 1996. *A Modern History of the Kurds*. London: I.B. Tauris.

McKiernan, Kevin. 2006. *The Kurds: A People in Search of Their Homeland*. New York, NY: St. Martin's Press.

Meiselas, Susan. 1997. *Kurdistan: In the Shadow of History*. New York, NY: Random House.

Miguel, Edward. 2004. "Tribe or Nation? Nation Building and Public Goods in Kenya versus Tanzania." *World Politics*. 56: 327–62.

Minorities at Risk Project. 2009. "Minorities at Risk Dataset." College Park, MD: Center for International Development and Conflict Management.

Moaddel, Mansoor, Mark Tessler, and Ronald Inglehart. 2008. "Foreign Occupation and National Pride: The Case of Iraq." Research Report, Population Studies Center.

Monten, Jonathan. 2014. "Intervention and State-Building: Comparative Lessons from Japan, Iraq, and Afghanistan." *Annals of the American Academy of Political and Social Science*. 656: 173–191.

Montgomery, Bruce. 2011. "Immortality in the Secret Police Files: The Iraq Memory Foundation and the Baʿath Party Archive." *International Journal of Cultural Property*. 18(3): 309–336.

Murray, Williamson and Kevin Woods. 2012. *The Iran-Iraq War: A Military and Strategic History*. New York, NY: Cambridge University Press.

Mylonas, Harris. 2012. *The Politics of Nation-Building: Making Co-nationals, Refugees and Minorities*. New York: Cambridge University Press.

Nakash, Yitzhak. 1994a. "The Conversion of Iraq's Tribes to Shiʾism." *International Journal of Middle East Studies*. 26(3): 443–463.

Nakash, Yitzhak. 1994b. *The Shiʿis of Iraq*. Princeton, NJ: Princeton University Press.

Nakash, Yitzhak. 2006. *Reaching for Power: The Shiʿa in the Modern Arab World*. Princeton, NJ: Princeton University Press.

Nalepa, Monika. 2010. *Skeletons in the Closet: Transitional Justice in Post-Communist Europe*. New York, NY: Cambridge University Press.

Nalepa, Monika and Grigore Pop-Eleches. 2016. "Religion and Anti-Authoritarian Resistance: Evidence from Communist Poland." Working paper, Department of Political Science, University of Chicago.

Natali, Denise. 2005. *The Kurds and the State: Evolving National Identity in Iraq, Turkey and Iran*. Syracuse, NY: Syracuse University Press.

Ngai, Mai. 2004. *Impossible Subjects: Illegal Aliens and the Making of Modern America*. Princeton, NJ: Princeton University Press.

Nixon, John. 2016. *Debriefing the President: The Interrogation of Saddam Hussein*. New York, NY: Blue Rider Press.

Nkpa, Nwokocha. 1975. "Rumor Mongering in Wartime." *Journal of Social Psychology*. 96(1): 27–35.

Olson, Mancur. 1965. *The Logic of Collective Action*. Cambridge, MA: Harvard University Press.

Osman, Khalil. 2014. *Sectarianism in Iraq: The Making of State and Nation since 1920*. London: Routledge.

Owen, Roger. 2007. "Reconstructing the Performance of the Iraqi Economy, 1950–2006: An Essay with some Hypotheses and Many Questions." *International Journal of Contemporary Iraqi Studies*. 1(1): 93–101.

Ozly, Onur. 2006. *Iraqi Economic Reconstruction and Development*. Washington, DC: Center for Strategic and International Studies.

Pasha, A. K. 2003. *Iraq: Sanctions and Wars*. New Delhi: Sterling Publishers Private Limited.

Pasternak, Avia. 2011. "The Distributive Effect of Collective Punishment." *Accountability for Collective Wrongdoing*. Editors, Tracy Isaacs and Richard Vernon. New York, NY: Cambridge University Press.

Patel, David. 2015. "ISIS in Iraq: What we get Wrong and Why 2015 is not 2007 Redux." *Middle East Brief*. Brandeis University Crown Center for Middle East Studies. 87.

Patel, David. 2016. *Islam, Information, and the Rise and Fall of Social Orders in Iraq*. Draft book manuscript, Crown Center, Brandeis University.

Pelletiere, Stephen. 1992. *The Iran-Iraq War: Chaos in a Vacuum*. New York, NY: Praeger.

Pellett, Peter. 2002. "Sanctions, Food, Nutrition and Health in Iraq." *Iraq under Seige: The Deadly Impact of Sanctions and War*. Editor, Anthony Arnove. Cambridge, MA: South End Press.

Perice, Glen. 1997. "Rumors and Politics in Haiti." *Anthropology Quarterly*. 70(1): 1–10.

Petersen, Roger. 2001. *Resistance and Rebellion: Lessons from Eastern Europe*. New York. NY: Cambridge University Press.

Podeh, Elie. 2014. *The Politics of National Celebrations in the Arab Middle East*. New York, NY: Cambridge University Press.

Posner, Daniel. 2004. "The Political Salience of Cultural Difference: Why Chewas and Tumbukas are Allies in Zambia and Adversaries in Malawi." *American Political Science Review*. 98(4): 529–545.

Posner, Daniel. 2005. *Institutions and Ethnic Politics in Africa*. New York, NY: Cambridge University Press.

Quinlivan, James. 1999. "Coup-proofing: Its Practice and Consequences in the Middle East." *International Security*. 24(2): 131–165.

Rabil, Robert. 2002. "Operation 'Termination of Traitors:' The Iraqi Regime through its Documents." *Middle East Review of International Affairs*. 6(3): 14–24.

al-Radi, Nuha. 2003. *From Baghdad Diaries: A Woman's Chronicle of War and Exile*. New York, NY: Vintage Books.

Randal, Jonathan. 1998. *After Such Knowledge, What Forgiveness? My Encounters with Kurdistan*. Boulder, CO: Westview.

Raphaeli, Nimrod. 2004. "Understanding Muqtada al-Sadr." *Middle East Quarterly*. 11(4): 33–42.

Razoux, Pierre. 2015. *The Iran-Iraq War*. Cambridge, MA: Harvard University Press.

Rear, Michael. 2008. *Intervention, Ethnic Conflict and State Building in Iraq: A Paradigm for the Post-Colonial State*. New York, NY: Routledge Press.

Reid, Donald Malcolm. 1993. "The Postage Stamp: A Window on Saddam Hussein's Iraq." *Middle East Journal*. 47(1): 77–89.

Roessler, Philip. 2011. "The Enemy Within: Personal Rule, Coups, and Civil War in Africa." *World Politics*. 63(2): 300–346.

Rogowski, Ronald. 1989. *Commerce and Coalitions: How Trade Affects Domestic Political Alignments*. Princeton, NJ: Princeton University Press.

Rohde, Achim. 2010. *State-Society Relations in Ba'thist Iraq: Facing Dictatorship*. New York, NY: Routledge Press.

Romano, David. 2006. *The Kurdish Nationalist Movement: Opportunity, Mobilization and Identity*. New York, NY: Cambridge University Press.

Rosnow, Ralph and Allan Kimmel. 2000. "Rumor." *Encyclopedia of Psychology*, Vol. 7. Editor, A. Kazdin. pp. 122–123. New York, NY: Oxford University Press and American Psychological Association.

Ross, Michael. 2012. *The Oil Curse: How Petroleum Wealth Shapes the Development of Nations*. Princeton, NJ: Princeton University Press.

Rouleau, Eric. 1995. "America's Unyielding Policy toward Iraq." *Foreign Affairs*. 74(1): 59–72.

Rozenas, Arturas, Sebastian Schutte, and Yuri Zhukov. 2017. "The Political Legacy of Violence: The Long-Term Impact of Stalin's Repression in Ukraine." *Journal of Politics*. 79(4): 1147–1161.

Rubin, Lawrence. 2011. "Documenting Saddam Hussein's Iraq." *Contemporary Security Policy*. 32(2): 458–466.

Rummel, Rudolph. 1997. *Power Kills*. New Brunswick, NJ: Transaction Press.

Sada, Georges. 2006. *Saddam's Secrets: How an Iraqi General Defied and Survived Saddam Hussein*. Brentwood, TN: Integrity Media.

Sakai, Keiko. 2001. "Modernity and Tradition in the Islamic Movements of Iraq: Continuity and Discontinuity in the Role of the Ulama." *Arab Studies Quarterly*. 23(1): 37–53.

Sakai, Keiko. 2003. "Tribalization as a Tool of State Control in Iraq: Observations on the Army, the Cabinets and the National Assembly." *Tribes and Power: Nationalism and Ethnicity in the Middle East*. Editors, Faleh Abdul-Jabar and Hosham Dawod. London: Saqi Press.

Saleh, Zainab. 2013. "On Iraqi Nationality: Law, Citizenship, and Exclusion." *Arab Studies Journal*. 21(1): 48–78.

Salti, Nisreen and Jad Chaaban. 2010. "The Role of Sectarianism in the Allocation of Public Expenditure in Postwar Lebanon." *International Journal of Middle Eastern Studies*. 42(4): 637–655.

Sanford, Jonathan. 2003. *Iraq's Economy: Past, Present, Future*. Washington, DC: Congressional Research Service.

Sassoon, Joseph. 2012. *Saddam Hussein's Ba'th Party: Inside an Authoritarian Regime*. New York, NY: Cambridge University Press.

Sassoon, Joseph. 2016. *Anatomy of Authoritarianism in the Arab Republics*. New York, NY: Cambridge University Press.

Schedler, Andreas. 2013. *The Politics of Uncertainty: Sustaining and Subverting Electoral Authoritarianism*. Oxford: Oxford University Press.

Schnytzer, Adi and Janez Sustersic. 1998. "Why Join the Party in a One-Party System? Popularity versus Political Exchange." *Public Choice*. 94: 117–134.

Schutte, Sebastian. 2017. "Geographic Determinants of Indiscriminate Violence in Civil Wars." *Conflict Management and Peace Science*. 34(4): 380–405

Scott, James. 1985. *Weapons of the Weak: Everyday Forms of Peasant Resistance*. New Haven, CT: Yale University Press.

Scott, James. 1990. *Domination and the Arts of Resistance: Hidden Transcripts*. New Haven, CT: Yale University Press.

Scott, James. 1998. *Seeing Like a State: How Certain Schemes to Improve the Human Condition Have Failed*. New Haven, CT: Yale University Press.

Shibutani, Tamotsu. 1966. *Improvised News: A Sociological Study of Rumor*. Indianapolis, IN: Bobbs-Merrill.

Shirk, Susan. 1982. *Competitive Comrades: Career Incentives and Student Strategies in China*. Berkeley, CA: University of California Press.

Singh, Naunihal. 2014. *Seizing Power: The Strategic Logic of Military Coups*. Baltimore, MD: Johns Hopkins University Press.

Sluglett, Peter. 2012. "Sectarianism in Recent Iraqi History: What It Is and What It Isn't." *The Shiʿa of Samarra: The Heritage and Politics of a Community in Iraq*. Editor, Imranali Panjwani. London: I.B. Tauris.

Staniland, Paul. 2014. *Networks of Rebellion: Explaining Insurgent Cohesion and Collapse*. Ithaca, NY: Cornell University Press.

Stansfield, Gareth. 2003a. "The Kurdish Dilemma: The Golden Era Threatened." *Iraq at the Crossroads: State and Society in the Shadow of Regime Change*. Editors, Toby Dodge and Steven Simon. Adelphi Paper 354.

Stansfield, Gareth. 2003b. "Contextual Analysis." *Iraqi Kurdistan: Political Development and Emergent Democracy*. New York, NY: Routledge Curzon.

Stein, Arthur. 1976. "Conflict and Cohesion: A Review of the Literature." *Journal of Conflict Resolution*. 20(1): 143–172.

Svolik, Milan. 2012. *The Politics of Authoritarian Rule*. New York, NY: Cambridge University Press.

Tilly, Charles. 1992. *Coercion, Capital and European States, AD 990–1992*. Cambridge, MA: Blackwell.

Totten, Michael. 2011. *In the Wake of the Surge*. Portland, OR: Belmont Estate Books.

Tripp, Charles. 1987. "The Consequences of the Iran-Iraq War for Iraqi Politics." *The Iran-Iraq War: Impact and Implications*. Editor, Efraim Krash. London: MacMillan Press.

Tripp, Charles. 2000. *A History of Iraq* (second edition). New York, NY: Cambridge University Press.

Tucker, Mike. 2014. *Now we are Free: Voices of the Kurds after Saddam*. Denver, CO: Outskirts Press.

Tullock, Gordon. 1987. *Autocracy*. Dordrecht: Kluwer.

Tyler, Tom R. 2006. *Why People Obey the Law*. Princeton, NJ: Princeton University Press.

Valentino, Benjamin. 2004. *Final Solutions: Mass Killing and Genocide in the Twentieth Century*. Ithaca, NY: Cornell University Press.

van Bruinessen, Martin. 1992. *Agha, Shaikh and State: The Social and Political Structures of Kurdistan*. London: Zed Books.

Viola, Lynne. 1996. *Peasant Rebels under Stalin: Collectivization and the Culture of Peasant Resistance*. New York: Oxford University Press.

Visser, Reidar. 2005. *Basra, the Failed Gulf State: Separatism and Nationalism in Southern Iraq*. London: LIT Verlag Munster.

Visser, Reidar. 2008. "The Two Regions of Southern Iraq." *An Iraq of its Regions: Cornerstones of a Federal Democracy?* Editors, Reidar Visser, and Gareth Stansfield. New York, NY: Columbia University Press.

Visser, Reidar. 2010. "The Territorial Aspect of Sectarianism in Iraq." *International Journal of Contemporary Iraqi Studies*. 4(3): 295–304.

Visser, Reidar. 2012a. "Sectarian Coexistence in Iraq: The Experiences of The Shiʿa in Areas North of Baghdad." *The Shiʿa of Samarra: The Heritage and Politics of a Community in Iraq*. Editor, Imranali Panjwani. London: I.B. Tauris.

Visser, Reidar. 2012b. "Iraq." *Militancy and Political Violence in Shiʿism: Trends and Patterns*. Editor, Assaf Moghadam. London: Routledge.

Visser, Reidar. 2012c. "The Sectarian Master Narrative in Iraqi Historiography." *Writing the Modern History of Iraq: Historiographical and Political Challenges*. Editors, Riccardo Bocco, Hamit Bozarslan, Peter Sluglett and Jordi Tejel. London: World Scientific.

Voller, Yaniv. 2014. *The Kurdish Liberation Movement in Iraq: From Insurgency to Statehood*. New York, NY: Routledge.

Walter, Alissa. 2016. "The Political Economy of Rationing in Iraq: 1990–2003." Working paper, Department of History, Georgetown University.

Warrick, Joby. 2015. *Black Flags: The Rise of ISIS*. New York, NY: Doubleday.

Wedeen, Lisa. 1999. *Ambiguities of Domination: Politics Rhetoric and Symbols in Contemporary Syria*. Chicago, IL: University of Chicago Press.

Weeks, Jessica. 2014. *Dictators at War and Peace*. Ithaca, NY: Cornell University Press.

Weinstein, Jeremy. 2006. *Inside Rebellion: The Politics of Insurgent Violence*. New York, NY: Cambridge University Press.

Wiley, Joyce. 1992. *The Islamic Movement of Iraqi Shiʿas*. Boulder, CO: Lynne Rienner.

Wimmer, Andreas. 2002. *Nationalist Exclusion and Ethnic Conflict: Shadows of Modernity*. New York, NY: Cambridge University Press.

Wimmer, Andreas. 2008. "The Making and Unmaking of Ethnic Boundaries: A Multilevel Process Theory." *American Journal of Sociology*. 133(4): 970–1022.

Wimmer, Andreas. 2013. *Waves of War: Nationalism, State Formation and Ethnic Exclusion in the Modern World*. New York, NY: Cambridge University Press.

Wintrobe, Ronald. 1990. "The Tinpot and the Totalitarian: An Economic Theory of Dictatorship." *American Political Science Review*. 84(3): 849–872.

Wintrobe, Ronald. 1998. *The Political Economy of Dictatorship*. New York, NY: Cambridge University Press.

Woods, Kevin. 2008. *The Mother of all Battles: Saddam Hussein's Strategic Plan for the Persian Gulf War*. Annapolis, MD: Naval Institute Press.

Woods, Kevin, David Palkki, and Mark Stout. 2011. *The Saddam Tapes: The Inner Workings of a Tyrant's Regime, 1978–2001*. New York, NY: Cambridge University Press.

Workman, W. Thom. 1994. *The Social Origins of the Iran-Iraq War*. Boulder, CO: Lynne Rienner.

Yildiz, Kerim. 2004. *The Kurds of Iraq: The Past, Present and Future*. London: Pluto Press.

Yousif, Bassam. 2010. "The Political Economy of Sectarianism in Iraq." *International Journal of Contemporary Iraqi Studies*. 4(3): 357–365.

Yousif, Bassam. 2012. *Human Development in Iraq, 1950–1990*. London: Routledge Studies in Middle Eastern Economies.

Zeidel, Ronen. 2008. "The Decline of Small-Scale Regionalism in Tikrit." *An Iraq of its Regions: Cornerstones of a Federal Democracy?* Editors, Reidar Visser and Gareth Stansfield. New York, NY: Columbia University Press.

Zeidel, Ronen. 2010. "On Servility and Survival: The Sunni Opposition to Saddam and the Origins of the Current Sunni Leadership in Iraq." *Iraq Between Occupations: Perspectives from 1920 to the Present*. Editors, Amatzia Baram, Achim Rohde and Ronen Zeidel. New York, NY: Palgrave MacMillan.

Zubaida, Sami. 1991. "Community, Class, and Minorities in Iraqi Politics." *The Iraqi Revolution of 1958: The Old Social Classes Revisited*. Editors, Robert Fernea and William Roger Louis. London: I.B. Tauris.

Zubaida, Sami. 2002. "The Fragments Imagine the Nation: The Case of Iraq." *International Journal of Middle East Studies*. 34(2): 205–215.

INDEX